James Morton is the author of the hugely successful Gangland series. He has long experience as a solicitor specialising in criminal work and was editor-in-chief of *New Law Journal* for many years.

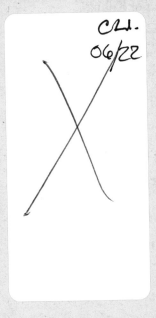

JAMES MORTON

EAST END GANGLAND

NEW EDITION REVISITED AND EXPANDED BY THE AUTHOR

SPHERE

SPHERE

First published in Great Britain in 2000 by Little, Brown and Company
Paperback published by Warner Books in 2001
This revised edition published in 2021 by Sphere

1 3 5 7 9 10 8 6 4 2

A CIP catalogue record for this book is available from the British Library.

ISBN 978-0-7515-8448-6

Typeset in Garamond by M Rules
Printed and bound in Great Britain by Clays Ltd, Elcograf S.p.A.

Papers used by Sphere are from well-managed forests
and other responsible sources.

MIX
Paper from
responsible sources
FSC® C104740
www.fsc.org

Sphere
An imprint of
Little, Brown Book Group
Carmelite House
50 Victoria Embankment
London EC4Y 0DZ

An Hachette UK Company
www.hachette.co.uk

www.littlebrown.co.uk

For Dock, with my love and thanks

CONTENTS

INTRODUCTION

It was about six in the evening on a Saturday in the autumn of 1962 when the Richardson Gang, or at least some of their employees, blew up my father's warehouse in Aldgate. It was nothing personal. My father, I am sure, had never heard of them nor they of him. The building just happened to be in the wrong place at the wrong time.

My father, who was a spice merchant, had a warehouse and office in Mitre Street just around the corner from where Jack the Ripper killed Catherine Eddowes. Although I went frequently to his warehouse – where as a child it was my delight to feed the cats since we did not have one at home – he never pointed out the connection with local history when we went to the Square to collect his car. He was a singularly incurious man and I doubt whether he even knew that he often stood on the cobbles where she died. Certainly if he did know, he did not pass this intelligence on to me. Now it is too late. The whole area has been pulled down to ease the flow of the traffic, speeding – well, that is perhaps not the right word – towards the heart of the East End.

At the time of the explosion the Richardsons were running what is called a long-firm fraud. The long-firm fraud has been one of the staple and most lucrative diets of the con-man. As far back as the 1920s it was estimated that as much as £4 million was cleared annually in London.[1]

In its simplest form, a warehouse or shop is taken by a front man who has no previous criminal convictions. Goods, usually toiletries, wines and spirits and other easily disposable items, are bought on credit and then sold perfectly properly through the shop. The supplier receives his or her money. More business is done with more and more suppliers until there is one big bang; a massive amount of goods is obtained on credit, knocked out at prices often below the purchase price in a great 'blow-out' or liquidation sale – which was where the local housewives benefited – and the premises are closed down overnight.

The beauty of a well-organised LF was that goods were bought from the wholesalers over the telephone by a 'blower-man', so identification of the purchaser was improbable. Managers of the shops knocking out the stuff were changed weekly or fortnightly. In those days it was difficult if not impossible for the police to find out who was actually running the show. In the 1960s a properly run small LF could, before it collapsed, expect to realise a profit of between £100,000 and £150,000, which was enormous money.

On this occasion the idea had been to remove the wines and spirits from the warehouse and have a fire, thereby doubling the profit by claiming from the insurance company for the so-called lost goods.

Apparently the plan had been to torch their empty warehouse at a weekend when no one was around, so the risk would be minimal. Unfortunately, after petrol had been poured all over the premises, the arsonists saw a courting couple in the street and, so to speak, held their hand. By the time the pair had gone, the fumes had risen and so, when a Guy Fawkes rocket was aimed at a semi-basement window, instead of igniting a fire which would burn nicely, the place literally blew up and demolished much of the street. The cats were unharmed. My father moved what was left of his stock to the generally much healthier area of the Borough, which was in fact Richardson territory. There he remained unmolested until his retirement two decades later, by which time the Richardsons were coming towards or at the end of their sentences. I don't think he even knew they had been imprisoned.[2]

Just why over the years has the East End offered so much fascination for outsiders when other areas, such as the Elephant and Castle, which have also had more than their fair share of crime and major criminals, have failed to generate any real interest? Perhaps it is a matter of semantics and it is the very word East which carries the air of the Orient with it. It was another world, one filled with the unknown and therefore the spice of danger, which gave it an attraction. Just as Harlem in the 1920s was the place for smart white New Yorkers to end their evenings, and Montmartre was where Parisians and tourists went to see, and be robbed by, the Apache gangs in Paris, so was the Railway Tavern in the East India Dock Road (also known as Charlie Brown's) the place for London's café society to visit for a *frisson*. The proprietor, in evening dress, would show them his collection of curios in what was in effect a museum and they would proudly sign the visitors' book. To have visited the East End, where policemen only went in pairs, and to have survived the experience was something to speak about. To an extent the East End was seen as another land and its inhabitants a race apart. Their poor physical condition was seen as one reason for British defeats in the Boer War, and in 1912 the convenient Anon was quoted as saying:

The first stage of decay had already been reached when the stolid, God-fearing puritan of two and a half centuries ago has given place to the shallow hysterical cockney of today.[3]

Jack London, who lived for a short time in the East End and described life there, wrote that to exist in the day-to-day

wheeling and dealing and fighting for food and work required a
social personality that was voluble and aggressive. Those outside
the area had a fear of the socially deprived mob dating back to 8
February 1886, when the London United Workmen's Committee
march to Trafalgar Square demanding employment took place.
The meeting had been addressed by Ben Tillett and John Burns,
but afterwards a small group went on a rampage, overturning
carriages, looting and, worst of all, breaking the windows of the
Reform and Carlton clubs. The demonstration was badly mis-
handled by the police. In charge was the seventy-four-year-old
District Superintendent Robert Walker in civilian clothes. He
was quite unable to cope and suffered the additional indignity
of having his pocket picked. The demonstrators made their way
to Oxford Street where they were turned back by Inspector
Cuthbert and fifteen men from Marylebone police station who
were due to go on night duty.

There were fears that this was the beginning of an uprising, but the majority of the marchers trotted off home singing
'Rule Britannia' and despite a careful lookout by the police
over the next few weeks no further demonstrations took place.
Nevertheless the incident was sufficient to establish the spectre
of 'The East End Mob' as an early, if as yet unlabelled, folk devil.
The Commissioner of Police, Edmund Henderson, resigned
the next day.

Years later Tillett spoke again. This time it was at a meeting
of dock labourers at Tower Hill on 7 August 1911, which was
once more watched by the authorities with some apprehension,
particularly when he urged that the Port of London should be
brought to a standstill:[4]

We are only fighting for the right to live; we are only fighting
our employers because hitherto they have refused to recognise

the claims we made. We were mere riff-raff, dockers, not men; now we are showing the employers that we are men with all the noble qualities that can be found in man. Brothers, we want to finish that period when the so-called docker or transport worker or coal porter or carman shall be looked upon as nothing. If we all drop tools the Lord Tomnoddys would rot from want of food.

This was one of the abiding fears of the general public, that the dockers would stop them from eating. It was also feared that the working classes would actually rise up out of the grinding poverty in which so many lived. It can be argued that many of the philanthropic improvement schemes had the ulterior motive of maintaining the *status quo* behind them. As the number of strikes at the end of the nineteenth century and in the first years of the twentieth century show, improvement in working conditions came slowly. There were, for example, tailors' strikes in 1889, 1906, 1909 and 1912; cabinet-makers' in 1896, 1900, 1911 and 1913; bootmakers' in 1891, 1901 and 1912, and Jewish bakers' in 1906 and 1913. It is against this background that crime in the East End must be set.

But back in the 1880s Henderson's successor, Sir Charles Warren, whose qualification for the post had been the governorship of the Red Sea Littoral, had fared not much better in his dealings with the East End. He was under constant criticism for failing to find Jack the Ripper. One of his less thought-through acts had been to engage a pair of bloodhounds from the entrepreneurial Mr Brough for £100. Their owner had a better sense of smell, at least for money, than his dogs, for they became temporarily lost.

The East End's reputation undoubtedly benefited from the rise in literacy and the growth of the popular lending libraries. Charles Dickens' unfinished *The Mystery of Edwin Drood* opens in an East End opium den. Later, in a Sherlock Holmes story, *The Man with the Twisted Lip*, a respectable man is seen disappearing into another den when he is supposed to be working on the Stock Exchange. Many of the popular Sax Rohmer novels had an East End setting, with the dastardly Fu Manchu plotting to overthrow the Western World.

The East End has always had its share of the famous and infamous. The Old Gravel Lane murders are mentioned by Thomas de Quincey, himself an early casualty of the opium trade. Claude Duval, perhaps the most gentlemanly of the high-waymen, lived in Colchester Road, Leman Street. A little later in time, a one-legged Welshman named Hughes ran a thieves' kitchen in Catherine Wheel Alley, and some maintain that it is he, rather than the usually favoured Ikey Solomons, who was the prototype for Dickens' Fagin.[5] The lovely Madeleine Smith, who years later would perhaps be fortunate to obtain a 'not proven' verdict in Edinburgh where she had been accused of poisoning her now-unwanted lover, went to school in Clapton. She was to have a small industry created around her trial arguing the merits of her guilt or innocence.

On the theatrical front, the celebrated actor David Garrick made his first stage appearance as Harlequin in Alie Street. Later a playhouse was named after him in Leman Street where it was said 'ladies can seat themselves without rats running over them'.

A curious feature of the East End towards the end of the nineteenth century was the so-called penny gaff. It was a form of theatre often played in a shop with a back parlour, with the dividing wall knocked down. There were usually two perfor-mances nightly, and the earlier house cost twopence. Ned Wright described a performance in *Cassell's Magazine*: 'It is difficult to conceive the strange power of fascination places of this kind acquire over these poor misguided boys and girls who attend them.' An evening would consist of something like a rough music hall and then the melodrama *Count Fribourg* or *The Murder in the Black Forest*. About a hundred young people sat on benches and there was also some sort of gallery. Wright thought that most had stolen the penny entrance money, although he had been obliged to pay double. A lady who danced the hornpipe to the point of exhaustion in the first half received six shillings a week and had to provide her own costume.

One very popular figure in this form of entertainment in which, like the Parisian Funambules, the players were not allowed to speak but could sign and discharge mock firearms, was Mrs Douglas Fitzbruce who appeared in such dramas as *Gentleman Jack* or *The Game of High Toby*.

James Greenwood describes her gallantly when she appeared as Dick Turpin:

> Dressed in buckskin shorts and highly polished boots she could not have been more than forty-five. Her husband who had been seen earlier putting up the poster advertising the performance was Turpin's colleague Tom King whom he accidentally shot. When Mrs Fitzbruce let fly at point-blank range there was such a whistling and stamping of feet that the dust from the plaster wash of the walls blew up a storm of dust. Afterwards patrons, if they had sixpence, could purchase pictures of Mrs. F. as Cupid and Lady Godiva.[6]

In creating and maintaining its image the East End was also fortunate to have a series of very public incidents. In the 1890s Jack the Ripper, one of the great serial killers, fascinated the public. Here was a man killing not a mile from the great British institutions such as the Bank of England and yet operating in conditions which those who worked in the bank and their families could only read and have nightmares about. And read and theorise about him they have done ever since. Richard Whittington-Egan, in his mammoth compilation of books and articles on the killings, estimated that at the end of 1998 there had been no fewer than 500 publications about the case.

In writing a book on crime in the East End there is an immediate problem in defining just what was and is the East End. Some parts are easy – Aldgate, Limehouse, the Docks, Stratford, West Ham, Hackney and Hoxton all fit neatly, but what of Hackney's neighbour Stoke Newington, which has an N postal code? What about Romford and Ilford? Certainly those are in Essex, yet they have been inextricably linked with the East End, its *moeurs* and its villains, and all have influenced criminal life in the East End. Indeed many of the old East End families have moved to Essex from where new generations ply their trade. Essex is also a gateway to the Continent and a route for drug imports.

I had intended to begin this account at the turn of the twentieth century, but I have slightly enlarged the parameters to start with the pogroms in Eastern Europe and the influx of the Ashkenazi Jews from the 1860s onwards – replacing the immigrant Irish who, with the successive Potato Famines of the 1840s and 1850s, had come to London and settled in the East End at the bottom of the social pile.

I have also included some of the particularly interesting domestic crimes such as the Lipski murder of his downstairs neighbour and the killing of Fanny Zeitoun, both of which give an insight into life in the late nineteenth and early twentieth centuries. I have, however, generally avoided the many non-gang-related East End domestic murders of the period and instead have concentrated on crime carried out for profit rather than for personal or political reasons. In the early years, however, most of the East End gangland murders were not commercially orientated but resulted from disputes over territory, wives and girlfriends and slights real and perceived. These have been included.

It would not be right, however, to omit the first murder on a railway. This world-wide distinction belongs to Franz Muller, a German tailor working in London who killed a jeweller, Thomas Briggs, in a railway carriage between Bow and Hackney Wick on 9 July 1864. Robbery was the motive and Muller snatched his victim's gold watch before throwing Briggs onto the railway line where, in fact, he died. In his haste, Muller overlooked £5 Briggs had on him and also took away the wrong hat. The watch-chain was eventually traced to a Cheapside jeweller with the appropriate name of Death, who described the customer as being foreign-looking and possibly German. Of course the case made the newspapers and a witness came forward to say he recognised the hat found in the railway carriage. He had bought two of them, one for himself and one for Muller. The police now discovered that Muller had sailed for New York and, anticipating the Crippen case by some fifty years, detectives took a faster ship. Muller was found with the missing watch in his possession.

He maintained his innocence and approached both Queen Victoria and German royalty to intervene on his behalf. At the end his nerve failed and, in one of the last public executions, he confessed before a large crowd. He was hanged by William Chalcraft on 14 November 1864. For a time, the type of hat he had left behind in the railway carriage was known as a Muller.

Once, this informal history would have ended, as journalist John Diamond puts it, when

> ... the Synagogues became mosques – broken-backed Jewish men who shuffled along Brick Lane have been transformed into broken-backed shuffling Bengali men.[7]

Now, as the television series has it, the only way to go is Essex.

My thanks are due to Harold Alderman, Julian Alexander, Albert Appleby, Steve Ashenden, Fred Bailey, the late Mickey Bailey, Pam Bailey, Frankie Bateson, the late Jeremy Beadle, the late J.P. Bean, Barbara Boote, Keith Bottomley, Hilary Clarke, Dave Critchley, Alan Dixon, the late Peter Donnelly, Mary Ewing, Micky Fawcett, the late Frank Fraser, the late Brian Hilliard, Rita Matharu, the late Jean Maund, Helen McCormack, Brian McDonald, Kelly Parkes, the late Silvia Perrini-Rice, Lillian Pizzichini, Thalia Proctor, the late Nipper Read, Pat Read, Rhiannon Smith, the late John Rigbey, Mark Roodhouse, Andrew Rose, Linda Silverman, Dot Swarc, Tony Thompson, the late John Warburton, the late Richard Whittington-Egan, the Curator of the Jewish Museum, Sternberg Centre, the staff of the Tower Hamlets Library, Bancroft Road, the National Archives, the British Library and the Newspaper Library then at Colindale, as well as many others who asked not to be named.

Once again, this book could not even have been started let alone completed without the total help and commitment of Dock Bateson.

NOTES

1. For details of the 100 plus long firms thought by the police to be operating in England in the middle of the 1920s, see National Archives (Nat. Arch) MEPO 2 2188.
2. See Robert Parker, *Rough Justice*, pp. 90–91; Charles Richardson, *My Manor*, pp. 124–5.
3. J.M. Whitehouse (ed.), *Problems of Boy Life*.

4. Nat. Arch MEPO 3 206.
5. Millicent Rose, *The East End of London*.
6. James Greenwood, *The Wilds of London*.
7. John Diamond, 'The Last Cockney' in *The Times*, 14 March 1998.

1

THE NINETEENTH CENTURY

The earliest of the great nineteenth-century East End murders were the so-called Ratcliffe Highway murders, which Thomas de Quincey calls the Old Gravel Lane murders and which took place in September 1811. On 7 September, a man named Marr sent his maidservant out to buy some oysters and when she returned she found the door locked. She went for help and when neighbours broke in they found that Marr, his wife, their baby and a thirteen-year-old apprentice had all been killed, their heads beaten and their throats cut. Now London was said to be in a state of terror with doors barred and gun dealers running out of stock as people prepared to defend themselves. On 19 September the bodies of the Williamsons – he was the landlord of the King's Arms in New Gravel Lane – and their elderly servant were found. They too had their throats cut. A lodger hearing noises went to investigate and, when he saw a figure standing over a body, escaped through a window and raised the alarm.

A labourer, John Williams, who was lodging at the Pear Street Inn near Cinnamon Street, was arrested. Within a matter of hours he hanged himself in his cell at Cold Baths Fields prison in Holborn. At any rate, that is the official story. What is certain is that his body was placed in a cart and escorted by parish officers and the High Constable of Middlesex (in full regalia) and driven through massed crowds past the homes of the victims. Since the practice was to bury suicides at crossroads, the body was then interred at St George's Turnpike and a stake driven through the corpse. Over a hundred years later workmen disinterred the corpse and the bones were shared out as souvenirs with a local publican having the skull.

Whether Williams was the murderer is very much more open to question, as is his apparent suicide. The police historian T.A. Critchley and the crime writer P.D. James have put together an interesting argument that Williams was innocent and was killed in his cell as a convenient way of closing the investigation.[1] It would not be the last time such a thing has happened.

It was shortly afterwards that the East End had its own version of the Glaswegian body-snatchers Burke and Hare. In 1831 John Bishop and his brother-in-law, Thomas Head, also known as Williams, drugged a fourteen-year-old Italian boy, Carlo Ferrari, who made a living exhibiting performing mice, in Nova Scotia Gardens, part of the Old Nichol which would later become Columbia Market. They killed him by first drugging him with rum laced with laudanum and then drowning him by lowering him head first into a well behind Bishop's house. They sold his teeth, but when they asked the surgeons at King's College for nine guineas for his body, the staff – suspicious of receiving a new corpse and one which did not appear to have died naturally – called the police. The pair had previously had two successes, the victims being an elderly woman, Fanny Pigburn, and another young boy. A crowd of some 30,000 is said to have turned out for their turning-off by hangman William Chalcraft at Newgate on 5 December. Their bodies were handed over to King's and St Bartholomew's respectively. Bishop claimed he had been a resurrection man for some ten years, the last five of which had been in partnership with Head and a third man, John May, who gave evidence against them.

The same year, Eliza Ross killed the eighty-four-year-old match seller Caroline Walsh in Goodman's Yard, now Royal Mint Street, for her clothes which she promptly sold. Ross seems to have been a dreadful woman who dealt in cat skins and whose greatest claim to fame, before the murder, was to have strangled and bare-handedly skinned the cat belonging to the landlady of the Sampson and Lion in Shadwell with whom she had quarrelled. Her common-law husband, Edward Cook, was acquitted after the jury heard that he had stared out of the window and had taken no part in the killing of the match seller. Ross was hanged on 9 January the following year.

The next case – which throws a little light on the emerging Metropolitan Police Force and their relationship with the community – came on 26 March 1863 when a respectable-looking man entered a shop owned by Matilda Moore and her husband at 96 Green Street, Bethnal Green, saying he wished to purchase some oats. Whilst she was looking for them he picked her pocket of a purse containing about £8. She discovered the loss immediately and, as he tried to leave the shop, hung on to his coat-tails. He then grabbed her by the throat and she had a heart attack. He escaped, leaving his coat and scarf behind.

Matilda Moore survived the immediate danger and went back to work, saying she could not identify the man, and it seems rather as if she told the police she wished the matter to be dropped. Inquiries into the scarf and coat came to nothing. Then on 7 January 1864 she died aged fifty-five years. The jury unanimously returned a verdict of wilful murder by a person unknown and the coroner suggested the only way to solve the matter was to offer a reward which would induce one of his 'Pals to Peach'.

A reward of £100 was suggested, but there was a dispute as to who should pay for the handbills and eventually the work was undertaken by the Commissioner for Police, offering £50.[2] The reward was never claimed.

The same year Henry Wainwright, a brush maker, died and left what was then a fortune of £11,000 to be divided between his five children. His son, also named Henry, had married two years earlier and carried on the business in the Whitechapel Road next to the Pavilion Theatre. A popular man locally, he owned a Georgian house in Tredegar Square as well as the shop. He gave readings of Dickens and lectured on 'the Wit of Sidney Smith' at the Leeds Mechanics Institute.

Unfortunately, after his marriage Wainwright had, in 1871, met Harriet Lane, the twenty-year-old daughter of a gas manager. She was educated, attractive and apprenticed to a milliner. All went well for a time, with Mrs Wainwright completely unsuspecting of her husband's second home. He had set Harriet up in a house in St Peter Street, Mile End, and on 22 August 1872 they had a daughter. A second daughter was born the following year and they moved to Cecil Court in the Strand before returning to St Peter Street. A notice was published in the *Waltham Abbey Weekly* that she had married a Percy King of Chelsea.

And then things began to fall apart. Wainwright was getting into a financial tangle by running two (and possibly more) homes. His brother William dissolved the partnership, with the result that Harriet's £5 a week was cut. In turn she became quarrelsome and turned to drink. Now Henry Wainwright introduced her to his brother Thomas whom, for the purposes, he called Edward Frieake. She supposed she was to be transferred; they thought they were going to kill her.

In early September 1874 Harriet became very drunk, created a stir outside the lodgings which she now shared with an Ellen

Wilmore and was given notice to quit. However, things improved and on 11 September her transfer to Frieake was apparently completed. She had tired of Henry and she was by no means averse to a new owner. That day she left to join Frieake and was never seen alive again.

Three weeks later Miss Wilmore received a letter from Harriet saying that things were even better. She and Frieake were off to the Continent and provided she renounced her old friends, marriage would follow. Both Miss Wilmore and Wainwright received confirmatory telegrams; but she was not satisfied and after consulting with Harriet's sister a private detective was instructed. All he discovered was that Edward Frieake was an auctioneer in the City and was certainly not the man with whom Harriet had apparently left the country. Her father called on Wainwright, begging to know whether his daughter was alive or dead and was told her former lover did not know.

Over the winter a paint room in the warehouse next to Wainwright's shop, also owned by him, began to develop a smell so strong that the tenants moved out from their rooms above it. As for Wainwright, things went from bad to worse and in June 1875 he was declared bankrupt. The warehouse was to be transferred to a new owner and it was imperative that Wainwright moved the body. Thomas, released from his role as Teddy Frieake and now the proud owner of an ironmongery at the corner of Southwark Street and Borough High Street, agreed to allow Wainwright to re-bury his mistress in the cellar of his shop. Unfortunately, it was not quite that simple.

On 11 September 1875, a year to the day since she had disappeared, the body of Harriet Lane came to light. Her body was dug up, but the quicklime in which she had been buried had preserved rather than destroyed the corpse, which Wainwright now wrapped in several cloth parcels prior to moving it. In the annals of crime, Henry Wainwright's behaviour must go down as one of the more stupid examples, for he then called in a youth named Stokes and told him to watch the packages whilst he went and called a cab. It should, of course, have been Stokes who was sent for the cab. When the inquisitive youth looked into the parcel, a severed hand fell out. There followed a sequence worthy of the Keystone Cops. Wainwright drove off and on seeing a ballet-dancer friend, Alice Day, invited her to join him and Harriet in the cab. Now he lit a cigar in an attempt to hide the ever-increasing smell of putrefaction. The astute Stokes, who had chased after him on foot, found two policemen to whom to tell his story. They laughed at him, but the youth was determined and eventually found another pair who this time listened to what he had to say. Wainwright now stopped at an ironmonger's and, when the police caught up with him and asked to be allowed to examine the parcels, offered them £50 each to go away. They refused what was then an enormous sum of money. In fact, since he was bankrupt it must be doubtful if, had they accepted, they would have received the bribe. Off went Wainwright, Miss Day and the pieces of Harriet to Stone's End Police Station.

Wainwright was charged with Harriet Lane's murder on 21 September 1875. The forensic evidence showed she had been shot twice in the head and her throat had been cut. He was hanged at Newgate prison by William Marwood on 21 December that year, an event to which some sixty people had been invited. According to reports he behaved with some dignity on the scaffold, rounding on the spectators saying, 'Come to see a man die, have you, you curs?'

His brother Thomas, charged as an accessory to murder, received seven years. For once virtue was rewarded and Stokes received, not the £50 the constables were offered, but £30 out of public funds.

The last decades of the century produced a series of seemingly inexplicable events which became known collectively as the West Ham Vanishings. On 13 May 1881, fourteen-year-old Mary Seward, described as young-looking for her age and said to be a trifle backward, disappeared. She had been playing at home in West Road, West Ham, most of the afternoon, but at 6 p.m. her mother told her to go and look for her nephew who had wandered away from the house. The boy was found and given a ticking-off, but Mary disappeared. Later there was a suggestion that she had been seen with a gypsy at a fairground. The Home Office put up a £25 reward and this was supplemented by the proceeds of a local concert.

At 10 a.m. on Saturday 28 January 1882, twelve-year-old Eliza Carter left her elder sister's house, also in West Road and only ten doors away from the Sewards, to go to her parents who lived nearby in Church Street. On the way she took some clothes to the laundry to put through the mangle. She was not seen again until at 5 p.m. she spoke to a school friend in The Portway opposite West Ham Park, telling her she was afraid to go home because of 'that man'. At 11 p.m. that night she was seen in the company of an ugly middle-aged woman dressed in a long Ulster and a black frock.

The next day Eliza's dress, which had buttons all the way down the front, was found in a local football field minus the buttons. There were traces of arrowroot biscuits in her pockets and the police believed they might have been used to entice her into the park. The buttons had been cut off and were thought to be worth about sixpence.

There was now disquiet in the neighbourhood that the Home Office seemed to value the lives of young girls so poorly; but although questions were asked of the local Member of Parliament, nothing came of it.

Curiously, on 13 September 1912 another Eliza Carter was murdered in West Ham. However, this was a lovers' quarrel and the seventeen-year-old was found with her throat cut in the arms of twenty-year-old William Charles Beal who had also cut his own throat. She had been nearly decapitated, but Beal's rather speculative defence was that it was she who had cut both his and her own throats. The jury made a strong recommendation for mercy on the grounds of his youth. It did him no good. Despite being described as not of very sound mind, he was executed at Chelmsford prison on 10 December 1912.

Another in the series of vanishings was said to have occurred the day before Mary Seward went missing, but this time it was a sixty-seven-year-old lady who disappeared from her home in Keogh Road. In the evening she went to a local shop to purchase soap and candles but when the postman and milkman called the next morning they were unable to obtain a reply. In turn the police failed to get a response and broke in. The soap and candles were in place and the grandfather clock in the hall had been wound up. The washing-up had been done and the bed made, but of the lady there was no trace. The case of the elderly lady is by no means as well documented in the local papers as the other vanishings, and may be an example of an urban myth.

Then for a time the vanishings stopped, or at least they were suspended until, in January 1890, three young girls disappeared within a very short time span. The only one whose body was found was fifteen-year-old Millie Jeffs who had been working as a nursemaid after leaving school the previous year. Curiously she lived twelve doors from the Seward home. One Friday evening she met her father Charles, a railwayman, after he finished work, and he gave her threepence to buy some fish at Bowmans in Church Street. She had not returned by 7.30 p.m. and a search was instigated; it lasted until 2.30 a.m. but produced no result.

On Valentine's Day, police officers searching for stolen lead broke the window of 126 West Road and found the body of Millie Jeffs in a cupboard. She had been sexually assaulted and strangled. At her burial in the East London cemetery a collection raised £250 as a reward, but her killer was never found.

Probably the young girls who were never found were kidnapped and used for the purposes of white slavery or child prostitution; there was generally an unhealthy market in young prostitutes at the time. Indeed there is also some evidence that prostitutes sold their children for the trade. In 1896 the beautiful auburn-haired Mary Carr, known as the Queen of the Forty Thieves, a talented thief who also worked the badger game, was sentenced to three years. She had posed for Lord Leighton as an artist's model and now had been found guilty of harbouring a boy stolen at Epsom racecourse at the City and Suburban meeting the previous year.

The case of Carl Wagner has often been included in the vanishings. He lived at 104 Victoria Dock Road, West Ham, where his father had a butcher's shop and he disappeared on 1 April 1882 and so fits neatly into the time scale, but his is a much more prosaic tale of childhood disobedience. The story is that his body, without any marks of injury, was found at the foot of a cliff in Ramsgate with no explanation as to how it got there.

In fact he had left his father's shop on 30 March with a bag containing the very substantial sum of £150 in gold and had gone to Ramsgate with John Walters, one of his father's employees with whom he had been told not to associate. But the body was not uninjured; there was evidence that he had been beaten with a screwdriver. Walters was recognised in the town as having bought Carl a pair of trousers and paid in gold. When told that a body had been found under the cliffs, Walters had replied that he hoped it was not that of his friend who had been with him the previous day but who had gone off with a woman. Somewhat fortunately he was acquitted of murder, but was immediately re-arrested and convicted of theft for which he received five years.

Six years later came Jack the Ripper.

The Whitechapel Murders have, perhaps, been the greatest and most lasting contribution to the lore and legend of the East End. Most aficionados who call themselves Ripperologists believe that the five murders which took place over the relatively short period from 31 August 1888, when Mary Ann Nichols was killed in Bucks Row, to 9 November, when Mary Jane Kelly was killed and then mutilated in Millers Court, Dorset Street, were the work of one man dubbed Jack the Ripper. The other three which are definitely attributed to him are Annie Chapman on 8 September at Hanbury Street and Elizabeth 'Long Liz' Stride and Catherine Eddowes at Berner Street and Mitre Square respectively, both killed on 30 September.

Two earlier murders took place which some attribute to Jack the Ripper. They were of Emma Elizabeth Smith on the night of 2–3 April and, four months later, on 7 August, Martha (or Emma) Tabram, who was also known as Martha Turner, in George Yard Building.

The first can certainly be ruled out, because Emma Smith survived after she was attacked and said she could identify one of the four men involved. She had been seen talking to a man with a white scarf shortly after midnight in Fairance Street, Limehouse, and then reappeared at George Street lodging house and told the deputy that she had been assaulted and robbed in Osborn Street. She was taken to the London Hospital where she was found to have had an instrument, not a knife, inserted in her vagina. She must have been in great pain as she staggered back to the lodgings, but had made no complaint to any police constable she must have passed in the street and was indeed reluctant to be taken to hospital. She died two days later of peritonitis. Unfortunately, it was not until 6 April that the police were informed. It is possible that her attackers were members of the Green Gate Gang or the Old Nichol Gang who operated in the area at the time as ponces and extortionists and as street robbers generally.

So far as Tabram was concerned, her body was first seen about 3 a.m. on 7 August on the first-floor landing of George Yard Building. She had been stabbed thirty-nine times. Earlier in the evening, along with a colleague known as Pearly Poll, she had picked up two soldiers and had been drinking with them in the Angel and Crown public house. The soldier with Tabram was identified and produced an alibi. It was thought that Tabram's killer was ambidextrous, and that two weapons had been used, of which one was a bayonet. All soldiers then stationed at the Tower of London were put on an identification parade, but Poll failed to pick anyone out. She was ordered to attend the inquest on Tabram and went into hiding. Found in Covent Garden, she was made to attend another identification parade, this time at Chelsea Barracks where out of pique she identified the first two men she saw. In turn they were able to provide alibis. Based on the fact that both killings were on a Bank Holiday Monday, Chief Inspector Walter Dew always believed that Emma Smith and Martha Tabram were genuine Ripper victims.[3]

There was another little flurry over the death of Catherine Millett – the so-called Poplar or Rainham Mystery. Catherine, sometimes called Rose Mylett, was found fully clothed lying in Clarke's Yard off High Street, Poplar, on 20 December 1888 by a Police Sergeant Golding. The Divisional Surgeon Matthew Brownfield saw nothing suspicious and the body was removed for a post mortem, at which time he suggested she had been strangled. However, his assistant Dr Thomas Bond, who earlier had examined the body of Mary Jane Kelly, did not agree and the inquest turned into a medical battle. Four doctors thought she had been strangled with a cord of the type used in those days to cut a bar of soap. Bond and the Coroner Wynne Baxter, who featured in so many of the East End inquests of the time, disagreed. The jury returned a verdict of wilful murder but no suspect, if indeed there ever should have been one, was ever arrested and for a short time there was speculation that Jack the Ripper had changed his methods.[4]

When it comes to it there are perhaps seven serious or semi-serious suspects with little if any evidence against any of them. In descending order there is Montague John Druitt, a failed barrister who committed suicide by weighting his pockets and drowning in the Thames. His cousin, Dr Lionel Druitt, at one time practised as a doctor in the East End, which gives him the opportunity to hide with his cousin and also to learn the rudiments of anatomy. At least he was favoured by the Assistant Chief Constable of Scotland Yard Sir Melville Macnaghten, but apart from opportunity, which is common to thousands, there appears to be no positive evidence against him.

Then there is public house landlord George Chapman, also known as Severin Antoniovich Klosowski, who was favoured by Chief Detective Inspector Frederick Abberline, one of the few senior officers involved in the actual hunt not to write his memoirs. He remarked to Inspector George Godley when some years later Chapman was arrested for the poisoning of various wives, 'You've got Jack the Ripper at last.' Just why Chapman should change his *modus operandi* from vivisectionist to poisoner is not clear. Nor is it clear why he should abandon his first career. As for ability, he had been some sort of field surgeon in the Russian army and could have acquired rudimentary skills there.

Dr Thomas Neill Cream was later convicted of poisoning a series of prostitutes. The evidence against him seems to be based solely on the fact that when he was being hanged his last words were 'I'm Jack ...' This may have been a muffled cry of 'I'm ejaculating', but his supporters take it as evidence of his guilt. A further complication to the flimsy case against him, in that he is recorded as being in prison in America at the time of one of the killings, is overcome by saying that bribery was rife and prison records inaccurate and he may have been released. There is also another fanciful theory, to which Sir Edward Marshall Hall subscribed, that he had a double, also a criminal, and they exchanged names and identities to provide each other with an alibi. Cream, when he was hanged, was repaying a debt by calling out 'I'm Jack the Ripper' – if that is what he intended to say – so clearing his doppelganger of suspicion.

The case against Cream may not be completely defeated by the fact that he was meant to be in prison. Certainly not if the case of John C. Colt, brother of the inventor of the revolver, is anything to go by. While in The Tombs prison in New York awaiting execution for the murder of Samuel Adams, Colt appears to have contrived his escape, with considerable help it must be said, by staging a fire and apparently committing suicide but in reality exchanging his position with a corpse. The coroner was aware of the deception and the jury was specially selected to investigate his death. Colt fled with Caroline Henshaw, the woman he had married hours before his escape, either to California or Texas.[5]

The Duke of Clarence, whose fiancée Princess May of Teck changed her name to Mary and married his brother George V, is favoured by many. Unfortunately, there is an almost insuperable flaw in the argument against him in that he was dead when one of the murders occurred. This is overcome by the ingenious and entertaining conspiracy theory that he had gone mad from syphilis and was being held in a private mental hospital. If this is correct, it means he was from time to time released or escaped, killed and found his own way home again.

If you do not fancy his Royal Highness – or a Masonic connection which is also on offer and which includes the Queen's physician Sir William Gull – then there is an argument against a man who may have been his lover and was certainly his tutor at Cambridge: James Kenneth Stephen, the son of the High Court judge. The reasoning is that when the Duke became engaged he sacrificed 'symbolic' women. The best evidence is that after Stephen received a blow to the head in an accident in 1886 he became increasingly deranged and was committed to an asylum in November 1892, dying three months later. Quite where he obtained the medical skill thought necessary to dissect the poor women is not made clear.

There are, however, two other doctors in the frame. One, Roslyn D'Onston Stephenson, was certainly peculiar – a journalist, medico, mage and, as Richard Whittington-Egan puts it, 'Man about Whitechapel'. As part of the case against him, it is suggested that the murders were black magic rituals.

A more likely doctor is the eccentric – if not plain mad – American Francis Tumblety who earlier had been arrested over the assassination of Abraham Lincoln. He was certainly in England at the time, was known to dislike women and had been inquiring about obtaining body parts in the East End before he broke his bail and fled back to America after being charged with indecency. The killings stopped after he left.

The case, such as it is, against each of the principal suspects has been rehearsed time and time again and it is entertaining although idle to look at some of the other names which have been suggested over the years. Sir Melville was by no means wholly committed to the theory that Druitt was the Ripper.[6] He also suggests a Polish Jew, Kosminski, in which he is supported by Chief Inspector Donald Sutherland Swanson, and a Russian doctor Michael Ostrog as possible suspects. Martin Fido is on the same lines on the Polish Jew theory. He has traced an Aaron Kozminski as being admitted to Colney Hatch, the North London asylum, on 6 February but, when it comes to it, favours another inmate Nathan Kaminsky who died there in 1889 under the anglicised name of David Cohen.

Other potential claimants to the title have included Frederick Richard Chapman, a Brixton doctor who died of a tuberculous psoas abscess on 12 December 1888. Given his illness, he could easily be eliminated; he would have been hardly able to walk, let alone dart about the alleys of the East End. The evidence against him is based on the account of a former police constable, Robert Clifford Spicer, who said he had arrested a doctor with blood-stained cuffs and a prostitute, but the pair had been released on the authority of his superior. Spicer had been discharged from the police on 25 April 1889 for being drunk and interfering with two private persons. B.E. Reilly concluded from some research that Chapman was really Dr Merchant, his name being a pseudonym – a chapman was a merchant. This was smartly blown out of the water.[7]

Francis Thompson, the poet, was another off-the-wall suggestion. The evidence against him is that he had some medical training, was a drug addict and therefore unpredictable, had a friendship with a prostitute and 'possessed a chaotic sexuality'. He also had lived in the East End and this familiarity suggests he would have been able to elude the police by darting into the back turns and doubles.[8]

As the years have passed, more and more outlandish theories have been produced. One of the more acceptable is that of Jock the Ripper expounded by Molly Whittington-Egan: William Henry Bury, who killed his wife and was hanged on 24 April 1889. He is said to have been known in Whitechapel and to have left a detailed confession which was never published but which made startling revelations about the Ripper murders. Other less likely candidates have included Mary Kelly's boyfriend Joseph Barnett; George Francis Miles, who was Oscar Wilde's boyfriend; and Charlie the Ripper, a fishmonger who had sexual difficulties.[9] In recent years on the strength of a diary, the authenticity of which is jealously supported and challenged, James Maybrick, possibly poisoned by his wife Florence in Liverpool, has come into the reckoning.

In a compilation of theories of Ripperologists, amateur and professional, in 1995 the identities were, as might be expected, widely spread. In Camille Wolff's compilation *Who was Jack the Ripper?*, Wilf Gregg lists no fewer than twenty-five suspects against whom some sort of plausible or implausible case has been made, and the actual list of suspects is probably three times that length.

As Donald Rumbelow wrote:

I have always the feeling that on the Day of Judgement, when all things shall be known, when I and the other generations of 'Ripperologists' ask for Jack the Ripper to step forward and call out his true name, we shall turn and look with blank astonishment as he does so and say, 'Who?'[10]

PC Ernest Thompson was thought to be the only person to have seen Jack the Ripper. He had only been in the service for six weeks when on 13 February 1891 he went out on night duty alone for the first time. He was walking through Chambers Street when a man came running out of Swallow Gardens towards the Royal Mint. Thompson saw a man under a lamp with a bag in his hand and he ran after him, but fell over something which turned out to be the body of Frances Coles. He was so upset he wandered about in a dazed state and was taken to the local station.

Over the years Thompson became convinced he would never die of natural causes, and indeed he was stabbed to death at Alder Street and the junction with the Commercial Road on 1 December 1900, at the age of thirty-two. The man he apprehended – Barnet Abrahams, a forty-one-year-old cigar maker – was allegedly behaving badly towards some women at a night coffee stall and when questioned moved away to open a clasp knife and returned to stick his knife into Thompson's neck. Thompson held onto the man, calling for assistance, and died with his hands still on the assailant's collar. Abrahams was defended by Charles F. Gill and claimed he had been given a severe beating by the police and so remembered nothing of the incident. The judge directed that the jury should find manslaughter and Abrahams received twenty years' penal servitude and died in prison.[11]

Thompson left four children all aged under four, and his widow benefited from a collection which raised £338. There is a small memorial to him and two other officers in Tower Hamlets cemetery: Richard James Barber who, on 2 March 1885 fell through a skylight when chasing James Smith, who received one year hard labour for theft; and William Paster who, at the age of forty-three, drowned whilst on holiday at Margate. He had tried to save a swimmer in difficulties on 24 July 1890.

What is certain is that the Ripper murders produced another wave of anti-Semitic feeling in the East End.[12] It was believed that only a foreigner could have carried out such abominable crimes, a theory argued from time to time by an Assistant Commissioner, Sir Robert Anderson. The theory was based, in part, on a report from *The Times* correspondent safely in Vienna. In 1884 a Jew named Ritter had been tried for the murder and mutilation of a woman in a village near Cracow. The reasoning was that there was a belief amongst fanatical Jews that the Talmud required such an act of atonement by a man who had had sexual relations with a Christian woman. The Chief Rabbi was keen and quick to scotch such a theory. So far as the Talmud was concerned, there was no such direction. But for a time, fuelled by the fact that one of the bodies had been found by a Jewish cemetery in Brady Street, there was the belief that the murder had been committed by one of the *shochets*, ritual Jewish slaughterers, and suspicion fell on a man called John Pizer (known as Leather Apron) who fitted the popular conception of Jack the Ripper.

A man of Jewish appearance, he was known to have abused prostitutes and after the Mary Nichols' murder he disappeared for a time. Rumour spread and many believed he was the Ripper. Eventually he was found by the police and taken into custody at Leman Street Police Station which, within half an hour, was surrounded by a crowd 'clamouring to get at him'. He provided an alibi but was kept in a place of safety until his name was cleared at the resumed inquest on Mary Nichols.[13]

The lot of the policeman in the East End at the time was not necessarily a happy one. Describing the Ratcliffe Highway as Tiger Bay, journalist James Greenwood interviewed a local police officer around 1870:

At times it is unsafe for our men to perambulate it except in a gang of three. They'd have the hair off a man's head if they could get a penny a pound for it.[14]

Describing his time in the East End ten years later, Chief Inspector Fred Wensley would have none of the officers walking in threes. He did allow, however, that an officer could expect a hard time.

Lambeth, however, was a model of probity and decorum compared with Whitechapel. Most of the inhabitants of my new division considered that they had a natural right to get fighting drunk and knock a policeman about whenever the spirit moved them. Bruises and worse were our routine lot. Gangs of hooligans infested the streets and levied blackmail on timorous shopkeepers. There was an enormous amount of personal robbery with violence. The maze of narrow ill-lighted alleyways offered easy ways of escape after a man had been knocked down and his watch and money stolen.[15]

One of the local sports, and one which continued for many years, was stuffing policemen down sewers. Norman Nettaway, who later himself served throughout the East End, recalls that his grandfather as a special constable received a certificate for pulling a constable out of a manhole.[16]

Wensley went to Whitechapel shortly before the turn of the century and never really left it. However the area might have been regarded by the ordinary citizen at that time, there is no doubt that it was the finest training-ground imaginable for a young detective.

Men and women ripe for any crime from murder to pilfering were to be found in its crowded slums and innumerable common-lodging houses. The off-scourings of the criminal population of Europe – Russians, Poles, Germans, Austrians and Frenchmen – found a refuge there. Many of them, British as well as foreign, carried knives or guns which they did not hesitate to use. Organised gangs of desperate men and lads, armed with lethal weapons, infested the streets, terrorising whole areas, blackmailing tradesmen, holding up wayfarers, and carrying out more or less open robbery in any direction that offered.[17]

Murders probably went uninvestigated and unrecorded and, unless there was clear evidence of foul play, those whose bodies were found near houses of ill-repute received open verdicts. To counter these hooligans there was a collection of what Wensley described, with perhaps some understatement in parts, as outstanding figures.

> Some of them, by present day standards, may have been a little rough and uncultivated, but they had the most wonderful knowledge of criminals ... They lived for their work.

Wensley was proud to have graduated from the ranks of men like 'Chinaman' Thompson and 'Johnny Upright' Sergeant John Thicke:

> I myself early attained the distinction of a nickname amongst criminals of the district. Those who spoke English called me Weasel – which I felt to be something of a compliment – and the foreigners corrupted it into 'Venzel'.

An assessment of his position nearly a century later puts his nickname in a slightly different context:

> Wensley knew his ground well and seems to have had an exceptional memory for detail, but he was unpopular with the Whitechapel immigrants who suspected him of corruption. Probably he knew rather less about the ways of immigrants than he tried to make out.[18]

One of the more curious aspects of detective work at the time, and one against which Wensley rebelled, was the practice of keeping detectives confined to their own areas, which gave criminals a relatively free hand since they could move districts in the almost certain knowledge that they would not be recognised.

A divisional superintendent did not like officers leaving his district to operate in another; and a local detective inspector resented detectives from other districts 'poaching' on his division. He would hint pretty broadly that if he wanted their aid he would apply for it.[19]

One of Wensley's earliest arrests as a young detective followed an attack on a Jewish shopkeeper and his housekeeper on 4 April 1896. With Harry Richardson, he was called to Turner Street between Commercial Street and the Whitechapel Road. They climbed into the premises through a back window and began opening the doors of the tenement. One was pushed back at them and when Wensley broke through they found the body of seventy-five-year-old John Goodman Levy. Upstairs in the front bedroom, which had been ransacked, was that of his housekeeper Sarah Gale. There was a hole in the ceiling and when they heard sounds above them Richardson volunteered to climb up. Wensley followed him.

On the roof they found the murderer about to jump into the street forty feet below, anticipating that the crowd of onlookers would break his fall. Wensley went back through the hole, down the stairs and was in the street almost immediately after the man jumped, knocking himself unconscious and injuring several of the spectators.

The robber was William Saunders (better known as Seaman), supposedly a sailor from Millwall but in fact a ticket-of-leave man who over the years had served twenty-eight years of penal servitude. On the last occasion he had walked into a chemist's shop in Whitechapel and asked for the loan of a hammer. When handed it, he hit the shopkeeper over the head and ransacked the premises.

It seems that for a time at any rate Seaman played the wronged lover. The woman at whose rooms in Millwall he was staying was brought in to make an identification, and she asked him why he had killed the pair:

> 'Revenge,' he replied. 'He did me the greatest injustice one man can do another.'
> 'Why, was that woman your wife?'
> 'No.'

And unfortunately the officer in charge then put a stop to this rather interesting conversation.

Later, Seaman's version of the crime was that he had known both Levy and Sarah Gale for some time and that Levy owed him some £70. The implication was that Levy had been acting as Seaman's receiver. On the morning of the murder he was let in by Levy and went upstairs to the girl's bedroom. She began shouting and kicking before he killed her and then went downstairs and killed Levy. It was then that he heard someone at the door.

The story was false at least in parts. There was no evidence that Sarah Gale had been killed in her room. So far as Wensley was concerned, there was an anonymous letter to back Seaman's implication that Levy was a receiver but no hard evidence. Seaman's statement ended:

> I then got on the roof from the inside and saw my only chance was to dive down off the roof head first. If it had not been for someone breaking my fall I should not have been lying in here. But there it is. Everyone has to die sometime. I know I am going to get hung and would not care if it was now, for I am tired of life.

However, in a curious way Saunders/Seaman still had a part to play in life. At the time of the Levy killing there had been a murder in Muswell Hill involving Henry Fowler and Albert

Milsom, who had battered a wealthy retired engineer, Henry Smith, to death. They had also tortured him to make him disclose the contents of his safe. Milsom had put the blame on Fowler, a giant of a man who in turn had repeatedly threatened his co-defendant. As the verdicts of guilty were announced Fowler threw himself on Milsom and, in a fight lasting some twelve minutes before he was subdued, the whole dock at the Old Bailey was smashed. When both were brought under heavy guard for sentence, Milsom made whining pleas for leniency which were mimicked by Fowler.

On 9 June, in the last triple execution held at Newgate, Seaman was put between Milsom and Fowler to prevent any further trouble. He is alleged to have said, 'Well, this is the first time in my life I've ever had to act as a peace-maker.'

By the end of the century the Rev. Samuel Barnett of St Jude's, Whitechapel, feared he had made no progress in bringing Christianity to the area. In a lament to *The Times* he wrote:

> After six years of work, after everything has been done which money can provide or thought can suggest, I have to confess that in the past year the church has been as little used as ever.[20]

Of course, one of his problems was that now many of his potential congregation were Jewish. And those who were not still did not seem to appreciate things.

NOTES

1. T.A. Critchley and P.D. James, *The Maul and the Pear Tree*.
2. Nat. Arch. MEPO 3 69.
3. Walter Dew, *I Caught Crippen*, pp. 95–103.

4. 11 Nat. Arch. MEPO 3 143; *The Star*, 24 December 1888; *The Advertiser*, 10 January 1899.

5. Charles Sutton, *The New York Tombs*.

6. Confidential memorandum, M.L. Macnaghten, 23 February 1894.

7. See *Daily Express*, 16 March 1931; B.E. Reilly in *City*, February 1972; Nicholas P. Warren, 'Dr Merchant was not Jack the Ripper' in *The Criminologist*, Spring 1992.

8. Joseph C. Rupp, 'Was Francis Thompson Jack the Ripper?' in *The Criminologist*, Winter 1982.

9. Molly Whittington-Egan, *Scottish Murder Stories*, Chapter 16.

10. Donald Rumbelow, *The Complete Jack the Ripper*, p. 141.

11. See Tom Divall, *Scoundrels and Scallywags*, pp. 104–5, and Frederick Wensley, *Detective Days*, pp. 4–5.

12. *Jewish Chronicle*, 14 September 1888; *East London Observer* (*ELO*), 15 September 1888.

13. Walter Dew, *I Caught Crippen*, pp. 109–11.

14. James Greenwood, *The Wilds of London*, p 1.

15. Frederick Wensley, *Detective Days*, p 8.

16. Conversation with author, 4 November 1999.

17. Frederick Wensley, *Detective Days*, pp. 13–14.

18. Andrew Rose, *Stinie*, p. 13.

19. F. Wensley, *Detective Days*, p. 39.

20. *The Times*, 7 April 1897.

2

IMMIGRANTS

In the 1850s some 18,000 to 20,000 Jews lived in London, around 12,000 of them in the City itself. The great Jewish migration to the East End of London began in the 1860s and gathered pace after the assassination of Tsar Alexander II in 1881. There had long been a Jewish presence in the East End and City of London, but these were the Sephardic Jews. The seemingly uncontrollable influx was of Ashkenazi Jews and, in a matter of years, the once-important Sephardic congregation had been reduced to numerical insignificance.[1]

By 1902–3 there were some 140,000 to 150,000 in the East End alone, with the area around Whitechapel High Street and Commercial Road East the most heavily populated. In 1901 there were at least 42,000 Russian-born Jews in Whitechapel. They were generally accepted in the community and in 1894 there were only ninety-nine Russians and Poles amongst the 1,972 aliens in British prisons. The number rose substantially and then, after the Aliens Act 1905, declined. Evidence to the Select Committee on Emigration and Immigration (Foreigners) showed they were committing only petty crime, which included counterfeiting and burglaries. They did not steal for food. The main complaint was that they did not wash.[2]

The Jews were the dispossessed. Following a series of anti-Semitic edicts by the Tsars who ruled not only Russia but Poland, for some years they had been restricted to an area known as the Pale of Settlement on the Polish–Russian border. They were debarred from taking employment in government projects such as roads and railways and state manufacturing – in effect, anything to do with modern industrial growth. This left them with traditional employment – tailoring, boot making, working in cigarette factories – and in all these endeavours they worked in competition with each other.

There were also other hardships and restrictions. Fit young Jewish men were subject to conscription at any age between twelve and twenty-five, where they could be required to serve for a period of thirty-five years. The mortality rate was high.

After the assassination of Tsar Alexander II by Jessie Helfmann, a seamstress, on 1 March 1881, an anti-Semitic campaign was launched in an attempt to deflect popular discontent. Apart from the pogrom in Kherson there were others in Kiev, Odessa and Warsaw, with some two hundred communities being the victims of arson, pillage and rape. One stated aim of the revolutionists was to have the troops defend the Jews against the Christians. The troops would either refuse or there would be a general uprising; it did not matter which. Now the Jews fled to England to find either a home or a resting-place before the longer journey to America.

During the winter of 1886–7 some 70 per cent of dock labourers, building craftsmen, tailors and boot makers in the East End were unemployed, many for over two months. Unemployment in the three preceding years was the worst continuous sequence of any period prior to the First World War.[3]

By 1887 it was estimated that one third of Tower Hamlets' population lived on or below the poverty line, and 55 per cent of East End children died before they attained five years, as compared with 18 per cent of children from other parts of London.

Typical of pious sentiments uttered for the jubilee of Queen Victoria was that written by the Reverend Simeon Singer, who would play a major part in the murder trial of Israel Lipski the next year:

> We are Englishmen and the thoughts and feelings of Englishmen are our thoughts and feelings.[4]

Despite this, there was considerable anti-Semitic sentiment being bruited in some of the magazines of the time:

> Foreign Jews of no nationality whatever are becoming a pest and a menace to the poor native born East-Ender – [they have] greater responsibility for the distress which prevails there probably than all other cases put together.[5]

It was said of St George's in the East, Shadwell, that a murder had been committed in every house in this depressing area just off the Commercial Road, and on 28 June 1885 one of the more famous crimes occurred there when the body of the six-month-pregnant Miriam Angel was found at 16 Batty Street, a rooming house where she lived with her husband, Isaac. She was twenty-one and came from near Warsaw. She had made him his breakfast overnight and he left her in bed when he went to work at 6.15 a.m.

Philip and Leah Lipski lived at 16 Batty Street and let the top room to Israel Lipski who was an unmarried stick maker – what we would call frames for an umbrella. Leah Lipski, his landlady (no relation), told the inquest held on 29 June and 1 July 1885 before Wynne E. Baxter that Israel had been a lodger for the last two years. He was a good worker when there was any, was of good character and had a fiancée, Kate Lyons, who steadfastly believed in his innocence. Batty Street was one of the poorest in the neighbourhood; average wages would be between eighteen shillings and a guinea and the rent six shillings weekly.

Shortly after 11 o'clock that morning, Mrs Angel's mother came round and went up to her daughter's room where she knocked and could get no reply. She and Mrs Lipski went into the room, saw Miriam on the bed and, thinking she had fainted, went for the doctor, John William Kay, in the Commercial Road.

He arrived at 11.30 a.m. and found a very different situation. Beside the German feather-bed was a glass tumbler containing stout. On the bed was the dead Miriam Angel. She had corrosive fluid running from her mouth and onto her neck and breast and her tongue was burned. Kay could find no bottle on the sheets, so he pulled them aside to see if it had fallen down and saw the face of Israel Lipski, protruding from under the bed. He gave him two slaps and he started; his mouth was injured with corrosive fluid in the same way as Miriam Angel's. The bottle, found at the foot of the bed under some clothes, was labelled Camphorated Oil, Bell and Co., 100 Commercial Road, corner of Batty Street. As for Miriam Angel, on her right eye and temple were marks of a serious blow probably made by a fist. There were no marks of violence about the genitals, but there was what appeared to be semen in the vagina. The girl's thighs were wide apart, and legs, thighs and genitals exposed; what is now seen as a classic position for the victim of a rape murder. When Kay gave evidence at the inquest on the second day he said it might be semen but there was no spermatozoa. When asked, Isaac Angel said that he had not had intercourse – described euphemistically as connection – with his wife on the morning of her death or the previous evening.

When Lipski recovered, his statement to the police was that he had returned to Batty Street from work during the morning when two men had taken hold of him by the throat, poured poison into his mouth and asked for his gold chain. Lipski said it was in pawn. He said they had told him, 'If you don't give it to us you will be as dead as the woman.' He suggested one of the men was a Simon Rosenbloom.

There was indeed a Simon Rosenbloom, but he gave a very different version of events. He said that he and Lipski had previously been apprenticed together and Lipski had offered him work when he met him the previous Saturday. Lipski gave him some work on the Tuesday and then said he was going out to buy a sponge and vice.

The nitric acid, said Charles Moore of Bell and Co., had been bought the previous Saturday, by someone who was not English. He knew the man was a stick maker from his clothes.

There does not appear to have been anything in the way of cross-examination of the witnesses, nor was there any evidence that Lipski had behaved oddly or shown any sign of sexual interest in Miriam Angel. The jury returned a unanimous verdict of wilful murder by Lipski, who was committed for trial at the Central Criminal Court.

He was tried in the July before Mr Justice James Fitzjames Stephen, who summed up heavily against him. In fact his whole trial was fraught with difficulties. A small public subscription raised enough money to pay for his counsel. His solicitor, a John Hammond who had a Jewish clerk, seems to have done the work unpaid. At first Gerald Geoghegan, one of the first-rank barristers at the Old Bailey, was briefed on Lipski's behalf; but unfortunately Geoghegan had a tendency to drink, particularly before a capital case which he feared he might lose. Although he was present throughout the trial he took no part and Lipski was defended by a commercial silk, A.J. McIntyre QC.[6]

At the time a prisoner was not allowed to give evidence on his own behalf. He could call witnesses and make an unsworn statement from the dock, but the danger in either of these courses was that the defence then forfeited to the Crown the final speech to the jury. Lipski remained silent.

The basis of the prosecution was that Lipski had seen the heavily pregnant woman through a window onto the stairs as he went to his attic room and, overcome by lust, had attacked her. The difficulty with this is that the purchasing of the corrosive argues a degree of premeditation. The other occupants of what was a small tenement building do not appear to have noticed any previous conduct by Lipski to suggest he was a potential rapist.

For a while there was considerable agitation that Lipski's conviction had been wrong, but on the day before his execution at Newgate, after days spent in prayer with the Reverend Simeon Singer, he made a full confession which satisfied some people for the time. His story was that he had gone into Miriam Angel's room to steal and, despairing of his impoverished situation, had taken poison himself. The confession has the smell of a compromise. It obviated the slur of an attempted rape, but it is difficult to understand since on the morning of the killing he had set himself up in a new business and had a loyal and supportive fiancée and her family.

It was rumoured that he had made an earlier confession which had been torn up whilst there was still hope of a reprieve. Was the confession genuine, or was it made when there was no hope of a reprieve on the instigation of Singer who feared public disorder in a climate of growing anti-Semitism?

Certainly the confession was wrong. In it Lipski said he had gone to the room to steal and had been surprised. He then poured the corrosive down Mrs Angel's throat and took some himself. This had taken place almost immediately before her body was found. The medical evidence, however, contradicted this. Mrs Angel had been dead some two to three hours before her body was discovered.

Lipski was hanged by James Berry at Newgate on 22 August. Berry, who had a history of accidents when hanging prisoners, once again miscalculated the length of drop required to break Lipski's neck and instead nearly decapitated him. When the black flag signifying a successful execution was run up at the prison, the crowd outside gave three cheers. Berry – sickened no doubt by his mistake, and moved by the Hebrew prayers chanted from the condemned cell – said he would not execute another Jew. After his death 'Lipski' became a Yiddish and anti-Semitic insult.

A subscription was set up to thank the solicitor Hammond for his tireless efforts for Lipski, but it closed with only three contributions. He died in 1917 leaving an estate of a little over £100.

It is thought by many that Lipski was the first Jew to be hanged in modern times, but this is not correct. William Marwood hanged Isaac Marks on 2 January 1874. He had been convicted of the Lambeth shooting of Frederick Bernard, at one time his intended father-in-law but whom Marks came to believe had cheated him in business.

Curiously, some thirty years later the body of another pregnant woman was found in St George's in the East with a man lying by her bed. The circumstances were, however, very different from the Lipski case and, on 30 December 1920 at Pentonville prison, Marks Goodmacher became only the second Orthodox Jew to be executed for murder when he was hanged. Russian born, he had served in the Tsar's army from 1898 to 1899. He came to England in 1908 and worked as a ladies' tailor's presser; he was then thirty-five. He lived at 57 Lambeth Street, Whitechapel, with his wife Sarah and they had a son and a daughter, Fanny. Goodmacher, a thoroughly evil-tempered man, drove his wife out of the home. When his daughter married Sion Zeitoun in 1919, at first they lived with her father at Lambeth Street but they soon moved.

Fanny had complained to a friend, Esther Albert:

> Oh I can't open my heart to you but this I can tell you, that my father loved my mother and because she left him his love has grown for me. He does not like me to go out or speak to anybody as he is very jealous of me. I must leave home through him.

Goodmacher began telling Zeitoun that his wife was having relations with other men. When that did not seem to have an adverse effect on the marriage, he then took to calling his son-in-law a ponce and spitting at him in the street. Relations were cut off but, to his fury, the couple still visited neighbours of Goodmacher; he said that if they went again he would cut the baby out of his pregnant daughter's belly. It was apparently a threat he made regularly.

Despite his threats and behaviour, Goodmacher expected his daughter to seek a reconciliation on the Day of Atonement that year. When she did not go round to Lambeth Street during the day, he was heard that evening cursing in his yard in Yiddish saying, 'Why don't she come and see me? Why hasn't she come today? I will kill her tomorrow. I will cut her in the stomach.'

At 8.30 p.m. on 23 September 1920, the police went to 17 Grove Street, St George's in the East, to the top-floor room where Fanny Zeitoun was lying fully dressed with her throat cut with a razor. Goodmacher was also lying by the bed with his throat cut. He was taken to hospital and survived.

He had cut all her clothes, torn a fur necklet to pieces, broken a set of spoons and generally done what damage he could to the room, almost certainly in her absence since there was little sign of a struggle. The police surmised that she had been in the lavatory in the basement when he arrived and returning to her room had found him there. From the bloodstains they concluded that her throat was cut from behind, right to left – Goodmacher was left-handed – near the fireplace, and it seems he then put her on the bed and tried either to staunch the blood or wipe it clean. He then cut his own throat. Blood dripped through the ceiling, and when they went to investigate at about 5 p.m., incredibly the neighbours thought Fanny must have had a miscarriage and had gone out afterwards. Her husband came home at about 8 p.m. to find her body. Goodmacher was charged with her murder and also the then offence of attempted suicide.

The defence relied on a plea of insanity at the brief trial at the Central Criminal Court on 18 November 1920, but it did not succeed. Dr Griffiths of Brixton prison was called in the hope that he would say the man was insane, but instead he gave evidence that although Marks Goodmacher was an hysterical and passionate man he could find no trace of insanity. In those days, and for some years subsequently, prison doctors rarely found their charges to be unfit for punishment, capital or otherwise.[7]

At the turn of the century, a favourite form of robbery was with the garotte. It was not the Spanish form of execution which involved a mask with a metal pin slowly tightened, but a neck hold which, properly applied, brought about unconsciousness. 'Properly applied' was the key phrase. Too much force and the victim died. You would come up to a man from behind, put your arms round his throat, with your fists on his throttle. If it went on for more than a few seconds he would choke, so you had to be skilled.[8]

A convicted garotter could expect a heavy sentence; five years and, worse, a 'bashing', eighteen strokes with the cat o' nine tails. The Reubens brothers were not sufficiently experienced and they paid the penalty. On 15 March 1909 the steamer *Dorset* berthed at the Victoria Docks and that night two officers, William Sproull (the second engineer) and McEachern (the second mate) went off on what was to be a drunken spree. They were not complete innocents. They expected to be tapped for money, and since they regarded it as insulting to give beggars bronze coins they carried with them a supply of silver threepenny pieces.

Around 2.30 the next morning the body of Sproull was found in Rupert Street just behind Leman Street. A policeman called by the night-watchman who found the body saw McEachern leaning against a wall in the Whitechapel Road. His almost incoherent story was that the pair had eaten somewhere in Aldgate and had then toured the public houses. They met two girls, Emily Stevens and Ellen Charge, and agreed to go home with them to 3 Rupert Street. Whilst they were with them the door burst open and in came the Reubens brothers, Morris and Marks.

Questioned by Inspector Wensley, who was called, the constable remembered that two rough-looking men had been peering through the shutters of a house in Rupert Street earlier in the night. From the place where Sproull's body was found, a trail of silver coins led back to 3 Rupert Street. Marks Reubens was arrested in the house and a young prostitute in Room 13 admitted that she had brought a man back to the room. As the police searched the remaining rooms Morris Reubens was found and admitted that Stevens and Charge had brought Sproull and McEachern back. When the men refused to hand over the rest of their money the brothers had attacked them.

When Morris Reubens was searched, a constable found that sewn into the leg of his trousers was a series of hooks on which swung Sproull's watch and chain. It appeared that after having sex with the girls, McEachern had decided to return to the ship rather than to stay the night, taking Sproull with him. The Reubens brothers had known the girls had gone back to Room 13 and probably one of them had signalled to the brothers who were listening outside the room. Instead of rolling the sailors whilst asleep, as would have been the normal practice if they wanted the remainder of their money – about £5 each – they were forced to attack them as they left. McEachern may have been hopelessly drunk, something which probably saved him, but Sproull put up serious resistance. Morris Reubens had a stick of hippopotamus hide and this was broken in the fight. Now Marks used a pocket-knife; Sproull was stabbed twice in the face and in the wrist as well as the body. They managed to get Sproull to the door and pushed him onto the street saying, for the benefit of a passer-by, 'Get out! You don't live here.'

At the trial at the Old Bailey Morris claimed he did not know his brother had a knife. Both said it was the sailors who had attacked them. They were unable to explain the watch and chain. The defence was not one which appealed to the jury, who convicted them both after a retirement of twelve minutes. Morris began to call out 'Mercy, Mercy' whilst Marks fought with the warders before they were led away screaming. They were hanged at Pentonville on 20 May by Henry and Thomas Pierrepoint. Marks is said to have apologised to Sproull's relatives and said, 'Goodbye Morris, I am sorry . . .'

Wensley wrote:

From that date, robbery with violence grew unfashionable in East London and few unaccountable dead bodies were found in the streets.[9]

It may be that a small industry was born with the execution of the Reubens brothers. A little later, Wensley was sent a whisky glass with a hanging man engraved on the base. The inscription was 'The Brothers Reubens – the last drop'. Similar items were a favourite gift at such events as Masonic ladies' nights until well into the 1960s.

By no means all immigrant crime was the fairly amateur mugging and rolling of sailors. In 1901 the middle-aged German woman Bertha Weiner, from Shadwell, came to grief along with her twelve-strong gang of housebreakers and thieves. Their targets were big suburban houses standing in their own grounds, and up to five of the gang would go on what were meticulously researched expeditions. The raids were carried out with seeming impunity.

Wensley claims that it was when he saw a number of men in the Shadwell area who appeared to have money and the leisure to spend it that he became suspicious. He began shadowing the area and discovered that many of the men lived in a house in Albert Street which was regularly visited by Bertha Weiner who paid the rent. She lived with a sailor, Rebork, in Ship Alley about a mile away. She had an auctioneer brother, Ludwig, who with his two sons lived in Tredegar Square, Bow.

According to Wensley, Bertha Weiner was the putter-up and financier. The men from Albert Street were the burglars and disposed of the articles to her. The better pieces were auctioned by her brother and nephews.

The raid scheduled for 28 October was aborted when Wensley's father was taken seriously ill and the next night a housebreaking took place in Willesden with the windows and doors forced, the silver and wines removed from the cellar and much of the owner's clothing taken. The police eventually raided on 31 October when eight men were arrested in Albert Street. One put on a pair of stolen socks and another had a hat taken in the burglary. Wensley went to Ship Alley and broke in the home of Rebork and Bertha Weiner at the same time as other officers raided her relations in Tredegar Square. One of the curious pieces of evidence against them was a small badge which had been presented to Sir Montague Sharpe, then deputy Chairman of Middlesex Sessions, by his fellow judges. One of the gang, Wald, a professional wrestler, wore it with pride, claiming he had won it in a tournament in Germany.

Bertha Weiner received seven years' penal servitude at the Old Bailey in December 1901 and, with the exception of a nephew, the others were sentenced to five years. The young Weiner received twelve months.

In his autobiography[10] published in 1931, Frederick Wensley wrote:

Any reader of the daily papers these days might come to the conclusion that Chicago is the only place in which organised bands of desperate criminals ever existed. The public have a short memory. It is not so very long ago that we, in the East End and some other districts of London, were engaged in stamping out groups of criminals, many of whom carried arms, and who waged a sort of warfare among themselves and against the public.

He continued:

In the early part of the century there was one gang of this class who had established a real reign of terror among certain people in the East End.

The victims were those same people who are always the victims:

In the main, however, the victims were persons who for some reason or another were a little shy of bringing their troubles to the notice of the police. Keepers of shady restaurants, runners of gambling dens, landlords of houses of resort, street bookmakers and other people on the fringe of the underworld were among those peculiarly open to trouble.

And of the others:

Sometimes small tradesmen were offered 'protection' against other gangs at a price. If they did not take kindly to this blackmail all sorts of unpleasant things were liable to happen to them ... Persons who had resisted their extortions had been brutally assaulted, their premises wrecked – in one case an attempt to burn down a building had been made – and any portable property stolen.

The principal East End immigrant gang which operated around the turn of the century was the forty-strong pack, the Whitechapel-based Bessarabians, sometimes known as the Bessarabian Tigers or the Bessarabian Fighters.

The Russian Jews with their ingrained terror of the police would, in practically every case, rather put up with the gangs than risk the consequences of complaining to the police ... we were continually having to let cases drop through lack of evidence.

They levied a protection toll on timid alien shopkeepers, proprietors of coffee stalls and so on. The faintest shadow of protest on their part at this blackmail and the gang descended on them in force armed with guns, knives and such weapons as broken bottles.[11]

In *Lost London*, the former Detective Sergeant B. Leeson gave another example of their methods:

Lists of people to be blackmailed were drawn up by the gangsters, and amongst these prospective brides provided the happiest and most productive results. A few days before the wedding ceremony a gangster would approach the bride's parents and threaten to expose all sorts of imaginary indiscretions of which their daughter had been guilty if their silence was not bought. The victims, fearful of the scandal that might ensue, invariably paid up.[12]

They ruled for almost a whole decade with their chief rivals the Odessians, so named because a man, Weinstein – also known as Kikal, the proprietor of the Odessa – took on the Bessarabians. He refused to pay protection money and, according to Leeson, fought them off with an iron bar when they came to demand their wages. The rival gang, which did not include Weinstein, took the name as a tribute to his courage.

For the next year or so there were the usual gang skirmishes. The Odessians threatened to cut off the ears of a leading Bessarabian named Perkoff. He was lured into an alley and one ear was removed before the local police arrived. In return, a coffee stall under the protection of the Odessians was attacked.

One of the final exploits of the Bessarabians came in 1902 when Barnet Badeczosky, Joseph Weinstein and Max Moses (who boxed at Wonderland under the name Kid McCoy and had no connection with the better-known American fighter) attacked Philip Garalovitch in Union Street. This was also an example of the power the gang wielded.

It is not now possible to decide whether this was simply robbery or had a political motive because Garalovitch was an ex-Russian police officer. At the magistrates' court the former officer said that Weinstein had gone up to him saying, 'Hello, you gave me two years' imprisonment in Russia.' He had replied, 'I only did my duty.' Badeczosky then knocked him to the ground and took his watch from his chain. Max Moses took £6, his hat and his umbrella. When Garalovitch's companion, a man named Rosenberg, tried to stop him, Moses hit him. By the time the case appeared again in the court witnesses had been threatened and Garalovitch had sensibly gone to South Africa. Barnet Badeczosky and Joseph Weinstein were discharged, and Max Moses was fined £3 with the alternative of one month's imprisonment for his assault on Rosenberg: so apart from having to pay a lawyer, he made £3 from the deal.

The effective end of the Bessarabians came in October that year following an attack by them on a Yiddish music hall held in the York Minster, a public house in Philpot Street off the Commercial Road, where a number of Odessians were thought to be. There had been trouble the previous Saturday and witnesses spoke of Bessarabians going up and down the Commercial Road asking the whereabouts of their rivals.

One man, sometimes called Henry Brodovich but also known as Kaufmann, was stabbed to death. In the ensuing confusion the public was either less discreet or more likely less frightened than usual and names were named. As a result Max Moses, Samuel Oreman and Barnet Badeczosky were arrested. 'If that man had not died £15 would have squared it,' said Moses. He was said to have shouted, 'I'll give you India Rubber Mob,' pulling on a knuckle-duster.

It was clear that witnesses were at risk and the stipendiary magistrate Mead issued a warning that those convicted of threats would face imprisonment. This intelligence failed to percolate to Woolf Selvitzky, a restaurant keeper said to be the leader of the Bessarabians, and Marks Lipman, because the following week they were promptly convicted of an assault on Marks Mieland. Selvitzky had punched him, saying, 'My pal is in trouble through you.' Two months' hard labour each.[13]

A week later, a Woolf Kigesky and Joe Zelkowitz each received a month's hard labour. They had been endeavouring to raise funds for their friends' defence and shopkeeper Morris Goldberg had refused to pay until threats were made.[14]

Meanwhile the committal proceedings on the murder charge continued and, somewhat against the perceived wisdom, E.S. Abinger, who would later have difficulties in the defence of Steinie Morrison, called witnesses to show that Moses was indeed the victim of a planned attack. Evidence was called that people including the dead man, Henry Brodovich, who was said to have been armed with an iron bar, had been out looking for and threatening to harm Moses that night. For the present it did neither him nor the others any good. They were all committed for trial. What must be remembered is that almost all the evidence except that of the police was translated by interpreters.

Alleged heads of the Bessarabians kept popping up. Presumably after the imprisonment of Selvitzky, Woolf Schaberman had taken over, for he was described as the head of the gang when he appeared charged with being concerned in the robbery of Max Goldman, a butcher, and stealing the watch of Harris Harman. This seems to have been a curious affair. Schaberman is said to have knocked Goldman down and then bitten him before stealing £8 in gold and his chain. Harman's watch was found in Schaberman's possession. It is difficult now to say what exactly happened or, indeed, who was batting for whom, because the police officer in the case said that Goldman had been very drunk, and despite the finding of the watch Schaberman was discharged.

With their leaders in prison the Bessarabians faded from power, although they were still hired to break up Anarchist and Social Democrat meetings. When not working they could be found playing cards in a Romanian restaurant at the corner of Setters Street and the Commercial Road. Meanwhile the police chipped away at the Odessians. Many went to America where they joined forces with the local crooks. One known as 'Tilly the Burglar' is said to have become a Chicago policeman.[15]

There is no doubt that the Odessians and the Bessarabians committed crime for money and perhaps power in the community. The position of the so-called Anarchists and Socialist Jews is less clear. Certainly the latter spent some time and effort in provoking the Orthodox. Troubles broke out in September 1904, when for a week the Socialist Jews battled with the faithful. On 17 September there was a free fight with Jews returning from Shul, and two days later, on the Monday, the Socialist Jews hired a hall opposite a Whitechapel synagogue and drove a food van through the streets. For their sins they were stoned and in turn they pelted a synagogue. The police rather took the side of the Orthodox Jews but it was not a position which found favour with Cluer, the stipendiary magistrate. Abraham Greenstone, the manager of the restaurant, was discharged on payment of the interpreter's fee and Cluer said that he hoped that next year if there was trouble the Orthodoxy would be the ones brought before him. He added that the Chief Commissioner of Police should take a strong line even if it meant a thousand Orthodox Jews in the dock.

[It is] disgraceful that a class of persons who for centuries have been distinguished as the victims of the fiercest persecutions should, when in the one free country of the world, turn upon those who disagreed with them upon religious points: their own co-religionists and stone and persecute them.

Later in the day he displayed something of an anti-Semitic attitude altogether when he dealt with Samuel Harris, described as an English Jew, who had robbed Esther Tobias of a watch and chain: 'And this is the Day of Atonement. I thought they all stopped indoors on that day.'

His comments did not pass unnoticed. A correspondent replied:

> There are no more law abiding people in the world than the Orthodox Jews; but Socialists whether Jews or Gentiles – well they are Socialists.[16]

It was the East End-based Socialists who, over the next few years, would feature in a series of some of the best-known cases of the twentieth century. Their home-from-home in London was the Anarchists Club, patronised by the Russian nobleman Prince Kropotkin who advocated that need rather than work was the only criterion for the distribution of property. Hand in hand with that philosophy went the one of expropriation – that is, the taking away of property from the individual for redistribution amongst the many. In theory this was not a licence to steal for oneself, that being a truly bourgeois concept. Whether in practice it was always adopted is another matter. By the first decade of the twentieth century there were many expropriators amongst the immigrant community of Whitechapel.

Two of the first who came to the notice of the public were Paul Hefeld and Jacob Lepidus who, on the morning of 23 January 1909, carried out what became known as the Tottenham Outrage.[17] Hefeld had for a time worked at Schnurmann's Rubber Factory in Chestnut Road near the police station. Lepidus had worked in a local furniture factory. They knew the timing of the wages run to a bank in Hackney carried out by chauffeurs Joseph Wilson and Albert Keyworth, and at 10.30 a.m. as Keyworth got out of the car with a bag containing £80, the firm's wage bill for the week, Lepidus leaped on him. Wilson, who had begun to drive away, stopped the car and went to help his younger colleague. Lepidus pulled Wilson off and it was then that Hefeld shot a bystander, George Smith, in the shoulder before the pair ran into the maze of streets which would eventually take them to Tottenham Marshes.

They were chased by two constables, PC Tyler and PC Newman, who in turn were followed by a number of other off-duty policemen who had been in the nearby section house. Wilson restarted the car and collected Tyler and Newman. Now an excited crowd took up the chase. Wilson caught up with the robbers in Mitchley Road and Newman ordered him to run them down. Both held their ground and shot at the car, hitting the radiator and windscreen. Both Newman and Wilson were slightly injured. A stray bullet hit a young boy, Ralph Joscelyne, in the chest; he died almost instantly.

Now an officer was sent back to the police station to obtain guns and Tyler and Newman split up to try to head them off before they reached the Marshes. When they were 20 yards away Tyler called on Lepidus and Hefeld to surrender. Instead of obeying, Hefeld shot him in the neck. Newman borrowed a gun from one of the crowd, fired and missed. Tyler was taken to the Prince of Wales Hospital where he died.

The men made their way north-east, reaching Stonebridge Lock, trading shots with their pursuers who had now been joined by footballers who had been playing on the Marshes. Generally the crowd followed at a safe distance, but when Sidney Slater came too close he was shot in the thigh for his pains. Now some men out duck-shooting shot at the pair, hitting Lepidus in the head.

The chase had lasted an hour when they shot William Roker in the leg and then saw a No. 9 tram going down the Chingford Road. This they commandeered; the driver hid under the seat and they forced the conductor to drive. Meanwhile the police had obtained a horse and cart to chase them. Hefeld shot the animal, overturning the cart and throwing the officer onto the pavement. They then jumped from the tram and took over a horse-drawn milk float, shooting the milkman in the arm and chest. They made slow progress through Walthamstow and then stole a horse-drawn grocer's van. Lepidus took the reins and Hefeld kept the police – who were now pursuing on bicycles – at a distance. The horse tired and they abandoned the van, making on foot for the River Ching, a tributary of the Lea. Hefeld, much the bigger man who in his time at Schnurmann's had been known as The Elephant, was now himself exhausted and when he reached a tall paling fence he told Lepidus to go on and save himself. As the police approached he shot himself in the head; he was overpowered and also taken to the Prince of Wales Hospital.

Lepidus on his own was also tiring. He crossed into Epping Forest and occupied the Oak Cottage of Charles Relstone, a coalman. There were two young children inside, but a police officer and a baker from Walthamstow, who had been in the van of the chase, broke in and took them out. Now two detectives, Charles Dixon and John Cater, climbed through a window. Another officer, a PC Eagles, borrowed a shotgun and ladder and climbed in through the back bedroom window. He saw Lepidus but could not make the shotgun fire and climbed down. Lepidus himself had almost run out of bullets by now; he had only two left and did not shoot at Eagles.

Eagles then joined Cater and Dixon and the three went up the stairs. Dixon pushed the bedroom door open and Lepidus fired. The police riddled the door with bullets and then peered through the holes. Eagles took Dixon's revolver, put his arm round the door, fired two blind shots and then crashed into the room, firing at the same time as Lepidus who shot himself in the head. He was dragged into the yard of the cottage, where he died at 12.45 p.m. The chase had lasted two and a quarter hours. All that was found of the £80 was £5 in silver which Lepidus had been carrying. It was suggested but never proven that he had pushed the money up the chimney of the cottage where it was later found by the Relstones.

The chase had covered six miles, during which the robbers had fired an amazing 400 rounds of ammunition from their automatic weapons. Hefeld died on 12 February when he contracted meningitis from his injuries and shock. The only words he uttered during the whole time were shortly before he died when he whispered, 'My mother is in Riga.' He and Lepidus were buried in an unmarked grave in Walthamstow cemetery.

PC Tyler's widow benefited from a collection of £2,000. She was, however, only to receive the income during her lifetime. She later married another police officer. The grocer whose horse had been hijacked claimed £2 10 shillings because it had been unable to work for four days after its efforts. The owner of Oak Cottage, where at first the dying and bleeding Tyler had been taken, claimed for damage to carpets and a tablecloth. In all, apart from the robbers, three people died and fifteen of the pursuers suffered gunshot wounds. One officer, a PC Bond, 'contracted a chill through taking up the chase when only partly dressed'. Ralph Joscelyne's mother never recovered from the death of her son. She kept the shoes he was wearing when he was killed until she died nearly fifty years later. They were buried with her.

The outrage produced another round of anti-immigrant feeling. With the successive waves of immigrants, wages had been low in the area for years and there had been rioting in 1902. Now an English shopkeeper told a reporter:

They [the immigrant community] change their homes every two weeks. If the guardians relaxed their vigilance for a single week they would go back to their old trick of sleeping twenty-five in a room. Here and there you find a decent, clean man or woman, but nearly all of them are downright riff-raff. I have been here a good many years and I have watched this and other roads go down since they infested them.[18]

Another unsuccessful attempt came in November 1909 when an Okhrana agent persuaded four men and a young woman to throw a bomb at the Lord Mayor's Show. Others more sensible, including the anarchist Rudolph Rocker, discovered the plot and it was abandoned.

Two years after the Tottenham Outrage, two or possibly three linked incidents once more raised a considerable amount of anti-immigrant and therefore anti-Semitic feeling in London. The first was the Houndsditch murders of two police officers. The second was the siege of Sidney Street and the third the death of Leon Beron. It is certain the first two were connected. It is certainly possible that the third was linked as well.

Since 1906 the focal meeting point for the non-Orthodox intellectual Jew had been the Anarchists Club opened by Prince Kropotkin in Jubilee Street, which in previous incarnations had been a Methodist Free Church and a Salvation Army depot. It could take over 800 people in the lower hall, and in the great hall there was a stage. The second floor held a library and reading room. It was financed through dances and other fund-raising activities, and donations by the sweat-shop workers. It was a hive of revolutionary talk as well as a home for Okhrana agents of the Tsarist regime who spent a considerable amount of time and effort persuading the members to misbehave.

One of the groups of anarchists was the Lettish Socialistic Revolutionary Party known as Leesma – the Latvian for flame – composed almost entirely, as its name suggests, of Latvians. It was on one of their members, Jacob Fogel, that suspicion fell following the Tottenham shootings when it was thought that somehow he had acquired the missing £80.

At the time he was living at 29 Great Garden Street in lodgings provided by Charles Perelman, a Russian photo-enlarger, sharing a room with another Lett known as 'Bifsteks' who was courting Perelman's daughter Fanny. Also in the building was a watchmaker, William Sokoloff, known as Joseph, a man whose misfortune it was to work regularly in premises that were burgled whilst he was there or very shortly afterwards. Once the police began their inquiries they were asked to leave and, in a case of fat and fire, in moved Fritz Svaars, a locksmith who shared his room with another Latvian, George Gardstein. Svaars was wanted for an American bank robbery and Gardstein for one in Germany. The back room on the ground floor was let to Fanny's friend Nina Vassilleva, who worked as a cigarette maker and became Gardstein's mistress. The anarchists were common figures in the area. Arthur Harding recalls Gardstein as being 'the gaffer, the top man':

> The most peculiar thing about them was that they always walked in the road, never on the pavement. I can see the idea, if anyone's lying in wait for you to arrest you they wouldn't wait out in the road, they'd wait in a doorway, they could see in the road. They always marched along in the roadway with their womenfolk in the middle of the road; they numbered sometimes as many as twelve or fifteen people, men and girls – the girls were good-lookers, gypsy-style: we would have liked to be friendly with them. We knew they were crooked, but we were told they were on the run from the Russian secret police; that fact alone gained them our sympathy. They had to live, they had to pay their lodgings, and they needed the money for their politics when all's said and done. That's why they did these robberies.[19]

Towards the end of 1909 Perelman and his family moved to Wellesley Street, giving Svaars and Gardstein notice to quit. Gardstein took a room and Svaars went back to Riga in a futile attempt to see his wife; he was captured by the secret police and tortured before being released. When he returned to London the following summer he decided to send for her and, if possible, emigrate to Australia. In the meantime he took up with a seamstress, Luba Milstein, and they rented two rooms at 59 Grove Street together. In the enforced absence of Fogel, Gardstein was now the effective leader of the Leesma group and he called daily, as did Peter Piaktow (known as Peter the Painter) who arrived from Paris in October 1910. They were joined in the autumn by Max Smoller, a noted jewel thief known to Sokoloff. It was Smoller who said he knew of a jeweller's shop in Houndsditch whose safe not only held a quantity of jewels but had an added attraction: it was rumoured that some of them belonged to the Tsar.

Directly behind Harris's shop in Houndsditch was a cul-de-sac, Exchange Buildings, and the plan was to tunnel through between the houses. Smoller rented No. 11 and Nina Vassilleva moved in. She slept downstairs on a sofa. Smoller and Sokoloff shared a bedroom upstairs. It was immediately clear that there was no way in from No. 11, but it was possible to get in through No. 9 and Svaars rented the premises saying it was for storing Christmas goods.

Work was to begin on the Jewish Sabbath, Friday 16 December, and continue throughout the weekend. The advantages were obvious. The shop would not open on the Saturday and the streets would be almost deserted. Gardstein and Smoller, along with Yourka Dubof, a locksmith, and Svaar's cousin, Jacob Peters, were to begin work, with the others waiting to come in as relievers; 59 Grove Street was to be a rendezvous if things went wrong, and Piatkow stayed there so that Luba Milstein – who disliked him intensely – would stay out of the way.

The plan was doomed from the start. Despite the fact that it was a windy night, the hammering could be heard in Houndsditch. It was also heard by Max Weil who lived over the shop next to the jeweller's. About 10 p.m. he called the police at Bishopsgate Police Station and a temporary constable, Walter Piper, went to Exchange Buildings. There was a Jewish family at No. 12, the Solomons, and they told him no one was working in the yard. At No. 11, however, Gardstein opened the door and Piper simply asked whether 'the missus was in'. Told she was not he went away, apparently satisfied.

In fact a number of police were now rounded up and seven positioned themselves in Exchange Buildings. Sergeant Robert Bentley went to the building and asked Gardstein, who again opened the door, whether anyone was working inside. Gardstein half closed the door, but Bentley followed him in and suggested he should look to see if anyone was in the back. When he went into the back room he was shot in the neck at point-blank range by Peters. Sergeant Bryant, who was behind, was shot in the arm by Gardstein. Both staggered into the street where Ernest Woodhams, who went to help Bentley, was shot in the leg by Gardstein. Peters then emerged and shot Sergeant Tucker in the heart, and a plain-clothes officer, Arthur Strongman, pulled his colleague away. DC James Martin took no part; he panicked and hid in a nearby house, claiming later that he had fallen, stunned, in the street.

The men now burst from Exchange Buildings and Walter Choate caught hold of Gardstein only to be shot in the leg by him. He held on and was shot a number of times, with Peters hitting him again at point-blank range. With amazing bravery he still held onto Gardstein until, as he finally fell, he left a target and one of Smoller's bullets hit Gardstein in the back. Dubof and Peters then half carried Gardstein into Cutler Street, followed by Nina Vassilleva with Smoller behind her.

The shooting took less than a minute and twenty-two bullets were fired. The police were unarmed.

Tucker was dead on arrival at the London Hospital and Choate was taken there on a handcart; he died in the early hours of the morning. Bentley was taken to St Bartholomew's where, although he recovered consciousness, he died on 11 December.

A number of people saw the escape but the only person able to recognise any of the party was a tobacconist, Isaac Levy from Walthamstow, who had been working late. Gardstein was taken back to Grove Street and Nina Vassilleva went for a doctor who sent her away. Luba Milstein was sitting up in the back room with her friend Sara Trassjonsky, a mentally unsound hunchbacked little seamstress, and she was the one who was left to nurse Gardstein as first Smoller, Piaktow and Joseph left, followed by Milstein. When she went to see an old friend, Karl Hoffman, Svaars, Piaktow and Joseph were there already. She was persuaded to return to Grove Street to collect any incriminatory photographs or papers. At 3 a.m. a Doctor Scanlon, who had a mainly immigrant practice in the Whitechapel Road, was persuaded to come to see Gardstein, who said he had been shot accidentally by a friend and adamantly refused to go to hospital. Scanlon agreed to return the next morning but, fearful that his clientele might see him as an informer, did nothing until noon when he rang Detective Inspector Wensley. It was arranged that there would be no raid until he had left the premises, but by the time he reached Grove Street Gardstein was dead and the only person in the building was Sara Trassjonsky, now thoroughly unhinged, idly throwing papers onto the fire.

Arrests followed. Sara Trassjonsky was detained on the spot

and on 17 December a Russian musician, Nicolas Tomacoff, who came to Grove Street to see his friend Fritz about a Christmas play at the Anarchists Club, gave the police the names and descriptions of the men he had seen at the house.

He took them to Osip Federoff's lodgings where Federoff was arrested. The next down was Luba Milstein, who was turned over to the police by her brothers. Nina Vassilleva fled to the country but, on her return, was interviewed by Wensley. He did not arrest her immediately in the hope that she would lead the police to the rest of the gang.

In fact it was Tomacoff who now became their main hope. He was put up in a hotel and given new clothes which cost £2.4s.6d. In fact he was something of a disappointment because although he gave them Nina Vassilleva's address they already knew it. On 22 December he did, however, lead them to Jacob Peters, who promptly put the blame on Fritz Svaars. The same day Dubof was arrested in Shepherd's Bush; in turn he offered up thin pickings. He admitted he knew the house in Grove Street and that he had been there on 16 December looking for work. Now he was identified by Levy as one of the two men – Peters was the other – who had carried Gardstein away from Exchange Buildings.

Charles Perelman came forward with the information that Joseph lived with a Betty Gershon at 100 Sidney Street between the Mile End Road and the Commercial Road. Perelman was the crucial informant and told the police that Svaars would move lodgings on the evening of 3 January and that Joseph would follow when he heard that Svaars was safe. In the early hours of 3 January, 200 police were called to Arbour Square Police Station for a briefing. All were unmarried since it was feared there would be heavy casualties – when Gardstein's room had been searched 100 rounds of assorted ammunition and a loaded pistol had been found. At 3 a.m. they had evacuated the neighbours and surrounded 100 Sidney Street. They also cleared the families from No. 100. Two men, they were told, were sleeping in the stock room. But they decided not to rush the room, since the stairs could be held against a wave of officers and the casualties would certainly be unacceptable.

The action began at 7.30 a.m. when a policeman ran across the road and threw stones at windows in the house. This brought a volley from the Anarchists, and Detective Sergeant Leeson received a chest wound. He clearly thought he was dying and what were meant to be his last words were:

> Mr Wensley, I am dying. They have shot me through the heart. Give my love to the children. Bury me at Putney.[20]

Fortunately, when the doctor took off Leeson's coat and shirt it was clear that the bullet had passed straight through his chest. In any event it was a signal for the police to retreat. They were hopelessly outgunned in terms of firepower and during the morning requested the help of troops stationed at the Tower of London. This required the permission of the Home Secretary and, with the regiment of Scots Guards, Winston Churchill himself came to the siege. It was estimated that from both the troops and those in the house thousands of shots were fired. It was also estimated that some 100,000 came to watch, with neighbourhood residents charging 10 shillings a head for spectators to stand on their roofs.

At 1 p.m. smoke was seen coming from the garret window and it was apparent that the second floor was alight. It was thought that the men had deliberately set fire to the house before trying to escape in the smoke and confusion, but the better thought is that a bullet had struck a gas pipe which had ignited. The troops reopened fire. Svaars leaned from the window and was shot instantly. As the wind blew the smoke away from the ground floor momentarily, the body of Joseph could be seen lying on a bed in a ground-floor room. Then part of the building collapsed.

It was then that the legends started. Although most newspapers identified the bodies as those of Joseph and Svaars, some believed that one was that of Joseph Vogel. The *Daily Mail* thought that Peter the Painter had been in the house.

The subsequent trial of the survivors was in a way both a triumph and a fiasco for British justice. The triumph was that despite the fact that three policemen had been killed there was no question of railroading the defendants. Indeed it was just the opposite. Although Sara Trassjonsky, Luba Milstein, Nina Vassilleva, Peters, Federoff, Dubof, John Rosen and Hoffman were arrested and stood trial, when it came to it not a single person was convicted.

The case for the Crown was not really handled very well. Archibald Bodkin, who later became Director of Public Prosecutions, opened the case against them by saying that Peters, Dubof and Federoff were concerned in the murder of the police officers, that the two women were accessories after the fact to murder and that all five were involved in the attempted burglary of Harris's shop. At the time they were the only ones in custody. Over a period of weeks they were joined by the others. Bodkin had taken the view that since Gardstein had opened the door of No. 11 Exchange Buildings, he was the one who had also opened fire on the police.

The first to be acquitted was Luba Milstein, who was found to have no case to answer at the Guildhall Justice Room after Bodkin accepted there was no evidence against her. She was released on 21 February. Hoffman was acquitted on 8 March and Federoff on 15 March. The identification against him was dubious and all that could be said against Hoffman was that he was a friend of Svaars. Sara Trassjonsky was released the same day.

The trial of Peters and Dubof, accused of murder, and Nina Vassilleva, with harbouring a felon, opened at the Central Criminal Court on 1 May before Mr Justice Grantham. There were also charges of being accessories to murder and conspiracy to break and enter. Rosen was charged only with conspiracy.

The principal witness against them was Isaac Levy, the shop manager, who said he had seen the two men with Gardstein and Vassilleva tagging behind them. He withstood a good deal of hostile cross-examination but on the second day the judge decided that, since there was no corroborative evidence of the identification, the murder charges against Peters and Dubof could not stand. Nor could it be said that Vassilleva knew a murder as opposed to a wounding had been committed. That charge must also go. This left the conspiracy case of which, at the end of the eleven-day trial, the only significant piece of evidence remaining for the jury was the fingerprints of Vassilleva. By now it was a question of humour in court and, to sycophantic laughter, the judge summed up:

> The male prisoners are aliens in this country for their own good. That is not to say it is for the good of this country.

Earlier, when Peters had given evidence that he had attended an LCC school to learn English but had in fact learned more Yiddish, Grantham had commented, 'It is a pity that the ratepayers should be called on to teach Yiddish.' Now the judge rather suggested that the lack of evidence was due to the cowardice of the unfortunate Levy in not following the quartet more closely until he came across a policeman.

The men were acquitted. Vassilleva was convicted, but the jury recommended that there be no deportation order. She was sentenced to two years' imprisonment, but her conviction did not stand long. The Court of Criminal Appeal ruled that the judge had misdirected the jury and that, merely because she was living at 11 Exchange Buildings and had undoubtedly told lies, this did not constitute sufficient evidence to prove a charge of conspiracy. Her conviction was quashed on 21 June 1911.[21]

Initially Churchill did not come out of the siege too well and when he appeared in newsreels the galleries booed him roundly. He set up a commission into compensating those who had lost property as a result of the siege and it turned out that one family, the Fleischmanns, far from living in some poverty, had (before their house was destroyed) actually owned something of an Aladdin's cave complete with fur coats, diamond rings and silver spoons as well as an evening-dress suit. The committee was not impressed and awarded Fleischmann just a quarter of his claim of £900, which of itself was half the total sought by all. There had been a £500 reward for the capture of Svaars, Peter the Painter and an unnamed woman. Since only one of the three was either arrested or killed, Charles Perelman was awarded a third of the bounty. New clothes for Tomacoff, which apart from his accommodation was all he received.

When Nina Vassilleva was released from prison her former friends had turned against her and she was looked after by the Anarchists Millie and Rudolph Rocker, who had found a solicitor, William Crocker, to act *pro bono* for her. For a time at any rate Nina believed that the whole of the Houndsditch incident had been an elaborate snare for Gardstein, deliberately murdered by Max Smoller. Throughout the rest of her life she remained in the East End, working first for the cigarette manufacturers Adbullah where she could be seen sitting in the shop window hand-rolling the tobacco, and then for the Soviet Trade Delegation. She died in St Bartholomew's Hospital on 24 February 1963.

The writer Richard Whittington-Egan visited her a few years

before her death, finding her suffering from arthritis and, 'Large, run to bulk, with white hair, short and straight, and faded blue eyes'.

I found her occupying, in poverty, a top floor front, looking out over London chimney pots, at 99 Brick Lane. It was a terrible climb for someone so disabled.

The room had blue wash painted walls. Furnished with a bed, one hard chair, and a gas-ring, illuminated by a single naked bulb, it was a cheerless place. A Greek Catholic, she had a positive welter of religious objects on display, spilling over everything.

Nina's account was slightly different from the orthodox one:

Nina knew Gardstein well, but denied that she had been his mistress. She told me that it was a popular canard that she had been Peter the Painter's girlfriend. She had, in fact, never known him, and her first meeting with Sara Trassjonsky was when they were both in Holloway. She told me that she was not one of those at Exchange Buildings, and denied that she had nursed the dying Gardstein.

She also, most interestingly, confided that it had actually been the fire brigade who had caused the fatal blaze at 100 Sidney Street. They had deliberately set fire to the gas meter, and Churchill had forbidden any attempt to extinguish the flames.

By one of those coincidences which make life bountiful, showing at that very time at a small cinema round the corner was a film 'The Siege of Sidney Street' in which Nina was magically transformed into the beautiful young woman of half a century before. It was passing strange to watch on the screen a young actress playing the part of the old lady I had just left. I had, in fact, invited her to come with me to see the film, but she did not want to. It had all been so long ago . . . and so sad.[22]

Sara Trassjonsky was admitted to an asylum, where she died. A small present was sent to the police in 1912 by Nina Vassilleva to be forwarded to Trassjonsky. This they did. The enigmatic Peter the Painter may have died in Philadelphia in 1916. One version of his identity is that he was the brother of Casimir Pilenas, the interpreter at Thames Police Court who had been used to take statements in the Houndsditch trial.[23] Jacob Peters went back to Russia to become a hero of the Revolution but died in 1928, the victim of a Stalinist purge. Luba Milstein, left pregnant by Svaars, gave birth and went to America in January 1912, followed by Karl Hoffman; they lived in and around New York until their deaths in 1961 and 1973 respectively. Smoller's wife had left the country with her children during her husband's trial; he had already escaped to Paris. The other defendants, Dubof, Rosen, Hoffman and Federoff, simply disappeared into anonymity. Meanwhile the body of Leon Beron had been found on Clapham Common on 1 January 1911 whilst London and, to a lesser extent, the rest of the country was still recovering from the Houndsditch police shooting which had provoked yet another wave of anti-Semitism:

> It is doubtful if there is more than a score of English families living within a radius of 500 yards of Sidney Street. Certainly there is not a single English tradesman there; the public houses are tenanted by Jews and foreigners and foreign drinks are almost solely consumed.[24]
>
> . . . the borough has been inundated by a swarm of people fitly described as the scum of Central Europe.[25]

Earlier in the article 'The Alien Immigrant', the leader writer of *The Times* had put things clearly: '... the average immigrant is insanitary in his habits: he is personally unclean.'[26]

Certainly public feeling in the area ran high, with Councillor Castle of the Stepney Bow Council urging a resolution be passed asking that the whole of the Aliens Act be put into effect and, as that in itself was insufficient, stronger legislation should be passed:

> For fifteen to twenty years the Borough has been inundated with the scum of the earth driving out the native population. [Shouts of No.][27]

Although it lingered on until 1915, another casualty was the Anarchists Club:

> Press agitation against the Anarchists and 'criminal aliens' reached a new crescendo. Police watch on the club and members increased. In the eyes of the local public anyone who walked along in a Russian blouse was considered a suspicious character and sometimes assaulted.[28]

It is difficult to judge who was the more unpleasant man – Steinie Morrison or Leon Beron; possibly the latter. Beron was born on 17 April 1863 at Gulvaki, Poland. His family moved to France where, it was alleged, his father amassed the fortune of £26,000. David Beron, his brother, later said it was £60,000.[29]Again, what Leon Beron did for a living is unclear. He was probably a locksmith and almost certainly a burglar. Without doubt he was a receiver. Certainly there were no outward signs of wealth. Arthur Harding recalls:

We used to see Behren [sic] at the Warsaw Restaurant in Osborne
Street at the bottom of Brick Lane. The watch-chains we used to
pinch, we'd go there and sell them to him. With gold chains he
used to pay you 27s. 6d. for 9 carat gold and 56s. for 18 carat,
and about £4 for 22 carat which was very rare.[30]

Beron may have been a front man for Ruby Michaels, regarded
at the time as the doyen of local receivers. If Beron could not be
found in the Warsaw Restaurant then he could often be found in
a shoe shop around the corner. He was always well dressed and
throughout his life had a passion for jewellery, gold and women.
In the early hours of a morning he was frequently seen coming
out of one of the Whitechapel brothels.

He owned slum property in Russell Court, St George's in the
East, which was let to prostitutes and on which he had a mort-
gage. He lived with his younger brother David, regarded as being
of low intelligence, at 133 Jubilee Street for which he paid 2/9d.
rent, with David contributing the ninepence. His other brother,
Solomon, who lived in Rowton House, said at the inquest that
Leon had no money to speak of.[31]

Whilst in France, Leon Beron had married a Frenchwoman,
Adele, by whom he had a daughter. He later had his wife committed to Colney Hatch Mental Asylum in North London where
she died in May 1902 of general paralysis of the insane. She had
almost certainly contracted syphilis from her husband. At the
time of his death he was walking with the rounded gait which
could be the sign of locomotaxia.

Steinie Morrison, a great poseur who sometimes claimed to be
Australian, came to England in 1898. He was at least partly educated and had something of a gift for languages because, as the
author Andrew Rose points out, at a time when criminals had a
hard time making their mark let alone writing, he spoke Russian,

Yiddish, German, French and, by the time of his trial, could write in English and speak it without the need for an interpreter.

His first traceable offence in this country was committed the year he arrived when, under the name Moses Tagger, he was given one month at Worship Street Magistrates' Court for stealing ledgers from his employer. Next, as Morrie Stein, he received two months for being found on enclosed premises; then, as Morris Jagger, it was six months at North London Quarter Sessions for burglary. In mid-April 1900, as Morris Stein again, he received fifteen months. Released in the summer of 1901, almost immediately he was seen carrying property away from a domestic burglary at Cambridge Park. This time he received five years.

Sometime after his release from that sentence he made the acquaintance of Max Frank, a Lithuanian Jew who was a receiver and pimp operating from 116 York Road, Walworth. On 14 January 1906 Stein was arrested again and this time racked up five years plus a year and eighty-three days for breaking the terms of his licence. After attacking a prison officer he received twenty-three strokes of the cat.

On his release he lived for a time at 5 Grove Street near the headquarters of the Houndsditch gang where he paid Minnie Honigman 3/6d. rent, but returned to Frank and the prostitute Florence Dellow in York Road.

When Beron's body was found, his watch and chain and a £5 gold piece he carried along with his day-to-day money (which could amount to £70) were gone. He had been beaten and stabbed and his skull fractured. On his forehead was carved a series of cuts which could be seen in the form of the letter 'S'. One interpretation of this was that it was the initial letter of the Russian word *spic* or double agent. A reward of £500 was offered for information leading to the conviction of his killer.

On 8 January Inspector Fred Wensley arrested Morrison but

not, he said, for murder, simply for failing to report a change of address. Wensley took with him five other detectives, explaining this by saying he knew Morrison carried a gun. Morrison never left custody again.

As to the murder charge which followed, the evidence against him was that he knew Beron and had been seen with him in the East End shortly before midnight on New Year's Eve. He also knew South London as he had worked in a bakery in Lavender Hill. He had given a parcel to a waiter in the Warsaw café, saying that it contained a flute, but the waiter believed it was far too heavy for that. Morrison also had a £5 piece which the prosecution claimed was from the robbery.

There was some evidence that Beron and Morrison had quarrelled in the past and there were minute spots of blood on the defendant's collar. Additionally, there was identification evidence from two taxi drivers who put him at Clapham Common at the time of the murder. There was also a hotly contested 'verbal' – an allegation that Wensley, when he went to arrest Morrison, had said 'Stein, I want you for murder.' There was some allegation that at Leman Street Police Station Detective Sergeant Brogden had said to Morrison that he was being detained for murder.

The trial started on 6 March and both Morrison and his counsel, Edward Abinger, did what they could to alienate the judge and jury. It was common then for the defendant to be required to stand during his or her trial, but when the judge offered Morrison a seat in the dock he refused and stood with his hand on his hip throughout the proceedings. Worse, Abinger was continually at war with the judge, the relatively amiable (for that era at any rate) Mr Justice Darling.

Meanwhile there had been an attempt to get at some of the witnesses. Lewis James Ward, Charles Macnamara and Charles

Haines, along with Lawrence Rappolt, had been charged with assaulting Alfred Stephens, one of the witnesses who put Steinie on Clapham Common. The defence argued that it was a domestic matter and that Stephens had made advances to Ward's wife, but they were convicted. When Ward came to be sentenced his counsel pleaded that he should not be sentenced to hard labour.

Mr Justice Darling: 'It will do him no harm.' (Laughter.)

The police were convinced that the instigator of the attack was Max Frank, but there was no evidence to connect him. There was, however, some evidence that Rappolt was part of a racecourse gang.[32]

The evidence against Morrison was not strong. As for the blood on the collar, he was both a fastidious man and sensible enough to have had his collar washed eight days after the murder. In fact he gave evidence that he possessed some six collars. The identification evidence was suspect and a John Greaves from the RIBA was called to point up the inadequate lighting at the Clapham Common cab rank.

Unfortunately Abinger decided to cross-examine the waiter about a period of time the man had spent in a mental hospital after a failed suicide attempt. Attempted suicide was then a felony and the introduction of this evidence entitled the prosecution to put Morrison's own convictions before the jury. If he had managed to avoid this trap Abinger had dug for Morrison, there was no possibility of escape because Abinger then accused another witness of being a brothel keeper.

Morrison also attempted to call alibi evidence from two young sisters with whom he said he had been at the Shoreditch Music Hall on New Year's Eve. Jane Brodsky gave evidence that she and her sister had gone there, had seen Morrison sitting in the same row and leaving the theatre at the end of the show. Esther Brodsky said they had paid five pence, but Muir was able to show that to get into those seats that night a person would have had to be in the queue at 7.15 for the 9 p.m. show. The girls said they had not queued and had gone straight into the seats. When he came to give evidence Morrison said he had arrived at about a quarter to nine after spending the earlier part of the evening in the Warsaw. He thought Harry Champion and Gertie Gitana had been on the bill, along with a boy and girl acting as man and wife. Certainly Champion and Gitana had appeared, but the boy and girl act had not been on the bill until the following week. Morrison had been to the theatre on 2 January.

The jury retired a bare thirty-five minutes before convicting him. Morrison now told the court that money found on him had come from a bank fraud.

It was the custom for the judge to remark that he wholeheartedly agreed with the verdict of a jury in a murder case, but Darling pointedly did not do so. He had already warned the jury that merely because Morrison had called a false alibi did not mean he was guilty. Ikey Foreigner was not the same as a straightforward Englishman. Indeed he had already summed up as best he could for an acquittal.

It is possible in Scotland to return a verdict of 'not proven'. An English jury cannot do that, but for all that, if they come to the conclusion that the case is not proven ... they give what is after all an equivalent verdict. If it is not proven then they must not say, 'Oh, it is not proven but we find him guilty'; there is only one verdict which an English jury is permitted to give.

Now he advised Morrison to say nothing more and that he should leave matters to his lawyers. When he came to pass the death sentence he used the traditional closing words, 'And may God have mercy on your soul.'

Morrison would have none of it. 'I decline such mercy. I do not believe there is a God in Heaven either,' he shouted.

He came before the newly formed Court of Criminal Appeal on 27 March and it was clear their Lordships did not like the conviction. Nevertheless they felt they could do nothing about it.

> Even if every member of the Court had been of the opinion that he personally would have acquitted the prisoner the Court must yet have upheld that conviction, unless they were of the opinion that the verdict was so perverse that no reasonable jury would have given it.[33]

When canvassed by Home Secretary Winston Churchill on the question of a reprieve, Darling allowed that whilst he personally thought Morrison to have been guilty he did not think the evidence strong enough to justify a conviction. Alverstone, who led the Court of Appeal, thought he had been badly defended by Abinger. There was a consensus of opinion that had Morrison been defended by either Marshall Hall or Curtis Bennett he would have been acquitted. *The Times* was in chauvinistic mood:

> ... the East End counts among its population, a large number of very dangerous, very reckless, and very noxious people, chiefly immigrants from the Eastern and SouthEastern countries of Europe. The second impression will be that these people add to the difficulties of the situation by their extreme untrustworthiness, since lying, especially in the witness-box, appears to be their natural language.[34]

Despite this, a petition with 75,000 signatures was raised calling for Morrison's reprieve. On 12 April it was announced that the death sentence was commuted to one of life imprisonment.

In 1912 there was an attempt to have Morrison's case reconsidered and Ethel Clayton, the woman with whom a Hugo Pool was living, went to the Home Office to give evidence and was questioned by Inspector Ward. She said that on the night of the murder Pool had left home at about 11 a.m. and had not returned for three days. When he had done so he tore up a bloodstained shirt and burned it, threatening her if she mentioned it. When Ward asked with whom the man had been that night she had replied, Steinie Morrison. Morrison was not a good prisoner and he did his time the hard way. He constantly protested his innocence and was truculent, abusive and violent to warders and prisoners alike.

I never saw him laugh. He swore to me, not once but a dozen times that he had not killed Leon Beron.[35]

In November 1913 it was thought that there might be an attempt to free Morrison and the Governor of Parkhurst Prison was alerted. He wrote back that the man was guarded and there was no fear of any attempt being successful. Nevertheless, for a time a watch was kept on Morrison's sister and two friends, Tom O'Sullivan and Joe Collins.

Steinie had one moment of pleasure when he learned that Inspector Ward had been killed in a Zeppelin raid during the war: 'I had become convinced that there was no God, but I think I shall alter my opinion after this.'[36]

Accounts vary as to the circumstances of his death. Certainly he was starving himself at the time. Some say it was another protest of his innocence, but there is a version that he was annoyed by a kitten kept as a pet by other prisoners and that in a fit of temper he threw it on a furnace. He received the No. 1 punishment of bread and water and after he had undergone that he began to starve himself as a protest for what he saw as another injustice.

> They put him in a padded cell, but there he refused to eat anything. Because of this a doctor ordered him out and into the prison hospital ward where I was working on special duty. He was too ill to be dangerous to himself or anybody else. Poor Steinie, they put him on a mattress on the floor and took the strait-jacket off him. One of the screws told me to lift his head up. He looked at me, sort of puzzled, as if he didn't know where he was. That was how he died, in my arm peaceful as a kitten. The man who'd murdered an old man and a cat. He died for the cat.[37]

Another version is that whilst being force-fed he accidentally choked to death. Shortly before he died he wrote:

> In this prison during the last 12 months alone about a dozen life sentence prisoners (all guilty of murder) have had their sentences reduced to 12 years or less. I am innocent. I have done close on 10 years and still I am forgotten about. Such is the justice of England.[38]

Whichever account is true, he died on 24 January 1921. Much to the annoyance of the Court of Criminal Appeal, a considerable time was spent at the trial discussing whether Morrison had mentioned the murder when he was arrested. Abinger felt that if he had not done this it was a most important point in his favour. It is difficult to see why. The whole East End must have been buzzing with the story and Morrison must have known that with his record he was a 'usual suspect'. A young officer, George Greaves, was called to give evidence to contradict Wensley and the others. He suffered very badly in a hostile cross-examination and after the case he was transferred to Ruislip. Despite appeals to be allowed to return, he remained in the country and resigned at the end of the year. *Police Review* thought he had been 'very badly treated'. He said that when he intervened he expected instant dismissal, and *John Bull* thought, 'The treatment which he has received is tantamount to dismissal'. Edward Abinger, in his memoirs, *Forty Years at the Bar*, wrote that he thought the evidence should 'not have hanged a dog'.

It was another ten years before the Court of Appeal quashed the conviction of the Liverpudlian insurance broker William Wallace on the grounds that, whilst there was nothing wrong with the conduct of the trial or indeed the verdict of the jury, each member of the court felt a lingering doubt as to his guilt. They were right to feel doubt. It is now almost universally accepted amongst those who have studied the case that Wallace did not kill his wife.

Was the Morrison conviction a correct one, and if not why was Beron killed? Was it something more than a simple robbery? Was there a political motive? There are a number of attractive rival theories.

Assuming Morrison did kill Beron, it is highly unlikely he was alone. Wensley believed that he and the man Hugo Pool carried out the murder. Benjamin Leeson, who was a junior officer in the case, thought that Morrison was guilty but that another man was also involved. Amongst others, the writers Eric Linklater and Julian Symons both have Beron murdered on behalf of the Leesma anarchists who feared he was an informer.[39]

On the other hand, Andrew Rose believes he was murdered simply because he was a criminal (rather than a political) informer, and there is no doubt whatsoever that he was a heavy player in crime in Whitechapel. All three, amongst many others, believe Morrison was completely innocent.

In his book of the trial Fletcher Moulton adds a fascinating afternote which gives some support to this theory.[40]

It appears that Mrs Maud Rider, an Englishwoman living in Paris, overheard a conversation on a tram about 10.15 one morning whilst travelling on the Avenue Kleber between Trocadero and the Arc de Triomphe. One of the participants was a French Jew, short, fat and bearded, with an old-fashioned curly-brimmed bowler. The second was a Frenchman who spoke poor English and the third a tall good-looking 'foreigner' who spoke fluent cockney English but with a foreign accent.

The Frenchman said in French, 'What are you doing in the affair Steinie Morrison?'

After being told to speak in English he continued, 'All right. Are you going to do anything?'

'No, Gort's (or Cort's) life is more valuable to us than his.'

'Yes, but we cannot let him hang. Can't you write a letter?'

The conversation continued. Mrs Rider watched the three men leave the tram separately and she followed the third to the Hotel d'Amiens in the rue des Deux Gares. She reported the matter to the director of the Paris edition of the *Daily Mail* who forwarded it to the Commissioner of Police in London, who took no action. The French police were never able to identify Cort or Gort, but some other names which Mrs Rider noted down were those of a gang of international criminals. One of the difficulties Mrs Rider faced in gaining credibility was that she was a woman. She compounded this by being a writer of romantic fiction.

One of the most ingenious of theories is that offered by

Abinger during his closing speech, that Beron had been killed by his brother Solomon. The motive could be that instead of living in Rowton House, Solomon Beron would thus acquire his brother's rooms and some of his clothes. He was undoubtedly unbalanced and in fact had attacked Abinger during the trial. He too would die in Colney Hatch. Their father was in a home at Clapham and Leon could have gone there at his brother's behest. Unfortunately there is really no evidence to support this particular flight of fancy. Given his precarious mental state, it is difficult to see how he would have had the wit to clean up his clothes and dispose of the property, let alone carve the 'S' on his brother's forehead and so divert attention. Unless of course the 'S' stood for Solomon. Another argument against this theory is that the descriptions of the other man at Clapham with Leon do not tally.

The next theory, favoured by Wensley, is that the killing was a straightforward robbery by Morrison and Hugo Pool. Despite the way that Muir opened the case against Morrison, that it was a lone killing, few really thought this was the case. The marks on Beron's head had a certain symmetry. Someone surely had to hold a lantern whilst the cuts were made. One of the problems with any of the robbery theories is why they should take Beron to Clapham. There were a number of open spaces in the East End and there were any number of alleys in the area in which to kill a man. Why should Beron travel across London with Morrison anyway? One suggestion has been that Morrison knew of a brothel in Clapham and Leon Beron, always keen on prostitutes, went in search of pastures new.

In recent years the most attractive theory has been that Morrison was set up to take the fall for the gang who had murdered Beron because he was a police informer – the mutilations on the forehead were certainly similar to markings on Polish informers. The legs of the body were crossed, so signifying double crossing. If this seems fantastic, think of the practice of Mafia killers dropping three dimes by a body to show that he was an informer. The similar but older version is that Beron was killed by the Leesma anarchists either because he was a political informer or he was suspected of being one.

Lapukhin, one of the heads of the Tsarist police, who died in Paris in 1928, tied the death of Beron to the Sidney Street siege and maintained that he had Peter the Painter working as a spy keeping observation on the Houndsditch thieves:

> I never could understand why the English made the mistake of naming this man as one of the criminal gang for they must have known he only consorted with them in furtherance of his duty which was to keep me posted regarding the activities of the gang.

Lapukhin claimed that the gang were really political assassins whose real aim in life was to assassinate the Russian royal family when they visited England or France. There had been some delay in fixing the details of the tour and this caused financial problems which meant they were obliged to carry out a robbery to survive. Certainly they had some success in their struggle for survival. Twelve months before the Houndsditch shootings they had successfully robbed a Post Office in North London, carrying away the safe on a wheelbarrow.[41]

The former policeman went on to say that when Peter the Painter disappeared he turned his duties over to Beron who had also been an agent of the Russian police. Lapukhin's version was that the nihilists were bent on killing Beron and, with the participation of Morrison, he was lured to Clapham Common on the pretext of buying stolen jewellery.

I am equally certain that the case against Morrison was not that on which he was convicted. Morally I suppose he was guilty, but I was able afterwards to supply the English authorities information that caused them to revise their theory and I think it was this information more than any other that caused them to go back on the death sentence.[42]

NOTES

1. D. Swarc, 'Background and conditions contributing to Jewish prostitution in the East End of London 1890–1914' (unpublished manuscript).

2. Thomas Arnold, Supt. H Div. Evidence to the Select Committee on Emigration and Immigration (Foreigners). Parliamentary Papers X (1889).

3. See W.W. Roston, *British Economy of the Nineteenth Century*, p. 49.

4. *Jewish Chronicle*, 25 June 1886.

5. 'Judenhetze Brewing in East London' in the *Pall Mall Gazette*, 18 February 1886. See also Simeon Singer's reply in the edition of 23 February.

6. Nat. Arch 1 265. For a full account of the case, which argues Lipski's innocence or at least that there was not sufficient evidence on which to hang him, see Martin L. Friedland, *The Trials of Israel Lipski*.

7. Nat. Arch. MEPO 3 285A.

8. Raphael Samuel, *East End Underworld*, p. 112.

9. See Nat. Arch. 1 1124 F. Wensley, *Detective Days*, p. 92.

10. F. Wensley, ibid

11. George W. Cornish, *Cornish of the Yard*, p. 4.

12. B. Leeson, *Lost London*, p. 147.

13. *ELO*, 1 November 1902.

14. ibid, 8 November 1902.

15. According to Leeson, Moses also went to America on his release and became a successful businessman.

16. *ELO*, 24 September 1904.

17. Lepidus may well not have been his name but it is used here for convenience. If it was correct he was probably the younger brother of Leister Lepidus who was killed in Paris on 1 May 1907 when a bomb he was carrying exploded in his pocket.

18. Donald Rumbelow, *The Houndsditch Murders*, p. 28.

19. Raphael Samuel, *East End Underworld*, pp. 136–7. Harding has it that Nina Vassilleva went mad after being beaten up by the police following the Sidney Street shooting. He is clearly wrong. It was Sara Trassjonsky who went mad, and there is no suggestion that she was beaten up.

20. In his memoirs Wensley omits the Putney request. F. Wensley, *Detective Days*, p. 172. Harding is particularly scathing of Leeson who he says '... was potty. He got scared and went to Australia where he imagined he met Peter the Painter on a train.' Raphel Samuel, *East End Underworld*, p. 318. The story of Leeson and Peter the Painter appears in Benjamin Leeson, *Lost London*. Rather more likely is that these rather anodyne memoirs were bolstered for publication.

21. (1911) 4 Cr App R 228.

22. Richard Whittington-Egan, 'Miss Nina and the Anarchists' in *New Law Journal*, 11 January 2000.

23. B. Leeson, *Lost London*, and Sir William Crocker, *Far from Humdrum*. Crocker's father represented both Trassjonsky and Vassilleva. The story is discounted by Donald Rumbelow, *The Houndsditch Murders*, pp. 184–5.

24. *ELO*, 7 January 1911.

25. *Morning Leader*, 12 January 1911.

26. *The Times*, 21 December 1910.

27. *Morning Leader*, 9 January 1911.

28. Louis Bailey, quoted in *East End Jewish Radicals*, p. 292.

29. David Beron, 'a miserable looking man', was charged with begging. He was found to have on him £25. 10s. gold; 6s. 11¾d. bronze. He told the court that at one time his father had property worth £60,000. After a week in custody for reports he was discharged. *ELA*, 21 and 28 November 1914.

30. Raphael Samuel, *East End Underworld*, p. 134.

31. Montague William Cory, later Baron Rowton (1838–1903) devised the concept of hotels for working-class men, which provided lodging and catering and which had the advantages of a club at the lowest cost. Despite considerable opposition, the first of these was opened in Vauxhall in 1893. It was a great success and another five followed. The one in Whitechapel opened in 1902.

32. Nat. Arch MEPO 3 202.

33. *Morrison* (1911) 9 Cr App R.

34. *The Times*, 16 March 1911.

35. George Smithson, *Raffles in Real Life*, p. 122.

36. Charles George Gordon, *Crooks of the Underworld*, p. 20.

37. Wally Thompson, *Time of My Life*, pp. 47–8.

38. *Daily Mail*, 26 January 1921.

39. Eric Linklater, *The Corpse on Clapham Common*; Julian Symons, *A Reasonable Doubt*.

40. H. Fletcher Moulton, *The Trial of Steinie Morrison*.

41. 'Peter the Painter' in *Morning Leader*, 9 January 1911.

42. Secrets of Sidney Street', in *Empire News*, 8 March 1928.

3

THE GRIZZARD GANG

At the turn of the twentieth century and for the first decade of the 1900s, the great receiver of stolen goods and 'putter-up' of burglaries throughout London was Joseph 'Cammi' Grizzard. More or less every major burglary could be laid at his door or that of his subordinates who would bring the jewellery to him in Hatton Garden or to his home in the East End to fence for them.

Born in 1867, by the early 1900s he was described as being of middle height and somewhat portly build, favouring a blond moustache and diamond rings on his fingers. Sir Richard Muir KC, who would later prosecute him, thought:

... [he] possessed rather a fine face with nothing in it to tell the world of the evil, intriguing brain that had been responsible for some of the most amazing coups in the whole history of crime.[1]

Christmas Humphreys took a rather different view:

... his impudence and swaggering self-assurance served to create a personality which dominated the smaller fry who hung about the 'Garden' and turned them when required into willing if not able tools.

Like so many criminals he was a great man with a twist in his character which made him prefer to go crooked where he might go straight.[2]

Grizzard was first convicted at Thames Police Court on 1 May 1880 and received fourteen days for larceny. He did not then appear before the courts for some twenty years when he was charged with a heavy burglary including seventy-eight gold watches, twenty-four gold chains and seventy diamond, pearl and sapphire rings at a jeweller's in Richmond, Surrey, in which he was said to have been involved with David Jacobs, a cutter known as 'Sticks'. Despite an eyewitness who claimed to have seen him outside the shop at 5 a.m. on the night of 19 November 1902; a woman who said she had been sold a bracelet from the stolen jewellery by Grizzard; and a remark that he thought a piece of iron exhibited in court must have been his jemmy, he was acquitted.[3] Over the next few years Grizzard would come to be recognised as one of the highest quality receivers in London.

His greatest coup came six years later when he masterminded the jewel robbery at the Café Monico in Regent Street which led to the appearance of John Higgins and the former lightweight jockey Harry Grimshaw at London Sessions.

On 20 June 1909 a French dealer, Frederick Goldschmidt, left Paris and travelled to London bringing jewellery with him and staying at De Keyser's hotel. It is not clear how Grizzard came to hear of this, but he had Goldschmidt watched; almost certainly Grizzard maintained connections in Paris who would inform him of the vulnerability of certain dealers. Indeed Goldschmidt seems to have been doubly unfortunate because another gang, which included the English-born American Eddie Guerin, then still almost at the top of his form, was also seen at the hotel watching him. It was really only a question of who got to him first and, past the post, it was Grimshaw.

It became clear that Goldschmidt never put his case down in public except when he washed his hands, and on 9 July he was followed to the Café Monico. When he went to the lavatory he put his bag beside him and as he reached out for the soap, he was pushed off balance and the bag was snatched by Grimshaw. As Goldschmidt chased after it his passage was blocked by Higgins. The jewels, worth some £60,000, were never found. Had the pair struck the previous day the haul would have been nearer £160,000.

Even more than today it was apparent that only a handful of people had the ability to organise such a theft and dispose of the goods. Within a matter of hours the police obtained a search warrant for Grizzard's home at 73 Parkholme Road, Dalston, and found him at dinner with his guests, three potential buyers. Grizzard and his company sat at the dinner table while the police searched the house, but nothing was found. After they had gone, Grizzard drank his now cold pea soup and at the bottom of the bowl was a diamond necklace which was then cleaned and sold. Another version of the story was that the necklace was hidden in his wife's underwear. Delicacy prevented officers of the time searching ladies thoroughly.

Higgins – defended by the talented and fashionable but dishonest solicitor Arthur Newton – ran an alibi defence that he had been with a police officer in the Old Bell public house in Holborn.[4] The officer accepted that he had been with Higgins but not at the crucial time. It was then announced that he also intended to call a character witness, a Mr Goldsmith. The cross-examination by Sir Richard Muir soon put a stop to this idea:

Q: What other names do you know him by?

A: Cammi, a nickname.

Q: Did you know that he has been tried at the Old Bailey for receiving as recently as 1903?

Silence.

Q: And that he has been arrested for the Monico robbery?

Higgins received fifteen months and Grimshaw three years' penal servitude to be followed by five years' preventive detention. It was thought that altogether six men were involved in the snatch.

But then Grizzard's fortunes began to decline. The next year he was back in the dock when he was arrested and charged with both receiving stolen jewellery from a burglary in Brighton and harbouring Samuel Barnett who had failed to appear at North London Sessions some fourteen months previously. This time, unusually, the police did find a criminal to give evidence against him. Arthur Denville Sassoon Collinson, then doing five years on the Moor, said that for the six months prior to his current unhappy experience he had worked as a burglar for both men. On 8 March 1910 at the Old Bailey Grizzard received five months in the Second Division for feloniously harbouring Barnett. Barnett, wanted for burglaries around the South of England, had been given bail but had fled abroad in 1907. On his return he had been found living at Grizzard's house.

Grizzard was also behind the theft of jewellery from Vaughan Morgan, son of Sir Walter Vaughan Morgan, the City Alderman. Frank Ellis was his butler from 1904 until 1911 when he left to set up as a bookmaker. Before he left he was asked to find another footman and he obtained a man named Robinson through an agency. In the three weeks before Ellis handed over, Robinson began betting with him. Ellis also knew William Bangham, one of Grizzard's men and a known jewel thief. By November 1911 Ellis's business was not going well and he was raided and heavily fined as an illegal bookmaker. He then persuaded Robinson to let him into his former master's house, and there was a successful trial run when nothing was taken. The second raid was successful, but the police dismissed the idea that there had been a break-in; so far as they were concerned it was an inside job. Robinson was arrested and discharged after naming Ellis, who was arrested but remained silent. He received twenty-one months' penal servitude. No amount of persuasion would make Ellis give up Grizzard.

One reason for the loyalty was that Grizzard would help friends who came to grief with the police, and their wives and children whilst they were away. He also had an unswerving loyalty to those with whom he worked. Unlike many a receiver his word was his bond; he paid what he promised. To a certain extent, to him crime was a sport. Again and again his friends tried to persuade him to settle down. He was a comparatively wealthy man and could have afforded to retire, but it was the chase that counted.

Grizzard's men included the burglar James Lockett, who also used the names Preston, Harry Graham, Lockhart and Jim or James Howard, who was described by ex-Superintendant Charles Leach as 'Lockett-the-lion-hearted – the man who never knew fear'.

At one time Lockett had worked with, and probably had been emotionally involved with Mary Carr, the then Queen of the Forty Thieves. He had certainly worked with the accomplished 'Blonde' Alice Smith, who came within an ace of stealing the Ascot Gold Cup in 1906 and later with Harry 'The Jockey' Grimshaw.

Lockett had convictions in both Italy and America and on 14 February 1906, under the name of William Preston, he had received five years at Liverpool Assizes for the attempted robbery of a man called Hutchinson, a travelling jewellery salesman. His partner 'Long Almond' received ten years. Along with two others, picturesquely known as 'Red Bob' and 'Shirty Bob', they had trailed Hutchinson for some weeks and by scraping an acquaintance with him discovered he was going to Liverpool. They watched him leave his hotel and went to his room to search for the jewels. Unfortunately for them he returned to find Lockett standing holding the stones. He was released on 15 November 1909.[5]

Apparently at one time Shirty Bob owned a fashionable club but when 'Chicago' May Sharpe knew him around the turn of the century he was a hotel thief working, amongst other places, the Langham Hotel. Although she often names criminals such as Dab McCarthy and Ruby Michaels, she does not identify 'Shirty Bob'.

Long Almond's name was Arthur Norton and he was regarded as one of the – if not *the* – finest safe-crackers of the period. Always impeccably dressed and a resident in the best hotels, he would cultivate the bank clerks who frequented the hotels' bars and billiard rooms with a view to obtaining an impression of the keys they carried. Just before the Liverpool fiasco he had been released from another ten-year sentence after a raid on a branch of the Bank of Sunderland in Newcastle. This time he had persuaded a clerk to accompany him to a Turkish bath, and when the man had taken off his clothes Norton went through his pockets for the keys. It was something of a surprise that he had actually gone to the hotel, and there was speculation that he had unwisely regarded it as 'a soft job'.[6]

Lockett had also been in the wars before the Liverpool case; the previous year he had been arrested over the theft of £10,000 of jewellery in Colmore Row, Birmingham. He and a woman had been visiting a number of jewellers where she had pawned jewels. Almost immediately after the theft she had left for America. Some of the jewels were later found in the possession of a New York pawnbroker. Almost certainly the woman was 'Blonde' Alice Smith who once fought 'Chicago' May Sharpe over the latter's lover, Baby Thompson. As for Lockett, he was put on an identification parade and was not picked out.

Now in 1910 Lockett was reported to have an interest in a motor-car business in Finchley and what was rather charmingly called a 'cinematograph palace' in Golders Green purchased with the proceeds from the Birmingham theft, although according to police files, he spent little time with either. Instead he was occupied as the working lieutenant of Grizzard in a series of substantial jewellers' shop burglaries in the West End during the winter of 1911–12.

Then in 1913 came Grizzard's greatest coup and most abject failure – the theft of a string of sixty-one pearls, one of the finest collections then assembled, with an insurance value of £130,000.

The international dealer Max Mayer had offices at 88 Hatton Garden and on 20 June 1913 sent the string to his agent in Paris, Henri Salomon, who had unfulfilled hopes of finding a buyer. On 15 July the necklace, in a leather case along with two drop pearls and a round pearl, wrapped in blue paper, marked 'M.M.' and sealed by Salomon, was returned by registered post through the postal authorities in Paris.

There was nothing remarkable in this process. The standard way of sending jewellery at the time, it was regarded as far safer than having a messenger carry it around, as Goldschmidt had found to his cost a couple of years earlier. On 16 July Mayer received a letter from Salomon saying the pearls were on their way and, in fact, the box arrived in the same post.

But instead of the pearls there was only the considerably less valuable cargo of eight lumps of sugar on a bed of cotton wool, all wrapped in a piece of newspaper from *Echo de Paris* dated 2 July. There were now twin problems. First for Salomon to explain just what he had done and eliminate himself from inquiries, and secondly for the thieves to dispose of pearls which were readily identifiable. Salomon came immediately to England, producing a receipt for the package. The French police and Chief Inspector Ward were able to trace the box's transfers from Paris to Calais through to the Central Sorting Office in Hatton Garden. There was, it seemed, no possibility that the box had been tampered with whilst in the hands of the postal services. The postman who had been given the box to deliver had signed for it and produced a receipt from the commissionaire at Mayer's office. He had never come under suspicion and had worked for the Post Office for over thirty years.

It was then discovered that there was an additional seal on the box to hide a cut in the paper, but this seal was also stamped 'M.M.'. Much to the wrath of the French postal authorities, the police now believed the theft had taken place on their side of the Channel, but there was no evidence of this and if the postal workers were to be believed the theft could not have occurred in transit. This left Salomon, but the police were quite willing to rule him out which left no one. A £10,000 reward was posted and an extensive description of the pearls was circulated.

Then at the beginning of August two jewel dealers in Paris, cousins Mayer Cohen Quadratstein and Samuel Brandstatter, heard that Leiser Gutwirth in Antwerp might have the secret of the whereabouts of the pearls. Brandstatter visited Gutwirth and was told the pearls were indeed available, but not for £20,000 which he was offered: he wanted double. Brandstatter said he must consult with his partner and wrote to Gutwirth, who was now in London, saying he had a buyer 'for the article'.

He was immediately summoned from Paris, but the price was now £50,000.

The cousins – who throughout were only interested in the reward – met Gutwirth, Grizzard and one of Grizzard's colleagues, Simon Silverman, in a Lyons teashop in Holborn. According to Christmas Humphreys, Silverman was a diamond broker who lived with his mother and sister at Bow. 'Those who knew him in Hatton Garden described him as a greasy, always smiling little hunch-backed Jew. He was always apologetic and polite to everyone, too much so for the blunt and honest English mind and none too popular.'[7]

Grizzard took out a cigarette, asked an apparent stranger for a match and a box was thrown to him. When opened, there were the three separate pearls. They were taken to be weighed; the box was sealed and it was agreed that only the price was in question. For amateur detectives the cousins behaved with great skill. They kept negotiations going for some ten days whilst they contacted the assessors, the firm of Price & Gibbs, and were given 100,000 FF to use in negotiations. Unwilling to have the men caught without the pearls, the police bided their time.

On 25 August another meeting took place in Holborn, this time at the now long gone First Avenue Hotel. The cousins, joined by Spanier, a French jewel expert employed by the assessors, met Silverman and Grizzard. The necklace was produced and the three stray pearls were purchased for 100,000 FF. Over the next few days Grizzard and his team were followed and the meetings were watched by detectives in disguise.

Meanwhile Grizzard was taking some precautions himself. He had made Brandstatter and Quadratstein remain in the room in the First Avenue Hotel for five minutes while he left with the money and the necklace. He also recognised one of the detectives set to watch him, and now he employed Lockett to watch the watchers. His antennae also picked up the signal that the whole thing was a trap and he arranged for the necklace to go to Amsterdam to be sold for £40,000, but Gutwirth and Silverman would not agree and Grizzard allowed himself to be overruled.

Now the police decided that the best way to follow Grizzard was not by having him tailed by a plain-clothes detective but by the simple expedient of using a uniformed constable seemingly going about his ordinary affairs, and accordingly a detective was put in uniform. On 3 September he followed Grizzard, Silverman and Lockett to a meeting at what was then the British Museum Underground station. The trap was sprung and after a fight the three were arrested.

The trouble began at Bow Street where the prisoners were taken. When they were searched there was no necklace. Their houses were searched, they were charged with stealing and receiving the necklace, but by the end of the evening there were still no pearls.

Nothing was found until a fortnight later when a matchbox containing pearls was found in St Paul's Road, Islington, when a piano maker saw the box in the gutter. He thought they were imitation pearls, but nevertheless took them to the local police station where the police agreed with him and they were registered as such and sent to the Lost Property office at Scotland Yard where an officer in the case saw and recognised them as genuine. Apparently when Lockett's wife had heard of her husband's arrest she had thrown the pearls away. So Mayer received most of his jewels back.

Just how was the snatch worked? Was it done in France? In fact, as with most of the best plans, it was all deceptively simple. Grizzard knew Mayer and that he received large quantities of jewellery. What he was hoping for was not pearls but diamonds which could easily be recut and disposed of without any great difficulty.

Silverman then took an office at 101 Hatton Garden and began to chat up the postmen. One by the name of Neville, either for money or accidentally – and although nothing was proven it really must have been the former – provided an opportunity for Silverman to take an impression of the seals on a package addressed to Mayer. From then on it was relatively simple to obtain a die, and once the defendants were in custody a die maker named Gordon came forward to say that he had made one for Silverman.

On the morning of the robbery the postman making the delivery went to 101 before 88 and – negligently, for he was not charged either – was distracted so that the package could be opened and the substitution made.

Prosecuted by Sir Richard Muir, Lockett and Grizzard received seven years' penal servitude and Silverman five years at their trial in November 1913. Silverman was to be deported after his sentence. Gutwirth was sentenced to eighteen months with hard labour. He had tried to disassociate himself from the others.

I was dragged into it. I have been eighteen years in Hatton Garden, my Lord, always straight-forward. I do not know what made me do it. I ought never to have done a thing like that. It is not my business. Mine is a straight-forward business.

Despite the fact that he had been in England for twenty-five years and was a married man, he too was recommended for deportation:

Mr Justice Lawrence: That may be, but he is an alien and we do not want such aliens here.

Their appeals were dismissed in December. After the arrests of the four principals the police had gone looking for eighty-two-year-old Daniel McCarthy, a long-standing member of the Grizzard gang and other teams. He was charged with them after admitting that he had changed some of the francs provided by Spanier, but the technicalities of proving anything more against him were too great and he was discharged.

A police report prepared after Grizzard's arrest establishes his high place in the pantheon of criminals of the time:

> He is a diamond merchant by trade, but has no established business premises. He does undoubtedly do a little business, but the greater portion of his time is taken up by organising crimes, and buying and disposing of stolen property. Much has been heard of him during the past fifteen years as having been connected with many serious crimes. A large number of statements made by prisoners are in our possession showing that they have disposed of property to him, but unfortunately we have been unable to prosecute him for a lack of corroborative evidence.

Grizzard found conditions in jail little to his liking and he began to try to scheme his way out. Like so many thieves, he came to a long prison sentence late in life and prison, particularly in those days, takes the stuffing out of many a man. Grizzard was no exception. There is a theory that those who have received regular sentences can cope better than those who have perhaps only served a few months. Lockett knew and understood what penal servitude was all about. Grizzard did not and, while Lockett appears to have accepted his sentence and conditions stoically, Grizzard became an informer on some of his former competitors. He was in his fifties and apparently in poor health because he spent much of his time in the prison hospital. In any event Grizzard was an old man by the standards of the day. He had a heart condition and was suffering from eczema. He wanted out and now, reneging on the principles which had kept so many men loyal to him, he wrote to the authorities naming George Hanlon as a man wanted for three robberies. Hanlon was well known; he had done three years in Paris and five here. Grizzard hoped that when his wife lodged a petition for his release it would be supported.

Grizzard may have been a master crook but spelling was certainly not his long suit. On 11 October 1915 he wrote from Parkhurst giving information that an American whom he knew only as 'Yankee Johnny' and a German whose name he did not know were two of the best burglars in London. The German was kept under cover by a Jim Trott in Manchester and 'Yankee Johnny' was a great friend of Harry Snell:

> The German may have his mustarsh off – Oftern – nows. A man
> Rogers used to live in the Westend has a money lender.

As for his health, he was suffering from 'diebertus' and 'skin diesiese'.

Grizzard was giving good information. 'Yankee Johnny' was John Talbot, an American safe-breaker who lived in Darwin Street in the New Kent Road. The German was Max Baum. James Trott did live in Manchester and had a police record. Harry Snell lived at 83 Hungerford Road, Holloway, and was a bookmaker suspected, rather like Grizzard, of being a financier and putter-up.

The gang had been relatively quiet since the arrest of Grizzard and Lockett, but George Hanlon was indeed wanted for stealing a mailbag from St Pancras station on 24 August 1913. He lived at 14 Wroughton Road, Wandsworth, where the bag minus the contents was found. And for that matter, the house was also minus Hanlon who was now thought to be living in Streatham.

Rogers was believed to be Swiss and was certainly an associate of Hanlon. He was also believed to have gone back to Switzerland. Sergeant David Goodwillie recommended that Grizzard have a reduction in his sentence, but nothing came of it.

But Grizzard was not finished and in 1917 he wrote again, informing this time on a Bernard Hedgis who was serving three years, alleging him to be one of the most dangerous criminals in the country. He also disclosed some of his own past. Hedgis had come from Africa at the end of the Boer War and knew a foreigner, Idleman, who lived in a boarding house in Russell Square kept by his wife. Hedgis was a dealer in stolen jewellery. Grizzard had been summoned there and later went over to buy jewellery in Paris for some £4,000. In fact this was a trick. Grizzard had been 'put out' and robbed. Hedgis, he claimed, also robbed the English in South Africa and then later went to South America living off women.

Sadly, apart from naming Hedgis and another prisoner, 0394*, he peached on his old friend Silverman saying he had been working with Lockett for some ten years. He hoped that his letter would be of assistance. The country, he thought, should be protected from the likes of Hedgis. At least he did try to row Lockett out, writing that neither he nor Lockett knew anything of the pearl necklace before it was stolen. Indeed, according to him, Lockett had apparently been recruited to save the gems after they had been stolen.

Again the police made inquiries and found that Hedgis and Samuel Morris Natenson had been recommended for deportation when they were sentenced to three years' penal servitude on 8 December 1914. They would have been entitled to nine months' remission. When the police checked things out they found that the men had not yet gone to Brixton to await their deportation, and that Natenson was not in fact due for deportation; he was to be allowed to join the British Army and did indeed join the Royal Artillery. Hedgis was to see a recuiting officer with a view to enlistment and on 14 April he too joined the Artillery. He denied even knowing Grizzard, and Detective Inspector Wensley, now having one of his most talented opponents in custody, was implacable. Poor Cammi was to be told that in his view the information was of no value to the police. He would remain where he was until he had completed his sentence.[8]

Despite his health and distaste for prison Grizzard just could not stop. In 1922 he was charged with receiving the proceeds of an ingenious fraud on a firm of London jewel dealers which netted some £10,000, and again Muir prosecuted him. Grizzard had arranged for Major Harrison – actually ex-Major Harrison since he had been cashiered – to purchase jewellery on approval from Bedford & Co. in Aldersgate High Street. He advanced Harrison £3,000 to establish a line of credit and Harrison played his part well. The jewellery was to be shown to a Colonel who would shortly be returning to India. It was a simple, well-established confidence trick. The initial purchases were paid for; more jewellery was bought and paid for and then £10,000 of jewellery was handed over for approval. The idea was for it to be smashed, or sold at a discount, on the Continent; but after a quick attempt to sell it in Hatton Garden, Grizzard and another member of the conspiracy, the American-born Michael Spellman, received only £900 for it in Antwerp. Foolishly he returned to England where he was found to have another collection of stolen jewellery in his possession and more gems were traced to Grizzard.

Spellman and Grizzard had worked together over a number of years. They had first met in America when Grizzard absented himself from London for a period. It was thought that Spellman had backed out of participating in the Great Pearl Robbery because his wife was ill.

In August 1922 Grizzard was arrested and in the October received twelve months, as did Spellman. The gallant major fled to Canada where shortly afterwards he received two years for a similar fraud. Whilst awaiting trial Grizzard was found to be suffering from both tuberculosis and diabetes in an aggravated form. He was taken home where he died on 15 September 1923, aged fifty-seven. He wrote a note for Spellman leaving him 'all the spoils you have done me out of and my place in the underworld as Prince'.[9]

On his release unfortunately Spellman did not behave as well towards those from whom he bought as Grizzard had done. Operating out of Hatton Garden and Duke Street, Houndsditch, he was known to screw burglars down for the last penny. It was from an anonymous tip-off that the police arrested him in the autumn of 1925 and he received a further twelve months with hard labour for receiving.

James Lockett had been released from penal servitude in 1919. He married a second time and became a bookmaker. He had not committed – or at least had not been convicted of – any further crime in the next decade, by which time he was sixty-seven. Whilst inside there had been a curious incident over his house in Powis Gardens, Golders Green, which had been sold for £425 to a Mrs Saxby who wanted to use it as a bed-and-breakfast. Now she reported to the police that the estate agent was pestering her to buy it from her. What was the reason for this? The police did not know. They had thoroughly searched the place – throughout which there was a host of electric alarms – when Lockett was arrested, and they could not believe his family had left anything behind when they moved out. They advised Mrs Saxby to search the house again and report back. There is no record that she did.

Towards the end of his life Lockett fell from his place as an aristocrat of crime. In 1938 then aged seventy-six he received six weeks at Bow Street for loitering at a Post Office with intent to steal from women's handbags and he was again before the courts in 1940. He died the next year in Edmonton.[10]

Harry Grimshaw, who had taken the fall for the Café Monico robbery, continued an independent life of crime. Born in Bolton in the 1890s, he had been a successful jockey who could go to the scales at a pound or two over six stone, and in 1895 he won the valuable Manchester November and Liverpool Cup handicaps. Later he rode in Austria and Germany before returning to England, relinquishing his licence in 1904, and he then worked as a tic-tac man. He first appeared in court two years later when he was bound over for stealing a purse, but the same year he received three months for theft. From then it was a step up in class and he became the known associate of jewel thieves working on the Continent. October 1907 saw him receive twenty-one months at North London Quarter Sessions for the theft of a ring and he followed up with three years for a handbag snatch. In 1912 he received a total of eight years following a conviction for theft at Marlborough Street Police Court. He was released during the war from his sentence and served well in France, but failed to report on his discharge and was returned to prison to complete his sentence. He was once more associated with a team of continental jewel thieves and in the spring of 1923 was suspected of being involved in the theft of a jewel case at Dover Harbour. It was thought he had returned to the Continent, but in fact he had gone back to the Northern racetracks and in October, described as wearing a smartly cut blue suit, he was given twenty-one months for receiving. At the time the police described him as one of the greatest of hotel thieves, with his speed being blinding. His colleague Frederick Johnson earned nine months for theft at Middlesbrough Quarter Sessions. Grimshaw's other colleague, Elizabeth Murray, said to be a French woman, was sentenced at

Durham the following month for the theft of the jewellery worth £290. Grimshaw died shortly after.

Another of Grimshaw's associates was the noted woman thief 'Blonde' Alice Smith who once fought the notorious 'Chicago' May Sharpe. After Grimshaw went to prison for the Pearl Robbery in which she had been an outside decoy, she went to America where she was involved in a £20,000 blackmail scheme with Charlie Smith, May Sharpe's new lover. She also served seven years in the States for a jewel robbery. In 1926 she served a period of three years for theft and was again imprisoned for another jewel robbery in December 1929.[11]

There are many accounts of the Great Pearl Robbery, including that of Christmas Humphreys. It is also given prominence in the memoirs of both Muir and ex-Superintendent G.W. Cornish who, as a young officer, was part of the investigating team. In *Cornish of the Yard* he gives a slightly different – and one more favourable to the Yard – account of the retrieval of the pearls.

In his time Eddie Guerin was one of the great safe-breakers and thieves of the early twentieth century. He was a known associate of both Grimshaw and Daniel McCarthy, and it may be that at the time of the Pearl Robbery he was in fact working for Grizzard. Born in England, Guerin worked in France and was sent to the French penal colony Devil's Island from which he escaped. He was the only survivor of the three escapees and it was said, with no evidence to support it, that not only had he killed (which he admitted) but that he had eaten his companions (which he did not). In 1906, represented by Sir Richard Muir KC, normally a senior prosecutor, he successfully fought an attempt to extradite him to France after a robbery at the American Express offices. That year Guerin was shot and wounded near the Russell Square Underground station by his former mistress 'Chicago' May Sharpe and her then companion.

Over the years Guerin remained in England working with the Titanic Gang and drifting into petty crime. In his later years he repeatedly appeared before the magistrates' courts up and down the country, usually on charges relating to shoplifting and pickpocketing. His last appearance in court was in 1940 when he received six weeks' imprisonment for theft. He died in hospital on 5 December 1940 in Bury, Lancashire, where he had been sent as a war refugee.[12]

There were, of course, other receivers and putters-up to replace Grizzard, although they may not have operated in the plush conditions in which he chose to work. Israel Myers was seventy-nine when he appeared at the Old Bailey charged with receiving. Born in the East End, he went to America where he had built up a fortune before returning to Houndsditch where he bought the George and Dragon. His second, much younger wife left him and he became a receiver. By the time he had remarried and his third wife was about to give birth to their second child, he was acting as receiver of some 25 per cent of the property stolen in the Metropolitan area. He pleaded guilty to five counts; his counsel urged that this was his first lapse and emphasis was placed on his unblemished past. The *Empire News* commented sourly, 'There were indisputable facts to disprove most of this.'[13]

Myers had been on remand for three months when Sir Ernest Wild sentenced him to a total of a year's imprisonment.

One of the biggest of the receivers of the time was Joseph Betts who, at his trial for receiving stolen jewellery, described Duke's Place off Middlesex Street where he conducted his business:

There are at least three or four hundred dealers there every Sunday even in a bad time like this and in summer I have seen as many as a thousand there. Dealers lay their goods out on the ground, on clothes and on stalls so that anyone who wishes to purchase anything can examine the article.

He went on to say that the Tsar of Russia's jewels had been broken down and sold in the market. His explanation did him no good; he received five years. After he was taken into custody, high-class burglaries were said to have ceased for a time in London.[14]

That, of course, may have been press hype. The police and press were always keen on elevating villains. Samuel Cohen, described by Detective Inspector Edward Greeno as 'a modern Fagin', received two years at the Old Bailey swiftly followed by two more for receiving and conspiracy at Winchester Assizes. He was regarded as having been behind much London crime for a number of undetected years. Or it may have been a successful attempt by the police to put the boot in at Betts' trial, because not long after came the trial of 'the best safe-breakers in the world', one of whom was an East Ender, James Flood, whose real name was Wood. The team, which consisted of him, as the putter-up and arranger, John Russell from Liverpool and two wild colonial boys – 'Daredevil' Dennis Harris, then aged sixty, from Australia and a South African, John James, both of whom had in their younger days been steeplechase jockeys – was caught on 28 November 1924 *in flagrante* in a burglary in the Euston Road. Flood/Wood received fifteen months and, to teach colonials not to come to England to rob safes, Harris and James were each sentenced to three years' penal servitude. Russell received six months in the Second Division.[15]

NOTES

1. S.T. Felstead and Lady Muir, *Sir Richard Muir*, p. 130.
2. Christmas Humphreys, *The Great Pearl Robbery of 1913*, p. 8.
3. *The Times*, 20 January 1903.

4. Arthur Newton was one of the most sought after London solicitors in the period 1890 to 1912, acting in the Oscar Wilde trial as well as in the Crippen and McDougal murder cases. He was given six months for conspiracy to pervert the course of justice in the Cleveland Brothel scandal and received three years in 1913 for a land fraud. After his release he established a dubious marriage agency, and died in 1930.

5. 'Chicago' May Sharpe. *Chicago May – Her Story*.

6. *Morning Leader*, 15 February 1906; *The Umpire*, 18 February 1906.

7. Judge Christmas Humphreys, *The Great Pearl Robbery of 1913*.

8. Nat. Arch. MEPO 3 236B.

9. *Empire News*, 25 October 1925.

10. *The People*, 19 June 1932; *Reynold's Newspaper*, 7 August 1938; *Westminster & Pimlico* News, 5 July 1940.

11. *Empire News*, 8 December 1929.

12. Eddie Guerin, *The Man from Devil's Island*; Brian McDonald, *Gangs of London*.

13. *Empire News*, 'Aged Spider Man of the Underworld', 9 September 1923.

14. *Empire News*, 22 February 1925.

15. Nat. Arch MEPO 3 483, *The Star*, 30 January 1925, G.W. Cornish, *Cornish of the Yard*, Ch. VII.

4

PROSTITUTION

It could never be said that prostitution in the East End was a way out of poverty, but it was an existence into which many young women, particularly Jewish women, were forced. Commercial prostitution was prohibited under Rabbinic laws as a form of idolatry. Part of the reason was the wish to disassociate the Jewish faith from other Middle Eastern religions in which sex played a large part. In East Europe, prostitution was almost unknown amongst the Jews until the nineteenth century.

In 1905 in Warsaw there was an *Alphonsenpogrom* in which the citizens attempted to drive out the pimps. In that city in 1889, 22 per cent of licensed prostitutes were Jewish; in 1910 in Minsk 33 per cent of official prostitutes and half the female patients in the VD ward were Jewish.

In the East End it was estimated that approximately a thousand Jewish women a year worked in prostitution. Some 20 per cent of brothel-keeping convictions were against Jews. One reason was that young women in rural communities in Eastern Europe were effectively sold by their parents from economic necessity. Girls were also enticed away from their families with promises of marriage and jobs. It is impossible to think that the families did not at least suspect what would befall their daughters. About a thousand unaccompanied girls a year arrived at the East End Docks alone. It is almost impossible to imagine the confusion they would feel with the bustle and with little command of English. It is no surprise therefore that many fell prey to offers of seeming kindness in the form of lodging.

> The scenes at the landing stage are less idyllic. There are a few relatives and friends awaiting the arrival of the small boats filled with immigrants; but the crowd gathered in and about the gin-shop overlooking the narrow entrance of the landing stage are dock loungers of the lowest type and professional 'runners'. These latter individuals, usually of the Hebrew race, are amongst the most repulsive of East London parasites; boat after boat touches the landing stages; they push forward, seize hold of the bundles or baskets of the newcomers, offer bogus tickets to those who wish to travel forward to America, promise guidance and free lodging to those who hold in their hand addresses of acquaintances in Whitechapel or are friendless. A little man with an official badge (Hebrew Ladies Protective Society) fights valiantly in their midst for the conduct of unprotected females, and shouts or whispers to the others to go to the Poor Jews' Temporary Shelter in Leman Street. For a few moments it is a scene of indescribable confusion: cries and countercries; the hoarse laughter of the dock loungers at the strange garb and broken accents of the poverty-stricken foreigners; the rough swearing of the boatmen at passengers unable to pay the fee for landing. In another ten minutes, eighty of the hundred newcomers are dispersed into the back slums of Whitechapel; in another few days the majority of these, robbed of the little they possess, are turned out of the 'free lodgings', destitute and friendless.[1]

All too often, however, the lodging turned out to be a brothel. The white slavers were looking for single and unaccompanied girls. Another reason for the descent into prostitution was that a married woman was unable to obtain a divorce without a 'get' from her husband and so remarry. Without financial support prostitution became a necessity. To overcome isolation from religion, some Jewish prostitutes and pimps set up their own synagogues and burial grounds in New York and Rio.

The Radcliffe Highway was known as the poor man's Regent Street because of the prostitution. In 1887, at any time there would be between twenty and thirty Jewish prostitutes at the East India Dock gates. Prostitutes' pubs included the Globe and Artichoke, the Gunboat, Malt Shovel and, the doyen of them all, the White Swan at the Shadwell end of the Highway, known as Paddy's Goose. The proprietor had, during the Crimean War, recruited for the Navy 'in a small steamer with a band of music and flags'. Despite this apparently wholly successful display of patriotism the proprietor soon fell out with the authorities.[2]

Flower and Dean Street in the heart of Spitalfields was regarded as perhaps the roughest of streets of the East End and one notorious for prostitution. In the early 1870s the Reverend Samuel Barnett gave notice to the Guardians to have the area demolished under the so-called Cross Act: the Artisans and Labourers' Act which had been passed thirty years earlier and which was designed as an answer to the challenge presented by criminal slums. The notice followed a severe outbreak of cholera in the street. Although the improvement scheme was signed in 1877 nothing was done because the authorities fought shy of making 13,000 people homeless in a time of severe depression. It was not until 1883 that part of Flower and Dean Street was demolished and the Charlotte de Rothschild Buildings were constructed. This now created quite separate communities in the street.

In October 1885 efforts were being made to clear out brothels from Lady Lake's Grove and Oxford Street leading into Bedford Street. Messrs F.N. Charrington and E.H. Kerwin went round the houses with a black book. As parishioners, if they gave notice to the police of the keeping of a disorderly house, on conviction the overseers of the street would pay them £10 under the Act of 25 Geo II c 36 s.5. They were attacked with fish and other filth and the next day they were stoned. One feature of the attack was the 'extreme scarcity' of the police. They had watched a police officer visit the brothel of a Mrs Hart in Canal Street.

Indigenous prostitutes suffered from the Jewish immigrants:

> Also, Jews had moved into those houses where certain rooms had been used for vice. Initially they would occupy one room, and persist in staying, notwithstanding the insults and provocations by the bordello operators. Eventually the Jew would take over a second room, and, in the long run, tough Jewish puritanism proved formidable against its more permissive antagonist. The demi-monde could see no profit or pleasure in remaining, and eventually took off to more lucrative areas.[3]

At the turn of the century, Sol Cohen ran the Jewish Association for the Protection of Girls and Women. His research into the white slave trade showed that many of the girls had been prostitutes before going to South America but, indeed, in many cases there had been no coercion. The Association was involved in 125 cases in 1900, 128 in 1901, and there was a massive leap in 1902 when 206 girls who had disappeared were thought to have been abducted or exported to South America.

His experiences were rather different from those described in a Metropolitan Police report of 1906 which recorded that cases of procuring innocent girls for immoral purposes were few and far between. There were perhaps half a dozen genuine instances, but they were mostly French and Belgian girls brought to work here before being sent to South America or South Africa.[4]

An interesting case of a Jewish procurer was that of Matthew Gammersbach of Hertford Road, Dalston, who was deported in 1906 following a conviction for living off the proceeds of prostitution. He had been sentenced to three months' hard labour and ordered to pay £22. 6s. 0d. costs. He was found back in the country when he should, at the very least, have been in Belgium. His story was that he was obliged to defend an action brought by one of the girls, a Miss Montyai, who was claiming the not inconsiderable sum of £1,110 from him. He was allowed to stay for the action, which he lost, but he was shadowed throughout by police officers who found him talking to other undesirables in disreputable public houses.[5]

However, the Home Office was not wholly deaf to the worries of the vigilance groups and on 17 October 1912 a small White Slave Traffic Squad was launched. It consisted of one CID inspector, one CID constable, two uniformed constables in each of C, D and H divisions and one constable in E and L. The constables were to be given seven shillings a week to enable them to perform their duties in plain clothes.

Thirteen months later, on 7 November 1913, John Curry, the Detective Inspector in charge of the squad, reported:

At the time of the formation of the Branch the country was being aroused by a number of alarming statements made by religious, social and other workers who spread the belief that there was a highly organised gang of White Slave Traffickers with agents in every part of the civilised world, kidnapping and otherwise carrying off women and girls from their homes to lead them to their ruin in foreign lands, and were thereby reaping huge harvests of gold.

I have to state that there has been an utter absence of evidence to justify these alarming statements, the effect of which was to cause a large shoal of complaints and allegations [many contained in anonymous letters] to be received by police, against persons of all classes.

The year's work had produced a total of fifty-one arrests. Two were for procuring; and two for attempting to procure. Forty-four were living on immoral earnings and the three who were aliens and who were suspected slavers were deported. There were, however, undoubtedly gangs with international connections. One such was headed in London by Aldo Antonious Celli (alias Carvelli, Shanks, Cortini, Ferrari and Leonora) who had convictions in Australia and was said to be of Swiss origin. Girls recruited in Belgium were told they would be taken to Wellington, New Zealand. On 30 November 1910 he and a Frenchman, Alexander Nicolini, pleaded guilty to a general conspiracy to procure women within the King's Dominions and he was sentenced to six months' hard labour and deportation.[6]

Inspector Curry thought that 'the Criminal Law Amendment Act 1912 has had a salutary effect on foreign ponces'. Happily, there was 'No case of unwilling or innocent girl' being recruited into white slavery and anyway, 'Mostly [they are] Jewesses of Russian or Polish origin [who] go to Argentina and Brazil.' The size of the squad was accordingly reduced.[7]

He was probably correct when he said that most were Jewesses, but note the anti-Semitic tone. With the pogroms, poverty and the forcing of the Jewish community in Russia away from rural communities into the city, there was undoubtedly a trade in young Jewesses.[8]

One such case where the victims escaped was followed by the prosecution of Joseph Karmeler and Sam Scheffer who had prepared mock marriage certificates in Hebrew and who were trying to lure young girls on board a ship bound for South America. The girls very sensibly went to their parents, as a result of which, in an unsuccessful effort to save himself from the inevitability of prison, Karmeler, who was known to have a direct link to a brothel in Rio, was obliged to hand in a written statement:

Dear Judges
    I am innocent of these charges … This is written not with ink but with the blood and tears of my eyes.

He received fifteen months' imprisonment and Scheffer three months more. Each also received twelve strokes of the cat.[9]

In fact, possibly because there was no money around, prostitution was not that much of a problem in all parts of the East End and it was confined largely to the Pennyfields, Limehouse and Aldgate areas. Nor, of course, were all prostitutes Jewish.

The 'brides', or prostitutes, were mostly down the other end of Brick Lane where the lodging houses were in Flower and Dean Street. The Seven Stars next to Christ Church School was mostly used by the ladies of the town, and the Frying Pan on the corner of Thrawl Street and Brick Lane was famous for being the centre of the red light district.[10]

The lodging houses charged fourpence, sixpence and a shilling, and some allowed 'husbands and wives'. In 1902 a survey of some twenty-three prostitutes found that their average age was twenty-seven and that they stayed in the same lodging house for weeks rather than for long periods. Set against this were Elizabeth Stride and Catherine Eddowes, both of whom were

Ripper victims and who lived in the same lodging house for years. Common lodging houses were allowed to accommodate a maximum of 323 people and one of the principal owners was the very popular Jimmy Smith of Bancroft Road who was regarded as the governor about Brick Lane.

Smith was a man of all trades who had started life selling coal in Flower and Dean Street. He would deliver it at a price for those who could not carry it home and, with the money earned, he invested in the common lodging houses. He was also a liaison between the police and street bookmakers.

At the time of the Ripper murders it was estimated there were at least sixty-three brothels and 1,200 prostitutes operating in W division. The Home Secretary wished to close down the East End brothels, but Sir Charles Warren rather pragmatically thought they should remain in place. Driving away brothel keepers would simply demoralise the rest of London.[11]

There was an echo of Jack shortly after the turn of the century when, at about 7.30 a.m. on 26 May 1901, twenty-eight-year-old Annie Austin was heard moaning in a cubicle in a lodging house at 35 Dorset Street, Spitalfields. She had been separated from her husband for about ten days. When she was examined by a doctor it was found that she had been stabbed in both the anus and the vagina. When he asked her if she knew who had done it, she said it was by the man who had come in with her the previous night but whose name she did not know.

She died in the London Hospital on 27 May. She was unfortunate because, through a series of administrative blunders, she was not examined for some twelve hours. The police had been called but did not arrive in time to interview her and instead she had told the doctor her story. She said she had slept with the man and then, as he was getting up to leave in the early hours, she felt a sharp pain as if a knife had been run inside her. She described her attacker as short, with dark hair and moustache and a Jewish appearance.

The hostel was managed by a Henry Moore and his wife. His brother-in-law, Daniel Sullivan, sometimes acted as his deputy and it was he who took her to hospital. The lodging house rules, observed in their breach, were that only married couples should share a cubicle. The manager said that customers were insulted if they were asked whether they were married.

On 30 May, Austin's husband was arrested and charged with her murder. At the inquest the pathologist reported no signs of a struggle and that, somewhat ironically, Annie Austin was healthy but for long-standing syphilis. Moore said that he had allowed the man and woman into the premises and that it was he who, the next morning, had sent for Dr Dale and had called a cab for her to go to the hospital. His wife, Maria Moore, said she had been up and about all that night but had heard no screams. One of the unanswered questions was when had the man slipped away, or if indeed he was part of the hostel staff.

Both Sullivan and Moore came under suspicion because for some reason they gave the wrong cubicle number to the police. At first they said Austin had been in cubicle 44 rather than the correct number 15. Was the street door unlocked before her screams were heard? If so, it would indicate that the man had left. If it was still bolted, it would almost certainly be that the killer had remained on the premises.

Maria Moore seems to have made some effort to divert attention. She made a positive identification of Austin's estranged husband, but he was able to give a cast-iron alibi. There was also some suggestion that Daniel Sullivan had been the man with Annie Austin that night, but he provided an alibi that he had shared a bed with a man named Timothy Batty at 10 Paternoster Row. The coroner, once again Wynne E. Baxter, took the view that the alibi was not conclusive but in the absence of any contradictory evidence the jury should give weight to it. Discharging Austin, he said he regarded the whole of Mrs Moore's evidence as perjured. If the Director wished to bring a prosecution on new evidence that would be up to him. The Director did not.

As the final police report reads, they felt the man was known to the lodging house habituées and was being protected by them. Clearly they had a hard time during their investigations.

> From the first to the last we have to deal with a class of witnesses that are as low as they can well possibly be and it is difficult to know when they are speaking the truth. In some instances they lie without any apparent motive.
>
> Although we never despair I fear that nothing further can be done to elucidate this mystery and the perpetrator of this crime unfortunately goes unpunished as a result of the scandalous conduct of nearly the whole of the witnesses in this case. Thomas Divall (Inspector).

Apart from anything else the police were not happy that they had had to pay out the then not inconsiderable sum of £5 to sober people to round up the witnesses and make them keep their appointments.

Certainly, whilst prostitution down in the East End at the turn of the century was rife it could not necessarily be called a lucrative trade:

> There were two kinds of girl. Those who went up West and mixed with the toffs. They would get as much as ten shillings a time or even £1 and they would ride home in hansom cabs ... The girls who stayed at Spitalfields were very poor. That was what you called a 'fourpenny touch' or a 'knee trembler' – they wouldn't

stay with you all night ... Even if you stayed all night with the girls like that it was only a couple of shillings.[12]

Dock prostitutes were known as trippers-up. Three or four would band together when ships docked and it became a battle of wits to separate a sailor from his money. The sailors' defences included pads in which they kept their money which they wore in their shoes, pouches sewn in waistbands and leather bags under shields attached to belts.[13]

NOTES

1. Charles Booth (ed.), *Life and Labour of the People in London*, vol. 1, pp. 582–3.
2. Kellow Chesney, *The Victorian Underworld*.
3. W. J. Fishman, *East End Jewish Radicals*, p. 58.
4. Nat.Arch. MEPO 2 558.
5. Nat.Arch. MEPO 2 1006.
6. Nat. Arch. MEPO 3 197.
7. Nat, Arch. MEPO 3 184.
8. See Edward J. Bristow, *Prostitution and Prejudice: The Jewish Fight Against White Slavery 1870–1939*.
9. *ELA* 11 August 1915.
10. Raphael Samuel, *East End Underworld*, p. 109.
11. Stepney MoH Report 1902 ; D.G. Browne, *The Rise of Scotland Yard*.
12. Raphael Samuel, *East End Underworld*, p. 109.
13. For an account of some of the schemes and counter-schemes see James Berrett, *When I Was at Scotland Yard*, Chapter 3.

5

THE TITANICS

With the improvements in transport, visiting criminals increased from the 1880s onwards. The Americans, such as Annie Grant who masqueraded as the President's daughter, preferred to stay in the West End except for visits to receivers such as Ruby Michaels. One of the smarter foreign gangs which did work the East End was the Italian Sacred Cross gang who worked a series of frauds, paying fleeting visits to the East End in the late 1880s. By the time their victims realised they had been cheated – usually by their money being switched for newspaper – Lorenzo and Rosina Moreno and Domenic and Mary Moretti were safely back in Turin. Their end came in May 1891 when all four appeared at the Old Bailey charged with stealing £300 from a Catholic priest. The women were acquitted but the men received five years' penal servitude apiece.[1]

As with other cities, each area of London had its own local gangs, each of which occupied a certain amount of territory even if only a street. Sometimes they expanded into the territory of others in the locality, and in the case of the bigger organisations such as the Sabinis and the Krays into completely different areas such as Soho. The East End was no exception and, given that until well after the Second World War the area was almost a series of villages, there was a proliferation of gangs who at the beginning were named simply after streets rather than areas.

One of the earliest of this period was the Green Gate Gang, from the road of the same name, which seems to have been principally a fighting gang but whose members were quite capable of straying out of their area to take on rivals.

In the spring of 1882, Thomas Galliers and James Casey stood trial at the Old Bailey for the murder of Frederick Willmore who was beaten up on the Sunday before Christmas 1881 and died from his injuries on 14 January the next year. There were about twenty in the Green Gate Gang who attacked Willmore and another man from the Dover Road or Lambeth Boys. Encountering the pair on the Embankment, they had asked where they came from. On being told, they said 'we pay (meaning hit) the Lambeth chaps' and 'trashed them with square brass buckled belts'.

Thomas Galliers was said to have had a public house door-strap with a large brass buckle on which was engraved a gate, which he wore as a belt. He received ten years for manslaughter but the jury disagreed over Casey, who had made a self-serving statement whilst awaiting trial. Many of the remainder of the gang had been involved in a riot in Bethnal Green the previous month and received between twelve and eighteen months' hard labour.[2]

Twenty years later the problem was just as acute.

The shortening of the hours of labour, together with the absence of any guidance in the use of the leisure hours is the cause of many of the social problems of the day. The young people have the whole of the evening to themselves. From seven till bed-time they can do what they please. We practically make them a free gift of one-third of the working year. But we offer nothing in the place of work except the street. Their own idea of employing their idle time is to do nothing to amuse themselves, and as the street is the only place where they can find amusement for nothing, they go into the street.[3]

Outside fighting gangs there were layers of criminal activity on a semi-organised basis. The lowest status was called the kinchin lay, or stealing from children who were delivering washing for their mothers. There was also the organisation of children to beg. In 1902 Jane Kelly, also known as Steele, was sentenced to five years' imprisonment for kidnapping an eight-year-old boy, Willie Crawford, and forcing him to beg. She had lured him away from outside his home in the Bethnal Green Road with the promise of cakes and sweets and had then toured the neighbourhood getting him to offer vestas (matches) to passers-by. The child had finally tired of the game and had tried to run away in the Costers' Market in Whitecross Street, but she had held onto him. A crowd gathered and a policeman came; she told him the child was hers. She had earlier served eighteen months and seven years for previous similar offences, and fifteen months from an unexpired sentence was added to the five she received at the Old Bailey.[4]

One of the senior indigenous gangs to flourish was the Blind Beggar Gang – a team of skilled pickpockets who were not averse to roughing up their victims if they complained. They took their name from the Blind Beggar public house in the Mile End Road. One story about them – concerning an attack on a travelling salesman in which an umbrella ferrule was pushed through the victim's eye by a man named Wallis – relates that, acquitted of murder, he was driven back from the Old Bailey in triumph in a phaeton drawn by a pair of bays. This whole story, like so many tales of these early gangs, is probably apocryphal and is based on the true story of James Vaughan (who went under the name of Ellis) who was charged with manslaughter following the death of a cabinet-maker, Frederick Klein, in September 1891 on a train at Farringdon Street. He and his wife had been subject to a series of anti-German taunts. Vaughan had stabbed Klein in the eye with an umbrella. He was convicted and sentenced to twelve months with hard labour.[5]

Generally the gangs of late Victorian East London seem to have been more concerned with territory and having a good fight with their rivals rather than profit. From the 1880s onwards there were a number of gangs who called themselves the Forty Thieves, one of which operated out of the Commercial Road in Whitechapel. They were led by nineteen-year-old John Carey who had convictions for robbery before. In 1896 he and John Road, one year older, were convicted of another robbery when they were seen in that road by a police officer kneeling over their victim and going through his pockets. Carey seems to have belonged to two gangs because, in March 1897, he was described as being one of the most dangerous men in East London and sentenced to five years following a major fight when some fifty-odd Bethnal Green Boys clashed with the Broadway Boys from Hackney. A number of shots were fired from weapons said to be on sale at £1 a time in the local markets. What is amazing is that, apart from that of Carey, lenient sentences of six months were handed out.

There were, however, exceptions and the first home-grown gang which organised itself for profit rather than territorial fighting seems to have been the fifty-strong Titanic Mob. They came from the very rough area of Nile Street, a market street off Shepherdess Walk near the City Road police station, and had their headquarters in the Duke of Portagus public house there. Their specialities were robbery and pickpocketing at race meetings, railway stations, at the music hall, football matches and, continuing the old tradition known as kirk-buzzing, in church. They do not seem to have been averse to burglary either.

They were highly regarded in the trade, partly because they only robbed men. Arthur Harding recalls that in 1908 his gang fought the Titanics following an argument over the protection of a coffee stall in Brick Lane. The Titanics seem to have been much the smarter of the sides:

> What they done was crafty. They set a trap for us. They was well in with the police and directly the fight started the police were there. They got hold of us – including Cooper who had a loaded gun on him. It wasn't an offence to carry a gun, but we got a week's remand for causing an affray. I always had it in for them afterwards. I thought, 'You twisters – you always have the bogies on your side.'

Some suggestions are that the Mob was named in tribute to the liner but this cannot have been so because there are references to members or associates operating at the 1908 London Olympics when Edward Spencer, also known as Edward Emms, received four years, well before the liner was launched. They were also known as the Swell Mob and sometimes as the Finsbury Boys.

An early leader was George Measures, whose career lasted nearly twenty years. Other early members included Billy Chandler, whose family later founded the bookmaking empire; Arthur Tresidern or Harding, who later defected to the Vendetta Mob based around the Blind Beggar public house in the Whitechapel Road; and the former bare-knuckle fighter Harry Bargery, who had a string of aliases and convictions going back to 1899.[6] At least an associate was the almost legendary thief Eddie Guerin. Another man who was suggested as an early leader was

Alf White from King's Cross, whose career spanned nearly half a century and who went on to much greater things.

The Titanics were also a fighting gang who fought the so-called first Battle of Nile Street in January 1908, possibly against the Sabini brothers. Certainly they battled two years later in Shaftesbury Avenue with the Elephant Boys from the Elephant and Castle in South London over territorial rights to Soho.[7]

The second Battle of Nile Street took place after the First World War and saw the Titanics pitted against the Sabinis. They were again involved in a major street fight with the Elephant Boys in 1919 and 'sank as soundly as their namesake', wrote Brian McDonald, whose uncles had led the Elephant Boys.

They survived until the early 1920s when they were broken up by the Flying Squad after raids on them following a pickpocketing expedition at an Arsenal football match.[8] Five members of the gang were caught at Euston Square station picking pockets in something which sounds more like robbery. One member of the gang had been holding the iron supports on either side of the door of the trains, so preventing passengers from getting on or off, whilst the others picked pockets.

Their ages showed that pickpocketing was not necessarily a young man's game. They appeared at Marlborough Street on 10 September 1921 when Alfred Mclennan (fifty-three), James Parrott (forty-six) and Richard Canter (forty-four) were committed to the Sessions for sentence. Dominic Mack (fifty-six) and George M. Measures (thirty-nine) each received twelve months' hard labour. This and further arrests signalled the end of the Titanics.

Certainly the gang had already splintered and Alf White had joined up with the Sabinis to fight off the predations of the Brummagen Boys over protection of the Jewish bookmakers on southern racing and trotting courses.

A further raid took place a few days later when other members were found to be working on the Underground at Baker Street station. Although only short sentences were handed out to members, from then on it would seem the team splintered finally and broke up with Fred Gilbert now heading the Finsbury Boys who in turn allied themselves with the Elephant Boys.[9]

It was not, however, quite the end of the Titanics. In August 1922 there was another fight between the Sabinis and the Titanics and the next month four Titanic men were charged over a jewel theft when gems valued at £3,000 disappeared in the relatively new sport of smash and grab, from James Walker's jewellery business in the Edgware Road. Peter Thornley, described as a chauffeur, told the police the leader was a 'straightforward man, and he does not work, all he does is raid and plunder'.[10]

The old Clerkenwell villain and so-called Godfather Bert Rossi recalled, 'The police said they'd been broken up in the early 1920s and maybe that's how Alf White came to join up with Darby [Sabini] but I know there were bits of the Titanics still around in Hoxton during the Second World War'.[11]

Many of the early gangs seem to have been relatively informal associations, something which continued throughout the century. One, led by the engagingly named One-Eyed Charlie, hung out around Clark's coffee shop near a railway arch in Brick Lane. According to Arthur Harding, a major villain of the time and later chronicler of the East End, they do not seem to have acted much in concert. The leader, Charlie Walker, had tuberculosis and, true to his name, had also lost an eye. Another of the gang, Edward Spencer, seems to have been the only 'complete all-round criminal'. A well-built man who took a great pride in his appearance and was known as 'the Count', he was a thief and robber. Most of the others were pickpockets and 'tappers', van draggers, watch chain or handbag snatchers, or petty blackmailers. The Walker team flourished, if that is the right word, until about 1904 when Charlie Walker died in a prison hospital, and re-formed some years later with some younger men, of whom Arthur Harding was one and he became the leader. Although he did not regard his loose 'connection of youngsters' as a gang, it was a much more cohesive organisation than in Walker's time:

> We were a collection of small-time thieves ripe for any mischief ... We were ready to steal anything. Sometimes we went in couples, sometimes alone – it was only when there was a big fight on that we went as a gang.[12]

Whether the local residents actually agreed with Harding's definition is a different matter entirely. Harding caused a great deal of nuisance at the evidential hearings of the Royal Commission into the Metropolitan Police by alleging that Inspector Wensley, after failing to have him convicted on a series of robberies, had framed him for an assault on an officer, something Wensley strenuously denied. Various local shopkeepers were brought along to give evidence of the activities of Harding and his definition of going in couples. One of the witnesses, William Southey, a hosier with two shops in the neighbourhood, thought the Harding team was some thirty strong.

> There is a gang of lads and young men that hang about the corners of Brick Lane and my corner is unfortunately a very convenient corner for these young men because they can see four ways. They are a regiment of soldiers; they do not talk to each other. They use dumb motions. If they were going to rob a man and they saw it was convenient to take his watch they

would use their fingers, their head and the movements of their body. Harding is the captain of the gang and has been for many, many years ... Whilst he was doing 20 months it was paradise.

A publican, Frank Rayner, manager of the Old Crown off Brick Lane, said that another of their activities was tapping local shopkeepers to pay their fines: 'As soon as the thieves "fall" as they call it they terrorise the neighbourhood with a paper for something to help him pay the fine.'[13]

Sixpence was apparently the going rate.

It was their activities as a gang that earned them the name the Vendetta Mob, but it was largely a question of what was in a name. One of Harding's ventures, along with his friends Dido Gilbert, Tommy Taylor and Danny Isaacs, whether as the Vendetta or an independent gang, was the holding-up of card games in the Jewish spielers and taking the proceeds, often as little as £3 or £4 a time. Harding justifies the activity by claiming the victims were all crooked men who regarded the raids as little more than a minor inconvenience: 'Yiddisher people make a laugh of it. They said, "Give them a few bob and get rid of them."'[14]

Eventually, however, the card players became bored with these raids in which they were made to stand with their hands in the air and they recruited some of their own to deal with Harding and the others. A meeting at Mother Woolf's public house in Whitechapel saw the Vendettas badly beaten. Finally Ruby Michaels, fearing there would actually be fatalities if the raids escalated, explained the facts of life to Harding through his henchman Tommy Hoy.[15]

Ruby Michaels was the most noted receiver of stolen property. He was the biggest buyer of stolen jewellery in East London. His headquarters was the Three Tuns in Aldgate. He had several front men – Leon Behren [sic], the man who got killed in 1911, was one of them. They picked the stuff up from the daylight screws-men at the spielers and took it to Ruby at the pub. Anyone who had any diamond rings to sell, they took it to him, and the buyers came from all over the world. In Portland I met a crook who had come all the way from America to buy something off Ruby.[16]

Michaels had a long and successful career. He was friendly with 'Chicago' May Churchill Sharpe, and it was she who tipped him off that Tim Oakes, who was regarded as King of the Panel Workers and who owned an antique shop in the City Road, was unfortunately also a police informer.[17]

In 1907, shortly before Sharpe was arrested for shooting at Eddie Guerin, her former lover, Michaels put up a jewel robbery for her in the Strand. A young Italian thief, Louis Lorenzano, who worked with Sharpe and her then partner Charlie Smith, was to be the coachman and drive her in an open barouche (on which had been placed a temporary coat of arms) to the jeweller's not far from Charing Cross. Usually the jeweller was left on his own during the lunch period. Lorenzano, fine in livery and with a birthmark painted on his cheek, was then to go into the shop and ask the jeweller to come to the carriage as his mistress was an invalid. Smith was then to snatch a tray of diamonds which were on display. Unfortunately the jeweller noticed Smith working on the hasp and staple which secured the jewels and ran after him. To maintain her cover, Sharpe found herself obliged to buy a solid gold collar button. As she remarks, Michaels was 'out his expenses'.[18]

However, Michaels generally kept a low profile, surfacing in court only in 1915 when he and Aaron Lechenstein – who, in his salad days, had been a police court interpreter – pleaded guilty at the Old Bailey to trying to bribe a police officer to allow them to conduct illegal gaming in East End clubs. The payment was to be £10 a week for each of three clubs totalling £1,500 a year, and an amber cigarette holder was delivered to the officer as a mark of esteem. The proposal had followed a raid in the previous June when a club owner had been fined £500, and Michaels thought that prevention was the best cure.

Under the direction of his superiors the officer played along with them, and the pair were arrested at a meeting to which they had brought a document for him to sign. There was clearly money about because Michaels had Sir Edward Marshall Hall KC to defend him. The receiver was, he said, now paralysed and prison would be a death sentence. Chief Inspector Wensley put his oar in, saying he had known Michaels as a gambler and receiver for some twenty-four years, but Marshall Hall won through. Michaels was fined £100 and Lechenstein, said to be in a poor financial way, a mere £10.[19]

Another crime of the period which was prevalent in the East End and was viewed by judges with extreme disfavour was organised horse-stealing. On 12 April 1913 three members of a gang specialising in stealing the animals for sale as food received lengthy periods of imprisonment, with the leader Schofield drawing six years. He had been selling meat for consumption for fifteen years, but it was not clear whether this was horse or ox. The others received twelve and nine months.[20]

Guns were easily obtainable and their possession was not unduly punished. Arthur Harding bought his first in about 1904. A Royal Ulster Constabulary revolver cost 2/6d. in Brick Lane, others four or five shillings.[21]

Nor were shooting incidents regarded by the courts with the gravity of today. Three years earlier Charles Callaghan had been convicted of the wounding of John Bailey who had been shot in the thigh at his home. Callaghan's counsel pleaded that his client should be bound over to come up for judgement and when Warburton (prosecuting) suggested it was nearly an attempted murder, crossly remarked, 'You've had your pound of flesh.' A police officer giving evidence thought Callaghan was a 'Good employee during the day but at night he associates with thieves and rogues'. Judge Rentoul KC did actually consider a bind over. He adjourned the case until he had spoken with other judges, after which he sentenced Callaghan to the modest six months' hard labour.

What appears to have happened is that the members of the Bailey family had attacked him in the White Hart in Shoreditch, hitting him on the head with a hammer. Nothing daunted, he had collected some friends and visited the Baileys' home. Later Callaghan would be sentenced along with Harding for his part in the Old Street affray.[22]

John Bailey was one of a family who came out of the Nichol, an area in Hoxton. Although one was a burglar, Harding did not regard them as thieves but more as fighting men – the father Alf being a particularly vicious man.

Perhaps, as today, it depended on the quality of the defence for in 1908 George Askew, a member of the Globe Bridge Gang, shot George Etherington of the Bow Road Gang and received a relatively lengthy fifteen months' hard labour for his pains.[23]

Even immediately after the First World War the possession of firearms was not regarded as anything much out of the ordinary. On 15 February 1919 Edward Joyce, described as a commission agent, struck Joe Palmer, the referee at The Ring, with the butt of a pistol after Palmer had disqualified Con Houghton in the ninth round for persistent holding in his contest with Dick Moss. Later 'Gossip of the Game' thought that 'if one or two other gentlemen had been attacked there was a sort of rough justice but not Palmer.'[24]

However, Arthur Harding was very much more than a villain pure and simple. He was a great baiter of the police and as such fell seriously foul of Wensley. Before that happened he had played a considerable part in the Royal Commission into the Metropolitan Police in 1908, and had assisted in the prosecution of a number of officers for assault.

The catalyst that sparked the Commission was one of those cases which need never have happened. However, once it was in the public domain a great deal of capital was made of it to the general discomfort of all concerned.

On 1 May 1905, Eva D'Angeley was arrested in Regent Street for 'riotous and indecent behaviour' or, in plain language, prostitution. The charge was dismissed after a Mr D'Angeley told the magistrate that he was married to the lady and that she was merely waiting for him, something she had done on a regular basis. Better still, the Sub-Divisional Inspector MacKay told the court he believed the D'Angeleys to be a respectable couple.

The experienced Marlborough Street magistrate, Denman, dismissed the charges and so another desert storm blew up with allegations of harassment, bribery and corruption. A Royal Commission was set up to inquire into methods and discipline in the force.[25]

The case was not the only one before the Commission, however. Another was that of a PC Rolls who, it was alleged, had planted a hammer on a cabinet-maker sleeping on a bench at London Fields and had then arrested him. The case was dismissed at the North London Police Court by the eccentric magistrate Edward Snow Fordham, who was continually at loggerheads with the police and who was not invited to give evidence to the Royal Commission. Rolls was later prosecuted at the Central Criminal

Court and received five years' penal servitude. Another officer was allowed to resign.

This led to the formation of the Public Vigilance Society, and such success as the public had in establishing any misconduct by the police was largely due to it and to Earl Russell, who appeared for the Society and who later wrote modestly:

> I was instructed by a curious body called the Police and Public Vigilance Society run by a fanatic called Timewell. He was prepared always to believe anything he was told against the police and to resent with some indignation the demand for proof which a lawyer always makes. However, we selected about twelve of the likeliest cases, and in spite of the extreme poverty on our side and the whole force of the Treasury and the police against us on the other we succeeded in getting home seven of them, largely on my cross-examination of the police.[26]

One of the cases which they 'succeeded in getting home' was that of PC Ashford, who is described by Arthur Harding as having a nice wife 'but always after the women. He wasn't intelligent enough to catch a thief, but he was good at perjury and he could do a man an injury by strength.'[27]

In August 1906, Ashford came across a young man named Gamble out walking with a prostitute, Ethel Griffiths. It appears he wanted the girl for himself and told Gamble to clear off. In turn Mrs Griffiths told Ashford she did not want him and the officer then knocked Gamble down and kicked him. A police sergeant, Sheedy, came up and told Gamble to get up and fight like a man. Then when he saw how badly the man was injured, he told Ashford to go away as he had done enough. Gamble was in hospital for four months and was operated on four times; he later spent nearly a month in a convalescent home. One member of the Commission compared his injuries with those which would have been sustained by falling on a railing.

This was one of the cases in which the Public Vigilance Society was aided and abetted by Harding, who discovered two witnesses and arranged for the Commission's investigator to take statements from them. Later another witness was produced. The Commission found that PC Ashford was guilty of the misconduct alleged, that is kicking Gamble, but that he did not intend to do him the serious injury which resulted. In Sergeant Sheedy's case, it was found that he had not stopped the assault and that he had failed to make a report to his superiors. So far as the investigation of the incident by an Inspector Hewison was concerned, this had aborted when he found no trace of Gamble's name at the London Hospital – he had been wrongly listed under the name Pearce. The Commission found that Hewison had done 'all that could be reasonably expected'.

The aftermath was the prosecution of Ashford. Proceedings were commenced immediately after the Royal Commission published its findings and, at the Old Bailey in September 1908, the jury was instructed to disregard the evidence of Ethel Griffiths because she was a prostitute. The defence also claimed that there had been no proper identification of Ashford as the kicking officer. After a retirement of two hours by the jury, he was found guilty and sentenced to nine months' hard labour. Leave to appeal was refused.

Within days of the appointment of the Commission its members had been inundated with letters and postcards alleging corruption, perjury and bribery, often in language 'foul and intemperate'. From these, nineteen cases, including that of Mme D'Angeley, were closely scrutinised and a variety of witnesses came before the Commissioners, who sat on sixty-four occasions over a period of eleven months.

Unsurprisingly, the Commission became increasingly bored with the East End evidence, exonerated the police and declared that, far from harassing street offenders, they were kind and conciliatory to them. True, in some nine cases there had been reprehensible conduct but, by and large, the Commission found, 'The Metropolitan Police is entitled to the confidence of all classes of the community.'

The Times for one was enchanted.

> We have no hesitation in saying that the Metropolitan police as a whole discharge their duties with honesty, discretion and efficiency.

The Hoxton Mob was the generic name given to a succession of gangs from around Hoxton Street over the next forty years. One of the early versions had its headquarters at the Spread Eagle public house and, amongst other interests, they were into the protection of the local clubs and spielers such as Sunshine's, a card and billiard club in an alley off Shoreditch High Street. Harding is dismissive of them:

> They weren't such good-class thieves as the Titanics. They were more hooligans than thieves. They worked ten- or twelve-handed. They all finished up on the poor law, or cadging. Their leader died a pauper, whereas the leader of the Titanics ended up owning a dog-track.[28]

Another local gang leader of the time was Isaac Bogard, known as Darky the Coon. Although he was Jewish he was so dark-skinned that some references to him are as a black man and his mob was accordingly known as the Coons. Although when giving evidence he described himself as an actor, Bogard had a long criminal record which included a flogging for living off immoral earnings. On 10 September 1911 at about 8.30 in the evening, he was set upon by Harding and the Vendetta Mob in the Blue Coat Boy in Bishopsgate. Bogard and his team ran a string of prostitutes in Whitechapel High Street and the quarrel had been about their ownership and the protection of a stall in Walthamstow Street market. Harding describes the fight:

> As it was we did a lot of damage. The Coon had a face like the map of England. He was knocked about terrible. I hit him with a broken glass, made a terrible mess of his face. I knew I'd hurt him a lot, but not anything that could be serious.[29]

Bogard, who in evidence at the subsequent trial said his throat had been cut, was taken to the London Hospital where after he had been stitched he discharged himself. But the next weekend there was more of the same for him when he was attacked once again by Harding and friends on the Sunday evening.

The outcome was dramatic. The police arrived and arrested both Bogard and George King on charges of disorderly conduct, to appear at Old Street Magistrates' Court on the Monday. Meanwhile Harding – then known as Tresidern – and his Vendettas met at Clark's, the coffee shop in Brick Lane, to rally support against the Coons who were about to commit the one really unforgivable crime: they asked for police protection.

Accounts vary as to exactly what happened, as they do to the precise lead-up to the earlier battle and the arrest of Bogard, but there is no doubt whatsoever that Bogard and King were besieged at Old Street by Harding and the Vendetta Mob until Wensley arrived from Scotland Yard in a horse-drawn vehicle to restore order.[30]

Money was again found from somewhere, because Harding and the others were defended privately, Harding by the well-known barrister Eustace Fulton.[31] It did him little good, for in December 1911 the team appeared at the Old Bailey in front of Mr Justice Avory who, when passing sentence, gave this little homily:

> This riot was one of the most serious riots which can be dealt with by law, for it was a riot in which some, at least, of the accused were armed with revolvers, and it took place within the precincts of a court of justice.
>
> I wish to say that the condition of things disclosed by the evidence – that a portion of London should be infested by a number of criminal ruffians, armed with loaded revolvers – ought not to be tolerated further, and if the existing law is not strong enough to put a stop to it some remedial legislation is necessary.

Harding received twenty-one months' hard labour to be followed by three years' penal servitude. His career was sketched by Wensley when giving the antecedents of the convicted men before sentence:

> When he was fourteen – he is now only twenty-five – he was bound over for disorderly conduct and being in possession of a revolver.
>
> At the age of seventeen he became a terror to Bethnal Green, and captained a band of desperadoes. In all he has been convicted fourteen times, yet he was one of the complaining witnesses before the Police Commission.
>
> He has developed into a cunning and plausible criminal of a dangerous type. I have never known him do any work.[32]

Wensley records that after Harding's imprisonment peace returned to the East End – for a little while anyway. Bogard certainly functioned until the 1920s when he was then what was euphemistically described as the 'governor' of the market stall-holders in Petticoat Lane and Wentworth Street. During the War he had served with gallantry and was awarded the Military Medal.

Associations were formed and broken. For example, the 'top man of the Jews', Edward Emmanuel, at one time had a working arrangement with Harding, then broke with him and joined up with the Sabinis, in turn broke with them and in the 1920s, working almost as an independent, was regarded as a great fixer with the police.[33]

Nor was it impossible for uneasy truces to be established with the police. Another of Harding's *bêtes-noires* was an officer he called 'Jew Boy' Stevens, yet at one time he and Emmanuel were going out with two sisters and Stevens with the third.[34]

The Old Street siege was undoubtedly the pinnacle of Harding's career, but he served another five-year sentence in 1915. From then on he seems to have had the sense to be an employer and manipulator rather than a front man. Two of the men he employed were destined to become East End legends and links with the present and they, along with Charles Horrickey, made as fine a trio as could be wished. The pair were Jack 'Dodger' Mullins and Timmy Hayes, known in the early part of his career at least as Dick Turpin.

The best known of the three, Jack 'Dodger' Mullins, was born probably about 1892 – there is no record of his birth at St Catherine's House – into a respectable family. The belief in the Underworld is that, as with many of the families, he had a half-Irish, partly Jewish or even gypsy background, but according to his family they had been in England since at least the beginning of the nineteenth century and there was no Jewish blood.

He was a small man, about 5' 6" tall, slightly built, with dark curly hair and a scarred face. Albert Appelby, his nephew, recalls him as a quiet man with a dry sense of humour who 'never brought any of his activities near the family' to whom he was close; as close that is as his prison record would allow. Every Christmas he would send Fred, his driver, to collect his sister Louise for a Christmas get-together:

One year Fred did not arrive.
    'You're a new face,' said Louise. 'Where's Fred?'
    'In hospital.'
    'Nothing serious, I hope.'
    'No, someone threw some flowers at him.'
    'Well, he shouldn't have to go to hospital for that.'
    'Trouble was, they were still in the pot at the time.'

Mullins may have been fearless on the streets, and in the First World War when he received the Military Medal, but like so many others he was terrified of his common-law wife, Minnie Dore, a big woman and East End matriarch of the old school. Louise kept a spare room vacant for him when Minnie was on the warpath:

'Hiding from the police again?' the neighbours would ask.
    'No, from Minnie,' his sister would reply.

Mullins' great friend was Timmy Hayes, who was even smaller than he was but just as violent. Ex-Detective Chief Superintendent Ted Greeno describes them in his memoirs:

When there was no racing Dodger and Tim once tried to earn a little protection money in London's East End. There the tradesmen paid tribute to the local hoodlums to 'protect' them and Dodger told the owner of a billiards hall, 'You don't want to pay that Yiddisher mob of yours. I could eat the lot of them. Now what are you coming across with?'

'Nothing,' said the billiards man.

Dodger gave him a day or two to think it over, then he tore down the racks and smashed the tables and chairs, snapped the cues and threw billiard balls at the lights. It didn't take long and I didn't need telling who had done it.[35]

On 2 July 1926, Mullins received four years and Hayes nine years at the Old Bailey after being found guilty of blackmail and assault. The police described the pair as 'pioneers of gang warfare in East London and on the racecourses'. Mullins said he could prove the case had been got up by the Sabinis and 'some of the Yiddisher people' in order to get him and Hayes out of the way.

What really did for Hayes was that since 1908 he had served twenty terms of imprisonment and one of penal servitude. He had also been charged with being a habitual criminal. By 1910 he had three convictions for wounding. At the Old Bailey, in his defence to that second charge, he claimed that after he came out of prison on 2 May he had been a volunteer railway worker for eight days during the General Strike before committing the offence on 17 May. This, it was argued, showed that he had exhibited 'a desire for work inconsistent with the habit of crime'.

Once again money was found to pay for Hayes' appeal. He was represented this time by J.D. Cassels KC, who cannot have appeared cheaply. His solicitor on that occasion was George Edjali, the Parsee who had been wrongly convicted of horse mutilation and whose case had been championed by Sir Arthur Conan Doyle.

The formidable Mr Justice Avory, who had been prosecuting

counsel in the case of Adolph Beck and who was now regarded as a hanging judge, would have none of this sort of specious argument about work:

[But] this Court has said over and over again that the mere fact that a man has done some honest work after he has served the sentence for the offence last before that with which he is now charged, is not by itself a reason why the jury should not find him to be a habitual criminal.[36]

Arthur Harding claimed the success of Mullins' light sentence for himself, saying he had used him and Hayes in conjunction with some of the Watney Streeters as strike-breakers in the General Strike of 1926 and continued to work with him over the next few years. He is a bit ambiguous about Mullins' level of violence:

Dodger lived by tapping people for money. They gave it him because they were frightened. I once watched him kick a little white dog to death. 'It bit me,' he said.

And on another occasion he wrote, 'He was a thief but not a violent type.' And yet again he described him as 'one of the biggest terrors in London at the time'.

Mullins probably worked as an enforcer on the increasingly popular dog tracks and was certainly having a violent time in 1930 because, along with George and Charles Steadman and Henry Barton, he was arrested for demanding with menaces and assault at the Argus Club in Greek Street. The quartet had first asked for drinks which were served and then demanded to know whether there were any 'Raddies' on the premises. Unfortunately for a man named Costognetti there was one; he received a beating and a woman who tried to protect him had her blouse torn. Eventually the charges were dropped.

Harding seems to have finally fallen out with Mullins around that time, when Mullins came round for a loan. Harding was now married with four children and his wife shouted from the bedroom window for them to go away:

> They foully abused her, using the most filthy language that I had ever heard even from the prostitutes of Dorset Street.

Now, Harding did what he had found most reprehensible in the conduct of Bogard some twenty years earlier: he involved the police. Not that he was averse to a little dealing on the side.

> Mullins got six years for demanding with menaces. The other chap got less. His people straightened me up – they gave my wife £50 or £60 so I was lenient in my evidence. It was the best thing I ever done when I put Dodger Mullins where he belonged. I should have been at everybody's beck and call when there was a fight on if I hadn't done so.

The quarrel with Mullins effectively ended Harding's association with crime; he was now no longer regarded as one of the fraternity. Perhaps he feared for himself and his family when Mullins was released because 'it became like a craze with us to get away'. In 1932 Harding moved from Brick Lane to a flat in Leyton and then bought a house in Canterbury Road for which he paid £675. His last court appearance seems to have been when he was acquitted of being a suspected person in 1932.[37]

Meanwhile Mullins was in Dartmoor prison at the time of the celebrated mutiny on 26 January 1932 when fighting broke out in the chapel and, with the mutineers in control, the officers' mess was attacked and the prison set alight. The army was called in and a number of prisoners were shot and injured. Mullins went into his cell and shut his door. The prisoners opened it and he shut it again.

His release brought no fortune to his friend Wally Challis who collected him from Dartmoor. On the way back he knocked someone down in the motor car he was driving and received five years himself.

In later life Dodger maintained his low profile. Albert Appelby recalls:

When my mother died my son and I went looking for Dodger with whom we'd lost touch. We'd heard he'd been over Dalston way and we went and asked people in the area. No, no one knew him, never heard of him at all. Then we asked a newspaper man and this time I said it was to tell him his sister had died. The man said he thought we should ask in the butcher's shop on the corner. They didn't want to know at first. They'd never heard of him either but I said again it was about Dodger's sister. The man called up the stairs, 'Jackie, get your Dad, your Auntie's died.'

Mullins attended his sister's funeral, but that was the last time the Appelbys spoke to him. His final conviction seems to have been in August 1956, when his age was given as sixty-four and he was sentenced to twelve months' imprisonment for theft at Inner London Sessions. He had by this time racked up fifty-one convictions. Equipped with a stick, he would barge into his intended victim entering a tube train while his co-defendant, a man named Simmonds, would be standing behind ready to pick the pockets at the moment of impact. Then, as the train doors closed, they would jump clear and move off down the platform. His barrister, Neil McElligott, later the fearsome stipendiary

magistrate at Old Street, said that Simmonds was the 'dip' and
Mullins was simply playing the lad to the artful dodger. He
received twelve months' imprisonment.[38]

Frank Fraser recalls him in 1948 in his later years:

> The last time I saw Dodger Mullins was in 1948 when he was
> on a J.R.[39] in Wandsworth. He was standing at the end of A
> wing. Little did I know that forty years later I'd be on the same
> spot as Dodger and I could see people looking at me knowing
> I'd been there forty years previous. Between us we went back
> eighty prison years.
>
> I liked him. What he really was was a thieves' ponce. I knew
> him in 1943 when I was just out of Chelmsford. We were in
> the Queen's Club in Queen's Road, Peckham. It was a licensed
> afternoon drinker for when the pubs shut at 3.30. Bertie Wymah
> had a row with Lennie Garrett and smashed a glass in his face,
> then Lennie chinned him and a couple of Canadian soldiers
> got involved and we all steamed into them. I remember Dodger
> saying, 'Get out of here quick, son.'[40]

Mullins did not always take his own advice and suffered for
it. The previous year he had been badly knocked about by two
men, Johnny Dove and Mickey Harris, in an Old Compton
Street club after he had remonstrated with them in the lavatory
for cat-calling during a performance by Billy Hill's sister, Maggie.
He was saved from further punishment by Billy Hill himself who
'cut them to pieces'.[41]

In old age Mullins still maintained a presence. In the last
years of his life he was a close friend of the Krays and once, when
Johnny Nash and Joey Pyle walked into the Kentucky Club in
Stoke Newington, he took Reggie Kray aside and said that if
there was trouble he was on their side, producing a Beretta to

prove it. Kray explained that while he was most grateful there was no need – they were all on the same side.[42]

He died following a car accident after a tour of drinking spots in the East End. Taken to hospital, he contracted pneumonia some days later.

Dodger Mullins' son was Jackie Dore. Again Fraser recalls:

He brought the boy up as his own but his wife had the boy by someone else before she met Dodger. How do I know this? Jimmy Brindle was driving past Sadler's Wells in Rosebery Avenue in one car and Jackie in another. We'd left Aggie Hill's Cabinet Club and were on our way to the Duchess of Kent. We're all nicked and when Jimmy said something about, 'My friend Jackie Mullins,' the copper said, 'No, you mean John Dore.' After that I asked Jackie and he told me.

By November 1914 Timmy Hayes had racked up ten previous convictions. Then he recorded his eleventh and his co-defendant William Driscoll his ninth when they received three months' hard labour apiece for pickpocketing. He would later live in Essex and is popularly supposed to have been the father of Lilian Goldstein, known as the Bobbed-Haired Bandit. His son Jimmy would keep up his father's good work.[43]

The third of the trio, Charlie Horrickey, 'another typical half-breed' – by which Harding means half-Jewish, half-Irish, 'as ignorant as hell' – was charged with grievous bodily harm, together with Harding, after cutting Moey Levy's throat in the Whitechapel Road in 1926.

Moey Levy, one of a family of seven, along with his brother Bobby was one of the big names in the East End at the time. He began life working for the Jewish gaming clubs and married an English girl, Polly Cash. He then worked as a bookmaker in

Brick Lane where the Jewish kept to one side of the street and the English to the other. Later he and a man called Gardiner kept a club over a confectioner's shop on the corner of Middlesex Street.

NOTES

1. Old Bailey Papers t18910504-443; Tom Divall, *Scoundrels and Scallywags*.
2. Nat.Arch. CRIM 1/13/6.
3. Sir Walter Besant, *The East End and Its People*.
4. *ELA*, 9 and 16 August 1902.
5. Old Bailey Papers, t8911019-790. In some accounts the Wallis story is attributed to a Tottenham-based gang.
6. *Surrey Comet*, 13 July 1901; *Pall Mall Gazette*, 27 December 1917; *Police Gazette*, 22 November 1919.
7. Brian McDonald, *Gangs of London*, pp 97 *et seq*.
8. There is mention of them in the memoirs of a number of police officers of the period. George Ingram gives a fictionalised account of a fight in Nile Street with the 'Sabatis', who are clearly the Sabinis, in *Cockney Cavalcade*. Edward T. Hart also fictionalises the fight in *Britain's Godfather*, although he names some of the combatants who were undoubtedly Sabini men of the period. He suggests that at one time Fred Gilbert was a member of the Sabinis and they only split apart after the Nile Street fight. Some writers, however, say the fight was a complete fiction. See also S. Felstead, *The Underworld of London*.
9. Brian McDonald, *Gangs of London*, p 111.
10. *Pall Mall Gazette*, 19 September 1922; *Birmingham Daily Gazette*, 20 September 1922; *Westminster Gazette*, 22 September 1922, *Aberdeen Press & Journal*, 26 October 1922.
11. Bert Rossi, *Britain's Oldest Gangland Boss*, Ch 4.
12. Raphael Samuel, *East End Underworld*, p. 148.

13. See evidence of William Southey and Frank Rayner, questions 23,123 *et seq*, Royal Commission into the Metropolitan Police 1908, Nat. Arch. HO 45 10523 140292.

14. Raphael Samuel, *East End Underworld*, p. 120. Gilbert was killed in the First World War, Taylor became a ponce and, according to Harding, died of syphilis in 1915. Harding later fell out with Isaacs over a girl they both knew and whom, so Harding believed, he was beating.

15. From reports in the local papers Hoy was clearly a man with whom to be reckoned. At least twice he was charged with shootings. He was friendly with Billy Chandler of the bookmaking family and was an expert dealer at faro. See *ELO*, 9 January 1909, 28 January, 11 February 1911.

16. Raphael Samuels, *East End Underworld*, p. 134

17. A panel was a brothel or low boarding house in which theft from the customers was rife.

18. May Churchill Sharpe, *Chicago May – Her Story*, pp. 116–17.

19. *ELO*, 18 September 1915. It was around this time that it was decided that, as a sufficient number of immigrants now spoke English, the services of a full-time Yiddish interpreter could be dispensed with at Thames Magistrates' Court.

20. *ELO*, 14 April 1913. They were defended by the West Ham solicitor, Charles Sharman.

21. Donald Rumbelow records the 1905 case of a Russian stopped at Dover Harbour on his way to London with enough arms to start a small war. He had in his luggage forty-seven automatic pistols and nearly 5,000 rounds of ammunition. None was confiscated. That year a firearm could be purchased over the counter for sixteen shillings. If the buyer was caught the maximum penalty was £5. *The Houndsditch Murders and the Siege of Sidney Street*, p. 41. In fact offences involving firearms rarely merited much more than a paragraph in the local paper and days rather than weeks in prison. In August 1914 William Voase

and other members of the Bow Road Gang attacked Frederick Alvin, all armed with belts and one with a revolver. Voase received fourteen days' hard labour. The member locked up for the most time in a year became the gang's captain. *ELA*, 28 August 1914.

22. *The Times*, 19 September 1905.

23. Raphael Samuel, *East End Underworld*, p. 109.

24. *The Mirror of Life* and *Boxing World*, 15 February and 1 March 1919.

25. As for the D'Angeleys, MacKay had conducted further inquiries and now came to the conclusion he had been mistaken in his assessment of the pair. How could he have been deceived in the first place? Did not he or his colleagues know the French girls who worked his area? Could he not tell D'Angeley was a pimp? Why did he not ask for a short adjournment to make proper inquiries? Meanwhile both the D'Angeleys had retreated to Paris and sensibly stayed there, despite the requests of the police who offered to pay the lady's fare back so that she could give evidence to the Commission. Sadly from the point of view of Anglo-French relations, their return to France had been hasty. When they caught the Dover packet they had not had time to pay for their lodgings, and had left behind a few empty trunks.

26. Earl Russell, *My Life and Adventures*, pp. 304–5.

27. Raphael Samuel, *East End Underworld*, p. 191.

28. ibid, pp. 147 et seq.

29. ibid, p. 154.

30. Bogard maintained in court that he had once been a member of the Vendettas but had left and tried to become respectable. This was what had done for him. For the competing accounts of just who was the most heroic see Raphael Samuel, *East End Underworld*, p. 154 *et seq.*; Chartres Biron, *Without Prejudice*, pp. 251–3; and Fred Wensley, *Detective Days*, pp. 103–6.

31. Harding says the Sabinis from Clerkenwell put up funds for the defence which, if he is correct, means that the family was operating

many years before they are usually credited. Raphael Samuel, *East End Underworld*, p. 120.

32. *Illustrated Police News*, 23 December 1911. Dido Gilbert, part of the spieler robbing team, received 15 months. Charlie Callaghan, who after his brush with the Baileys became both a thief and also a thieves' ponce, received a prison sentence. He had an unfortunate record of being hit over the head; his antipathy to Bogard had resulted from his being hit over the head following a quarrel in the Horns in Shoreditch High Street. Later he worked for a bookmaker.

33. Others in the Emmanuel gang included Jacky and Moey Levy, and Bobby Nark who would also go on to work for the Sabinis.

34. Jack 'Jew Boy' Stevens in fact came from Hampshire where he had been a groom and gardener before he came to London and joined the police. A swarthy man, he grew a beard and so could pass as Jewish. He rarely appeared in court and once when, after some undercover work, he did, he appeared clean-shaven. The next day he was back in his beard which a wig-maker had furnished. On his retirement he bought and ran the White Horse in Harlow. See *Reynolds' News*, 31 May 1925.

35. Ted Greeno, *News of the World*, 15 November 1959.

36. (1926) 19 CAR 157. For more of Hayes' career see also *ELA*, 9 April 1910. Edjali was the son of a Parsee clergyman who was sentenced to seven years' penal servitude after five horses, three cows and a number of sheep were killed or mutilated in Staffordshire where his father was a parson. After three years and a substantial campaign, in 1906 he was released on ticket of leave. The following year he was granted a free pardon. For an account of the case see Richard and Molly Whittington-Egan, *Mr George Edjali*.

37. Raphael Samuel, *East End Underworld*, pp. 132, 148, 185, 218–19, 235, 245.

38. *The Star*, 28 August 1956. I am very grateful to Albert Appelby and his family for their recollections of Mullins and for allowing me to use the family archives.

39. Judge's Remand when a man was held for reports prior to sentence.

40. F. Fraser, *Mad Frank and Friends*, p. 13.

41. F. Fraser, *Mad Frank*, p. 52.

42. Reggie Kray, *Villains We Have Known*, p. 20.

43. *ELO*, 14 November 1914.

6

THE SABINIS

Although they operated principally from Saffron Hill, Clerkenwell, any account of East End crime between the Wars without including the Sabini family would be sadly lacking. Over two decades they and their Hoxton and Hackney allies and opponents dominated street and racecourse crime until, at the beginning of the Second World War, the brothers – along with their formidable friend Papa Pasquale, known as Bert Marsh – were interned as enemy aliens, appropriately enough at Ascot racecourse.

They are mentioned regularly enough, but writers have not always been clear about how many brothers there actually were. For example, Charles and Darby Sabini are often referred to as the same man when in fact Charles was an older brother. Darby Sabini, when it suited him, was quite prepared to be known as Fred Sabini who was in fact the eldest.

In all there were six brothers, beginning with Frederick, born in 1881, who according to police files traded as Bob Wilson at the Harringay Greyhound Stadium and took no part in the other brothers' affairs. There is no note on the files as to what he did before greyhound racing became popular at the end of the

1920s. Next came Charles, who was two years younger and was a list supplier working for the bookmaker Joe Levy in what the police saw as a protection racket. He owned shares in West Ham Stadium and was thought to be 'slightly mentally deranged'; certainly by 1940 he had spent some time in mental hospitals. Then came Joseph who on paper was the villain of the family. He had served in the First World War in the Royal Welsh Fusiliers and then the Cheshire Regiment, and had been wounded in France. He had then been invalided out and received a twelve shillings a week pension. On 12 October 1922 he was given three years' penal servitude for his part in the shooting of Fred Gilbert in Mornington Crescent. The police thought, however, that after that he had split from his brothers and there was no evidence that he was operating behind the scenes. He traded as Harry Lake at Harringay. George Sabini was the youngest of the brothers – there was a sister who was a cripple – who had no convictions and worked at both Harringay and White City. He was not regarded as being any part of the gang, but it was noted that his name alone would provide him with protection. Of the brothers it was principally Darby and Harry who provided what was euphemistically called protection and what, in reality, was demanding money with menaces from the bookmakers.[1]

Ullano, sometimes Octavio, better known as Darby Sabini, was born in 1889 in Saffron Hill, Little Italy. His Italian father died when he was two and the family was raised by their Irish mother. Sabini left school at the age of thirteen and joined Dan Sullivan, a small-time boxing promoter and bookmaker who later worked for Bella Burge at The Ring at Blackfriars. At one time it was thought that Sabini could, in the words of Marlon Brando, 'have been a contender'. Whilst still in his teens he had knocked out the fancied middleweight, Fred Sutton, in the first round.[2] Unfortunately he did not like the training required and instead became a strong-arm man for Sullivan's promotions at the Hoxton Baths. Later he was employed by George Harris, a leading bookmaker of the time, again as a strong-arm man.

Harry, always known as Harryboy, was educated at St Peter's Roman Catholic School in Clerkenwell and then went to work for an optician. During the First World War he worked in a munitions factory. He then became a bookmaker's clerk, working first for Gus Hall and later for Walter Beresford. When the latter died he became a commission agent. By 1940 he was a wealthy man with money in bonds for his children's education, bank accounts and a number of properties. His solicitors regarded him as a 'conveyancing client'. He was also a Life Governor of the Northern Hospital.

After the First World War attendance at racecourses boomed, particularly at the southern tracks at which trotting was also a popular spectacle. Before the War the Birmingham gangs had established a hold on racecourse protection and now they sought to advance their empire. Under the leadership of Billy Kimber from Bordesley in Birmingham, who described himself as a bookmaker and punter, and the heavy gambler Andrew Townie, they metamorphosed as the Brummagen Boys despite the fact that most of the members came from the Elephant and Castle area of London. They had a fearsome reputation, being said to be willing and able to kill rats by biting them. Their organised racecourse protection began in around 1910 and for a time Kimber's mob took control of southern racecourses such as Newbury, Epsom, Earls Park and Kempton. There were also other gangs operating from Leeds, Uttoxeter and Cardiff, with links throughout the country. Later Kimber's men also had a loose alliance with one of the metamorphoses of the Hoxton Mob. In fact Kimber was not a layer but instead controlled the best pitches on the courses, leasing them out on a half profit but no loss-sharing basis. Kimber, according to some accounts, was well regarded and it was looser elements out of his control who terrorised the mainly Jewish bookmakers in the cheaper rings at the southern courses. The southern bookmakers accepted the imposition fairly philosophically.

Racecourse protection worked in a number of ways. First, there was the question of the pitches themselves. The Sabinis and their rivals simply bullied the hapless bookmakers away from their spots and then sold or let them to their cronies. One way of preventing a bookmaker from attracting any business was to surround his stand with thugs so that the punters could not get to it to place their bets. Then there was the bucket drop. If a bookmaker wished to avoid this trouble he would drop 2/6d. in a bucket containing water and a sponge carried up and down the line between races. The sponge was also used to wipe out the odds next to the printed sheet of runners on the board. If the tribute was not paid, then the odds would be wiped at inappropriate and totally inconvenient times. The sheets of runners had themselves to be purchased; costing about a farthing to produce, they were retailed by the Sabinis to the bookmakers for another half a crown (2/6d). Chalk had to be purchased, and a stool cost ten shillings to hire for the day. Other manoeuvres included starting fights near a bookmaker's pitch, claiming a non-existent winning bet, and having other pitches put so close to the non-paying bookmaker that he physically could not operate. Quite apart from that there was the straightforward demand for a non-repayable loan of £5 or £10. The sums may seem small, but added up it came to big money and the racecourse business was a profitable one. When a gang went to a course like Brighton they could clear £4,000 or £5,000. At Epsom on Derby Day, it could be £15,000 to £20,000.[3]

Now the Sabini brothers, 'The Italian Mob', who were said

to import gangsters from Sicily, began to put together their organisation. The fact that 'there wasn't an Englishman among them'[4] did not mean they could speak anything but English. The Sabinis may have had no great command of Italian, but they had command of the police:

> Darby Sabini got in with the Flying Squad which had been formed about 1908 or 1909; they got in with the racecourse police, the special police, and so they had the police on their side protecting them. Directly there was any fighting it was always the Birmingham mob who got pinched. They was always getting time, five year sentences and that.[5]

With the arrival of the Sabinis and their superior relation-ship with the police, Billy Kimber and his gang retreated to the Midlands. For some time the factions lived in an uneasy relation-ship. Kimber and Co. worked the Midlands and northern tracks; the Sabinis, along with a gang called the East End Jews, the London and southern ones.[6] In some versions of the legend the meteoric rise of Darby Sabini can be traced back to a fight he had in 1920 with 'Monkey' Benneyworth, a leader of the Elephant Gang, when Benneyworth deliberately tore the dress of an Italian girl serving behind the bar of the Griffin public house in Saffron Hill. Benneyworth was knocked out and humiliated by Sabini. When his broken jaw had mended he returned with members of the Elephant Gang, but they were driven out of Little Italy by Sabini with the help of young Italians who looked on him as their leader.[7] Now, with them behind him, he saw the opportunity to muscle in on some of the smaller gangs who were providing protection around the racetracks. Although the big gangs such as the Broad Mob from Camden Town, the mainly Jewish Aldgate Mob and the Hoxton Mob could boast a membership of up to sixty, they could be spread thinly because they were obliged to operate several tracks a day. The Sabinis moved in in force.

The next five years saw a long-running battle over control of on-course bookmakers. On the one side were the Sabinis, allied to the Jewish bookmakers from Aldgate. On the other were Billy Kimber, George 'Brummy' Sage and Fred Gilbert from Camden Town. Kimber's Brummagen Boys did not give in easily and the fighting continued throughout the year. The file on the Mornington Crescent shooting appeal against internment provides a good, although probably incomplete, list of the major bursts of violence.[8]

A bookmaker under the Sabinis' protection was threatened at Sandown Park and was beaten up when he refused to pay a £25 pitch fee. Darby Sabini sent a retaliatory force to Hoxton. He himself was caught at Greenford trotting track on 23 March 1921 and escaped a bad beating from the Brummagen Mob by shooting his way out of trouble.[9] It was one of the few occasions when he was arrested. Charged with unlawfully and maliciously endangering life, he was acquitted after arguing self-defence, fined £10 and bound over to keep the peace on a charge of possessing a five-chamber revolver without a certificate. Inspector Heaps told the court that about twenty Brummagen people tried to get at Sabini, shouting, 'Come on, we've got them on the run. The police are frightened of us too.' Sandy Rice and Fred Gilbert were charged with being suspicious persons, but since they could not be linked to the Sabini incident they were discharged the following week.[10]

On 26 March, Robert Harvey was beaten at London Bridge Station. He had been suspected of welshing at Greenford. The next day there was a serious piece of violence. Billy Kimber, 'accompanied by a number of other roughs' who may, or more likely may not, have been trying to pour oil on the troubled waters, was found shot on the pavement outside Sabini's house in King's Cross. He had apparently gone to 70 Colliers Street to remonstrate with Alfie Solomon and produced a revolver. Solomon took it away from him and Kimber was shot with his own weapon. On 27 April 1921 Solomon was acquitted of attempted murder when the jury accepted his claim that it was an accident. Reprisals for the Greenford incident came quickly. On 4 April at 'The Ascot of North London', Alexandra Park, a small frying-pan-shaped track which closed in the 1960s and which was known as Ally-Pally, the police were informed of a likely showdown. By 1 o'clock, all they had found were two Birmingham bookmakers' touts who had been beaten up. Later, however, two Jewish taxi drivers, chauffeurs to the Sabinis, were caught in the Silver Ring by the Birmingham men. One was shot twice as he lay on the ground; he too could not identify his shooter. A further reprisal came later that spring at Bath when Billy Kimber and his men attacked the East End Jews found in the Two Shillings Ring.

The quarrel between Sabini and the Jewish element in his contingent and outsiders continued throughout the summer. Fallers included David Levy of Bethnal Green who went to prison for three months at one of the magistrates' courts which were specially commissioned at the Derby meeting. He had been found carrying a pistol with soft-nosed bullets. His explanation was that he had been told that if he and his brother Moses went to Epsom they would be shot by 'The Sunderland Kid'. Nothing daunted, they had gone to the course. Levy had eighteen previous convictions for assault and two for larceny.[11] This was clearly a small part of the celebrated battle on Derby Day. It appears to have been engineered by Reuben Bigland, the Birmingham tycoon known as 'Telephone Jack', following a complaint by the publisher and later convicted swindler Horatio Bottomley. He complained that it was wrong that Italians such as the Sabinis should be depriving 'our boys' of a living, particularly after the latter's gallant fight in the First World War. The outcome was a punitive expedition by the Brummagen Boys, who were fuelled by the knowledge that the previous evening one of their men had been attacked in Covent Garden and had needed seventy stitches in his legs alone.

After the Derby itself, won by Steve Donoghue on the ill-fated Humorist, the Birmingham Boys left the course and blocked the road with their charabanc to lie in wait for Sabini and his friends. Unfortunately for them the Sabinis had already left the scene and the first cab in sight – which was duly attacked – contained their allies from Leeds. In the ensuing fracas one man lost three fingers. Twenty-eight men were arrested by a Sergeant Dawson, who at first thought the affray was a Sinn Fein riot and removed the sparking plugs from the charabanc. He then held the men at gunpoint until help arrived.[12]

It is curious how throughout the history of organised crime the victims will align themselves with their oppressors who, in turn, through that alliance somehow gain a quasi-respectability. After bookmakers at Salisbury races had been forced at gunpoint to pay a levy for the privilege of having a pitch, in 1921 they formed themselves into the Bookmakers and Backers Racecourse Protection Association (BBRPA), today a highly respected organisation. Eight stewards were appointed at a wage of £6 per week, including Darby Sabini, Alf White and Philip Emmanuel (son of Edward) who became the association's vice-president. Another curious steward was Fred Gilbert.[13]

It is said that at the time Darby was earning £20,000 a year. This may be an exaggeration but, taken at the lowest level, sixty sheets sold at 2/6d made a working man's wage for the week and there is no doubt the brothers did far better than that. It did not last long for it was soon apparent that the stewards had reverted to their old ways and were demanding a shilling for every list sold.

Emmanuel senior also set up a company providing layers with tickets for the punters. There is also a suggestion that in 1922 he was now controlling the Sabinis. In September of that year their services were dispensed with by the BBRPA.[14]

Violence may have spread away from the racecourses, but 1922 was a vintage year in the battle for supremacy on them. On 23 February 1922 Michael Sullivan and Archie Douglas, both of them Brummagen Boys, were slashed in Coventry Street by a Sabini team consisting of Alfred Solomon and his brother Harry, Alfred White, James Wood and a man named Mansfield.

On Good Friday, Fred Gilbert was slashed about the legs in the New Raleigh Club in Jermyn Street by the Italians led by Alfie Solomon. He declined to bring charges. The Derby meeting that year, when Captain Cuttle won after spreading a plate on the way to the start, passed off quietly. But two months later, the Sabinis were back in the dock charged after a fight in Mornington Crescent, Camden Town, during which shots were fired at Fred Gilbert who had been out walking with his wife and some friends when he was ambushed. For once the Birmingham men were able to give the names of their attackers to the police, but by the time the case was heard they had forgotten them.

Things did not stop there and real consideration was given by the Jockey Club to shutting down the courses on which there was trouble. There had been persistent stories that a son of the boxer George Moore, a Gilbert man from West London, was stabbed to death in a club off the Strand, or perhaps in Tottenham, but the police report specifically denies this. What is clear is that the Sabinis and their rivals fought for supremacy on street corners, on trains, on the roads and at the racecourses.

On 29 July 1922 there was an affray just outside the Red Bull in Gray's Inn Road. William John Beland said that he had heard shots fired from a public house. He went to the scene but was stopped by Fred who said, 'Go the other way or I shall blow your fucking brains out.'

Beland had also been down at the canal bank off Caledonian Road at the beginning of 1920 when Gilbert and George Droy were fighting. When Gilbert was getting the worst of it he took a razor and slashed Droy across the shoulder. Trixie Droy, a manufacturing optician, came to his brother's assistance and for his pains Gilbert shot him in the shoulder.

On 22 August 1922, Jewish bookmakers actually went to the police complaining that George 'Brummy' Sage and Gilbert had demanded £10 from them as they waited for a train to the races. Samuel Samuels said that he was at Waterloo Station on 19 August when George Sage came up to him and said, 'You Jew bastard. You're one of the cunts we're going to do. You're a fucking bastard Jew and we are going to do you and the Italians and stop you going racing. I want to be the governor here.'

Jack Delew from Yorkton Street, Hackney, said he had been in the Rising Sun at Waterloo on the same day when Sage, Jim Brett and Gilbert approached. Sage caught hold of Harry Margolis and said, 'This is one of the bastards, do him Fred, through the guts.' Gilbert then pressed a large service revolver into Margolis' body and said, 'Give us a tenner and you can go.' Jim Brett, aka Stevens, pulled a butcher's knife on Delew and asked, 'Shall I do him?' when a man, Sullivan, entered and said, 'Let them alone. They'll do later.' He then said there were fifty of them and the Sabinis and Alf White would be done in for certain.

Earlier that same day the Sabinis, including Alf White – now Chief Steward of the Racecourse Protection Association – Joseph Sabini, George West aka Dai Thomas, Paul Boffa and Tommy

Mack, arrived at Mornington Crescent in a fleet of taxis and shot at Gilbert.

There was a good deal of ducking and diving by friends of the Sage and Brett contingent in respect of their bit of bother, as a result of which on 24 November John Gilbert, Joseph Smith, Thomas Ackroyd and George Moore were found not guilty of perverting the course of justice by getting Margolis to give false evidence. It had been alleged that on 12 October, when Margolis went to the Old Bailey to give evidence, he was met by George Moore whom he knew from the races. Moore said he was ashamed of him giving evidence. Margolis went with him across to the Wellington coffee shop and there saw Joe Smith and John Gilbert. Later he went with Gilbert and met Fred Kimberley who had offered money to change his story. Overall neither of the cases could be seen as noted successes by the prosecution. On 1 November, Gilbert, Jim Brett and Sage had all been found not guilty of demanding with menaces. No one bothered about the shooting of George Droy.[15]

Meanwhile most of the Sabini gang involved had been acquitted of the Gilbert shooting in Camden Town. Alf White was convicted but acquitted on appeal. 'The sooner the Bookmakers Protection Agency is disbanded the better,' said Mr Justice Roche. Joseph Sabini was not so fortunate. He received three years which he was serving in Maidstone when Alf White, together with George Drake and another unidentified man, decided his conditions should be improved. To this end they approached a warder Matthew Frygh and offered him £2 to deliver letters for him. Frygh reported the matter and the recently released White found himself back in the dock along with Drake. The police wanted to charge George Sabini but there was no evidence against him. It had been thought he had masterminded the whole thing but, on closer inspection, it turned out that the 'George Sabini' who had visited his brother in prison had been another of White's men. This time White received eighteen months and Drake six months more. They appealed and because White had an arguable point of law he lost no remission when his appeal was dismissed. Drake apparently had a good service record, being the batman to an RSM in the British Expeditionary Force in France. Now Lord Justice Swift had a little judicial fun at his expense.

> It is clear that society is not safe unless Drake is in the army or in prison and as the court cannot send him into the army what are we to do? One thing is certain. If the sentence stands he will not be able to bribe another warder from outside.

The unfortunate Drake lost his appeal and with it his remission.

At the Doncaster St Leger meeting the Brummagen team sent word that no bookmakers or their employees would be allowed to attend Town Moor. As a result, in open defiance, Sabini and his men 'protected' the London bookie, Walter Beresford, putting him safely on the train to Doncaster where it was met by Kimber's men who then allowed only him and his staff to go to the racecourse. It is often suggested that this was an act of generosity by the Sabinis. Beresford had employed Harry Sabini – or was it the other way around? – for years.

The next trouble spot was at the Yarmouth autumn meeting, a course claimed by the Sabinis as theirs. They arrived the day before the meeting to search the public houses in the town to see if the Brummagen men had arrived. They had not. Instead they were met by Tom Divall, an ex-Chief Inspector of the CID and a superior of Wensley and Leeson down in Whitechapel, but now working for Wetherbys. Divall, something of a supporter of the Midland team, calmed things down.

Divall wrote of Kimber that he 'was one of the best' and of another incident:

> Just to show what generous and brave fellows the aforesaid Sage and Kimber were, they would not give any evidence or information against their antagonists, and stated that they would sooner die than send those men to prison.[16]

One explanation of the Sabinis' success and longevity comes from Billy Hill:

> There were more crooked policemen about than there are today. The Sabinis received protection from certain elements of the law. If a thief or pickpocket was seen on a course, a Sabini man would whiten the palm of his hand with chalk and greet the thief with a supposed-to-be 'Hello'. In doing so he would slap the thief on the shoulder, just like a long-lost friend. The whitened hand-mark would identify him to the law. Then they knew without doubt that this man was safe to be nicked for being a suspected person.[17]

According to Divall it was Beresford who in 1923:

> ... brought the two sides together, he is still continuing in the good work, and I am very pleased to see the two crews are associating together, and, in addition, to have their principals assuring me that no such troubles will ever occur again.

The Sabinis and Kimber did agree to divide the racecourses between them and the racecourse wars died down. Now, with the Sabinis controlling the South, where there were more meetings, and Kimber and his friends the rest, the bookmakers were firmly in their hands. But if by then Darby Sabini had made his peace with that fine fellow Billy Kimber, for some time he had been under threat from other sources inside his own organisation. Some of the troops decided to seek a higher percentage of the takings. The four Cortesi brothers, Augustus, George, Paul and Enrico, known as the Frenchies because they were born in Paris, were deputed to act as shop stewards to put the case. Almost immediately afterwards part of the Jewish element in the gang, to become known as the Yiddishers, also formed a breakaway group. In true business fashion the Sabinis negotiated. The Cortesis would be given a greater percentage. The Yiddishers were given permission to lean on one, but only one, of the bookmakers under protection.[18]

However, peace did not last long. The Yiddishers began to side with the Cortesis and with defections amongst the troops to the Frenchies, the Sabini position was substantially weakened. In the autumn of 1922 the new team had effectively hijacked the Sabini protection money from the bookmakers at Kempton Park. Retribution was swift. As a result of the reprisals, Harry Sabini was convicted at Marylebone Magistrates' Court of an assault on George Cortesi. More seriously, one of the other leaders of the breakaway group was attacked, for which five of the Sabini troops were sentenced to terms of imprisonment for attempted murder.

Then on 19 November 1922, just before midnight, Darby and Harry Sabini were trapped in the Fratellanza Club in Great Bath Street, Clerkenwell, by six Cortesi men including Enrico (Harry) and Gus Cortesi, regarded as the wildest of the brothers, along with Sandy Rice. The heroine of the evening was Louisa Doralli, the club secretary's daughter, said to be in love with Harry Sabini. First, she knocked Gus Cortesi's hand as he shot at Darby and the bullet went through a window, then she stood in front of Harry when Enrico tried to shoot him. Harry pushed her away and took a bullet in the stomach. Darby was hit with a full wine bottle. He also suffered a greater indignity. As he told the magistrates' court, his false teeth were broken as a result of the blows from the bottle. He was also able to confirm his respectability:

> I am a quiet peaceable man. I never begin a fight. I've only once been attacked. I've never attacked anyone ...
>
> I do a little bit of work as a commission agent sometimes for myself and sometimes for someone else. I'm always honest. The last day's work I did was two years' ago. I live by my brains.

He had only once carried a revolver and that was the time when he was attacked at Greenford Park. Indeed he turned out his pockets in confirmation that he was not carrying a gun.

The Cortesi brothers, who lived five doors from the Fratellanza Club, had been arrested the same night, but only after the local community, trying to prevent Enrico's arrest, had skirmished with the police. They appeared at the Old Bailey on 18 January 1923.

The trial judge, the eccentric Mr Justice Darling, endeavoured to talk to the Sabinis in Italian and when he discovered they could not speak the language he rather lost interest in the proceedings. He had also tried to explain the Rape of the Sabine Women in Roman mythology to no great effect. Augustus and Enrico each received a sentence of three years' penal servitude. George was found not guilty, as were Paul Tomasso and his brother Alexander, known as Sandy Rice. A recommendation by the Grand Jury that the Cortesi brothers should be deported was not followed by Mr Justice Darling.

> I look upon this as part of a faction fight which has raged between you and other Italians in consequence of some difference which

the police do not entirely understand. You appear to be two lawless bands – the Sabinis and the Cortesis. Sometimes you are employed against the Birmingham people, and sometimes you are employed against each other. On this occasion you were carrying out a feud between you and the Sabinis. I have the power to recommend an order for your deportation. I am not going to do it. I can see no reason to suppose that you two men are worse than others who have been convicted in these feuds and have not been recommended for deportation.

A rather sour note on the Home Office file reads: 'It is a pity that the Cortesis were not charged with the murder of the Sabinis.'

Meanwhile anonymous letters to the police detailed a series of incidents for which the Sabinis were said to be responsible. The principal correspondent was 'Tommy Atkins' who said he had been victimised and, if the police cared to contact him by putting an advertisement in the *Daily Express*, he would reveal all. Meanwhile he alleged that Edward Emmanuel and a Girchan Harris were financing the Sabinis and that they had a number of members of the Flying Squad in their pay as well. The police inserted the advertisement suggesting a meeting, which was declined by 'Atkins' who, nevertheless, did supply details of some twelve incidents including an attack by James Ford and George Langham (also known as Angelo Giancoli) on bookmaker John Thomas Phillips in Brighton. He also reported the story that the brother of George Moore had been killed and that the *Evening News* racing correspondent J.M.D. had been attacked at Newmarket. There was a suggestion that Billy Westbury had been injured so badly that he was now 'mentally insane'.

The police could find no trace of the death of Moore's

brother and reported that poor Billy Westbury had suffered 'minor injuries'. It was correct, however, that J.M.D. had indeed been attacked.

In June 1923, Darby and Harry Sabini, along with George Dido, were arrested at Epsom races and charged with wounding Jack Levine, known also as Maurice Fireman. The allegation was that they had used knuckle-dusters on the unhappy bookmaker. They were fortunate in that the incident had been witnessed by Sgt-Major Michael O'Rorke VC, a resident of a local veterans' hospital, who saw no knuckle-dusters and Fireman as being the aggressor. Dido gave evidence that he had been wearing a ring which might have seemed at a glance to be a knuckle-duster. Asked where it was, he said rather piteously that he had pawned it to pay for the defence. Not Guilty.[19]

One of the most serious incidents came in 1924 when Alfie Solomon stood trial for the murder of Barney Blitz, known as Buck Emden, who had nine convictions for wounding and assaults on the police including one at Old Street Magistrates' Court when, on 20 July 1916, he had been ordered to pay £20 compensation for striking an officer with a bayonet.

The police only managed to persuade a bare half-dozen of the forty-odd present in the Eden Street Club where the killing took place to come to give evidence. One defaulter was the fishmonger, soon to be boxing promoter, Jack Solomons. He wished he could help, but since he had been drinking all evening he could not give an accurate recollection even though he had been sober enough to play faro when he arrived at the premises.

The story is that Darby Sabini arrived at the flat of Sir Edward Marshall Hall KC brandishing a bundle of white £5 notes in an endeavour to persuade the great man to appear for Solomon. He was sent to see Hall's clerk and Sir Edward accepted the brief. Solomon's defence was that he had seen Edward Emmanuel being assaulted and struck a blow with a knife to save his dear old friend. As for his part, Emmanuel, who had now left behind his East End upbringing and was living in Golders Green, wished he could cut off his own hand if the act would bring Emden back to life.

Some felt that the real villain of the piece and the person who had set it all up was indeed Emmanuel, who was alleged to have controlled things from the Tichbourne Club in Paddington, and Scotland Yard received another anonymous letter.

> I feel (rec 25 Sept) I must write and tell you something about the poor man that was stabbed in the Eden Street Club. The man who started the row was Edward Emmanuel who I know went there with Solomons. He is making his brags all over the East End that his money will keep him out of this affair. I know him and know he paid this man Solomons to do this poor man some injury. The police must know this Emmanuel he has had gambling houses all over London and it was because he had a previous row with this poor man that took him there with Solomons who is also a villain and this is not the first one he has stabbed. Make Solomons say who he went to the club with and who broke the glass and hit the poor man on the head. Please take notice of this letter and make this Emmanuel come forward. I only wish I had curage (sic) to come and see you and tell you more you will find out this is true. He professes to be a very good man by helping poor jews and that is why they will never say anything about him you have got his photo at Scotland Yard if you look it up I am a poor woman who has suffered through these gambling dens.[20]

The Solomons referred to is obviously Alfred Solomon who, on his release from prison, went bent on his former associates and supporters, writing to the police asking for protection as he had been going straight and working the racetracks when he was threatened at Clapton by a gang headed by Dodger Mullins. The police thought differently, saying that Alfred Solomons was 'a dangerous rascal and his enemies are far more in need of protection than he is'.[21]

Without their leaders the Cortesi faction had folded, but 1925 was a vintage year for gang fighting in London. The list of incidents is formidable. According to the newspapers, on 15 February there was a razor slashing in Aldgate High Street, and another slashing took place at Euston Station on 24 April. On 21 May, ten armed men raided a club in Maiden Lane looking for the Sabinis or their men. Later that night shots were fired in the Harrow Road. On 30 July, three men were wounded in a club in Brighton. There was an incident when men fought on Hampstead Heath on 3 August. Five days later a man was attacked in the Marshalsea Road in the Borough, and on 16 August, twenty-four men fought in Shaftesbury Avenue. Four days after that there was a pitched battle when fifty men fought with razors on the corner of Aldgate and Middlesex Street.

The police, asked for their comments, were dismissive, saying that the fight at Middlesex Street had been a minor incident and the fight in Shaftesbury Avenue was total invention. They accepted the Maiden Lane incident and that Monkey Benneyworth had been involved. In connection with the Hampstead Heath fight, there was no evidence that racecourse gangs were involved. As for allegations that Flying Squad officers were standing by watching some of the incidents, this was totally incorrect; indeed the newspapers should be ashamed of themselves for such irresponsible reporting. However, in the House of

Commons the Home Secretary, William Joynson Hicks, vowed to stamp out the racecourse gangs.

And just as swiftly as they had arisen so did the street fights die away. Darby Sabini moved to Brighton where, in October 1929, he was fined £5 for assaulting bookmaker David Isaacs. After an incident at Hove Greyhound Stadium, he had attacked him in the Ship Hotel and then in a billiard saloon. When Isaacs was asked why he had not brought witnesses he replied, 'How can I get witnesses against a man like this, when everyone goes in fear of their life of him?'

It was not until the 1930s, by which time the Sabinis had expanded their territory into greyhound racing, that they again came under serious threat from another team.[22] This time it was from their former ally Alf White whose family and friends had been getting stronger over the years and were now set to challenge their previous allies. Trouble had been brewing for some time and Sabini had not been able to control the disparate interests of the Jews and the Whites, the more right-wing arm of the organisation. There was also the small matter of the pitches on the open courses at Epsom and Brighton which were outside the control of the racecourse stewards, as well as bookmaking at point-to-points, let alone the dog tracks where, according to the son of a man who ran a pitch, 'they terrorised the bookmakers'.

Meanwhile, from the 1920s onwards the Sabinis had been branching out, taking interests in the West End drinking and gambling clubs and installing and running slot machines. They were also extending their protection to criminals. If a burglary took place the Sabinis would send round for their share.

Burglars and thieves had no chance. If they wandered 'Up West' they had to go mob-handed. And they had to be prepared to pay out if they were met by any of the Sabinis. If they went into a club it was drinks all round. The prices were usually doubled especially for their benefit. If they did go into a spieler they never won; they knew better than to try to leave while they were showing even a margin of profit. If one word was spoken out of place, it was all off. The Sabinis, who could rustle up twenty or thirty tearaways at a moment's notice anywhere 'Up West', stood for no liberties, although they were always taking them.[23]

The family was also undoubtedly behind one of the best of the bullion robberies of the 1930s, the very carefully planned gold snatch at Croydon Airport. Gold used to be shipped from the airport and, on 6 March 1936, three boxes of gold bars, sovereigns and dollars intended to be sent by Imperial Airways to Brussels and Paris disappeared. The boxes had been placed in a safe room and amazingly only one man, Francis Johnson, remained at the aerodrome overnight. He had to leave the actual building at 4.15 in the morning to receive a German airliner which was landing. An impression had been made of the keys to the safe room and, while Johnson was on the tarmac, the gold was stolen.

A cab had been hired from King's Cross and driven to the airport where the boxes were loaded and brought back to Harringay. Cecil Swanland, John O'Brien and Silvio Mazzardo (known as Shonk after Darby Sabini slit his nose because he had gambled away the day's takings) and a Sabini man who lived off Saffron Hill were arrested. The police found wrappers and seals from the gold in Swanland's room but there wasn't a trace of the gold itself. The evidence included identification and, since it was clearly not strong, the mandatory confession to a cellmate. Mazzardo and O'Brien were acquitted. Swanland's defence was that by the time the boxes arrived at his home they were empty. He had a number of old convictions mainly for forgery, and had already served seven, five and six years' penal servitude. This time he received a seven-year term. None of the gold was recovered. Bert Marsh, who had earlier been acquitted of the murder of a

Monte Colombo brother at Wandsworth Greyhound Stadium, was suspected of being the actual mastermind.[24]

But the Sabinis and the Whites were not without rivals. In 1937, the crime writer and novelist Peter Cheyney wrote in the *Sunday Dispatch* that there were five major London gang districts: Hackney, Hoxton, North East London, North London, and the West End, this last being 'worked over' by a loose alliance of the Hoxton, Elephant and Castle Boys and the Hackney Gang as well as the West End Boys. Until 1927, wrote Cheyney:

> . . . the Hackney Gang was supreme in the West End. Then came the battle of Ham Yard when the gang suffered a severe reversal in terms both of blood spilled and prestige lost.

Apart from the gangs which ran their areas there would be splinter teams such as the squad of pickpockets from Aldgate who worked the nearby City.

After his unfortunate incident at Maidstone prison, White had maintained a low profile as far as the courts were concerned until, in July 1935, he and his sons William and Alfred junior each received twelve months' hard labour for assaulting John McCarthy Defferary, the licensee of the Yorkshire Stingo in the Marylebone Road, at the Wharncliffe Rooms on 17 April that year. The fight had been at a dance in aid of St Mary's Hospital and Defferary lost the sight of his left eye. There was a suggestion that Carrie White, Alf's daughter, had been given £12 taken from the victim.[25]

On 28 April that year, Frederick Ambrose had written to the police alleging that Alf White was 'one of the Worse Race Course Pests and blackmailers that ever put foot on a racecourse' and the file contains another series of letters suggesting White had the police in his pay.[26]

Now when the Whites appeared at the Old Bailey they were supported by some forty members of the gang and fighting broke out. There were no arrests. The guilty verdict was thought to be very much against the weight of the evidence and the writer of an internal Scotland Yard memo said 'success in such an appeal would, in the matter of Law and Order, be a catastrophe'. There had been a threat against prosecuting counsel, Horace Fenton, and for a time he was given police protection.

As for the racecourses, the last major pre-war fight took place when, at Lewes racecourse on 8 June 1936, the Bethnal Green Gang in alliance with the Hoxton Mob and probably sponsored by Alf White, ran riot. In retaliation for an incident at Liverpool Street when a member of the Whites had his throat cut, thirty members of that firm went to the races with the specific intention of injuring two of the Sabinis. They did not find them and instead set upon the bookmaker Arthur Solomons and his clerk, Mark Frater, known to be friendly towards the family. After a running battle sixteen men were arrested. As always serious money was available and they were defended privately at Lewes Assizes by the very fashionable J.D. Cassels KC and G.L. Hardy, but on pleas of guilty the ringleaders, who included Jimmy Spinks and other Hoxton men, drew five years' penal servitude from Mr Justice Hilbery who imposed a total of fifty-three and a half years on the defendants.

It was after that that an accommodation was reached. The Sabinis should have the West End, the Whites the King's Cross area. They became known as the King's Cross Gang and Alf White would hold court in the Bell public house or Hennekeys in the Pentonville Road exercising strict discipline amongst his followers. 'No bad language was allowed,' says John Vaughan, a former police officer from King's Cross. 'First time you were warned. The next time – out.' It had been the same with Darby

Sabini; women were to be treated properly; Italian youths could not drink before they were twenty. His had been a reasonably benevolent dictatorship.

Darby Sabini lost another battle when, following a series of unfavourable articles, he sued D.C. Thomson, the proprietors of the offending *Topical Times*, for libel. On the day of the action he failed to appear and costs of £775 were awarded against him. He did not pay and bankruptcy proceedings were commenced.[28]

The Sabini empire was effectively destroyed by their internment at the outbreak of the Second World War. Darby Sabini had moved to Brighton with, according to Saffron Hill legend, two sacks of gold, where his daughters were educated locally – again Saffron Hill legend said it was at Roedean, but there are no records of the girls there – and where he had a penthouse flat in the Grand Hotel. Harryboy, who escaped internment, was sentenced in 1942 to nine months' imprisonment for perjury when attempting to prevent that fate. Their business interests were now up for grabs. For a time their West End interests were shared by the Whites, Jack Spot and the Elephant Gang, with the Whites increasingly the dominant force.

Another old Sabini man to gravitate to Brighton was Patrick Daley who in August 1937 received six months in the local magistrates' court. He had been leaning on bookmakers at Brighton races, demanding two shillings from each of them. When arrested, he hit a detective and it had taken a further six policemen to get him to the station. Up until 1926 he had twenty convictions for assaults and thefts but had then given up drink and become a bookmaker. He had, he told the court, lost his money some eighteen months previously which accounted for his present actions. In return the chairman told him he was a 'dangerous man'.[29]

Just what were Darby Sabini and his brothers like? A picture taken of the Cortesis and the Sabinis before the Fratellanza shooting shows Enrico Cortesi in a straw hat sitting in the middle of the group like the captain of a cricket team. To his left is Darby, less than middle height, with the flat cap he always wore and a shirt with no collar. He wore a dark brown suit with a high-buttoned waistcoat, a black silk stock and the light checked cap; he had selected this outfit when he was twenty and wore it for the rest of his life – indoors, outdoors and, so it is said, sometimes in bed. To Cortesi's right and in the background is handsome Harryboy Sabini who wore highly polished spring-sided boots. Brother Joe liked cherry checks, whilst George wore a grey fedora.

On 17 June 1943, Darby Sabini, under the name Fred and having by then been released from internment, was convicted of receiving wine and silver worth £383 which had been stolen by soldiers from the Uckfield house of a retired Sussex magistrate. The jury had rejected his defence that he thought that he was buying goods from a hotel which was being sold up. The Recorder Gilbert Paull, passing sentence, told him in the time-honoured words judges love to use to receivers: 'It is men like you who lay temptation before soldiers. If there were none like you there would be no temptation to steal.' Sabini, who was said to have no previous convictions, received three years' imprisonment.

After the war Harry joined his brother in Brighton. Darby's son, also named Harry, had joined the RAF and was killed in action in Africa. In the late 1940s Darby functioned as a small-time bookmaker with a pitch on the free course at Ascot – a danger to no one, certainly not the up-and-coming Jack Spot and Billy Hill.

When he died in Hove in 1951 his family and friends were surprised that he apparently had so little money. One story goes that the man who had been his clerk, Jimmy Napoletano, was stopped when leaving the country on his way to Italy with £36,000. Sabini's wife returned to live in Gray's Inn Road, Clerkenwell. She died in 1978, the same year as Harryboy.

Darby Sabini, who with his wife is buried in Hove Old Cemetery, lives on in fiction and film as the Brighton gang leader Colleoni in Graham Greene's *Brighton Rock*. One of the key scenes in both book and film is the meeting between him and Pinky in the Brighton hotel. The slashing of Pinky at the race meeting is based on the Lewes battle of 1936.

NOTES

1. Nat. Arch. HO 45/25720.
2. There is no trace in boxing records of this bout. It is, however, possible that the contest took place at a fairground booth. Until the 1960s, when it was banned by the British Boxing Board of Control, it was common for licensed boxers to take on all comers at booths. Sullivan was himself part Italian and on one occasion broke up a fight at The Ring between the Sabinis and the Hoxton element.
3. Raphael Samuel, *East End Underworld*, p. 184.
4. ibid, p. 182.
5. ibid, p. 183.
6. There were numerous tracks in the South, many of which such as Gatwick, Lewes, Alexandra Park and Hurst Park have now closed down. In addition, trotting was popular with courses at such places as Greenford and Hendon.
7. 1 Benneyworth is something of a shadowy and unsung figure who reappears over the years. On 8 August 1935 he was involved in the beating of a pickpocket by the name of Flatman in the Waterloo Road.
8. Nat. Arch. MEPO 3 158.
9. *Glasgow Herald*, 25 March 1921.

10. Nat. Arch. MEPO 3 366

11. *The Star*, 1 June 1921.

12. Nat. Arch MEPO 3 346. It is often suggested that Jack 'Dodger' Mullins was one of those involved in the attack. If so he escaped arrest. Humorist began to haemorrhage after the race and died within a few weeks. A post-mortem showed he had won with only one sound lung.

13. The Bookmakers and Backers Racecourse Protection Association, *What It Has Done and What It Can Do with YOUR Help* (NAB File, 'History' 1921); The Bookmakers and Backers Racecourse Protection Association General Committee, Minutes, 12 September 1921.

14. South PA Folio 47, 15 May 1933, 'Printing of Lists', The Bookmakers and Backers Racecourse Protection Association General Committee, Minutes, 15 May, 12 June, 4 September 1922.

15. Nat.Arch. MEPO 3 366.

16. Tom Divall, *Scoundrels and Scallywags*, p. 200.

17. Billy Hill, *Boss of the Underworld*, p. 4.

18. Arthur Tietjen, *Soho*.

19. *News of the World*, 24 June 1923.

20. Nat. Arch. MEPO 3 373

21. Ibid.

22. In February the faithful James Ford received two months' hard labour for an attack on William Farmer who was said to be taking control of Belle Vue Greyhounds. *The Times*, 25 February 1929.

23. Billy Hill, *Boss of the Underworld*, p. 5.

24. Just as bookmakers' pitches on the racetracks had been controlled so it was with the new sport of greyhound racing. Marsh and Bert Wilkins were involved in a fight over who should work at the pitches and Massimino Monte Colombo was stabbed to death on 1 September 1936. They were acquitted of murder and received short sentences for manslaughter. See James Morton, *Gangland*, pp. 20–21.

25. The White appeal against his conviction in the Gilbert incident

appears in the Law Reports under (1922) CR App R. 60 and also in Nat. Arch. MEPO 3 910.

26. Reprinted in *Making Crime Pay*. Cheyney was writing a decade later and in fact the battle took place at the end of 1923. The following January George West (forty-three) and James Ford (thirty) had wrecked the New Avenue Club in Ham Yard for which they went to prison. West had a long record beginning in 1898 when he served two months for larceny, interrupted by a career when he boxed as Dai Thomas. In October 1922 he had been acquitted of the attempted murder of Fred Gilbert in the Mornington Crescent shooting. This time West received nine months and Ford six.

   In February 1927 Freddy Ford (no relation of James), who ran the Musicians and Artists Club, an *alter ego* for the New Avenue, went to prison for receiving, along with a man named Chandler. The club was described by Inspector Wensley as patronised almost exclusively by thieves – male and female. If, by mistake, a genuine patron stumbled into the club it was rare that he left with his money. *Empire News*, 13 February 1927.

27. For an account of the battle, see Edward Greeno, *War on the Underworld*. Greeno, on whose recollections it is not always safe to rely, gives credence to the story that a Sabini man was killed in the Benneyworth raid on Maiden Lane.

28. *The Times*, 16 December 1925.

29. *Empire News*, 8 August 1937.

7

CHINATOWN, MY CHINATOWN

I was glad when I was through Pennyfields. It was the only street in the miles of East London that I traversed day and night that inspired me with any real fear.

Until my visit to the Asiatic Sailors' Home I had always considered some of the Jewish inhabitants of Whitechapel to be the worst type of humanity I had ever seen.[1]

At the end of the eighteenth century most of the Chinese population had been discharged from vessels and were living in poverty until the ships were ready to sail again. In 1814, the East India Company was required to provide food, clothing and lodging for them (Report on Lascars and other Asiatic Seamen 1814–15). They were mainly employed through the East India Company and it was only at the turn of the century that Chinatowns began to develop. The 1851 Census for England and Wales showed there were 110 London residents born in China of whom thirty-two were British subjects and seventy-eight foreigners. Ten years later the number was almost double and in 1901 had reached 545, most living in Stepney and Poplar where over 20 per cent worked in the laundry industry.

There were anti-Chinese riots in the East End in 1908 caused by the fear of sailors that with the companies using more Asiatics their jobs would be lost. Several Chinese boarding houses were ransacked.

The Chinese were not the only targets. As early as 1736 there were anti-Irish riots in Spitalfields when cane weavers protested about undercutting. Two Irish heavers, Murphy and Duggan, were hanged after an affray between sailors and coal-heavers in 1768 at Wapping (Annual Register, 25 May 1768). This time the Irish had been in revolt about their own poor conditions of employment. After the disturbances in the spring of 1768, five Irishmen were hanged in Sun Tavern Fields off the Ratcliffe Highway in front of a crowd said to number 50,000. Then in 1786 seven Irishmen were hanged after an affray at Shadwell.[2]

It is difficult to know just how accurate were the tales in books such as *Women and Crime*, but they certainly enthralled the readers and added to the mystery of Limehouse. In this autobiographical episode Cecil Bishop, the Scotland Yard officer turned private detective, is asked by J.W., 'a well-known London man', to find his young wife who has disappeared.

It was thought that she would be found 'in some East End Joss House'.

I received information that the girl was in a particularly unsavoury den in Limehouse. I visited the place with J.W. We were received by a Chinaman whom I persuaded to show me the women addicts then in his house. One of the women answered the description of the girl for whom I was searching. She was largely undressed, as it so often happens that proprietors of opium dens will remove the clothes of sleeping clients so that they may not leave the den until all their money is spent. I told the Chinaman that I should take the woman away with me, and when he heard that I was an ex-Scotland Yard officer he consented. Some Chinese clothes were found and we returned to J.W.'s house in the West End. But no sooner had I placed the girl on a couch than my companion groaned and told me that we had brought the wrong woman.[3]

Unfortunately Bishop does not disclose what he did with the unfortunate girl, but he returns to the den saying that he wishes to find a girl who took morphine. The Chinaman explains that he only sells opium and recommends him to another den. Because the proprietor of the second establishment knows and loathes the detective, Bishop puts on a disguise, one of the key features of which is a wooden leg – rather, it seems, like Tony Hancock playing Robert Newton playing Long John Silver. He visits his own wife who fails to recognise him and so, satisfied with the disguise, off he goes back to the East End where he buys the girl for £50, the price the Chinaman tells him he would receive from white slavers. He gets a nearby labourer to help him carry the girl out, but all does not go smoothly.

[We were] halfway down the short flight of stairs, the labourer carrying the girl, when the floor collapsed and we were precipitated into the cellar. In the fall most of my disguise came off and the Chinaman recognising me, drew his knife and rushed me.

Now follows a bit of verisimilitude and instruction for those readers who might venture into Pennyfields.

A Chinaman has a peculiar way of stabbing. He rushes at his enemy with a knife held on a level with his hip. He then slashes low down, once right and once left. It is seldom that more is needed. One does not observe the Queensberry rules on these occasions, so I kicked my Chinaman with my wooden leg and he collapsed. We got the woman away safely, but shortly after arriving home she died. The effects of the fall had been too much for her drug-weakened heart.[4]

Because of the various spellings of Chinese names the man in question may have been Tung-Tse-Ana-Tse, known as Mr Johnson or Mr King, who was regarded as one of the major financiers of the trade.

One of the first and certainly the best known of the major Chinese drug dealers was Chan Nan, known as Brilliant 'Billy' Chang. Born around 1886 he was a stocky figure barely 5 feet tall with patent leather shoes and a fur-collared melton cloth coat. He called himself a general merchant and an Admiralty contractor and was described as 'the unemotional yellow man, his narrow slit eyes blank, his face a mask. He had a Chinese wife and three yellow children.'[5] Chang, gap-toothed with dark hair swept back, was apparently the son of a well-to-do Chinese businessman and he was sent to England in 1913 to pursue a commercial career or study medicine; accounts vary. Instead he opened a restaurant in Regent Street and started drug-trafficking on the side from his private suite. In a short time he was looked on as the leader of drug-traffickers in the West End. White women fascinated him and he trafficked in them. Those who attracted him would receive a note via a waiter.

Dear Unknown,

Please don't regard this as a liberty that I write to you. I am really unable to resist the temptation after having seen you so many times. I should extremely like to know you better and should be glad if you would do me the honour of meeting me one evening when we could have a little dinner or supper together. I do hope you will consent to this as it will give me great pleasure indeed, and in any case do not be cross with me for having written to you. Yours hopefully, Chang.[6]

Curiously, since these were clearly pre-printed and their recipients could not possibly think they had suddenly induced an irresistible urge for Chang to write to them, he had a high success rate. From there it was often a short step to drugs and degradation.

In 1917, several men in Birmingham were arrested with correspondence showing that Chang was a leader in the drug business, but although there was a period of police surveillance nothing came of it. Chang was almost certainly the supplier of the drugs which led to two well-publicised deaths. After the Victory Ball held in aid of the Nation's Fund for Nurses at the Albert Hall, Billie Carleton, a pretty young actress who had been addicted to drugs for a number of years, collapsed and died. Born in 1886, the illegitimate daughter of a chorus singer Margaret Stewart, she was described as:

a frail beauty and delicate . . . all of that perishable, moth like substance that does not last long in the wear and tear of this rough and ready world.[7]

In fact she was a tough young woman who had been one of Cochran's young ladies and appeared with Gertrude Lawrence and Bea Lillie in the revue *Some* at the Vaudeville Theatre in 1916. Along with the sinister Reggie de Veulle, she took parties to Limehouse where she was supplied with drugs by a Chinese, Lau Ping You, and his Scottish wife Ada, who had a house at the eastern end of Limehouse Causeway under the railway bridge which leads to the Isle of Dogs.

The inquest showed she had died of cocaine poisoning and was addicted to opium smoking. It was common knowledge that Chang had been a close friend but her companion of the night before had been Reggie de Veulle, described as having an 'effeminate face and mincing little smile' and who had designed Billie Carleton's gown for the ball. The son of a former British Vice Consul at Le Mans, de Veulle had been part of a scheme to blackmail William Cronshaw, a well-known homosexual of the time.[8] Prosecuted by Sir Richard Muir, he was lucky to be acquitted of Carleton's manslaughter but he received eight months' hard labour for supplying her with drugs. Ada Lau Ping received five months also for supply, whilst her husband was altogether more fortunate. Liable for deportation, he appeared in front of one of the few magistrates who thought that a little smoking was no worse than a glass or two of whisky and was fined £10.

Also attending the Carleton inquest was Sui Fong, later described as the Yellow Snake of the Underworld when he, Yong Yu and Long Chenk all received three months and were recommended for deportation at Marlborough Street. Fong's wife was described as an Austrian Jewess and Yong Yu had married an English girl. Fong had come over at the turn of the century as a steward on a liner and had been linked with one of the most spectacular gambling dens where, after the gaming had finished, orgies took place. He had been seen near the White Swan (known as Paddy's Goose), the celebrated public house on Radcliffe Highway, and was a marriage broker between the Chinese and English girls.

Then, on 6 March 1922, Freda Kempton, a dancing instructress, was found dead also from an overdose of cocaine. She was to have married a Manchester businessman the Monday after her death. A friend recalled that she had promised to give up dancing and the man had sent her money for clothes.[9]

This time Chang did feature; he had been with Freda the night before and faced a hostile series of questions at her inquest. 'She was a friend of mine, but I know nothing about the cocaine,' he told the coroner. He had given her money but not drugs. 'It is all a mystery to me.'

There was no mistaking the thrill that passed through the court room as the Chinaman in his matter-of-fact fashion referred to the bedroom incident and went on to speak of the present of £5 which he gave to the erring girl on that occasion.[10]

The coroner ruled that there was not sufficient evidence to link Chang with the death of Freda Kempton, but not before he had taken the opportunity of delivering a little homily:

> [It is] disgraceful that such a dangerous drug as cocaine should be handed about London helping to ruin the bodies and souls of inexperienced girls.

The jury recorded a verdict of 'suicide during temporary insanity'.

> When the jury returned the verdict Chang smiled broadly and quickly left the court. As he passed out several well-dressed girls patted his shoulder while one ran her fingers through his hair.[11]

In the flurry of unwelcome publicity after Freda Kempton's death, the police used two out-of-work dressmakers, Gertrude Lewis and Mabel Smith, to whom they paid £3 to act as undercover agents. Chang's premises at 107 Regent Street were frequently raided, and in one which netted six Chinese in West London four were found to be waiters at his restaurant. Eventually he sold his restaurant and, to the annoyance of the formidable Mrs Kate Meyrick – who had her own club at No. 43

and who certainly did not want police attention – became a partner in the Palm Court Club in Gerrard Street.[12] He then moved
to live and conduct his operations at 13 Limehouse Causeway.
The premises were almost derelict, with an unoccupied shop
on the ground floor, and he let out the second floor to Chinese
seamen. It was the middle floor which Chang used for himself
and which excited the public. The great bed was a 'divan of
luxury'. Silver dragons were everywhere, as was costly furniture
all derived – so the press and police said – through drug-dealing.
'This man would only sell drugs to a white girl if she gave herself
to him as well as paying.'

The method of dealing from there was simple. Couriers such
as Violet Payne, euphemistically described as a failed actress,
who had a number of aliases, bought the drugs in Limehouse
and took a taxi to the West End to sell them on. At the end of
May 1923 Paddington chemist James Burnby and his wife Mary
were convicted of supplying heroin to Payne. According to the
statement she had made to the police, over a period of years she
had taken stolen property to Mrs Burnby who had supplied her
with heroin and had allowed her to fix in the kitchen behind the
shop. One one occasion blood had sprayed all over the cooker
and Mrs Burnby had cried out, 'Don't die here.' When arrested,
she is alleged to have said, 'Oh, do overlook it this time for the
sake of my poor dear husband.'[13] She received six months and
he a mere two.

Brilliant Chang was arrested on 23 February 1924. The police
had been keeping watch on the Commercial Tavern public house
in Pennyfields and 15 Limehouse Causeway which was a Chinese
restaurant. Violet Payne had been seen to flit from one to the other
and when stopped she was found to be once more in possession of
drugs. When pressure was put on her, she mentioned his name. A
small packet containing cocaine was found under a loose board

in Chang's kitchen cupboard. Since he did not wish to alienate the Old Bailey jury and more particularly the judge, he ran the defence that it had been put there without his knowledge rather than that the police had planted it. The jury did not leave the box before convicting and he was sentenced to fourteen months in the Second Division and recommended for deportation. During his imprisonment he continued to be something of a thorn in the flesh of the authorities because although he could write in English perfectly well he insisted on writing in Chinese. Since none of the warders could read Mandarin and so censor his letters, they had to be sent to the Home Office for translation.

He was deported in April 1925, taken by cab to the Royal Albert Docks where his family had reserved him a suite on the boat. Whilst in prison he had been sent numerous letters from women friends, and he was allowed these but not to speak for long with the well-wishers. He left to calls of, 'Come back soon, Chang.' During his six-year reign in England it is estimated he made over £1 million from drugs-trafficking, most of which he had remitted home.

It was thought he might indeed be back.

Chinese physiognomy is practically a blank page to the average Englishman. They all seem alike. Chang may return as Han Fat Sang, his appearance slightly altered.[14]

Shortly after Chang's imprisonment Lily Brentano, whose real name was Rumble, said to have been living with him in Pennyfields, received six months' hard labour for dealing. No cocaine was found on her but she had been heard talking ambiguously with two women described as Big K and Brixton Peggy.

Now there were reports that he had disappeared when the ship docked at Marseilles, Port Said and again when it finally reached

China. At Marseilles a number of Chinese had gone on board when the ship docked and Chang had left with them, only to be spotted by a detective. In Port Said he disappeared completely.

After a spell in the East or Middle East he returned to Europe. There were then rumours that he had gone blind and that he had died, but it is thought that some of these were cover stories put about by himself. There were also reports that he had gone to Zurich, and was controlling the London drug traffic through his old accomplices, intending to flood the Thames Valley area. According to one source he was visiting a south coast town on a monthly basis aided by a new lieutenant, the Dutchman Henri Boom, who had been deported only a matter of weeks previously. He was certainly in Paris in the summer of 1927 because in September that year he was arrested after allegations that he was dealing in drugs and had been responsible for the disappearance of girls in the Latin Quarter. He was also suspected of setting up the rolling of clients by prostitutes. He was finally given bail in the sum of 200,000 francs and absconded along with a young woman called Suzanne Fichet with whom he had been living. In 1929, there were reports that he was wanted concerning the death of Minna Spermel, a German cabaret singer. He was also linked to the addiction of another actress, Marie Orska, who had been confined to a mental hospital after attacking her understudy with a knife.[15] What actually happened to Chang remains a mystery.

The British authorities had been convinced that with the compulsory retirement of Chang they had struck a major blow against cocaine and opium dealing and, if statistics do not lie, they were correct. Between 1921 and 1923 there were sixty-five cocaine prosecutions a year. The figure had dropped to five between 1927 and 1929. Over the same periods the opium prosecutions had declined from 148 to thirty-six.

Almost immediately after the conviction of Chang, down went one of his successors. Ah Wong had been his factotum when Chang was running the West End, and after his master and mentor had been driven to the East End he took over. It was thought that at the time of his conviction in June that year he was making £100 a week.

The next month the opium den of Chong Sing in Limehouse was raided. When the police burst through the door bells began to ring and the only two people in the house, described as 'such as might have been fashioned for the opium den of a mandarin', were Chong Sing and his brother New Mok Sing. There were a number of warm pipes, and the other smokers had disappeared through a series of secret passages. Chong Sing received three months' hard labour and was recommended for deportation. It was thought that his brother was not involved in dealing and he was fined £3 or twenty-one days. The fine was paid. The police believed they had finished another major dealer.

The public galleries of the magistrates' courts were invariably packed with members of the Chinese community when the drug and gaming cases were heard. Reports often speak of stoic English women, forever outcasts from their own society, watching the sentencing of their husbands. In his book of reminiscences of his life as a London magistrate, Horace Cancellor, who spent much of his time sitting at Thames Magistrates' Court before and after the First World War, wrote in his chapter 'The Heathen Chinee':

> Distasteful as such unions seem to our Western minds, the magistrates seldom receive complaints against husbands from white wives. On the other hand the women often give evidence to screen their yellow spouses and show in court that they have taken lessons in the art of lying from their lords and masters.

They appeared laden with jewellery. They were treated well unless they were perceived to fancy another man.

He was not alone in his dislike of mixed marriages. The Rev. W.H. Lax, who had a parish in Limehouse, displayed a singularly un-Christian attitude to some of his parishioners.

There is something inherently revolting about this union of European girls with black men or Asiatics, and by entering into such unions and marriages girls are fomenting a danger which, I am convinced, will give rise to a great conflagration in the future.

The Chinaman is a gregarious creature. He will not live alone. When an English girl takes on the responsibilities of a Chinaman's household she finds that he will bring ten or twenty men to the house.

He lives in a crowd. The crowd will probably live with him, and while it is not my desire to indulge in wild charges I am certain that these girls suffer a moral degradation which, in many cases, ends in their becoming the hireling of any Chinaman who happens to desire her.

The streets abound with little, slant-eyed babies with the high cheek-bones of the Celestial, yet possessing the pink-and-white colouring of their European mothers. This combination of Asiatic and European qualities is a grave menace to the peace and well-being of the community.[16]

But the magistrate Cancellor seems to have been fascinated by one particular man:

In the centre of the space a tall thin Chinaman always stood in the front row ... I felt sure that he was there for the set purpose of exerting will power on my mind.

He turned out to be the treasurer of the community, who came to pay the fines, but this did not satisfy Cancellor: 'No doubt he was trying to hypnotise me into making the penalties light.'

He nearly obtained his revenge when the man appeared in the dock on gaming charges and Cancellor saw it as the opportunity to send him to prison. Unfortunately he was only present and not taking part in the gaming, so the kindly magistrate was thwarted.[17]

All sorts of excuses were offered for possessing opium, mostly that it was used by the Chinese as an alleviation of consumption; but one of the most ingenious, if ultimately unsuccessful, was that of James David Jackson, a commission agent, who said his wife had picked up the bottle at Goodwood Races and after winning three bets decided it was a lucky charm and to keep it as a mascot. Six months.[18]

In July 1923 the police struck another blow to drug operations in the East End.

The negro rolled, struck, kicked and bit like a savage.

He looked like a beast of prey and almost foamed at the mouth ... the raving maniacal nigger was braceleted.[19]

This dispassionate account was of the arrest of Jack Kelson after buying cocaine from a Chinese café on Limehouse Causeway. At the time he was almost certainly operating for his superior, Eddie Manning. Kelson, who had been looked on as one of the safest runners between Limehouse and the West End, like Manning also dabbled in the white slave trade. Eddie Manning is often regarded as a successor to the Chang dynasty but in reality he was a contemporary. He was considered to be one of the Big Four dealers in the West End, obtaining his supplies from Limehouse. Born in Jamaica, his real name was McManning and he came to

England in around 1914, working as a labourer until 1916 when he was discharged for ill-health. He was then a jazz drummer and an actor in small-time touring reviews, at the same time running prostitutes and selling drugs from his flat in Lisle Street. The other three in the quartet were Alexander Iassonides, his wife Zenovia and his nephew Leonidhas. Unfortunately for the quartet Manning became fascinated by Madame Iassonides, by all accounts a striking woman who, much to the fury of her husband, eventually went to live with Manning.

In September 1920, Manning received a sentence of sixteen months for shooting at three men in a fracas at Cambridge Circus. If the witnesses can be relied on, Manning had been in Mrs Fox's Restaurant in Little Compton Street when 'American' Frank Miller – who was a pimp, and had just been acquitted at the Old Bailey of receiving – tried to extract, extort probably being too strong a word, £1 from him and insulted a girl by throwing a lighted cigar in her face. Manning chased after and shot at him and the others.

It was his first conviction and Mr Justice Greer took the view that he had been more sinned against than sinning, saying how much he regretted having to sentence a man of respectable character but that foreigners had to be taught that guns could not be discharged on London streets. Even then the police were not totally fooled. There was much more in the matter than met the eye, said the officer in the case. It may be that the men had been turned on Manning by the jealous Iassonides. Certainly that was suggested later. Two of the 'victims', Miller and Charles Turnick, said to be his brother, disappeared after giving evidence in the police court. Manning cannot have been doing too well at the time. He was living with a prostitute, Doreen Taylor, and some fifteen pawn tickets were found when her premises were searched.

On his release he went to live with Madame Iassonides, and

now cocaine injections at ten shillings each and lessons in how to apply the drug were available at the Berwick Street cellar café owned by the pair. On the side Manning ran prostitutes and also illegal and crooked roulette parties, as well as '... dope orgies [at his flat in Lisson Street] at which scenes of the wildest debauchery were witnessed'.[20]

He had also come to notice over the death of Freda Kempton, and now a former army officer, Eric Goodwin, died from a drug overdose at Manning's new flat in Hallam Street, Marylebone. He gave evidence at the inquest to the effect that he had never known Goodwin take drugs, but Manning was now well in the frame.

A successful police raid on Mrs Iassonides' flat at 33 Regent's Park Road in April 1922 resulted in her receiving six months and her deportation. She was followed in quick succession by her nephew in the September and the estranged Alexander the following March. He had survived one case when drugs were found beneath the stair carpet of the Soho café run by his nephew. A tame doctor appeared to give evidence, saying that Alexander was a kind man whom he could not conceive being involved in drugs. The magistrate said it would be unsafe to convict.[21]

Manning also received six months for the Regent's Park raid, but since he was British he could not be deported. After their release Madame I. and her nephew retreated to Paris from where she maintained a steady correspondence with Manning.

Just before the downfall of Kelson, Manning received three years' penal servitude for possession of opium, but he continued to survive if not to flourish for some years more. In 1927, he was fined for harbouring prostitutes and given six months for possessing cocaine. Then in 1929 he received what would be his final sentence. By now he too had been chased out of the drug-dealing world and was into receiving. Property worth £2,000, the result of a number of burglaries, was found at his flat. He was sentenced to another three years' penal servitude and died in E2 Ward at Parkhurst on the Isle of Wight, apparently from the ravages of syphilis. One of his great fears was of owls and when dying he heard one hoot. 'His body shook and his eyes rolled in abject terror.'[22]

Part of both the Manning and Chang empires passed into the control of William Allan Porter, who had been another pair of safe hands on the Limehouse run until, in December 1924, he was found with the equivalent of 2,000 doses of morphine on him and he received twelve months. He tried to bribe his co-defendant – a young Irishman, John Mason – to take the blame, and when the offer was turned down threatened to attack him in the dock. Porter had apparently always been a lieutenant rather than a captain and after his sentence he, too, faded into oblivion.

The so-called White Queen of Limehouse, May Roberts, was arrested at the end of December 1922 and charged with being in possession of black opium. She and an Albert Ellis were arrested at Ludgate Circus after a dramatic car chase through Trafalgar Square and along the Strand and Fleet Street. She had been followed since leaving her home in Limehouse. Ellis, a man of good character, appeared at Marlborough Street Police Court where conveniently at the back of the court he apparently said to the arresting officer, in the sort of remark which might well be regarded by the cynical as a 'verbal':

I have been a mug. I had best get it over. Can I be dealt with here? I don't mind getting a fine.

No doubt he did mind, however, when he received six months' imprisonment, as did the lady herself. In fact, Ellis had not been a mere mug. He had been actively engaged in the dope trade for several years along with his brother David Ernest Ellis and the sinister Max Faber, who eventually swindled the Ellis brothers and his Chinese partner with whom he ran a brothel in Hamburg, before retreating to Montreal. There he was known as Sheba Max and Big M, was the head of Maxie's Gang, and was an associate of some seriously big-time players. David Ellis had been convicted and fined in December 1915 on charges of illegally exporting opium.[23]

May Roberts was born and married in Liverpool. Before her marriage she had met Wun Loo, an assistant doctor on a ship, and after he had shown her Liverpool's Chinatown she became enamoured with him and left her husband. He died in a drug-dealer's fight, and her next amour was killed in Rotterdam either in a quarrel over drugs or possibly over her charms. She seems to have been a woman of immense character and some physical strength because she survived several attacks from other women and once when she had been swindled out of a drug deal went in search of her robbers with a gun. She is also credited with stopping the drug wars in Liverpool and putting together some sort of peace amongst the various gangs. At one stage it was suggested by the police that the distribution of the entire opium traffic out of England for consumption by the Chinese abroad was in her hands. Eventually she came to London where the newspapers referred to her as either the White Queen of Limehouse or the Queen of the Yellow Men.

In a reply which has all the hallmarks of the hand of an experienced journalist composing it, when asked about her predilection she said:

Whatever may be his faults the Chinaman has the power of fascinating a woman and of holding her in a way the White man cannot do. There is a subtle charm, a romance and a poetry about his lovemaking that makes the efforts of the average Westerner seem ridiculous. I have been told again and again that I ought not to have anything to do with Chinamen; that they have a degrading effect. I cannot see it. I prefer Chinamen to the Englishmen or other white men I have known. This preference may have its origin in some wild primitive instinct that may or may not be a reversion to a barbaric past as I have been told by a missionary, but the fact is that the preference is deeply ingrained in my soul and I cannot get away from it no matter how much I try ... I am not going to alter in this respect for anyone.[24]

When she was released from prison in the summer of 1923 she went to live back in Limehouse with another woman from Liverpool, Julia An Kitt, who had also married a Chinese, Choy An Kitt. It was all of five months before she in turn was arrested, claiming the drug had been planted. For a period she was regarded as the chief figure in running between the East and West Ends. She also had been born in Liverpool and ...

... for many years her worst fault was a flighty disposition and an insatiable thirst for the fleeting pleasures of life. No matter how carefully she chose her course, the moth that plays constantly near the flames of human passion must some day pay the penalty of scorched wings. And so it was with Julia. A man robbed her of her honour and then cast her aside like an old glove ... Presently she cut loose definitely from home ties and became a 'woman of the town'. She did not like any of the Chinese and Japanese seamen with whom she mixed, only accepting their admiration because it was profitable and with a secret feeling of contempt. But fate tricked her, for the lure of the Eastern character was stronger than her own will.[25]

She and Choy An Kitt had two children, and at first she acted as a runner for her husband before branching out on her own. Dressed as a poor Chinese woman, she would move around the Limehouse restaurants before changing into fashionable clothes for her visits to the West End.

Not long after that, Choy An Kitt left for Hamburg to conduct that end of operations as agent for Choy Loy with whose underling, Lum Chung, May Roberts now took up. An Kitt and Julia remained on good terms and he also supplied her with cocaine obtained from Germany which was much cheaper and on which she was able to make a profit of £10 an ounce. On a good evening she could handle one pound in weight. Along with Ellis, Julia An Kitt also received six months.

Running parallel with Brilliant Chang and Manning was the altogether more structured operation of the Japanese, Yasukichi 'Sess' Miyagawa. One account of his career has him as initially the tool of an international syndicate, ensnared by his fascination for white women which had led him into debt and so their clutches. He and his family had an import and export business on Ludgate Hill and this provided excellent cover for the repackaging of the drug. Miyagawa took over the English end of the business, importing from Germany and Switzerland and exporting to France, Japan and India, and again reimporting for consumption here. It was estimated that the contents of a 100 pound consignment could be disposed of within the hour. Given today's huge drug imports Miyagawa's efforts may seem puny, but he was exporting 500 pounds of morphine on a regular basis when the average quantity used per patient at the London Hospital was 8 ounces a year.

During October 1923 Miyagawa paid £37,000 to a Hamburg-based firm for heroin. He was also receiving substantial amounts of morphine from Switzerland and his monthly profits were thought to be in excess of £25,000, 'most of which was dissipated on a life of excess in the West End'.[26] Eventually morphine was seized at his premises in Ludgate Hill and he received four years at the Old Bailey, coupled with a recommendation that he be deported. His appeal was dismissed on 21 January 1924. He is described as:

[an] unassuming little Oriental, boots cracked and down at heel, a threadbare suit, and battered bowler hat, shuffling his melancholy way along the gutters of the East End. Spending but a few coppers on his meals in carmen's pull-ups, sleeping in cheap lodgings, and sometimes in doss-houses – not a detail overlooked in the part he so ably played, that of a down and out.

Yet Sess Miyagawa was a millionaire! Through a pair of horn-rimmed glasses a pair of soft brown eyes peered sadly and timidly. Who would have suspected that such a nonentity was a master criminal, the head and fount of a colossal narcotic trade employing hundreds of lesser crooks.[27]

The last of the old school to go was To Yit who lived at 32 Pennyfields. He had been around since the early 1920s and had been associated with practically every Chinese national who had been deported over the years. He had an English wife, Maud Alexandra, in Cane Hill Mental Hospital – admitted, it was said, as a result of his cruelty to her – and two sons.

In September 1929 he racked up the sixth of his convictions for drug and gaming offences but, because of his wife, the magistrate declined to deport him. The police raided his premises again in February 1930 and found nothing, but they then received a letter suggesting that they would find opium if they searched his other premises at 51 Pennyfields. Sunday around 4 p.m. was suggested as the optimum time. This time they struck lucky but, defended by a local solicitor, Edward Fail, To Yit was acquitted. The police agreed that the front door was always kept open and To Yit suggested that the drugs had been planted by the man downstairs who not only disliked him but wanted to take over the whole house. To add insult to injury the man, he said, ran English prostitutes from the basement.[28]

The magistrate may have had doubts but the Home Office had none. 'He is a worthless and particularly crafty type of Chinaman,' wrote an official, suggesting he be deported. What particularly worried them was not so much the opium smoking, although he was forever in clubs in the West End, but the fact that he ran a Fan Tan game at which the English lost their money at great speed.[29]

A. Maxwell, a Home Office official, wrote in a memorandum of 10 January 1933:

> Is To Yit the organising spirit, and are the people in the West End, his tools? Or is To Yit a tool for more important persons? If so, what are we doing about the more important persons?[30]

Clearly someone thought he was a mover and shaker for, after a short inquiry, along with his sons Edward and Alexander he was put on the SS *Glenamoy*, bound for Hong Kong, at 1 p.m. on 22 April at King George V Docks. Even then there were fears that To Yit might escape deportation. The boat was in a collision as it sailed down the Thames and had to return to the dock. Could the crafty Chinaman possibly have engineered this to effect his escape? The police hurried to the dock to make sure he stayed on board until the boat sailed the following Wednesday. After it did, a note was sent to the authorities in Hong Kong warning them of the impending arrival of this thoroughly unsavoury character.[31]

Not all Chinese kept their front doors open to welcome

customers. When Lai Chi (Chee)'s house at 17 Limehouse Causeway was raided in November 1929 the police had some trouble getting in. At the foot of the stairs there was an electric bell-push concealed under the linoleum. On the first floor there was a stout plank door across the staircase, locked and bolted. A trapdoor had been lowered over the staircase top and bolted with iron bolts. Lai Chi received the standard six months and was deported. The police were well pleased; they considered him to have been running a major opium den.[32]

But by now the authorities had cleared most of the large-scale Chinese dealers from the East End – that, or they had moved to other cities. For instance, one of the old Pennyfields school was found in Cardiff with a pound and a half of raw opium strapped in each armpit.

It may seem from the six-month sentences handed out at the time as compared with those convicted of drug-trafficking today that the courts dealt leniently with the inhabitants of Chinatown. But it was the deportation order which accompanied them rather than the almost tariff six months' hard labour, which was the real penalty. In financial terms the price of an ounce of cocaine was the annual wage of a girl in service, and those at the upper end of the trade such as Chang and Miyagawa made fortunes.

By the 1930s much of the drug trade in Europe was in the hands of the Eliopoulos family, Greeks from Alexandria of whom Elie was reputed to be the head and whose London offices seemed to be the Hellenic Club in Notting Hill. He was said to have been the chief accountant of the Constantinople Gasworks which he had defrauded. They had connections throughout Europe, not only with the East End dealers but with Paul Carbone in Marseilles and with the French concession in Shanghai, as well as links with the United States and Canada. The substantial hold of the Chinese on the East End drug trade had effectively been broken.[33]

One of the last survivors, Annie Lai, lived to feature in a television documentary. She had married Yuen Sing Lai in 1923 after arriving in Limehouse two years earlier. When he was deported to America following a conviction for wounding, she took up dealing, turned to the drug herself, became hooked and became a prostitute to support her habit. Apparently, her husband died in Hollywood in another fight shortly after his arrival. She maintained that there were prostitutes at Charlie Brown's pub, the Railway Tavern, but never in Chinatown. Many of her problems, she said, came from officials who expected her to repay their lack of interest in her dealing with sexual favours.[34]

Throughout the period there was an unhealthy trade in smuggling Chinese into the country. By the end of the 1920s the price was £50 a head.[35] By the end of the Second World War the Chinese had been largely absorbed into the East End community – if not socially, then as the main providers of alternative medicine.

In his articles in 1960 on the rebuilding of the East End, Tom Pocock thought that there was probably only one regular Chinese opium smoker left in Limehouse.[36] Others were perhaps not so sure:

> There was opium dens well after World War Two. Then in the sixties the Chinese moved up West. Before they moved to Soho they were a very strong force in the East End. They didn't sort of integrate, kept their own counsel. They'd go off to Gerrard Street to gamble. There was a lot of Chinese gambling down there.
>
> Then there was the Chinese herb shops. If you were ill you went to them to cure boils.[37]

NOTES

1. First quote: H. Thorogood *East of Aldgate*, p. 141. Second quote: Health Inspector Chambers Journal 81 (1904).

2. Annual Register, 26 July 1786.

3. Health Inspector in *Chambers Journal* 81 (1904), pp. 193–5.

4. Cecil Bishop, *Women and Crime;* 'Secret Chief' in *Empire News*, 10 October 1920.

5. *Daily Express*, 11 April 1924.

6. One of the letters is in a file on the Chinese and the drug trade, Nat. Arch. MEPO 3 469.

7. *Sunday Pictorial*, 1 December 1918.

8. *The Times*, 13 December 1918; *News of the World*, 15 December 1918.

9. *News of the World*, 30 April 1922. Other demi-mondaines of the period who died through drugs included Audrey Harrison and Vacera Steane. In April 1926 Violet Kempton, Freda's sister, alleged that her sister had been deliberately poisoned. 'Queer disclosures in Drug Tragedy' in *Empire News*, 4 April 1926.

10. 'The White Girl and the Chinaman' in *Empire News*, 30 April 1922.

11. *News of the World*, 30 April 1922.

12. Kate Meyrick was one of the most notorious night-club owners of the period. She served a number of terms of imprisonment and was a partner of the corrupt police sergeant George Goddard who would warn her of impending raids and who in 1929 received two years for conspiracy to pervert the course of justice. Mrs Meyrick becomes 'Ma' Maybrick in Evelyn Waugh's *Brideshead Revisited*.

13. *Empire News*, 27 May 1923.

14. *Empire News*, 5 April 1925; *East End News*, 6 May 1924.

15. See *World's Pictorial News*, 19 April 1924; *Empire News*, 14 November 1926; 22 May, 11, 15 September 1927; 8 September 1929; *John Bull*, 13 February 1926.

16. Rev. W.H. Lax, 'The Lure of Gambling' in *Empire News*, 3 October 1920. On the other hand Cyril Demarne writes, 'They seemed to be happy marriages and Chinamen could be seen playing with their children in the street on warm summer evenings.' 'The way it was – the recollections of a Poplar boy' in *East End – Then and Now*, p. 99. Annie Lai says that there were only three Chinese married women in Limehouse in the late 1920s.

17. H.L. Cancellor, 'The Heathen Chinee' in *The Life of a London Beak*, pp. 61 *et seq.*

18. *Empire News*, 29 July 1923.

19. *Empire News*, 29 July 1923. This was fairly typical reporting of the time. In the issue of 9 September that year, 'In black clutches at seaport towns', Rosie Sherella, who had drifted into Limehouse and bigamously married a series of men, concluded her story of degradation with the words, 'I am safe from the black man now forever.' Overall the popular papers offered an almost undiluted hostile and racist approach. For example girls were forever telling of their ordeals in Chinese laundries; e.g. 'In a Chinaman's House' in *Empire News*, 17 October 1920, 'Drugging Mystery of Chinese Laundry' in *Empire News*, 26 November 1922 and Lily Siddall, 'My Experiences in a Chinese Laundry' in *Empire News*, 3 December 1922. Miss Siddall had the misfortune to be employed in the Sheffield laundry in which Lee Doon killed the owner Sing Lee. In fact it was her worries over the disappearance of her employer which caused the police to make serious inquiries. For an account of the case see J.P. Bean, *Crime in Sheffield*. Even when the girls did not tell their stories but merely appeared in court to support their husbands and lovers, they were described in terms such as 'Vice was written plainly in their dimming eyes and whitened cheeks' in 'Menace of Darkness' in *Empire News*, 12 September 1920.

20. 'The Dark Tempter of Chorus Girls' in *Empire News*, 22 July 1923.

21. *News of the World*, 15 October 1922.

22. 'Black Dope King's Spell over White Women' in *Empire News*, 15 September 1929. Val Davis, *Phenomena in Crime*, p. 90. For an account of the Cambridge Circus shooting see also Nat. Arch. MEPO 3 424.

23. Nat. Arch. MEPO 3 469. For an account of the early days of crime in Montreal see James Morton, *Gangland International*.

24. 'White Queen of Yellow Dope Smugglers: Mystery of Woman's Strange Choice' in *Reynolds' News*, 14 January 1923. See also *Empire News*, 31 December 1922 and *Reynolds' News*, 7 January 1923. Another girl involved in the trade and who began her career as a lure for seamen so they could be robbed was Lily Ellis, who in October 1920 received five years for burglary and was regarded as one of the best thieves of the period. *Empire News*, 3 October 1920.

25. 'Snow Queen from East to West End' in *Empire News*, 2 December 1923.

26. *Reynolds' News*, 16 December 1923.

27. Val Davis, *Phenomena in Crime*, p. 92. Davis met Miyagawa during his sentence in Dartmoor. See also 'Evil Negro Caught' in *News of the World*, 22 July 1923. According to Davis, Miyagawa was succeeded by the German Loffenholtz Brandstaetter. If so Brandstaetter had a long run. He was found hanged in his cabin whilst being extradited to New York in the summer of 1936. This followed information given by Marie de Wendt or Marie Wenn, daughter of a German father and Chinese mother, after she had been picked up by the San Francisco police trying to import opium and had escaped to New York where she was arrested trying to impersonate a passenger on an English liner. See *New York Times*, 11, 14, 30 August; 5 September 1936.

28. There was often a good deal of money available to be spent on defence. For example, on 5 August 1921 J.G. Jones KC MP appeared on behalf of a Low Ping You accused of frequenting rather than running an opium den.

29. Fan Tan, a game played at enormous speed, depends on the total

number of buttons or counters left in a jar after a series of with-drawals of four at a time. Another game played at the time in Chinese gambling clubs, and about which the kindly Reverend Lax complained, was Peccapur or Puk-a-pu, meaning plucking pigeons, which was a form of lottery. Stakes were sixpence upwards and prizes of £25 were not uncommon. Cyril Demarne recalls that as a boy he would be sent to place bets in Puk-a-pu gambling shops. See 'The way it was – the recollections of a Poplar boy' in *East End – Then and Now*, pp. 98–9.

30. In fact, in one of its less anti-Celestial moods, the *Empire News* had posed this question thirteen years earlier: '... the men who control the traffic are not Chinese, they are Jew and Gentile scum.' 'Brain of the Secret "Dope" Traffic' in *Empire News*, 3 October 1920. It may have been Faber and the Ellis brothers to whom they were referring. Another East Ender, Monty Cohen, was a candidate for being behind the trade. A known associate of Manning and Madame Iassonides, in September 1923 he received four years' penal servitude, the longest sentence so far handed out for trafficking. Instead of solely preying on women he had used unemployed former servicemen, paying them £1 a day to distribute the drugs. See 'Women Slaves of Snow King' in *Empire News*, 16 September 1923.

31. Nat. Arch. MEPO 3 1049.

32. Nat. Arch. MEPO 3 434. For other accounts of devices to keep the police at bay see *Evening Standard*, 15 November 1929; *Daily Express*, 16 November 1929; and *The Star*, 18 February 1930.

33. Nat. Arch. MEPO 3 1047.

34. See *East End News*, 14 February 1930. She may well have been cor-rect about Charlie Brown's public house. Although he was a popular figure in the East End there were stories about gentlemen visiting the back rooms to meet with live exhibits. One of his possessions was the opium pipe Billie Carleton used before her death, and it was questioned from where he had obtained the item.

35. 'Traffic in Human Cargoes' in *Empire News*, 12 February 1928.
36. Tom Pocock, 'The New East End' in *Evening Standard*, 17 November 1960.
37. Michael Bailey: conversation with the author, April 1999.

8

THE RISE OF JACK SPOT

The rise of Jack Spot to be one of the two Kings of the Underworld in the immediate post-War era – the other was Billy Hill – can be traced to the mid-1930s and the rise of Sir Oswald Mosley's British Union of Fascists.

Born Jacob Comacho, which was later informally changed to Colmore and then Comer, on 12 April 1912 he made his name and his career on a myth.

Far better known as Jack Spot – either (he said) because he was always on hand if you were in a spot or, probably more likely if more prosaically, because of a mole on his face – he built his whole career on a story which, unbelievably, no one bothered to check for half a century. He had, he said, led a Jewish contingent which broke up a march on 4 October 1936 led by Sir Oswald through the East End of London – the so-called Battle of Cable Street. Using a club made from a hollowed-out chair leg replaced with aluminium, he had felled Mosley's bodyguard, the all-in wrestler King Curtis known as Roughneck. He had armed his long-term friends Moishe Goldstein and Bernie Schackter and together they scattered Fascists left and right until he was finally overpowered and clubbed unconscious. He was taken to hospital for a week at the end of which he was charged. His wife, the former Mollie Simpson, tried to see him but she missed visiting time. He had no money and the local Communist party paid for a solicitor. Unfortunately, instead of defending Spot, in court the solicitor ranted on about the prosecution and urged the Police Commissioner to ban Fascist marches. Spot was convicted and received six months.

It was all lies. There was no march. Mosley and his men remained on one side of a cordon as the police battled the anti-fascist element. When told to, Mosley's men obediently trotted off towards the Strand. Spot was never arrested and therefore there was no jail sentence. Nevertheless he made his reputation out of the incident, billing himself as a champion of the Jews – which he undoubtedly was – someone who would protect them. He undoubtedly did but it cost small shopkeepers and stall-holders a weekly fee.

His parents, Alexander and Rifka, were Polish Jews who had met and married in the East End. Alexander could not speak English. Spot was the youngest of four children. There were two older brothers, Piza and Irving, and a sister, Rebecca. Myrdle Street, Whitechapel, which ran parallel with the Romford Road, where they lived, was never the best address in the East End and times were hard for the immigrant Jewish and Irish communities in the early days of the twentieth century. 'It was dirt poor. You didn't earn enough to pay the six shillings a week rent,' said Gerry Parker, one of Spot's henchmen.

One brother was a tailor, his sister a dressmaker. After he left school, for a time he became a bookie's runner and he ran a typical fairground scam called *Take a Pick* at the major race meetings. The mug punters paid 6d to pull a straw with a winning number from a cup. If they were extremely fortunate they won a cheap prize while Spot cleared between £30 and £40 a day. Later the enterprise was extended to Petticoat Lane where *Take a Pick* earned him another £50 a morning. He was also an active bookmaker on the free courses. On a bad day he welshed, leaving before paying out on the last race.

The next year he joined forces with a leading figure of East End protection rackets. Strictly small-time, together they protected the Sunday-morning stall-holders in Petticoat Lane. He fell out with the man and they fought, leaving Spot the winner. Now he called himself the King of Aldgate. Whatever else has been said about him, he was a good fighter.

A contemporary recalls:

> Spotty wasn't a coward. I met him many times and by then he'd had some fucking terrible seeing to's. Jews weren't liked in the East End and Spot was known by the Jewish mob as a protector. There wasn't a Jew straight or crooked in the East End who didn't know Spot and if a Jew was in trouble he sent for him. On a Sunday I used to see the Jewish stall-holders at a café across from Ziggy shouting out in their Jewish accents, 'Is Jacky Spot in here?' They would be queueing up to give him various sums of money which was for what he called Market Traders Associations but which was then just protection money.

As a youth he drew two small convictions for loitering with intent to steal from motor cars in 1933, and in 1935 he was bound over for housebreaking. His only prison sentence was in April 1939 when he and his henchmen, Morrie Goldstein – known as Blueball because of the colour of one of his testicles – and Bernie Schackter were charged with grievous bodily harm. They had been running protection rackets in the East End and two of their victims were Hyman Jacob and Spot's one-time friend Nathaniel 'Itchky' Simmons. The Lord Mayor, then allowed to sit as a single magistrate, thought there was a doubt in Goldstein's case and discharged him. Spot and Schackter each received six months and that was when fighting broke out. Spot tried to get out of the dock and there were fights in the well of the court. Eventually the police broke up the fracas and managed to get them into the cells. There was more fighting outside the court.[1]

When he was released he became an enforcer, collecting subscriptions for an East End Stall Traders Fund run by Larry Sooper. This was a private association formed by stall owners who kept the Depression at bay by refusing to let any other new trader break in and set up a stall.[2]

Spot claimed it was while he was serving his sentence that he came to the notice of the one-eared – it had been bitten off in a fight – Arthur Skurry from West Ham and earned this very hard man's approval. Over the years Spot forged an alliance with the Upton Park gypsies who generally 'protected' small market stall-holders. Fighters they may have been but they were not smart and as the War ended the Upton Park Mob, with luminaries such as Skurry, Teddy Machin, Porky Bennett and Jackie Reynolds, effectively became Spot's boys.

His reign in the East End was not without skirmishes. The father of Bernie Perkoff, who established the fashionable London firm of solicitors Peters & Peters which represented Spot throughout most of his career, ran The Windmill, a pub in Whitechapel patronised by Spot in his earlier days and which was once wrecked by the Sabinis looking for him.

One of the many things held against him by supporters of the alternative king, Billy Hill, was his readiness to take his disputes to the courts. He may well have taken a beating from time to time as well as handing them out, but he would also enlist the aid of the police to prosecute his assailants. Frank Fraser remembered:

In 1948 Teddy Machin took a chopper to Jimmy Wooder at Ascot Races for Spotty. It was all part of a long feud. Before the war him and another beat Spot up and he nicked them, and both got some bird. That wasn't enough for Spot. In 1943 he cut Jimmy Wooder in a club in the East End, a very bad cut. Of course Jimmy didn't nick him but from then on Jimmy could never stop talking about how Spot had give evidence. That day at the races Jimmy was working on the bookmaker's box and Teddy Machin just started cutting him off at the ankles. Jimmy never nicked him and he didn't retaliate neither. Spot was really above Billy at the time and Jimmy Wooder just didn't have the power himself or anyone to go to for help.[3]

Unlike many major criminals of the time Spot had actually served in the War with the Royal Artillery stationed in Cornwall. Annoyed he was not given a commission, Spot raged on about how demeaning and wasteful it was for a man of his ability being obliged, for three years to shine his boots and buttons, to suffer from a sergeant's temper and to take orders from 'pasty-faced little runts with officer's pips'. Fight followed fight and he gained a reputation as a trouble maker. Eventually, following a short time with the Marines, he was sent to see a psychiatrist who recommended him for a medical discharge in 1943. He returned to the East End to find his parents dead and his brothers and sister scattered. One brother was, in fact, serving in the RAF.

Now, it is impossible to trace the accuracy of most of Spot's stories but, according to him, he gravitated to the West End where in November that year he became involved in a fight with a man named 'Edgware Sam' – in all Spot's stories the men are Manchester Mike, Bristol Bert and so on – in the grandly named Piccadilly Club, in reality a spieler in the Edgware Road. Spot's henchman Gerry Parker was told that the quarrel was over the serious matter of who should be served their tea and butty first. Other accounts suggest there was anti-Semitic bullying of the barman over not putting enough sugar in Sam's tea, which certainly makes for a more heroic account. Spot intervened and, after knocking Edgware Sam down, hit him with the metal teapot. Sam ran out of the club, some said to get a gun.

Whether Spot believed this or thought that Sam had gone to the police, he feared a prison sentence and, advised by his friend and mentor, the London club owner and receiver Abe Kosky, fled north to a land where the black market and organised crime were rampant. Goods were being stolen from the ships at Hull docks and the cash had to be spent somewhere.

Where illegal gaming and drinking clubs are established, protection is sure to follow. According to Spot, he helped a club owner, Jack Marks known as Milky, of the Regal Gaming Club in Brunswick Street, Chapeltown, Leeds, to clear out a Polish protection racketeer from his club, became the owner's body-guard and, as a reward, was given a pitch at the local greyhound track. Next he dealt severely with an ex-coalman who seemed to believe he had a no-loss betting account, expecting payment when he won and his losses to be erased. Spot swiftly disabused him. He also dealt with Liverpool Jack, said to be the leader of the toughest gang in Leeds, and apparently another formidable man 'London Alf' who was in the North at the time. Whether these men existed or were merely later good stories for the Sunday newspapers is a moot point. He certainly went to Leeds where local recollections of what happened differ from his own.

Whichever version is correct, from then on Spot's future in Leeds was assured. He undertook to protect members of the local Jewish business community against anti-Semitism and he certainly brokered a partnership between a leading northern bookie and Abe Kosky.

He also worked as what he described as a 'troubleshooter' for various other northern clubs until he heard Edgware Sam had been jailed for fraud. Perhaps fraud is too grand a word. It seems to have been for working the tweedle, a short-time con trick of taking a ring into a jewellers for valuation and then declining to sell it. At the last moment the grifter changes his or her mind and offers the ring once more. This time, however, the ring appraised by the jeweller has been switched and he is now offered a fake in the hope he will not bother to examine it a second time. In any event Spot returned to London, pleaded self-defence to the assault charge and was acquitted.

Now he was in great demand. He was regularly called back to the North to help club owners in the major cities.

The old spot man, Gerry Parker recalled:

In Manchester the old bookmaker Gus Demmy wanted a pitch and he couldn't get one. The man who was running them wouldn't talk to him. Jack called a meeting with him in the Midland Hotel and asked why his 'cousin' couldn't have a pitch. Everyone was Jack's 'cousin'. Jack gave him a dig – and remember a lot of big men can't punch their weight but Jack was well over six foot and 17 stone and he could. After that Gus got his pitch and Jack was made.

According to Spot's account of his life he assisted in establishing the proper allocation of pitches at northern bookmaking tracks, having to deal with such as 'Fred, leader of a big mob in Newcastle' along the way:

Newcastle Fred was not only a gangster but a racecourse operator as well. He thought he had the say-so on flogging out bookmakers' pitches, but he made a mistake when he tried to get nasty with me and a few of my pals at Pontefract races. There was a battle ... a proper free for all, and we had settled it before the police and racecourse officials got wise to it. We'd settled Newcastle Fred's business too.[4]

There were other accounts of the story including one from an eyewitness. One bookmaker recorded:

What Spot doesn't tell is that old Fred celebrated his 65th birthday a few days before Spot bravely kicked him with his pointed shoes into the racecourse dirt covered in blood. That's how courageous Spot was.[5]

Again it is difficult to assess the accuracy of the story. It could be said that the bookmaker who had 'scars tearing across the top of his scalp – relics of the days when he had to fight the slashing gangs who terrorised Britain's racetracks between the wars', was not wholly disinterested. He was Harry White, the son of Alf White who had challenged the Sabinis during the 1930s.

Spot had trouble in getting a pitch for himself at Doncaster races, having to stand up to another racecourse bully, and later claimed he assisted officials in the North to allocate pitches in a fairer way. It was something he maintained stood him in good stead when there were similar troubles at Ascot shortly after the War.

He was also well regarded in Birmingham and he moved, as required, between the cities. Spot was certainly back in London by the end of 1944 when, with the bombing over, things gradually returned to normal and with normality came the opportunities beloved by any criminal. In his book *Jack Spot, The Man of a Thousand Cuts,* echoing Billy Hill's earlier memoirs, he claimed modestly that:

I was the first man to realise that criminals could be organised, each crook becoming a small part of a master plan in which every cog and spindle operated perfectly.

I became the planner and master mind.

I became the Boss of the Underworld!

It was this sort of attitude which would eventually lead to his downfall, but for the moment things went accordingly and by the end of the War Spot was doing very well for himself. He claimed he had met with the American gangster Sam Clynes, said to be a former member of Murder Incorporated, and received a good deal of advice from the great man. The advice included how to treat members of his team if they went to prison. Clynes suggested a weekly pension of £20 for wives at a time when a policeman's wage was between £9 and £11. After Clynes' death he had, he said, paid for a funeral service and a headstone. As for the wives' pension unfortunately too often Spot failed to pay and in turn paid the penalty for it.

One problem with this story is that it is another almost total fabrication. The name Clynes is probably an amalgamation of James Hynes and Harry Kleintz. Hynes was certainly an American and, it was claimed, he was shot when the gangster 'Little Augie' Orgen was killed. Later, together with Kleintz, he came to England where, following a robbery on a jewellers, they both received five years on 28 June 1928 at Newcastle Assizes. Further long sentences followed and Hynes died in Parkhurst on 12 April 1943. Spot can never have met him. But why should that get in the way of a good story?

What was much more accurate was that Spot was running Botolph's, a gaming club masquerading as the Aldgate Fruit Exchange in the daytime, on behalf of Abe Kosky, now a black market millionaire, and running it extremely profitably. During the daytime, clerks in white collars and bowler hats arrived at their desks. At 5 p.m. they put on their hats and coats and left and the transformation began. The desks were shifted into an ante-room, the blinds were pulled down and soft lights were switched on. By 7 o'clock the place had been turned into what Spot described as 'the biggest gambling club London had ever known'. Play continued until 7 o'clock the next morning. 'We never had an argument much less a fight'. This was not surprising because apart from Spot, on the door was the fearsome Arthur Skurry who, despite fearing 'he would look like a poof', had been persuaded to exchange his cap and choker for a suit. The fact that half an ear had been bitten off only enhanced his status.

If there was a big winner Spot would arrange for him to be seen home by little Hymie Rosen, Moishe 'Blueball' Goldstein or George Wood. Quite apart from the pretence of masquerading as the Aldgate Fruit Exchange the real reason Spot's club stayed open and untouched was that huge sums were being paid weekly in bribes to the police.

It was reputedly taking £3,000 a week tax-free from illegal gambling. The figure may be accurate; certainly large sums of money changed hands there. George Stanley, the solicitors' clerk who claimed to have laundered the Great Train Robbery money, remembered:

There was a burglar known as Taters [George Chatham], best screwsman in London. He once went out and did a job, pulled in £7,000 and then went and did it all in a night playing chemmy with a Jewish bookmaker in Spot's club in Aldgate. It was a straight game but mugs always want to beat the finest and they never succeed. Tragedy really.

'We didn't serve drinks,' said Spot, 'drinks interfere with business and they can lead to people taking liberties or starting a battle.'

Kosky was born Abraham Schliman Cohen in August 1905 in Goodman's Fields, Hackney. His parents were Russian Jewish immigrants and Abraham was the oldest of four children, all sons.

He started his life working in a café but when, in September 1928, Kosky appeared at Old Street Magistrates' Court charged with frequenting a common gaming house, the New Criterion Club in Hanbury Street, he gave his occupation as jeweller.

In 1937, Kosky married Rosina Alice Aldridge but in the November, now a bookmaker's clerk, he lost control of a car that he had bought for £10 earlier that day. He hit seven people at a tram stop at the junction of Theobald's Road and Gray's Inn Road. Two men died from their injuries. Kosky was uninsured and Mr Justice Humphreys, who considered it the worst case he had heard, sentenced him to eighteen months' imprisonment.

In late 1947 Kosky was on the up and he moved to Bedford Court Mansions near Russell Square where he lived until his death. In October 1957, his first daughter Myra, a mannequin, married the property developer Eric Merton Miller. When the *Jewish Chronicle* announced their engagement, Kosky gave his occupation as 'turf accountant'.

Kosky, who had links to jewel dealers George Miesl and Matty Constantino in Hatton Garden as well as links to the New York Mafia, died aged sixty-two on 13 September 1967 at Hôtel Le Provençal, in Juan-les-Pins. According to the *Jewish Chronicle*, his estate was worth c.£39,000 before the payment of death duties.

The links with the Mafia may have been fragile. Bert Rossi, the old London villain, recalled:

Dino Cellini told me one day that once Meyer Lansky asked Abe Kosky to do him a favour. There was someone of theirs over here in a bit of trouble and Kosky got the charges dropped. Angelo Bruno said how much and Kosky named a figure which they thought was over the top for what he'd done so he was invited over to Las Vegas. Wined and dined, Abe saw reason and it was all sorted out but Dino said if he hadn't listened his grave was already dug.[6]

Spot, who saw himself as a Jewish Godfather in the East End, left a modest account of how his version of protection worked:

I didn't have to buy nothing. Every Jewish businessman in London made me clothes, give me money, food, drink, everything. Because I was what they call a legend to the Jews. Anywhere they had trouble – anti-Semitic trouble – I was sent for: Manchester, Glasgow, anywhere. Some crook go into a Jewish shop, says gimme clothes and a few quid, the local rabbi says, 'Go down London and find Jack Spot. Get Jack, he'll know what to do'. So they did and I'd go up and chin a few bastards. The Robin Hood of the East End. A couple of taxi drivers told me once, 'You helped everyone,' they said.[7]

After separating from the Sabinis the White family had had control of bookmakers' pitches on the free course at Ascot, Epsom, Brighton and at the point-to-point races, not yet under the aegis of the Jockey Club and the National Hunt Committee. It was an arrangement that had been going for more than thirty years.

During that time Alf White, Harry's father, had been collecting £2 a pitch from each bookmaker working at the point-to-points, something which went as a 'voluntary contribution' to the hunt committees which organised the meetings. Later Harry White expanded the job to include keeping out

welshers and pickpockets as well as a more structured organisation of the pitches. It was apparently a semi-formal arrangement
which appealed to police, hunt committees and, no doubt,
to Mr White.

Now Spot took over. First he dealt with the ageing Eddie
Raimo who had beaten up a Jewish bookmaker at Yarmouth
Races. Then another White man, Johnny Warren, mocked Spot
over the fact he was drinking lemonade in a Soho public house.
Spot followed him to the lavatory and knocked him about.
'Bump. Down in the piss he went,' he recalled.

There was another fight, this time at the point-to-point
races at Bletchley in February 1947. With little difficulty Spot
cleared the decks: the £2 pitch fee became £7. For the next
eight years he exercised such strict control over point-to-point
bookmaking that, for example, at the Puckeridge Hunt meeting in 1955 he refused to let betting take place on the Grand
National which was broadcast to the meeting over loudspeak-
ers. Meanwhile Harry White paid him 25 per cent of his
winnings.

Exactly how the denouement happened depends upon the version preferred. This is Harry White's account as related by Sidney
Williams in the *Daily Herald*:

His fear of Spot began in January 1947 in a club in Sackville
Street, off Piccadilly. He was drinking with racehorse trainer
Tim O'Sullivan and a third man.

Spot walked in with ten thugs, went straight up to Harry and
said, 'You're Yiddified' – meaning he was anti-Jewish.

White denied it. He said: 'I have Jewish people among my
best friends.' Spot wouldn't listen, and hit him with a bottle.
As White collapsed in a pool of blood, the rest of Spot's men
attacked O'Sullivan and the third man who was employed by

White. O'Sullivan was beaten unconscious and pushed into a fire in the corner of the club. The other man was slashed with razors and stabbed in the stomach.[8]

It is not totally surprising that Spot's version of events is a different one. His account in the *Daily Sketch* read:

But the biggest, toughest and most ruthless mob was the King's Cross gang, led by a bookmaker named Harry who had taken over the racecourse protection racket from the Sabini Boys. Their word was law, not only on the racecourses but in the clubs and pubs – even in the fashionable night-clubs of the West End.

He goes on to record that in an unnamed Mayfair club a challenge was thrown down and the King's Cross Mob 'partly wrecked' the place. A few nights later the 'same crowd' returned and were told that Jack Spot was a friend of the Guv'nor. 'F–– Jack Spot,' came the answer. 'He doesn't work for us – when we want him we'll call him.' There were other encounters until:

We finally ran them down at a place in Sackville Street off Piccadilly. Harry had seven of the toughest of his boys with him when I led my pals into the room. There wasn't any politeness this time. They knew what I'd come for. And I sailed right in.

At the first smack I took at them Harry scarpered. You couldn't see the seat of his trousers for dust . . .[9]

Clearly they are both talking about the same incident.

Later Spot met up with Teddy Machin, George Wood and Hymie Rosen and they went to Al Burnett's Stork Club in Sackville Street where Harry White and, said Spot, seven of his men were drinking. Spot knocked White down and in the ensuing fight Billy Goller had his throat badly cut. In the days when the death penalty was in force Spot had forgotten his own maxim, 'You must never cut below the line here, cause, if you do, you cut the jugular – and the hangman is waiting.' Spot was rushed down to Southend and hidden away in Benny Swan's B52 Club at the end of the airport runway while Goller was given the last rites. Amazingly he survived but it was not until he recovered and was paid off that Spot returned to London. When he did he went to see Harry White and said he now wanted 30 per cent of his racecourse takings.

By now Billy Hill had been released from his sentence for a fur robbery – Spot had met him at the prison gates – and it was time to oust the Whites. According to both Hill and Spot, they were finally routed in early July 1947. There had been a previously scheduled meeting as a preliminary to the main event at the Baski–Woodcock fight at Harringay Arena on 8 April that year, but the police had wind of this and had warned both sides to stay out of trouble. Now, according to both Spot and Hill, huge armies were summoned and searched for the Whites. In Spot's tale Harry simply vanished and the gang faded away. Hill has a rather more colourful version which included graphic accounts of the autumn 1947 battle in which the Whites are chased out of town; one man roasted on a fire.

In their respective biographies naturally each man plays a more heroic part in his version of the story, with a triumphant Spot telling his men, 'Get rid of the ironmongery'. As a result Sten guns, grenades, revolvers and ammunition were dumped in the Thames far from the prying eyes of Scotland Yard.

The West End now had new owners who ran it for nearly a decade. Hill and, to a lesser extent, Spot were essentially businessmen. Accommodations could be reached with anyone and since neither had any serious interest in vice it was easy to continue the *laissez-faire* arrangement with the prostitute-running Messina brothers.

> They were peaceful and highly profitable years in 1950 and 1951. Visitors and strangers must have found the West End a rather dull place with no running gang-fights and feuds ... The truth was that we cleared all the cheap racketeers out. There was no longer any blacking of club owners and restaurant keepers. In fact so peaceful did it all become that there was no gravy left for the small timers.[10]

NOTES

1. Mansion House Register 1939; *East London Observer*, 6 April 1939.
2. Hank Jansen, *Jack Spot, Man of a Thousand Cuts*.
3. Frank Fraser, *Mad Frank and Friends*.
4. *Daily Sketch*, 29 September 1958.
5. *Daily Herald*, 8 October 1955.
6. Bert Rossi, *The Last Godfather*.
7. Michael Ewing: *Evening Standard*, 6 January 1986.
8. *Daily Herald*, 3 October 1955.
9. *Daily Sketch*, 3 October 1955.
10. Billy Hill, *Boss of Britain's Underworld*.

9

WARTIME

Amongst East Enders, along with other docklanders and to a lesser extent other communities, the Second World War not only produced incredible heroism in the face of repeated bombing which resulted in the destruction of their homes, but also ushered in a new attitude amongst those who would not normally have consorted with criminals.

In terms of Wartime criminality the East End was really no different from other cities in Britain. It shared the problems of pilfering from the docks with Glasgow, Liverpool and Belfast. Edward Smithies, in his *Crime in Wartime,* lists the types of crime committed, adding only the black market to the usual suspects – theft, betting and gaming, prostitution and violence. In theory, under the Defence of the Realm Act, the looting of buildings carried the death penalty, but in practice deterrent sentences of up to five years were being passed in 1942.

The *Police Review* thundered against the looters as being 'Human Ghouls ready to profit from the suffering of their fellow men and women'.[1] Its columnist, 'Watchman', went on to remark on the increase in the number of women criminals during the first years of the War, something which had been in decline for some years. The women were charged with looting and fraud. 'Watchman' wished to see a flogging for a first offence and shooting for the second or third.[2] Smithies, however, gives the crime only two brief mentions, pointing out that of 228 cases in the Romford area some 43 per cent were carried out by men in official positions or positions of trust such as ARP (Air Raid Precautions) wardens, police and auxiliary firemen. One of the reasons for the relatively small numbers was that the authorities had anticipated the looting of bombed buildings and consequently had committed their resources to guarding them, leaving unbombed factories and warehouses at the mercy of thieves.[3] So breaking and entering increased during the last years of the War.

It was clear that there was an inordinate amount of pilfering from the workplace, to a great deal of which employers turned a blind eye. It was only when the level became unacceptable and, later in the War, companies were required to account more closely for the raw materials they obtained, that the losers began prosecuting. In the early years of the War, in the Hackney area alone, those firms and organisations which suffered included the ARP and borough councils, Ever Ready, tobacco companies, milk depots, London Transport, Bovril, the Post Office, Berger Paints, the Co-op, cinemas and the Metropolitan Police canteens. At the Ever Ready plant in Stoke Newington 13,000 batteries were stolen during a five-week period in 1941. Paint from Bergers, which cost thirty shillings a gallon retail, sold for fifteen shillings with four shillings going to the insiders. A group known as the Silver Ring was clearing £40 a week. At Shoreditch Sanitary Towels a whole shift of girls was stopped at the exit and their bags searched.[4]

It was not, of course, a phenomenon unique to the area, but with rationing and food shortages it created whole new markets in which the criminal and quasi-criminal could flourish.

> If anyone could get a bit of extra bacon then they were involved
> in the black market. My wife she would go all the way to the
> Elephant [from the East End] to buy silk stockings if she heard
> there were some on offer.[5]

Alcohol and tobacco were prime requirements, as were clothing and material which otherwise required coupons, themselves a target. In 1942, a tobacco company based in Hackney was losing some two million cigarettes a year at a cost of about £8,000, at that time the price of a small row of houses. Some of these thefts were of course for personal use and some for small-time barter, but a very large percentage of the goods found their way onto the black market.

It was now that the target of the professional criminal changed. As Smithies points out, no longer was the private home of the rich man the prime target; now the factory, the warehouse and the distributive network were the objectives and the proceeds went to supply the black market. And those who worked the black market were often deserters; either British or, in the later years of the War, Canadian and American servicemen.

Once a man had deserted he became almost *ipso facto* a criminal, for he would no longer have access to ration books and he would be forced to the black market if he wished to survive. By 1947, it was estimated that there were some 20,000 British, let alone American and colonial, deserters. It would be impossible to say how many took to crime, but it must have been a high percentage.[6]

Of course, the call-up was there to be avoided and a salesman in Brick Lane with advanced heart disease not surprisingly obtained an exemption certificate. He turned his illness into a cottage industry and successfully impersonated nine people, relatives and friends before he was unmasked and sent to Borstal. He had obtained up to £200 a time but had lost his money gambling. Those he impersonated received two years' imprisonment.[7]

It was only a repetition of the pattern of behaviour during the First World War, according to Horace Cancellor:

> In the East End where young Russian Jews and Poles born of alien parents on British soil had acquired a British nationality they refused to obey the calls to colours and raised the plea of being conscientious objectors . . . by hook or by crook they mean to let the British soldiers fight for them and stick to their soft jobs in the markets of East London.

The hooks and crooks included the assistance of solicitors since their parents were wealthy; forgery of special certificates, lies about their ages and faking diseases. Cancellor recalls that towards the end of the War one young man was given albumen so that his organs might appear unsound. He was kept in custody for two days, by which time all traces had disappeared. He gave evidence against his doctors and one was acquitted at Quarter Sessions on appeal; he had been defended by an eminent King's Counsel. If all else failed, Cancellor believed they fled to Ireland where as a bonus there was still horse-racing.

One home-grown crime involving visiting servicemen took place at Ilford in 1944. When American servicemen came on leave from bases in East Anglia, a gang posing as taxi drivers would take them to a secluded area and rob them. They claimed that they had done so because 'it was so easy'. The ringleader was sentenced to twenty-one months' imprisonment.[8]

Perhaps because he did not wish to admit the extent of its existence Lord Woolton, the Wartime Minister of Food, was somewhat dismissive of the black market which went hand in hand with rationing:

> The penalties for infringements of the food regulations were
> literally ruinous ... and the consequence was that [black mar-
> keteering] became so perilous an occupation that few indeed
> dared to embark on it.[9]

In fact his Lordship was probably in a minority of one. The
essence of successful crime is that it is not detected. As for the
deterrent element, when pickpocketing was a capital offence it
was still going on at the foot of the gallows of those convicted
of the crime. Whilst black marketeering may never have reached
the heights it did in America, it was still a very worthwhile and
lucrative trade. It began to emerge in 1941 in Petticoat Lane and
flourished also in markets such as Romford and Chelmsford,
both of which had reasonably easy access to the East End.

Smithies gives Romford as an example of the attitude of the
authorities to the black market. Apart from a thriving market
in coupon-free clothing, it was a centre for black market food.
In theory the poultry on offer was for breeding, but a reporter
found that many of the birds were less than prime physical
specimens and, blind and unable to stand, were good only for
the pot. The controlled price in the shops was 1/10d, whilst in
the market it was 3/6d. Farmers from East Anglia and the purchasers from the East End had known each other from pre-War
days and it was not long before word was passed around and
West End restaurateurs turned – swiftly followed by pickpockets, thieves and three-card tricksters – to the market. For some
time prosecutions were scarce and fines imposed by magistrates
in no way a deterrent.

In sharp contrast to this was the case of a fifteen-year-old
whose mother had died some weeks previously. While her fire-
fighter father was out at work she inadvertently left the light on
in their home. Despite her father's plea that it was almost a week

of his wages, the local bench fined her £2. Following comment in the local paper, readers paid her fine.[10]

By the end of the War, black market goods available in the East End included the then exotic oranges and bananas, and people were prepared to pay a shilling an egg with no questions asked.[11]

The authorities were also desperately keen on saving. Those found betting could expect a severe ticking-off, with substantial fines for the promoters. The North London magistrate, Blake Odgers, commented in the case of a prosecution of a number of men betting on a boxing match at a Stoke Newington cinema:

> I think the wickedness of this sort of thing is that here we are in a war, and we have had to stick it for nearly six years. You, all of you, ought to know that every spare pound ought to go either to war savings or be put into the bank and here you are going off with hundreds of pounds between you to a boxing match . . . and not only betting yourselves, but encouraging other people to bet. I cannot help noticing that nearly all the defendants took the oath in the Jewish fashion and cannot help remembering what people of that race and creed have gone through during these years. I think it is disgusting that people of the same race and creed who have not had the bad time they have had should behave themselves in this way, instead of doing what they can to finish the war.[12]

And a month later, fining Hyam Hyams £25 for allowing betting on snooker at the Vogue Social Club, opposite Stoke Newington Police Station, the same magistrate said:

> Do you mean to say that in these days of national savings these men could find nothing better to do with their money than take it to this club?[13]

Throughout the pages of local newspapers faces old and new appeared. On 5 January 1944 Jack Comer, described as a doorman at the Apex Social Club, Beaumont Grove, was fined forty shillings along with his cousin Solly Kankus and another dozen or so punters who, when asked, chorused, 'We all plead guilty.' Two weeks later Mrs Ettie da Costa, the proprietress, was fined £250. On 3 May that year, William G. Kray along with seven others was fined five shillings for playing Two-Up in Worgate Street.

. Thomas Holland had 'Roll 'em Down' tables at a bombed-out site in Stockmar Road. His great offence was encouraging juveniles to play this old fairground game which paid odds of 4–1. The fear was, as with fruit machines at a later date, that they would become addicted and go on criminal sprees to obtain the necessary funds. Holland was fined £5 with an alternative of two months' imprisonment. His appeal that the wooden boards should not be destroyed in view of the Wartime shortage was granted by the stipendiary magistrate, Daniel Hopkin, on his undertaking not to use them for gaming.[14]

Generally there had been worries about fairgrounds being breeding places for crime and in 1941–42 the London Diocesan CETS undertook a survey of fairs in London, many of which were in Hackney and Stepney. They found that 71 per cent of patrons were youths under sixteen. One of the principal games was a crane which could pick up packs of cigarettes, which in turn could be sold back to the management. Unfortunately the survey found that it might cost eleven shillings to win four packs of cigarettes which could be sold for three shillings. The estimated profit on a crane game was 75 per cent.

In his foreword to the survey, the magistrate Basil L.Q. Henriques, who later had a street named after him, told how the previous week he had dealt with a boy who had stolen £20 from his employers, all of which had been spent gambling at a fair in Aldgate over two nights.[15]

Food hoarding and wasting were great sins. In the summer of 1942, Rose Denyer was given a two-month sentence by Rowland Thomas KC for wasting food.

> I regard this as a most revolting, disgusting and outrageous case. You look well fed, you are 35 years of age and I am assured there is nothing wrong with you mentally and yet, in these days, when men are giving their lives on the high seas in order to bring us food, you are wasting enough food to feed many families. It's no good fining you. I should not get the money. The only thing I can do – and I do it without hesitation – is to send you to prison, where you will be fed at the expense of the State, free to yourself and I am sure with no waste.

The Bethnal Green Food Officer had found twenty-five large and thirty-two small loaves in varying stages of mould on her table along with spoiled prunes, jam and margarine. In a cupboard there were a further seventeen loaves.

An essentially East End crime was associated with the docks: the bribery by the police of foreign sailors. On 24 June 1940, officers went to the Hotel Central in Aldgate High Street to see two Dutch seamen, Hermanus Sneek and Pieter van Teijligen from the SS *Kelbergen*. Neither had permits to be absent from their ship and they were arrested. At Bishopsgate police station while Sneek's fingerprints were being taken, he said that it was cheaper to stay at 'an Hotel' than to stay on the ship overnight. Asked what he meant, he said that on 20 June when he returned to the Victoria Docks with van Teijligen they had been stopped by a policeman inside the gate who had taken away their passes and then demanded fourteen shillings and twelve shillings respectively to get them back.

The next day they returned at 11.30 p.m. but the policeman said it was an hour late and that while he would let them in on this occasion in future he would charge £2. This appears to have been a steady little racket, with Dutch seamen handing over whatever change they had left at the end of an evening to gain entry to their ships. On one occasion a bottle of gin was extorted.

Both the seamen were discharged at Mansion House Justice Room and the victims now became valuable witnesses. The offences were denied by the officers, who were not picked out on an identification parade, but once the case of Sneek had come to court the game stopped. One constable was dismissed from the service and two had their pay reduced by five shillings a week for six months. Two others had their good conduct allowance of 2/6d withdrawn, and these and three other officers were transferred.[16]

One of the benefits to the wartime criminal, both amateur and professional, was that absences could be more readily explained by the bombing and bodies could be buried in the rubble. The one-time Mosley supporter Frederick Lawton, who went on to become a Lord Justice of Appeal, believed he owed his successful career to being in Lambeth Magistrates' Court at the moment when Harry Dobkin appeared, charged with the murder of his wife Rachel. Theirs had been an arranged marriage in 1920 and although a son was born it was not a marriage which was in any way a success.

They had separated three years after the marriage and Rachel Dobkin had obtained a maintenance order. Over the years Dobkin, a poor payer at best, served a number of short prison sentences designed to remind him of the necessity of keeping up the payments. When he was out and about he seems to have been violent towards her. She took out assault summonses on four occasions, but the magistrates dismissed them all.

The Dobkins met in a Dalston café for tea on Good Friday,

11 April 1941, and after they left, at about 6.30 p.m., Rachel was never seen again. The next day her sister reported her as missing, blaming Dobkin, but the police did not interview him until 16 April, the day after a small fire broke out in the cellar of the Baptist Church in Vauxhall Road, South London, where Dobkin was a fire-watcher. On 16 April, twenty-three people were killed when a land-mine was dropped 250 yards from the church, which had already been blitzed in August 1940. The police circulated a description of the missing Rachel Dobkin and there the matter rested.

Then on 17 July 1942 a workman demolishing the remains of the church found her body. Professor Keith Simpson, performing the post-mortem, discovered the hyroid bone had been fractured, signifying strangulation. Dobkin was arrested. At his trial much play was made on Rachel Dobson's height. The corpse was 5' 1", but there was some evidence that Rachel had been 5' 3". If this had been the case Dobkin would have been acquitted. Eventually Rachel's sister, who maintained she was the same height, was measured. In shoes she was 5' 1". The jury took only twenty minutes to return a verdict of guilty.

Lawton defended in another East End Wartime murder. Lilian Hartney was found dead at about 5 a.m. on 6 August 1945 in Rich Street with her feet pointing to Grenada Street. Her dress had been neatly folded back to her stomach as if to deliberately expose her pubic hair because she had on neither pants nor stockings. She had bite marks around her nipples which appeared to show that the biter had two teeth missing in the lower jaw. She had been strangled.

The prosecution case was that she had been killed by her consumptive husband, Patrick, who had tired of her being out in Chinatown night after night and who said she had taunted him that sexually he was 'no good'. From a patch of urine in the

matrimonial bed it was argued that she had been killed at home.
When the police called they found her husband fully dressed.
The major, probably the only, point to be made for the defence
was that this consumptive husband could not have carried his
wife's body 250 yards down the East India Dock Road and he
could easily have dumped her in a nearer air raid shelter. The jury
agreed with Lawton that he could not. In any event, although he
did not know it, Hartney had only a few months to live.[17]

NOTES

1. 'Watchman', 'More notes on the Blitz' in *Police Review*, 7
   February 1941.
2. *ibid.*
3. Edward Smithies, *Crime in Wartime*, pp. 49 and 53. The statistics
   are from the *Romford Recorder*, 31 January 1941. One such case in
   the area was a twenty-eight-year-old removal contractor who, found
   guilty of looting a house, received a year's hard labour. *Romford
   Record*, 3 January 1941.
4. ibid, p. 31. Melanie McGrath recalls her grandfather was an ARP
   warden who spent his nights fishing and poaching game in Essex. 'By
   the late forties he was the only cafe owner in the East End to drive a
   Cadillac.' 'In Grandfather's Footsteps' in the *Guardian Weekend*, 20
   September 1997.
5. Fred Bailey in conversation with the author. Bailey also recalls
   a remark made by a tenant whose flat he visited, commenting on a
   supply of meat: 'The butcher – he's shagged everybody in this block
   including me.'
6. John C. Spencer, *Crime and the Services*, p. 52.
7. *Brighton & Hove Gazette*, 29 June 1940.
8. *Ilford Recorder*, 5 October 1944.

9. Lord Woolton, *Memoirs*, pp. 230–31.

10. *Romford Recorder*, 3 and 10 January 1941. *Police Review* was appalled by the general lack of enthusiasm for fining thoughtless people who left lights on in the blackout, suggesting that 2/6d was derisory compared with the risk to life such behaviour engendered. *Police Review*, 17 January 1941.

11. *Hackney Gazette*, 22 March, 9 August 1946.

12. ibid, 28 March 1944.

13. ibid, 12 April 1944.

14. ibid, 23 February 1944.

15. London Diocesan CETS and Churches, *Commission on Gambling, Funfairs and Delinquency: A Survey in London 1941–42.*

16. Nat. Arch. MEPO 3 2341.

17. DPP 2 1452, CRIM 1/1754, MEPO 3/2303.

10

THE FALL OF JACK SPOT

The downfall of Jack Spot may have been a long time in coming, but when it came he fell like Lucifer. It can be traced back in time as far as 1948 and in distance to London Airport. Not necessarily correctly, Spot has been given the credit for planning the robbery but now it is doubted he had the intelligence to plan such an operation. The better view is that the putter-up was his employer, the unsung Abe Kosky.

Before that Jack had seen himself as very much the senior partner in the Billy Hill–Spot duo, helping Hill when he was on the run in 1947 after a spell in South Africa. Hill had returned to England after a fight in Johannesburg with the club owner Arnold Neville and had gone to ground in East Ham, then in the control of Arthur Skurry and the Upton Park Mob. That year Hill went North to Manchester to do a highly successful job with two of Spot's assistants, Sammy Josephs and the formidable Teddy Machin, also from Upton Park. Hill then gave himself up and served two years – to be met at the prison gates in 1949 by Spot, whose team had been severely weakened by the loss of a number of men following an unsuccessful bullion raid.

The job on 28 July 1948, which was to have been the first

major post-War robbery, took place at Heathrow Airport – then called Heath Row. Sammy Josephs had discovered that cargoes were kept overnight on a fairly regular basis and the target was the bonded warehouse which contained nearly £250,000 worth of goods including diamonds and was due to receive £1 million in gold the next day. The job had been meticulously laid out with inside help, and the gang maintained a twenty-four-hour watch on Heath Row over a two-month period. Dummy parcels were sent from Ireland and Franny Daniels checked they had arrived when, as an authorised driver, he was allowed in the customs sheds. Then a warehouseman approached Donald Fish, chief security officer of BOAC, to report that he had been offered £500 to dope the coffee of the warehouse staff. The Flying Squad was called in.

The plan had been to drug the guards at the warehouse and at first the raid seemed to go according to plan. The messenger with the tea was intercepted, and barbitone was dropped in the jug. But at the last minute the guards had been switched and replaced by members of the Flying Squad. The tea was put on one side and the three 'guards' lay on the floor seemingly unconscious. The members of the gang entered, hit one of the detectives with an iron bar to ensure he was unconscious and then took the keys from his pocket. At the same time other members of the Squad attacked the robbers. Of the detectives, John MacMillan had his nose broken and a robber broke DI Peter Sinclair's arm. Five of the gang escaped. Teddy Machin fell into a ditch, was knocked unconscious and as a result was overlooked in the search for the escapees; Franny Daniels held onto the underside of a van and instead of being dropped off at the first set of traffic lights as he hoped was carried to Harlesden police station from where he made his way home. Scorched by the exhaust, he carried the burn on his shoulder for the rest of his life. The great burglar Billy Benstead escaped.

Sir Gerald Dodson, the Recorder of London, had a field day:

All of you men set your minds and hands to this enterprise. You were, of course, playing for high stakes. You made sure of your position by being ready for any situation with weapons of all kinds. This is the gravity of the offence. A raid on this scale profoundly shocks society. You went prepared for violence and you got it. You got the worst of it and you can hardly complain.

Edward Hughes received twelve years' penal servitude, Sammy Ross one less, and Alfred Room of Ilford received ten years. The very respected Jimmy Wood of Manor Park collected nine. George Wallis (who was really George Wood, Jimmy's brother) and Sidney Cook of Stratford picked up eight, and William Ainsworth of Dagenham a more modest five years.

In the East End it was said that the betrayer of the scheme was the former wrestler Alf 'Man Mountain' Dean, who had also appeared as a film extra. Shortly before their release, Dean took to his bed, so it was said, to keep out of the way of those on whom he had informed:

He just laid there the rest of his life. He died a few years ago – a very wealthy man. By the end he'd got some skin disease and it just used to come off in flakes.[1]

It is difficult to accept the reason for Dean taking to his bed as gospel. After all, a number of men on the robbery had escaped capture and had not sought him out over the years. That he took to his bed is certainly correct, however. When he was charged with selling condemned Argentinian beef, a court was convened in his bedroom.

Everyone was selling it. There must have been a container full in
Romford market alone.[2]

Some of those captured lived to fight again, but Room
became more and more unbalanced during his imprisonment.
On 20 January 1956, the day before his eldest daughter's wedding, he attacked his wife and John Wirth at Wirth's newspaper
stall outside the main gate at Ford's Dagenham with a knife
and a hatchet. He then committed suicide on the spot by swal-
lowing a potassium cyanide capsule. Although he had worked
on the stall himself for a few days, he had believed his wife was
having an affair with Wirth and had tried to persuade him to
sack her. Room had already tried to set fire to his daughter's
trousseau.[3]

Those men on the airport were such a good firm; really getting
dough. They were organised and sensible and intelligent enough
to be doing very well. When they were nicked and so many
got such bird it took the heart out of their organisation. Teddy
Machin was never really the same after it. He was a Spot man.[4]

When the Wood brothers came out of prison they transferred their allegiance to Billy Hill. Billy Benstead had already
moved. As for Spot, the police could never prove that he was the
organiser, but his interests were disrupted and under pressure his
gambling club in St Botolph's Row was closed.

In contrast, the first successful major post-War robbery was
the Eastcastle Street Great Mailbag Robbery of 21 May 1952
when £287,000 in hard cash was stolen from a post office mail
van. According to Billy Hill, the night before the robbery nine
men, all of whom had been selected and warned of the raid the
week before, had been collected and taken to a flat in the West

End where they were locked in before being fully briefed on the operation. Hill set a precedent on the necessity for keeping a tight hold on his men – one which was adopted by Nipper Read when he came to arrest the Krays in 1969.

The robbery was carried out with immaculate precision. The mail van had been followed every night for months as it left on its journey to Oxford Street, and cars had been stolen specifically for the raid. In the early hours of Wednesday morning one of the team had disconnected the alarm system on the mail van whilst the staff were on their tea break. It was kept under observation when it went to Paddington Station, then once it left there a call was made to the West End flat. Four men climbed into one of the stolen cars, a green Vanguard, and the other four into the stolen two-and-a-half-litre Riley.

As the van turned into Eastcastle Street the two cars blocked the driver's path. Six men attacked the three post office workers and then drove off in the van, leaving them on the pavement. It was driven to Augustus Street in the City where the cash was transferred into boxes on a fruit lorry – belonging to Jack Gyp, who was minded by Sonny Sullivan, one of Hill's men – which had been left there earlier. Only thirteen out of a total of thirty-one bags had been taken. 'The thieves were surprised,' claimed the police.

According to Hill the remaining bags were left because there wasn't any more room in the lorry, which was driven to Spitalfields market and parked there before it was moved round to the Borough, Covent Garden, Stratford and back to Spitalfields before finally being unloaded. The stolen cars were left in Covent Garden.

At the time Hill was seriously suspected of the robbery and it is now generally accepted that he organised it. Rewards totalling £25,000 were put up by the insurance companies, but despite intense police activity for over a year – headed by Superintendent Bob Lee, then second-in-command of the Flying Squad – there were no charges.

Hill pulled off a second successful robbery when in 1954 his team robbed a bullion lorry in Lincoln's Inn Fields. Again the police met with little success in obtaining convictions.[5]

Now Hill was very much in the ascendancy whilst Spot was in serious decline. What had begun as a partnership if not a friendship turned to emnity. One of the reasons was their mutual love of publicity. The second and probably equally potent reason was that Hill had taken up with Phyllis 'Gypsy' Riley, leaving behind his wife Aggie Hill who ran the Modernaires Club in Greek Court off the Charing Cross Road (which once belonged to Spot) and the Cabinet Club in Gerrard Street. According to Underworld legend they went on holiday together in September 1951 with Spot and his beautiful Irish wife, Rita, to the South of France and the women did not hit it off at all. Rita, it was said, considered Phyllis socially well below her.

There are complaints in various quarters today that former (and possibly current) criminals are making money from writing their memoirs. It is as if this was a new phenomenon; it is not, of course. From the days when Dick Turpin was hanged on the Knavesmire after his ride to York, the public had taken a healthy or unhealthy interest in the lives real and imaginary of criminals, and the 1950s were no exception. Both Hill and Spot were keen that their lives as King or Boss of the Underworld should be recorded for posterity and no doubt a fee. Hill had the benefit of Duncan Webb of *The People* to set out his account of things. Spot used the columnist Arthur Helliwell of the same paper to say he was going to retire and go into 'legit business'.[6] He did not.

Instead, in September 1953 he was involved with Hill in the cutting to pieces of Tommy Smithson and the same month was

arrested for possessing an offensive weapon under the Prevention
of Crime Act which had just come into force. Spot claimed that
as a protector of small-time bookmakers it was essential he carried such a weapon, but his explanation was not accepted and
perhaps luckily he was fined only £50. Superintendent Herbert
Sparkes – who would soon fall foul losing a libel action brought
by the safe-breaker Alfie Hinds – was having a clear-up of the
West End and was happy with the result.

Spot was now on the slide. The Jockey Club was helping the
big credit bookmakers prepare for the legalisation of off-course
betting, and the smaller bookmaker and his protector were being
squeezed. He was not being helped by mass defections of his
troops to Hill, and worse, this one-time hardman was becoming something of a figure of fun. Married life and domesticity
were suiting him. Now he was being openly mocked that when
the baby cried he had to go home to look after it. In his book
Spot wrote:

Billy Hill was a friend of mine. But he had his own way of working. His own personal ambitions and his own ideas and plans;
ambitions and ideas can sometimes clash.

On another occasion:

I made Billy Hill. He wrote to me when he was in gaol, wanted
me to help him ... Then he got to be top over me. If it wasn't
for me he'd never have got there. I should've shot Billy Hill. I
really should.[7]

Hill had this to say of the deterioration in their relationship:

Jack was becoming insecure and a bit jealous of me. He was an older man, you see, and once he got this persecution complex he was impossible to work with any more.[8]

'The worst thing I ever did,' he told an acquaintance, 'was to give Jack £14,000 from the Eastcastle Street job.' In September 1954 'The Amazing Confessions of Billy Hill' began in *The People*. The following month in a fit of pique Spot committed one of the cardinal sins of the big-time criminal. He attacked a journalist. Unsurprisingly it was Duncan Webb who was the target of his unwanted attentions. On 21 October, Spot summoned him to The Horseshoe public house in Tottenham Court Road and taking him round the back gave him a beating, breaking his wrist. Webb sued for damages and on 18 November at Clerkenwell Magistrates' Court Spot was fined £50 for inflicting grievous bodily harm. More seriously, this led to an action in the High Court and to Spot's eventual bankruptcy.

There was still time for him to have his version of events published in the *Sunday Chronicle* before, in August 1955 – amidst worsening relations with Bert Marsh and Albert Dimes who had the foresight to see the coming of the betting shop and who were far better prepared than Spot – he determined on action and sought out the man whom he saw as the leader: Albert Dimes. It was an almost fatal error.

There is no doubt that by the summer of 1955 Spot's career as a gang leader was just about in ruins. Things had deteriorated so much that he feared for his pitches on the course at the Epsom Spring Meeting. Frank Fraser and another hardman Billy Blythe were now more closely aligned with Hill than he was, and they would be at the meeting. So he called on the Kray brothers in their billiard hall in the East End to seek help. The Krays were never keen on Spot, nor, it seems, he on them. They had their day at the races, their first outing into the upper echelons of

Underworld society. Since Fraser was then in Long Grove Mental Hospital there was no trouble. At the end of the meeting they took their money and drove off.

As for Spot, he lamented:

> At first little things went wrong. When a raid was carefully planned and schemed, something would go wrong at the last minute. The man detailed to steal the getaway car wouldn't be able to steal it or a bunch of skeleton keys that should have opened a door failed to do so at the crucial moment.
>
> The men who'd been responsible for these slip-ups had been bawled out. But they hadn't cried. Instead they'd walked straight out on me and got themselves a job with another organisation.[9]

Slowly he lost both his gang and his reputation. The word was out in the Underworld that he was a grass.

'We'd had his sheet pulled from the Yard,' said the daredevil safe-breaker Eddie Chapman, who had been released from prison during the War for work in German territory, 'and there it was for all to see.'

On the other hand Hill's friends and allies, including Chapman and ex-boxer George Walker (brother of Billy, who was to go on to found the Brent Walker group of companies and whose daughter married into the aristocracy) remained staunch.

Once splits occur in Underworld factions, even the slightest quarrel or perceived insult can trigger a string of repercussions. One such incident occurred in Manzi's restaurant off Leicester Square when one of Spot's men, Bill Diamond, gave Johnny Jackson, a man more aligned to Hill, a backhander. Such a public display caused both a loss of face and loss of patience.

At the Epsom August meeting he had a run in with Bert Marsh who wanted a return of the pitches. But the real trouble came on 11 August. Spot was in his drinking club, the Galahad in Charlotte Street, when he was told Albert Dimes wanted to see him.

They met on the corner of Frith Street and Old Compton Street and, seeing Spot had a knife, Dimes ran away. Now Spot made a serious tactical blunder. Instead of letting Dimes go and so lose face amongst the watching Italians, he chased after him. Dimes turned and they struggled for the knife. The fight moved into a fruit shop on the corner of Frith Street where they fought almost literally to the death until ironically the Jewish lady fruiterer, Bertha Hyams, broke up the fight by banging Spot over the head with a brass weighing pan. Spot staggered to a barber's shop usually used by Dimes where he collapsed. Dimes was picked up by Bert Marsh and driven to the Charing Cross Hospital. Spot went to the Middlesex. Their injuries were horrific. Spot had been stabbed over the left eye and in the cheek, neck and ear. He had four wounds in his arm and two in his chest, one of which penetrated a lung. Dimes needed twenty stitches in his forehead. He also had a wound in his thigh and a stab in his stomach had just failed to penetrate the abdominal cavity. Both were charged with affray and grievous bodily harm.

Frankie Fraser, who was a close friend of Albert Dimes, recalled:

Me and Eva's husband, Jimmy Brindle and Tony Nappi were up Albert's house at 22 River Street in Clerkenwell where he lived at that time to see how he was getting on and we went downstairs, opened the street door and there were the police come to arrest Albert. I wouldn't let them in and Jimmy and Tony stood straight behind me. They were trying to push in but then Albert heard what was going on and said it was all right, let them in. I asked what he wanted me to do and he said I was to see Bert Marsh and then see Bill.

Jimmy had a motor and I went straight to see Marsh. At the time he had an illegal bookmaker's pitch in Frith and Old Compton with his partner, a man called Buster. I told him on me own and Bert just said, 'Leave it to me.' That's when the police conveniently found the knife just off Soho Square, the very knife Spot had used. Bert had picked it up just after the fight. It was very important in Albert's favour. I'd went with Bert when he put it in the square and then went with Hilly. There was then an anonymous phone call and the knife was found. It was a moody of course.[10]

But, almost miraculously, eleven days later their wounds had sufficiently healed for their appearance before Marlborough Street Magistrates' Court charged with wounding with intent to commit grievous bodily harm and affray. Clearly the tradition of the Underworld that the common enemy was the police and that one member should not give evidence against another did not apply to their defending lawyers. Counsel for Dimes said his client had acted completely in self-defence after being attacked by 'this other murderous, treacherous rascal'. Bert Marsh, who just happened to have been in Frith Street at the time, and who could not now abide Spot, loyally gave evidence favouring Dimes and was roundly attacked for his pains. There was clearly a case to answer, said the magistrate; Spot and Dimes were committed for trial at the Old Bailey where they were prosecuted by Reggie Seaton, later to become Chairman of the Inner London Quarter Sessions.

The way Seaton put the case for the Crown was that Spot had started the attack and that Dimes had at some time in the struggle wrested the knife from him and had struck back, going far beyond the limits of self-defence.

The trials which followed were genuinely sensational. At first Mr Justice Glyn-Jones refused an application for separate trials, which, on the face of it, was reasonable. The defendants were charged with making an affray. Unfortunately he had what would be described, in the world of Spot and Dimes, as 'a touch of the seconds'. The next day he asked counsel for Spot, Rose Heilbron, who was later to become the second woman High Court judge, and G.D. 'Khaki' Roberts, a doyen of the Bar acting for Dimes, what they had to say about making an affray in a public place.

Roberts argued that the reactions of a man fighting for his life could never be described as making an affray. Reggie Seaton for the Crown, accepting that view, then tried to take the affray into the greengrocery shop itself where the fight had ended. If, he argued, it was a public place, then Dimes' conduct after he had wrested the knife from Spot was capable of being an affray. This was not a view accepted by the judge, who withdrew the charge of affray against both Spot and Dimes from the jury and told them that, if they wished, they could acquit Dimes on the charge of wounding Spot:

> It is not for Dimes to prove that he was acting in self-defence. It is for the prosecution to prove that he was not.

The jury was not convinced and in the circumstances Glyn-Jones discharged them, saying that, 'A joint trial without the first charge would not be lawful.' He then directed Dimes be acquitted of possessing an offensive weapon, gave him bail and remanded Spot in custody. The separate trial of Spot was fixed to take place forty-eight hours later.

On 22 September Spot went into the witness-box to say that he had gone to Frith Street to meet Dimes following a telephone call which warned him off racecourses. He told the jury that he paid £300 for the pitches and, keeping one for himself, let the rest out at a fee. Now Dimes had told him, 'This is your final warning! I don't want you to go racing any more,' adding that he had been going on long enough and it was time someone else had his pitches. As for the fight:

> We started pushing each other. All of a sudden he pulls a knife out and makes stabs at me. I put my arm up, and it goes through my arm. I fight my way back to the door of the greengrocer's shop. He goes at me again and gets me in the face.

So far as he was concerned Dimes received his injuries in the struggle.

There was a witness to corroborate this version of events: a decorated Polish war hero Christopher Glinski, then an interpreter, who a decade later would feature in the Richardson Torture Trials and a number of other criminal cases both for and against the prosecution. Spot was right, he said:

> I saw Spot push the other man. Then the other man charged him. The other man took a knife out of his pocket. The man in the dock lifted his arms to defend himself. I saw the knife cut into his arm. Then I saw another blow cut his face ...

Glinski had got in touch with Peters & Peters, Spot's solicitors, after reading the reports of the magistrates' court committal proceedings and realising they did not tally with what he had seen. But there was more, and better, to come.

The eighty-eight-year-old Rev. Basil Claude Andrews came to court to say exactly the same thing. He was sure the darker man (Dimes) had attacked the fairer one (Spot). Although reporter Arthur Tietjen remarked to a colleague 'Anyone can see the old villain's bent', on the face of it here was an unimpeachable eyewitness. In scenes of triumph and jubilation Spot was acquitted. Immediately afterwards in a separate trial Dimes too was acquitted.[11]

But retribution was to follow. The police were informed by disgruntled bookmakers and friends of Dimes that far from being a saintly old man the Reverend Basil was an old rascal who welshed on his bets. His only course of action was to go to a newspaper, the *Daily Sketch*, longtime supporters of Spot, to publish his side of the story:

> I am fully aware that cowardly people who dare not come forward into the light of day are suggesting that I am a fraudulent witness and that I hoodwinked Mr Comer's [Spot's] legal advisers.
>
> I would recall to you that when I gave my evidence last week I gave it on my solemn oath, and I need not remind you that I am a Clerk in Holy Orders.

He went on to deny he had committed perjury, adding:

> Any financial difficulties due to my changes of address and my harmless flutters in the sporting world are only temporary, due to my age and inexperience.
>
> Those who are dunning me will soon be repaid if they have patience – some debts have been settled already.
>
> My innocent walk in Frith Street, Soho, that day has made me finish up in a nest of trouble, with enemies in an Underworld I never dreamed existed.

And for good measure:

> I would like to bring about a reconciliation between the parties in the strife who seem to have forgotten that, by what they have done, they are debasing the sacred Brotherhood of Man.

By the end of the year the Reverend Basil was back in the Old Bailey giving evidence, this time on behalf of the prosecution. The police, unhappy about the collapse of the Spot–Dimes case, had been busying themselves and now brought a prosecution for conspiracy to pervert the course of justice. Andrews admitted that he had given his evidence following a meeting with Bernard Schackter and Morrie Goldstein in the Cumberland Hotel at Marble Arch. His reward had been £25. The Reverend Basil was again believed. Goldstein was sent to prison for three years, Schackter for two, whilst Rita Comer, Spot's wife, was fined £50. No one seems to have thought twice about Glinski. They did, however, consider adding Bernie Perkoff, Spot's solicitor, to the charge of conspiracy – but in the end wiser counsel prevailed.

After the trial Spot announced that he was quitting Soho and the racecourses. He would, he said, open a small café. He would have been fortunate if he had done so. Soho was up for grabs once more, though Dimes does not appear to have been too interested. Meanwhile Ronnie Kray shot up a club in the depths of Italian territory. Dimes took over Spot's point-to-point interests. Newspapers reported that there were five major gangs each seeking to put their top man into the position vacated by Spot. Frank Fraser, along with Eddie Richardson, brother of Charlie, was re-establishing his business of putting gaming machines into Soho clubs. Billy Hill had now returned from Australia; he had decided to emigrate there but was refused entry when he turned up with Gypsy Riley. Curiously, however, the outbreak of gang violence anticipated with some relish by the press never quite reached all-out war.

However, there were to be further reprisals against Spot, who knew from rumours in the Underworld that he was due for punishment and repeatedly went to Paddington Police Station seeking protection. Nipper Read recalls:

He started by talking to Peter Beveridge, the Detective Chief Superintendent of the District, and worked his way down through the Detective Inspector and various sergeants until he ended up with me. He told me on numerous occasions that the other mob was going to do him and he often pleaded with me to do something about it, but as I pointed out unless there was more direct evidence there was nothing we could do. As a betting man Jack must have known that it was 6/4 on that he would become a victim eventually but it would have been impossible to offer him any sort of protection against a situation he had manufactured himself.

When the police could not help, Spot rented himself a personal bodyguard, Joe Cannon, the minder at the Miramar Club where he drank, paying him £50 a week.

Spot had thought seriously about buying a pub in Paddington and on 2 May 1956 he and Rita had been to look at the Little Weston off Praed Street when at about 9 p.m. they were attacked by a number of armed men. Spot was knocked to the ground with a shillelagh – recognised by his wife as one which in happier days he had given to Billy Hill – kicked and slashed. In hospital he made a statement giving the names of his attackers but later retracted it. Rita was made of sterner stuff; she named Frank Fraser and Bobby Warren as leaders of the attack. Both Hill and Dimes were arrested and questioned but never charged.

But where was Spot's minder, Joe Cannon, a man who had been in Portland Borstal, although rather later in time than another former pupil, Billy Hill? Spot had told him that he was taking Rita out for a meal in the Edgware Road and to meet him back at the flat. Cannon had taken his girlfriend Ellen out for the night and had forgotten the time:

... when I looked at my watch it was one o'clock in the morning, long past the time when I was due to meet Jack and Rita. Still, there was no use crying over spilt milk, so I spent the rest of the night with Ellen.

In a way I was lucky. If I had been with Jack when he made his way home I would have been dead or, at best, seriously injured ...[12]

After the attack and once it was realised that this was a police matter, there were the usual out-of-court negotiations. It was arranged that Cannon should go to Hill's office at Warren Street, just off Tottenham Court Road. According to his memoirs Cannon took the precaution of taking a .45 revolver with him to the rendezvous where he met Hill and Albert Dimes. The message he was to convey was that Spot knew Rita was set on going to court but that he, Jack, would talk her out of it. The *quid pro quo* was that Hill should stop the escalating aggravation between them. Hill was not pleased, telling Cannon that Spot was a wrong 'un and that he would get the same treatment if he remained his man. Indeed, it was only the kindly intervention of Frankie Fraser who put in a good word for Cannon which had kept him unmarked so far.

Dimes appears to have been the potential peacemaker. All that mattered now was that no one was arrested. Could Cannon fix it so that a couple of the Hill boys could get in to Spot's bedside so things could be agreed in person? One problem was the police sitting by his bed. The negotiator, Jimmy Wood, went with Cannon to the hospital and in whispers it was agreed that there was no point in nicking Fraser and the rest. Jack said he would persuade Rita not to go ahead. So far as Spot knew it was a genuine settlement negotiated by interested but not involved parties. As he was leaving, Wood was asked by Spot, antennae twitching, whether he had seen Hill recently. 'Haven't seen him for months,' was the reply. Unfortunately, instead of waiting for Cannon and Wood at the Fifty-One Club as arranged, Hill had come to the hospital where he was photographed with Wood and Cannon. Cannon and Spot realised they had been set up.

Fraser went to Ireland until matters had, so he thought, died down. He was only lured back when the police let it be known that the matter was closed and he was arrested at London Airport on his return.

Nevertheless, once the trial began Spot tried to do his best for his attackers. 'I do not recognise these men,' he told the court. 'I know that these men did not attack me.'

But Rita was quite prepared to go through with it. She was cross-examined vigorously by Patrick Marrinan on behalf of Bobby Warren, who put it to her that she was giving evidence to get rid of Hill, Dimes and friends so as to re-establish her husband as 'King of the Underworld'.

'I don't care about the other people. I just want to be left alone with my husband and children,' she replied, after earlier saying, 'I would be very happy if they let my husband and me alone. I'd like him to get just a small job.'

Was it right, Marrinan asked her, that on the day after the attack she had telephoned a Mrs Harry White and said, 'I'm going to get your husband ten years. I saw him with a knife in his hand stab my husband last night'?

'No,' she replied; she had said, 'I suppose you and your husband are pleased now.'

Harry White certainly must have been.[13] After the Spot–Dimes fight he had given an interview to his old friend Sidney Williams, spitting on the floor as he said: 'That's how frightened we are of Jack Spot and his men now. He hasn't got five men he can rely on to stand at his back.'[14]

Frankie Fraser – who by then had fifteen convictions and who had twice been certified 'insane' – had, said his counsel John Ritchie, been made use of by other persons for a foul purpose. Warren, with no convictions for violence, received the same seven-year sentence as Fraser.

On 11 July 'Billy Boy' Blythe and Robert Rossi were to appear to answer for the attack on Spot, and later William 'Ginger' Dennis joined them at the Old Bailey. Blythe received five years and the others four apiece.

Over the years there have been considerable doubts concerning Rita Comer's identification of the men who attacked her. Various of the convicted have claimed responsibility and exonerated the others but it now seems to have been a badge of honour to have been on the attack.

By now Jack Spot was himself back in the dock at the Old Bailey, accused of attacking 'Big Tommy' Thomas Falco, a driver for Dimes, outside the Astor Club, home of the brave, on 20 June 1956. Falco, who said, 'I work for Albert Dimes when we go to the races ... When he wins, I get wages,' had acquired forty-seven stitches as a result of this attack and maintained that as Spot had slashed him he had said, 'This is one for Albert ...'

A witness, ex-boxer Johnny Rice, who gave his occupation as a steel merchant but who was photographed within a few days on a bookmaker's stand at Brighton Races along with Tommy Falco and Harry White, remembered it as, 'This is one for Albert Dimes.'

At the committal proceedings, James Dunlop for Spot said of the allegation that 'it is a complete and utter fabrication from start to finish'. He would, he said, be calling a witness who had volunteered first-hand information.

The whole story came out at Spot's trial at the Central Criminal Court when that witness, Victor 'Scarface Jock' Russo, came to give evidence. He had, he said, been offered £500 by Albert Dimes to allow himself to be slashed so that Spot could be framed. The offer had come in a car in Frith Street. He had gone there and met Dimes, Hill, Franny Daniels and Johnny Rice after a back-room meeting at Peter Mario's restaurant in Gerrard Street, Soho. There Hill had said to Duncan Webb, the crime reporter, 'I want you to have a go at Spot this week,' and Webb had agreed to write up something to Spot's detriment in *The People*. How would they know that Spot did not have a cast-iron alibi? 'I will get Kye-Kye (Sid Kiki, a bookmaker) to find out,' said Hill. Russo had thought it over and then declined. Later he had heard of the slashing of Falco. When Spot had been arrested Russo had both gone to the police and telephoned Billy Hill telling him what he had done.

Hill gave evidence denying Russo's allegation. Almost all he would admit to was being Boss of the Underworld. Afterwards he held a press conference saying that Fraser and Warren were his boys and complaining that the police watched him day and night. Spot was duly acquitted and Hill was asked, would he make peace with Spot?

'I am a powerful man,' he said, 'and I don't have to make peace with anyone.'[15]

Spot went downhill. Webb obtained damages of £732 and costs in March 1956 and pressed for the money. On his bankruptcy examination Spot maintained that his memory had gone through too many bangs on the head. He had liabilities of £12,321 and assets of £125. He and Rita were evicted from their Hyde Park Mansions flat. He obtained his discharge in January 1957 and later that year with her earnings from newspapers – shortly after the attack she had been paid £300 by the *Daily Express* for posing with her husband – she opened the Highball Club in Bayswater.

In March 1957 Gypsy Riley was accused of attacking Arthur Ranns in the Miramar Club in Paddington. She was acquitted after the magistrate said the evidence was confused and whilst there had undoubtedly been a fracas he could not say who exactly was to blame. She had been defended by Patrick Marrinan (who regularly appeared for the Hill team) in one of his last cases before he was disbarred. It was generally thought that the fracas had been to show Spot that he no longer controlled Paddington.

Bayswater was not a success. Whilst still under police guard it was set ablaze on 13 August. It never reopened.

On 4 September 1957 Spot went to Canada on the *Colombia* travelling tourist class. He was seen off in Liverpool by Rita and the story was that he was going to see his sick brother in Winnipeg. After Spot sailed, Rita went back to Dublin. It was a quick visit for both because he arrived back in England on 15 September. Information had been sent by Scotland Yard to the Canadian authorities. Even before the boat docked Canadian immigration had announced there would be a full inquiry the moment he landed. Spot claimed to be an agent for a fruit and clothing firm in London but a deportation order against him followed shortly. The suggestion was he had been planning to open a chain of illegal betting shops.

He then drifted into employment as a meat packer working for J. Lyons at Cadby Hall, West London. He had also set up a second business selling stolen meat to local restaurants. He was finally caught stealing £1.10 shillings worth of bacon and was fined £2 after telling the West London magistrate 'I am sorry this has happened. I lost my job because of it. I have to look for another.' He omitted to mention a furniture shop in which he had an interest.

Known as the Professor, Spot had been popular amongst

his workmates. One man recalled him giving demonstrations of bookies' tic-tac, market spiels and showing them how to spot double folded notes, and the stab wounds over his body. Physically, however, the work had tired him.

He became estranged from Rita and once again changed his name, this time to Comacho. Over the years he could be seen at small-hall boxing tournaments in London, as perky and ebullient as in his prime.

One aspect of the bankruptcy is that it shows the depth of the slump in his fortunes that Spot was unable to raise the money. Perceived wisdom is that the acquittal in the Falco slashing case saw the end of his business interests in both the West and East Ends. It may be that this was something put about by Hill and the Italians but, on this occasion, perceived wisdom was wrong. Spot may not have been the force he had been but he still had a considerable number of interests. For a start there was the 41 Club on the corner of Dean and Greek Street, the home for some current and up-and-coming Soho faces, and the protection of hot-dog stalls in the West End. Then there was the Jewish connection in Petticoat Lane. Mickey Bailey, the East End face, recalled that even after the trials:

> They couldn't give him money quick enough. It was all, 'Where's Spotty?' Spot would sit and someone would write figures in the book. It was all one pound notes and half quids. It was protection.

Just how much control Spot did exercise is debatable. He claimed to have united the gangs from as far apart as Upton Park and Aldgate in the East, Forest Hill and the Elephant and Castle in the South, through to Islington, Shepherd's Bush and Clerkenwell. Possibly he never even aspired to 'running' Soho which was, at the time, synonymous with the 'Underworld', although he had clubs there and took a cut of £200 a week from another. He held court in the Galahad Club off the Tottenham Court Road. He was a family man living at Hyde Park Mansions in Bayswater with his beautiful wife, Rita, whom he had met at Haydock Park races and who had, for years, stood by him through the troubles which came his way. Perhaps, as has been said, he was too happily married to be a proper gang leader. Yet at his peak he maintained a style reminiscent of the American gangsters of the 1930s.

The crime reporter Michael Jacobson thought little of him:

I knew Spotty well and he was never more than just a thug. He had no initiative of his own. He was never a gang leader. Hill was.

On the other hand, Nipper Read, who as a young officer at Paddington knew Spot, thought quite well of him:

By the 1950s he was something of a grand old man. He had mellowed since his early days and was now well groomed with well tailored, usually brown suits, a brown fedora hat and hand-made shoes. He would leave his flat, walk across the road to his barbers and then down to the Cumberland Hotel where at a table in the corner of the Bear Garden he would hold court offering advice and wisdom to anyone who sought it. He looked like a successful businessman. He seemed to have modelled himself on the American *mafioso*, Frank Costello, but had neither that man's intellect, power or political connections.[16]

Later, in retirement, Spot would admit his mistake, one made by others before and after him:

The papers. All that 'King of the Underworld' thing. It was the worst day's work I ever did. Nobody even knew me before that and then suddenly everyone's trying to put one on me. That was my mistake, Nipper, publicity.[17]

His biographer, the American pulp writer Hank Jansen, perceptively thought there were other, more fundamental, reasons for Spot's downfall, which

... was *not* caused by authority, Spot's downfall was caused by his own inordinate pride, a touch of persecution mania and an unwillingness to admit he could be bested.[18]

Whatever the reasons, all this left a vacancy amongst the Jewish community in the East End and it was partially filled by Harry Abrahams. A contemporary says:

He was the sort of successor to Spot as far as the Jews were concerned but he never used the power he could have. His father had fought as Joe Brahams in the thirties and forties. Harry would have been world champion if he'd ever been in the ring.

Abrahams, who had worked on robberies with the Krays' self-styled lieutenant Albert Donoghue, was regarded as a quiet but hard man; a thief to start with and then acquiring a reputation in the East End. His father had owned the Wentworth Club in Mile End around the corner from the Krays' billiard hall.

There was a fire and Joe drank away the insurance money. He asked me and Harry to put up for the club but I didn't. I didn't see any point in watching my money being drunk away.

The work was bashing, debt collecting, putting someone in

place: anything that Spotty was doing apart from the racing. He could have had everything. The difference was that where Spotty wasn't averse to cutting his own people, Harry would just give them a dig.

Harry could hurt people and he wasn't afraid of anyone. He could have had what he wanted but he didn't have that ruthless streak to go and do it. He was offered financial gains beyond his dreams. Them Jews do love a Jewish villain.[19]

Rita died on 10 September 1988 at the Charing Cross Hospital. She had been suffering from cancer for some time. Jack Colmore, aka Spot, Comer, Comar, Comor, Comacho and probably other names died on 12 March 1995 at Nazareth House, Isleworth. He left no will and no letters of administration were taken out. As he had wanted, some of his ashes were later scattered in Israel.

NOTES

1. Conversation with author August 1999.
2. ibid.
3. For an account of the case see *The Times*, 18 September 1948. Shifty Burke's *Peterman* is an inside account of the robbery.
4. F. Fraser, *Mad Frank and Friends*, p. 34.
5. A suitably immodest account can be found in Billy Hill, *Boss of Britain's Underworld*.
6. *The People*, 13 October 1951.
7. *Sunday Times Magazine*, 8 August 1965.
8. John Pearson, *The Profession of Violence*, p. 85.
9. Hank Jansen, *Jack Spot: Man of a Thousand Cuts*, pp. 117–18.
10. F. Fraser, *Mad Frank and Friends*, pp. 61–2.

11. Arthur Tietjen, *Soho*.

12. Joe Cannon, *Tough Guys Don't Cry*.

13. Harry White's daughter was killed whilst filming *Ocean's 11* with Frank Sinatra and the Ratpack in America. White had close links with Frank Sinatra and provides an early link with transatlantic interests. A devout Catholic, whilst providing the betting for a church Donkey Derby, he discovered that the animal his son was riding was a heavy favourite. 'If it looks like fucking winning make sure you fall off,' he told the child, who duly obliged.

14. *Daily Herald*, 8 October 1955.

15. There are numerous accounts of the series of trials. One of the more entertaining is by Laurence Wilkinson, *Behind the Face of Crime*.

16. Leonard Read, *Nipper*, p. 54.

17. ibid, p. 58.

18. Hank Jansen, *Jack Spot, Man of a Thousand Cuts*, p. 191.

19. Conversation with author, August 1999.

11

HELPERS

Although criminals need doctors and lawyers to help them in times of trouble, English solicitors have rarely headed international gangs of thieves, but one exception was the West Ham solicitor Charles Sharman. When, around the end of the nineteenth century, police courts sprang up around London, they spawned a sort of second-class solicitor, neither quite as trustworthy nor quite as well regarded as his colleagues. 'A Police Court solicitor; being used to denote advocates of a less exalted type', wrote Travers Humphreys, the High Court judge, a trifle snobbishly.

One man not tarnished with those words was Sharman, who earned Humphreys' respect, striking him as one of the few natural lawyers he had encountered. Sharman had a large practice and a variety of well-connected associates. He had also acted for most East London villains of the time and, in 1922, he appeared for the twenty-year-old Frederick Bywaters in the celebrated Bywaters and Thompson murder case.

So it was with something approaching horror that Humphreys, briefed by the Director of Public Prosecutions, learned that his old police court adversary, now aged seventy-five, was charged with receiving a share certificate stolen from a Post Office mail-bag and with the forgery of a cheque stolen from the same bag. To his further amazement, he discovered that this kindly and courteous old man had for many years been suspected of heading a gang of international thieves specialising in stealing mailbags.

In 1922, a mailbag had been stolen on a train somewhere between Liverpool and London. Some of the contents had then been cashed in Antwerp and Brussels by an elderly gentleman giving the name of Johnson but who had been identified by a bank clerk as Sharman. Given Sharman's reputation, it was thought there must have been some mistake and the clerk could not possibly be correct. The matter was left on the file. A month later another mailbag went missing, this time on the Birmingham to London run. A transfer of £900 of Quebec rail-way stock went with it, only to end up with Sharman, who was now interviewed. He explained that a poor man had picked up the stock certificate in the street and brought it to his office. It was the sort of standard Quarter Sessions defence, but the DPP thought there was not sufficient evidence to prefer a charge. In 1924, yet another mailbag went missing between Bristol and Paddington. One of the stolen letters contained a £50 Mexican oil share certificate which was then sold in Manchester by some-one closely resembling Sharman. He provided an alibi that he was at home all day. However, he failed to convince the police that nine people were wrong when they identified him that summer as selling war bonds in Canada, which had been stolen from the same bag.

He appeared at the Old Bailey before Mr Justice Salter on 25 June 1925, charged with conspiracy to steal and receive mailbags. Defended by Sir Henry Curtis Bennett KC, his mitigation was that he had fallen into the hands of thieves who had been black-mailing him. Salter would have little of this:

So far as you are concerned, this is a most scandalous offence...
I am satisfied that you, as an experienced solicitor of the High
Court of Justice, have made yourself an associate of a gang of
very daring and very dangerous thieves and mail-bag robbers.
They required a man of your standing and knowledge of business to dispose of the booty for them. I hear that you have been
blackmailed. Thieves often blackmail one another. If you were
a younger man, I would have sent you to penal servitude for
seven years.

Sharman received three years' penal servitude, which in the
1920s meant Dartmoor, where the conditions were dreadful. It
was not a situation in which any man let alone a seventy-five-year-
old would wish to find himself. Yet, against the odds, Sharman
survived the sentence, dying in 1933. His ornate will left gifts to
various members of the judiciary. His estate was worth £175,000
in today's money.

In fact, Sharman had deceived many people for years on end.
He had begun his career in Chelmsford as a clerk to a solicitor.
It had been an unfortunate start because this bible-quoter had
already been involved with a young woman and had been rail-
roaded from the town. Sharman later obtained articles, and in
1888 was acquitted of misappropriation of funds, but was suspended by the Law Society for two years. About the same time,
he was made bankrupt and was not discharged until 1901. That
year he brought a prosecution against his clerk Edwin Porter for
sending him a letter threatening to accuse him of indecent assault
without reasonable cause. When the jury heard of Sharman's
track record Porter was acquitted in short order.

Sharman had begun fencing in a small way, taking gifts from
those whom he had successfully defended or their friends and,
it was said, enriching himself in the winding-up of estates in

lunacy. Just which was the international gang into whose clutches he claimed to have fallen is not known, but he certainly acted for the Sabinis, then in control of the London Underworld. Traditionally, the Sabinis were thought of as mere racecourse hooligans and club-owners but there was a good deal more to them than that and it is not impossible that Sharman was more than simply their solicitor. Other suggestions as to his associates include a mysterious 'international gang of gentleman crooks'.[1]

Not many of the Great Train Robbers benefited from their efforts but a man who did was almost certainly George Stanley. Over the years small criminal defence firms have often been run by a managing clerk acting unsupervised by the titular head of the firm. In East Ham in the 1950s and 60s, Lesser and Co was effectively run by Stanley. After his death Stanley's nephew told reporters his uncle had been given £2.6m from the robbery for safekeeping. Instead, he bought and renovated houses in Southend, making substantial profits. Unfortunately, wives and loved ones who came to his office for their weekly payouts do not appear to have been allowed to share in this mini property boom. Stanley continued to work into the late eighties as a clerk with another firm of solicitors. Aged ninety-seven, he died following a car accident in 2008.

Manny Fryde's pedigree was never quite clearly established. He probably qualified as a solicitor in South Africa and may or may not have been struck off there. Opinion is more or less equally divided. By the 1950s, however, he was working in London for a firm near Ludgate Circus as a managing clerk and an exceptionally powerful one at that, acting for many of the top class East End villains of the era. Some of his earliest clients were members of the Nash family, the collection of brothers from North London who tutored the Krays. In September 1958 sixteen-year-old Roy, one of the younger members of the family, was found guilty of the manslaughter of Alan Compton, stabbed at a dance in Cropley Street, Shoreditch, and was sentenced to five years.

In May 1960 Fryde also acted for Jimmy Nash in the Pen Club murder case in which Nash was acquitted of the murder of Billy Hill's friend Selwyn Cooney but was sentenced to five years for grievous bodily harm on the man. Nash appealed and now Fryde commenced an ingenious action for contempt of court against the *Daily Sketch* which, on 10 May, had published details of Nash's two very minor previous convictions. Leave was given to issue a writ but the Divisional Court thought that members of the Court of Appeal would in no way be influenced by anything which appeared in the *Daily Sketch*. Their Lordships also doubted any judge would read it anyway.[2]

A great Zionist who kept a list of known Blackshirts and sympathisers under the carpet in his office, Fryde on one occasion visited the home of a client charged with murder and when using the lavatory found a swastika painted on the ceiling. He promptly threatened to withdraw from the case. It took a good deal of persuasion (and no doubt an additional fee) for him to accept that the offending swastika was nothing more sinister than an Aryan symbol of light which had been painted by a previous tenant and had not been cleaned away.

In the early 1960s Fryde took Ralph Haeems under his wing. Haeems, the son of Bombay school teachers, had come to London to study engineering and had run out of money. He was now living in an East End hostel of which Fryde was a trustee. He offered him a job filing and also used him to collect his gambling winnings from local betting shops. Always a great and entertaining gossip, Haeems recalled:

He [Fryde] never carried less than £5,000 on him. One time he sent me to a small shop opposite the Law Courts and I handed in the winning ticket. The girl went for the manager who asked who I was from. I said 'Fryde'. He said, 'Here's the money and tell the effing bastard not to come in the shop again.' It was £12,000.

This was at a time when a newly qualified solicitor could expect to earn in the region of £20 a week.

Some years after the Krays were convicted, with the shades of the prison house, or at least the handcuffs, closing around him, Fryde took advice from a leading silk and caught the night plane to Majorca where he lived for many years. Eventually he returned to England and is buried in the Jewish cemetery in Brighton.[3]

NOTES

1. *Empire News*, 28 June 1925.
2. *Daily Sketch*, 10 May 1960; *The Times*, 12 May, 16, 22 June 1960.
3. James Morton, *Krays: The Final Word*.

12

UPTON PARK AND THE WATNEY STREETERS

The size and composition of a mob could, and indeed did, vary considerably depending upon who was out and about at any one time and who was currently allied to whom. Nevertheless there were some clearly defined teams, apart from the Sabinis and the Whites, both before the War and after. One of the most sizeable and influential as well as long lasting was from Upton Park.

'The Terror of Upton Park' said the *News of the World* when Arthur 'Porky' Bennett was jailed for eight years in February 1951 after slashing a customer in Ding Ah Ching's café in Pennyfields. One of a number of brothers, Porky Bennett was also dubbed 'King of the Dodgers' because, during his four years' Army service, he had racked up only five days on the parade ground. The rest of the time he had been a deserter. Three years before the café incident he had received a modest six months for running over his wife's legs.[1]

Bennett and his brothers – one of whom, Dickie, was in the long firm business and went to Malta after a confidence trick in which another East End villain was deceived over some gold – were well known in the area.

An East End face recalls:

Over the years Porky was a well-known face. Did a bit of minding, hurt a few people. Russy, another brother – 'you could best
describe him as "one of a crowd"' – was shot by Ronnie Kray in
the late 1950s or early 1960s.

He looked like doing it [dying] and at the time topping was
available. Mickey Smith and Albert Lovett were given the gun
to get rid of. Albert Lovett had a big scar on the side of his face
given to him by one of the Jones brothers. The cut was for mess-
ing about with his wife. It was to come out much later that Smith
had been an informer for years.

One day Lovett told me that Smith had brought the gun
round to look after and if the police had come anywhere near his
door he'd have grassed Ronnie up. He also told me of a family
called Francis in North London who were butchers and who
he had fitted up. They got two years each. It was put on them.
Lovett was a man with policemen as friends from the constable
on the beat to the Supes in the Commissioner's office. Lovett
died in around 1989. He just fell over.[2]

Bennett died in June 1999. Curiously he had been in the same
ward in St Andrew's as Albie Gerard, Alfie Gerard's brother.

But over the years the names that mattered around Upton
Park were George and Jimmy Wood – both of whom had been
on Spot's fateful London Airport robbery – Joe Carrington and
Teddy Machin. An old East End villain recalls:

If I was asked as a kid where I came from and said Upton Park
I'd be asked, 'Do you know the Woods?' That's how respected
they were.

The Woods were proper men. They were the nearest to

gangsters I ever met; always had big cars, beautifully dressed, always had a pocketful of money. They saw us boys as coming up and they'd always mark our cards. Never shy of putting their hands in their pockets for people. Hill and Spot fought to have them on their firms. From the Sabinis onwards, they all used Georgie and Jimmy.[3]

Another of the Upton Park Mob on the London Airport robbery had been Teddy Machin.

Those men on the airport were such a good firm; really getting dough. They were organised and sensible and intelligent enough to be doing very well. When they were nicked and so many got such bird it took the heart out of their organisation. Teddy Machin was never really the same after it. He was a Spot man.[4]

Indeed he had long been a Spot man and had taken a leading part in Spot's feud with Jimmy Wooder, who in turn had cut him before the War. Now, with Spot's star in the ascendancy, Machin took an axe to Wooder at Ascot races in 1948, cutting him at the ankles. Then, in October 1952, Machin and Big Jim Tibbs, along with four others, were accused of causing a disturbance at the Madeleine Members Club in South Molton Street:

In 1952 Machin was in custody for a long time for leaning on a club which Sulky used to manage in Mayfair. He got out of it eventually when someone saw Sulky.

Just before his death he was thought to have done Harry Barham, the bookmaker, who'd fenced the stuff for me years earlier and who had been going round collecting money he needed for his defence at the Bailey. But then it may just be convenient that Machin's dead and he's got the blame.[5]

The body of bookmaker Harry Barham was found in his car at 6.30 p.m. on 14 February 1972 in Windmill Lane, Stratford, in East London. He had been shot in the back of the head. For some years he had held the majority interest in bookmaking businesses in Islington and Holborn. In late 1971, however, he had lost and paid out £50,000 in personal bets, and he was awaiting trial at the Old Bailey on a charge of evading betting duty.

It was thought that if he could raise the duty he might escape with a fine, and that day he started to buy jewellery cheaply in Hatton Garden and sell it at an immediate profit. By 4 p.m. he had put together some £40,000, but it was not the sort of business venture that could be kept secret. A theory is that a middleman was sent to meet him to decoy him and then rob him. He was known to have had tea at Lesley's Café, a greasy spoon in Red Lion Street, Holborn, and was seen about 5.15 that afternoon cutting across traffic in Russell Square. A driver who had been inconvenienced took the number of the car and told police he had seen three men in it.

All sorts of reasons have been given for the killing, one being that it was to recoup money loaned to Barham before it was swallowed up in the anticipated fines and compensation orders. Another was that Barham had stumbled on a gang planning a major crime and had been killed to silence him.

In his last years Machin became increasingly unpleasant. Now he was drinking heavily and he acquired a number of enemies. On 23 May 1973, he was shot dead whilst walking near his home in Forest Gate. He had survived a previous attack when asleep in bed in Windsor Road, Forest Gate, in January 1971. The would-be assassin had broken the bedroom window with a milk bottle and then shot Machin in the legs and buttocks; a bullet had landed chest-high in the wall. It was said to have been a contract killing with £500 on offer to the successful killer. Machin fled for a time to Streatham.

> Machin was a tapper. You only had to meet him once and he'd be round your door the next morning blagging you for a score or a fifty.[6]

He also worked as chauffeur and minder to the enigmatic Albert, commonly called Charles, Taylor, forger, con-artist, and corrupter of the police.

The complainant in another potential police corruption case, Taylor conveniently died of a heart attack whilst on the way back to prison from the Old Bailey trial in which he was a defendant. Some in the Underworld maintain he was murdered. In the subsequent inquiry it was quite apparent that there were still high-ranking officers who had escaped Sir Robert Mark's purge.

In the autumn of 1976 Taylor was under investigation in connection with a dollar premium fraud. He was a well-known figure in the Underworld and it had been at his hotel, the Leigham Court, in Streatham, that an attack had been planned on Peter Garfath, the lover of Rusty Humphreys, wife of the pornographer Jimmy Humphreys. Whilst on the run in Holland, Humphreys had complained that a DCI John Bland of the Serious Crime Squad had framed him for the attack. Bland was a frequenter of Taylor's hotel. The information on Taylor was that he was being 'minded' by corrupt officers and that he was running the fraud.

Gilbert Kelland, then head of the CID, arranged for Bert Wickstead to lead an investigation. Wickstead selected his own staff but reported that he was being asked by a Deputy Assistant Commissioner from 'C' Department to explain their use.

Taylor was arrested and charged with a conspiracy to counterfeit gold half-sovereigns as well as with the dollar premium fraud.

Lodged well out of the way in Bedford prison he now began to make lengthy statements about his involvement with very senior officers and Barry Pain, Chief Constable of Kent, was called in to conduct an inquiry under s.49 of the Police Act 1964. Bland was suspended.

During the inquiry Wickstead received a call from the wife of a man with whom he had dealt as a junior officer in the Pen Club shooting in the East End in 1959. The man, then in custody, told Wickstead that he had received an offer to set him (Wickstead) up and was being supplied with dates and places where Wickstead was alleged to have taken money. Wickstead sought the assistance of the new Commissioner David McNee but with the death of Taylor the inquiry was closed down.

The Director of Public Prosecutions decided there was not sufficient evidence to bring charges. Bland resigned before disciplinary proceedings could be taken. The DAC in question, Dave Harries, also resigned at short notice on the grounds of ill-health, as did a Commander, Jock Wilson.[7]

After Machin's death, Alan Mackenzie was charged with his murder. The prosecution's case was that Machin, who had been having an affair with Mackenzie's aunt, had been treating her badly, effectively robbing her and refusing to allow her out without him. The defence was that it was Machin's own gun which had gone off accidentally when Mackenzie tried to take it from him. After a retirement of five and a half hours the first jury could not agree. On 6 December 1973, Mackenzie pleaded guilty to manslaughter, receiving a sentence of three years.

Hoxton was regarded as a very clannish place for its size, possessing, more than one person has said, more crooked people than anywhere else in the world. Before the War the undoubted head of what was known as the Hoxton Mob was Jimmy Spinks, described as:

... not very tall but he was built like a brick shithouse. He had no brains but he had courage. You could put him in a room full of men with knives and at the end he'd be cut to ribbons but he'd still be there fighting them off.[8]

The Hoxton Mob came a cropper at the Lewes racecourse in 1936 where they tangled unsuccessfully with the police after their attack on two Sabini bookmakers. Jimmy Spinks received five years.

Some mobs were subsumed by the Kray Twins. One such was the Poplar Mob who were based on a family by the name of Donovan.

When people talk about the Twins being in the ring they don't talk about how they could fight on the cobbles. They fought the Poplar Mob, who were really a family, on the debris next to a pub the Coach & Horses which was a bucket of blood itself. Billy, one of the family, had his eye just about out. After that the Poplar Mob was trash of the Twins.[9]

The longest surviving East End mob has, without doubt, been the Watney Streeters, of whom boxer and hard man McLean wrote:

This mob's always been about. As one lot get older, and move on to bigger things, younger ones move in and take over. Same name, different kids, year after year.[10]

It is the Watney Streeters who, since the early part of the nineteenth century when work was flowing down the river, have been greatly instrumental in controlling crime on the docks.

*

In sociological terms the East End has long been thought of as a 'deviant' area – one of physical and moral disorder, and much of that has centred on the Thames. The East Enders had lived off the spoils of the river for centuries before the construction of the docks and, as houses were destroyed to build them at the beginning of the nineteenth century, East Enders saw no reason to change their attitude. Policing of the land area of some 2,000 acres and a water area of 700 acres was not an easy matter. It was not helped by the fact that by the 1930s some 3,000,000 tons of imported and exported goods were being handled.

In the time of the magistrate Patrick Colquhoun's treatise, which did so much to establish a river police and which was a foundation stone for the Met, one in four West Indiamen ships were 'game' – that is, manned by officers and watchmen who for a bribe would allow looters known as the Light Horse on board.[11] The fee was between twenty and thirty guineas and the targets were sugar, coffee and Jamaica rum. Cooperers and watermen were in league with the night thieves. There was enormous overcrowding amongst the ships lying at anchor – 1,400 might dock, with berths only available for just under 900 vessels, and so control was minimal.

The so-called Heavy Horse were stevedores or lumpers who carried long narrow bags lashed to their thighs, which were concealed by large wide-legged trousers. Their prey was sugar, coffee, cocoa and ginger. In league with them were the rat catchers who would let loose rats so that a further visit had to be made and who would also collect parcels at night. Toshers stole copper from the ships' bottoms. Rat catchers would then steal what were called plumpers, full-weight packages, and would also pick up cargo spill or Greenacres, named after the murderer who left bits of his wife over London.[12]

James Greenacre, a grocer from the Kent Road, was hanged

on 2 May 1837 for the murder and mutilation of fifty-year-old Hannah Brown whose body parts he spread across South London. He was visited in the condemned cell at Newgate by MPs and the nobility whilst, at the other end of the social scale, pie-sellers increased their takings by selling meat pies as Greenacres.

One of the very few murders of a river police officer was that of Jacob Tolhurst, poisoned on 9 March 1876 when he accepted a drink from a man on East Quay whom he described as wearing a low-cut grey coat and a billy-cock hat. The liquor tasted of bitter ale. Within minutes Tolhurst suffered convulsions and crippling stomach pains. Taken to St George's Workhouse, he died within forty-five minutes. He had been given strychnia – a vegetable alkaloid derived from *nux vomica*. There was evidence that about the same time a man on a ship sailing from the docks died in similar circumstances, but no arrests were ever made and no further instances of this sort were recorded.

Before the creation of the Port of London Authority in 1909, policing of the docks had been in the hands of the dock companies themselves. The new police force was not viewed with much alarm. They were so badly clothed they were known as the 'Pantomime Police', but they must have had some effect because in 1919 some 1,500 people were arrested for cargo broaching. The problem had become so acute that a special branch called the Shipping Police, a plain-clothes force, was created to go into the holds of ships and watch cargo being loaded and unloaded.

To an extent the Shipping Police stamped out broaching, but it could not stop the pilfering by the crews and the theft of rum and port was prevalent. One method was known as 'sucking the monkey', the insertion of a metal pipe with a rubber tubing; the thief then sucked until the liquor started to flow. Another was 'spiking the cask' which involved boring holes in the barrel.

Children were employed, bringing in their father's dinner pail and returning with it full of tea or tobacco.[13]

The stipendiary magistrate Cancellor was well aware of the problem.

> It was hard to send a man who had borne a good character for many years to prison because he had put a tin of canned food or some packets of tea in his pocket on his way home from work. If everyone is encouraged to think they can commit one theft without more serious consequences than a small fine or being bound over to come up for judgment, pilfering will be so common that it will be a danger to the commercial life of the nation.[14]

Cancellor believed that during the First World War wholesale pilfering was organised by older dockers who used young boys now earning £4 a week when twelve shillings would have been the normal wage as a van boy.

Effectively, however, most of the organised crime in the docks of the last century was in the hands of the Watney Streeters, the oldest and largest of the East End gangs, sometimes called The Black Cap Gang because of the flat black caps they wore. Over its hundred years-plus in existence it may not have always been the most powerful, but it has certainly proved the most durable. It probably evolved from the 1860s when the Irish started flooding into the area and St Katherine's Dock was built to provide homes for some 15,000 people. Wapping was then an island with five bridges and the surrounding roads off Watney Street were effectively Irish colonies.

The Watney Streeters had begun life as a fighting gang. Mickey Bailey recalls:

> My own father was born in 1905 in Twine Court, so called because there were rope makers for the ships lived there. By the time he

came there were established gangs of Irish origin in the Wapping and Watney Street areas where they'd fight amongst themselves for spoils out of the docks. His elder brother Jimmy was born in 1891 and joined the Watney Streeters about the time my father was born and he had other brothers which followed him. My father told me it was a regular thing for them to go south side to Bermondsey and fight the Irish over there – a lot was to do with the work in the docks as well as thieving. To my way of thinking it was just muggish. They wasn't even fighting for any sort of money.

Round Watney Street there was so much inter-marrying you wouldn't know who was your cousin. In Wapping alone there must have been two dozen families called Sullivan.

They were good Catholic men. Up until the 1950s on Saturday night they would go to confession and on Sunday morning they would go to Mass to repent. Then they go straight into the pubs and within an hour the cobbles would be running with blood.

Many of Bailey's uncles were Watney Streeters of high rank:

Before the war my uncle Bob did a bloke Mike Carey and he became governor of the London Docks which had about 4,000 men. It was a straight fight on the cobbles. That meant my uncle had the books, the loans, the gambling, the receivers. It was all horses and carts with tea, cloth, suiting, cigarettes all coming out. My old man used to tell me they'd nick the smuggled watches from the smugglers. When I went to the docks betting shops were just becoming legal but bookies still had runners. The men didn't want to spare the time to go to them. It was years before they finally died out.

In those days the Streeters could be hired to go to the races and stand behind the Whitechapel Mob, such as Timmy Hayes and

Dodger Mullins, and the Jewish Mob who were not regarded as real fighters themselves, ranged against the Camden Town and other mobs. When the Sabinis came down the East End in one of their periodic demonstrations of strength they found themselves in an ambush organised by the Watney Streeters.

> In the Second World War there was something called the Golden Navy for anyone who'd had anything to do with docks and rivers, but they were so much trouble that they disbanded it and used them as a force to go and help out over the country at a moment's notice – Glasgow, Manchester wherever.[15]

To an extent the Watney Street Mob died out during the War. As with many families, Bailey's suffered terrible predations. His uncles Bobby and Mike died, both of cancer. Jimmy was killed and so was Joey. Bill was wounded and, as far as he recalls, Jerry was either killed or wounded. Another brother, Davy, joined the navy and his ship was sunk but he survived:

> Things started again in the docks after the War. I didn't really know that much that went on until I was a kid in the 50s. The first people I heard about was a family called Duggan. I didn't know them obviously. They were older than me. Then you had Billy Jones who was to get three years with Ronnie Kray over [the cutting of] Terry Martin. That was over his cousin Jacky Martin who was a Watney Streeter.[16]

After the War one family ran the business of taking on the unloading crews in the London dock:

> The Butlers were big in the docks. People paid them to work. They were instrumental in getting docker's tickets. In the early

60s a ticket would go for £200 upwards probably up to £500. It depended on who you were and who you went to. You may have been entitled to one but you might have to wait a year. If your family had no connection then a book could be got through wharfers, stevedores, docking firms. There were so many books a year on offer. Say ten books handed out by the Dock Labour Board. You would join a Union and from there when a book came up if there was no history in your family of work on the docks then the cost might be say three or four hundred quid.

A levy was also paid to the family for a licence to steal:

If you had a good job working in one of the holds where there was good cargo, you paid a levy for the stuff you stole and you had to give a kick-back from this thieved gear. Say if the stuff came to £18 you would give them a fiver back.

That was in the hands of the Watney Streeters and then it went to the Butlers, and Billy Jones who was with the Twins and was related to Pedlar Palmer, the boxer, controlled it for a number of years.

The Governor at that time was Jimmy Fullerton. From what I heard there were clubs, spielers sprang up at the end of the War all over Stepney, Limehouse and Aldgate and some Watney Streeters was running them. In 1948 Fullerton was killed in a car crash. He was in a Ford V8 Pilot with Olly Williams, the boxer who survived and became Jack Dash's minder. Dash sent Olly over to the Regency one night I was there to ask if the Twins could help over some business. It all got a bit heavy. It was after that Willie Malone took over after he and his brother Paddy came out from doing three years for cutting a black man who'd insulted their sister. This didn't do Willie's reputation any harm but he was known as a peaceful man. Peaceful but a bad man to upset. Willie formed an alliance with the Twins but he was also friendly with Billy Hill and Frank Fraser.

Before all this there was a war going on between Jimmy Fullerton and the Twins. When Fullerton was killed Willie Malone was the natural for the Watney Streeters. He already had his finger in a lot of the clubs plus he had a tea business. By this time he was a fairly wealthy man anyway. He was friends with The Dean. He had several people work for him in his factory who also worked in the clubs. It was kept a tight family affair.

The Dean was a black man, but he never mixed with other blacks; he kept himself to himself but he was not to be trifled with. He was friendly with both the Malones and the Twins. He still goes in a pub in Wentworth Street.

Pay-day was Thursday and so dice was a Thursday game. It was played on a stretch known as The Asphalt, a smooth surface of old-fashioned tarmacadam outside the Old Fire Station, Watts Street. It had the advantages of a highly polished surface, proximity to the pay station and it was a place from which approaching police could easily be seen.

My old gran (great-grandmother) after her husband died used to run a bookmaking business. She'd let you bet on tick and on a Thursday she'd call you in and she'd know exactly what was in your pay-packet and she'd have part of the debt. She'd say to my father, 'Owen, get your brother Bobby and do them Irish bastards.' If anyone knocked her Bobby would be sent round, told to collect the debt and interest and then to use the capital and buy himself a drink. It wasn't the money, it was the principle. When she died she lived next to Jikey Stevens who had a whole lot of betting shops. Billy Ambrose and Jerry Callaghan bought into them.

Her husband hadn't been a fighting man, but he had no compunction about paying the local villains and that included Bobby to collect debts for him. In a way Bobby was a good client of his.

As bigger and bigger vessels were needed for container traffic the Thames was too shallow for them. Docks at Tilbury were established and from 1961 gradually the Royal Docks closed. The last vessel to leave was on 7 December 1980.

NOTES

1. *News of the World*, 4 February 1951.
2. Conversation with author, August 1999. Mickey Smith and the Jones brothers are pseudonyms.
3. George Wood died in spring of 2000.
4. Frank Fraser in conversation with the author.
5. Conversation with author, 1999.
6. ibid, August 1999.
7. Lilian Pizzichini, *Dead Man's Wages*.
8. Conversation with author, August 1999.
9. ibid.
10. L. McLean, *The Guv'nor*, p. 110.
11. Patrick Colquhoun, *A Treatise on the Police of the Metropolis* (5th ed.).
12. Robert Huish, *The Life of James Greenacre*.
13. Charles Graves, 'Dock thieves' in *The Sphere*, 14 April 1934.
14. H. Cancellor, *The Life of a London Beak*, p. 54.
15. Mickey Bailey, conversation with author.
16. Ibid.

13

HEROES

In a poll to name the pantheon of East End heroes the Kray Twins would probably head the voting, leading by far comedians such as Bud Flanagan, actresses such as Barbara Windsor and sportsmen such as Kid Berg. Their rule in the East End can be said to have lasted fifteen years, shorter than that of Jack Spot and far shorter than that of the Sabinis, but theirs is the name which will for ever be associated with East End crime.

The sociologist D.M. Downes may have had it wrong in what has been described as his landmark study *The Delinquent Solution*.[1] He considered that there was an absence of delinquent gangs in the East End, with the norm being 'the fluid street corner clique, averse to any form of structure and organisation'. He missed altogether the juvenile gangs with a degree of structured organisation in Hoxton and Islington. Later, writing in 1968, Kenneth Leech noted:

> ... a number of well-known adult professional criminal cliques in the East End, but even these are not organised in such a way as to resemble the semi-bureaucratic criminal syndicates in the United States.[2]

Not everyone would agree. Martin Short, prolific writer on the Underworld and producer of the television series *Gangsters*, said:

It was very structured. Bosses in the East End would liaise with those in the North, South and West. Now the days of the big Mobs have gone ... People work in much smaller groups of four or five people and they're much more paranoid about each other.[3]

Certainly the major mobs could call on troops where necessary. An East End contemporary recalls:

The Twins had around twenty at any one time but they could call on people. They could phone people in Birmingham, Liverpool, Newcastle, especially Glasgow. They had a large following of Scots. The Nashes could call on a lot of people such as Ronnie Diamond and his mob in their day, call them out of Hoxton, Islington and their own ground, Little Italy. Then they could call on Curley John[4] – he was a villainous little bastard. Never stopped cutting birds and always took liberties with people he thought he might get away with. He married a rabbi's daughter.

He got stabbed and blamed Bobby Cannon – not the one from Paddington but a cousin of some sort – and made a death-bed statement. He recovered and someone went to see him. It turned out in the end it was a 16-year-old kid who'd done him. Then there were the Rileys, a whole lot of brothers – they were tied up with the Nashes and people in Notting Hill. George was the brightest of them. He was well liked.

And Spotty, he could call on any amount of the Yiddishers and there was some villainous fucking Yids.

Probably the nearest to the semi-bureaucratic United States syndicate, certainly in the East End, were indeed the Kray Twins, who maintained a fairly rigid system and hierarchy in and around Bethnal Green for the duration of their career until it ended in 1969. During that time they dealt with other organised and semi-organised gangs such as the Watney Streeters and the Donovans from other East London areas, and they treated with various individuals and teams who did not fall under their banner.

Not that a summons by the Twins for those outside the umbrella could be ignored. There were two kinds, as an East End face recalls. The first, the relatively innocuous one to their home at Vallance Road:

> Bill T. cut Mickey Barrie to pieces at the Le Monde which the Barries had with Philly Herbert at World's End off the King's Road. Philly had been having it away with Harry Abraham's wife and Bill went down to do him. He escaped out the back and so Bill cut Mickey Barrie who tried to intervene.
>
> Bill was called to the Twins a day or so later because Johnny Barrie had been over there complaining. As his punishment Bill was told to go to a porn shop in the West End and tell the guy to shut up shop and never come back and then to give the keys to the Twins. Bill didn't mind a bit but the Barries weren't happy. Bill had been told to go to Vallance Road and so he knew that nothing untoward would happen and there'd be no villainy.

And then the rather more formal call to one of their clubs. The same source remembers how he and the Jewish hardman Harry Abrahams went to the Regency on behalf of Bill Ackerman, a long firm dealer whom the Twins believed owed them money:

> Ronnie and Reggie were going to do Bill Ackerman who'd pulled a stroke and muscled into a long firm. Bill wasn't fully accounting for things and whether Harry's Jewish blood was siding with

Bill's Jewish blood I don't know, but he went to see the Twins on his behalf and I went with him.

Ronnie just said, 'You can fuck off back, Harry, and tell that fucking bastard he's got to pay.'

Once we got outside Harry wiped his forehead and said, 'At least that's all he's got to do.'

Next day I got a call from Ron who wanted to know why I'd been along. I said Harry was a friend of mine. He wanted to know if I was backing Harry against him and I said there was nothing like that. 'Did Ackerman give you a few quid?' he wanted to know. I said he gave us a monkey and Ronnie laughed and said he should have given us double. Ackerman had to go to the Regency the next day and Ronnie took another £500 from him and give it to us.

Much that has been written about the Kray Twins – Ronnie, the elder, and Reggie, who were born in 1933 in Stean Street – is the stuff of legend. Certainly they had an older and loyal brother Charlie, who was at one time in the Navy and was an early boy-friend of the actress Barbara Windsor. It has been suggested that he was the brains behind them, but the reverse is true. He was involved by them in their activities rather than leading them. Their grandfather, Jimmy 'Cannonball' Lee, was once a well-known flyweight boxer, and their father was a totter selling bits and pieces of antiques. And what is certainly not legend is that they were devoted to their mother, Violet.

All three of the brothers were keen boxers. One of their earliest bouts was at Cephas Street School where they went to fight four boys and won handily. The one to show serious promise was Reggie, a lightweight who was never beaten in his professional career. Ronnie, as a welterweight, won four of his six bouts between July and December 1951 but had a tendency to get himself disqualified. Charlie Kray had only a few bouts in his two-year career. He lost all three of his contests and he had not been in the ring for some time when he was knocked out in the third round at the Albert Hall by Lew Lazar, from the well-known Aldgate family, who went on to be a British champion.

As young men they would have razor blades stitched into their lapels so that anyone taking hold of them would have their hands cut. They also favoured nails protruding from their shoes, and knuckledusters. They were in their first serious trouble in 1950 following a fight outside Barries' Dance Hall in The Narrow Way, Hackney. One of those who gave evidence against them was Dennis Stafford; convicted of grievous bodily harm, they were sent down for Borstal.[5]

In fact the Twins' career almost ended before it started when Reggie was nearly stabbed by the very tough and well-protected Davy Levy. The blade passed harmlessly through his coat jacket. Levy came from a poor but large Jewish family in Mile End whose mother, nevertheless, had a pot of stew on the stove the whole day. 'If you went round any time you were always welcome to a bowl,' remembers one East Ender. It is said Kray kept the ruined suit as a memento for some time.

They began their club-owning career by simply commandeering the Regal in Eric Street. After that they took over the Green Dragon which, with its sister club The Little Dragon, features throughout club history of the period. Like other celebrated Underworld spots, such as the Blue Plaice Restaurant and the Artists' and Recreation Club in the Charing Cross Road, the Green Dragon passed through a number of hands. It was at one time owned by Bill Ackerman and run by Sammy Lederman, one of Jack Spot's workers who had the dubious distinction of appearing for the prosecution in both the Babe Mancini trial of 1941 and that of the Krays. On 2 June 1969 an armed robbery took place in the club in which a black gambler was shot. Shortly before that there had been an arson attack. In the 1970s it was taken over by Charlie Knight and Billy Bartram, the brother-in-law of docklander Willie Malone. In the spring of 1975 there were a number of shootings at the club including that of Georgie Plummer, the boyfriend of 'Blonde' Carol Skinner. Plummer had tried to prevent what appeared to be a contract shooting. No prosecution followed.

Later Reggie opened what was their best club, the Double R Club. It was probably financed in part by their profits from the other clubs and by poncing from local villains, in other words demanding a share of proceeds from a burglary or robbery in the East End.

The Twins also knew villains who were stealing cheque books by office creeping and then flew kites[6] to get equipment to set up a gymnasium over the Regal Club, itself just a drinker. It was here the Firm was born, helped by the loyalty derived from former prisoners whose families had been looked after by the Krays whilst they themselves were away.

The next serious trouble arose from the Twins' connection with the former boxer Bobbie Ramsey, part owner of The Stragglers, a drinking club at Cambridge Circus, combined with a long-running feud with the Watney Streeters. The story goes that one of the Streeters at the time, Charlie, had a small scam going with local Post Office drivers who would re-address parcels to places where he could collect them. Ronnie Kray wanted 50 per cent of the profits. Charlie was dilatory with payments and was listed by Ronnie as someone with whom he would soon have to deal severely. The opportunity came when Charlie had a fight with Billy Jones, another part-owner of The Stragglers. In return, the next night Bobby Ramsey, as Jones' partner, sought out Charlie and beat him up. Two nights later Charlie, this time with a complement from the Watney Street Gang, beat Ramsey unconscious outside the Artichoke pub in the East End.

Although not strictly involved, Ronnie apparently wanted to make an example of Charlie and to shoot him, but both Ramsey and Jones argued against this. Instead it was agreed that a severe beating would be handed out to the Watney Street connection in the Britannia public house on Watney Street territory. Ramsey and Jones went with the Twins, backed by a dozen others. They found the Britannia empty of Streeters except for a boy, Terry Martin, who was playing gin rummy with three friends. The Watney Street Gang had escaped through the back entrance. Martin was made to suffer for this display of collective cowardliness; he was dragged out of the pub, slashed with a bayonet and kicked about the head by Ramsey as the principally aggrieved party.

Instead of now doing the sensible thing and going home, Ronnie decided to look for the fleeing Watney Streeters. Driven by Ramsey, he was found with a revolver when the police stopped the car in Stepney around midnight. In the car there was both a crowbar and a machete. Ronnie explained the bloodstains on his shirt by saying he had had a nosebleed. There must have been some attempt to buy off Martin, which failed, and Reggie was also charged. He told the jury that bloodstains on his jacket might have come from boxers in the gym. On 5 November 1956 the Recorder of London, Sir Gerald Dodson, sentenced Ronnie to three years' imprisonment. Ramsey received five years and Jones three. Reggie was acquitted.

Charlie Kray senior wrote to the Court of Appeal in an effort to obtain a reduction in his son's sentence for the attack on Martin:

> It is my firm belief that he was intimidated into this brawl; more out of curiosity than any intentions of committing any violence

of which he was innocent. If you will at least believe me, sir, they are the most respectful and good-natured lads anybody could wish to meet, so kind to my wife and I and everybody in their thoughts and actions and only do good to everybody and with my guidance and my wife and son Charles (the eldest brother) they will make good.

Bobby Ramsey's club, The Stragglers, closed shortly afterwards.

According to Reggie the bad behaviour of Terry Martin caused such resentment in the East End that one man, John Hall, offered to shoot members of the family on Ronnie's behalf. Kray told him it did not suit his purpose at the present. Four years later on 3 June 1961 Hall, an avid gun collector and member of a rifle club, shot and killed two officers outside West Ham police station. He later shot himself in a telephone kiosk at Wanstead.

The Double R may have been the jewel in the crown, but even then there were numerous other interests, each paying a weekly tribute. By the early 1960s, although Reggie Kray claims that he disliked the protection business, feeling it was none too glamorous, he was looking after the remainder of Billy Hill's interests in the enforced absence of Frankie Fraser. He also claimed to be looking after the criminal and property owner Peter Rachman's interests in Notting Hill.[7]

Sometimes, however, people came to the Krays rather than their going out looking for things to protect.

The Krays would know the right guys who would open a club and approach them. Anyone opening a club would go to them. Young guys only respect someone who is a name otherwise the doorman is a target. It makes sense. I worked the Green Dragon in Aldgate. I got paid and there was £40 to the Twins over and above my wages. People who came to the club knew who I was and why I was there.[8]

They now had tabs on clubs, large and small, infamous and famous throughout London, each paying money from £10 upwards a week. Of the more famous clubs, the Colony in Berkeley Square paid £100 a week and the Casanova, off New Oxford Street, half that sum. The money from all subscribers to the Firm was collected on a Friday by Albert Donoghue, Ronnie Hart, Scotch Jack Dickson and Ian Barrie. It was known as the milk round and the collectors were treated just like the milkman making his weekly call.

In 1960, they acquired Esmeralda's Barn in Wilton Place off Knightsbridge. Once a fashionable night-club, it had declined into producing strip shows. With gambling legalised by the Gaming Act 1959, it had been granted a licence. The acquisition was brought about by the simple expedient of frightening the controlling shareholder, Stefan De Fay, into signing away his shares to them for £1,000. They had heard of the vulnerability of De Fay from Peter Rachman and, with implied threats being heeded, the club was theirs within six hours. De Fay stayed on the board of directors for the next two years but drew no salary. The day-to-day running of Esmeralda's and the Twins' financial affairs were now firmly in the hands of an adroit long-firm fraudsman, Leslie Payne, and in its heyday the Twins cleared £40,000 a year from the club.

All went well until Reggie Kray went to prison and Ronnie, lonely and frustrated and not the brighter of the pair, unfortunately started to take an active interest in the club, granting long lines of credit. When the punter could not pay, Ronnie took to threatening him. The serious players now began to drift away to find other more respectable clubs. A lesbian-orientated discotheque was started in the basement. The club continued its decline until 1963 when it went bankrupt with debts of £4,000.

By 1964 the Twins really did not have much of a prison record. It never seemed as if the police wanted to do – or, if they did, were capable of doing – anything about them. The Krays even had an illegal drinking club next to Bow Road police station. As is often the case, it was the press which precipitated matters. There was, it was said, some film of a homosexual peer and a gangster. The then Commissioner of Police, Sir Joseph Simpson, issued a statement denying a witch-hunt against titled homosexuals. The man who took the photographs obtained an injunction in the High Court to prevent the pictures being printed by the Mirror Group of Newspapers.

On 13 July the *Daily Mirror* ran an editorial:

> This gang is so rich, powerful and ruthless that the police are unable to crack down on it. Victims are too terrified to go to the police. Witnesses are too scared to tell their story in court. The police, who know what is happening but cannot pin any evidence on the villains, are powerless.

The next day Sir Joseph made a statement that he had asked senior officers for 'some enlightenment' on reports that inquiries were being made into allegations of a relationship between a homosexual peer and East End gangsters.

On 16 July the *Daily Mirror* led with the story 'The picture we dare not print', and described it as one of a 'well known member of the House of Lords seated on a sofa with a gangster who leads the biggest protection racket London has ever known.'

When it came to it the picture, which appeared a week later in the German magazine *Stern*, turned out to be a totally innocent one. It was Lord Boothby, who was also something of a television pundit, and Ronnie Kray sitting on a sofa. With the fuss that was made, it had been thought that at least the pair were naked. In fact the picture did not tell the whole story. Sitting on the other side of Ronnie was his and Boothby's lover, the talented burglar Leslie Holt. Lord Boothby instructed the fashionable, if louche, solicitor Lord Goodman and received £40,000 in damages. Ronnie received an apology from the *Mirror* but no damages. But, as John Pearson says, the apology kept the *Mirror* away from launching an investigation into him and Reggie.

Following questions in the House of Commons concerning extortion from club-owners and what action was being taken by the Home Secretary, the police began to make active inquiries into the Krays' affairs. A young Detective Inspector, Leonard 'Nipper' Read, at Commercial Street police station was asked if there was any reason why he should not conduct a detailed investigation into the Twins' business and personal interests. The implication behind the question was clear. Was Read an officer in their pocket? It was a question to which he rightly took great exception.

However, despite his efforts, Read could not obtain any hard evidence against the Twins. People were simply afraid to talk. What he did hear was that the main income of the Firm came from long-firm frauds, which are neither new nor difficult things to organise. The long-firm fraud has been one of the staple and most lucrative diets of the con-man. As far back as the 1920s it was estimated that as much as £4 million was cleared annually in London.[9] Then Read heard through an officer at Paddington that a club-owner, Hew McCowan, had been pressured to pay protection money for the Hideaway Club, a smart drinking place in Gerrard Street, Soho. The decline of the Twins themselves can be traced to McCowan's refusal to sell the Hideaway to them. As with many of these clubs, it was difficult to find out just who owned what. The Hideaway had previously been the Bon Soir, owned in partnership by Frankie Fraser, Albert Dimes and Gilbert France, who also owned the restaurant Chez Victor in Wardour Street. Later the Bon Soir had been managed by a young man, Sydney Vaughan, who had been in dispute with France and the club had closed in early autumn 1965. Now France had met McCowan at Vaughan's twenty-first birthday party and an agreement had been signed giving Vaughan *carte blanche* to run the premises. For this he had to pay Gerrard Enterprises, France's company, £150 a week. McCowan employed Vaughan as his agent and manager and spent some £4,000 on refurbishing the club, which opened for business on 16 December.

McCowan had foolishly mentioned that he was thinking of opening a club and it was arranged he should meet the Twins in the Grave Maurice in the Mile End Road. According to McCowan, Reggie had maintained it was essential that he have two of his men installed in the club to prevent trouble. Initially a figure of 25 per cent was suggested, which was to rise to 50 per cent. A table for ten was reserved for the Twins' party on the opening night, but no one appeared. Three days later a script-writer friend of the Krays, 'Mad' Teddy Smith, did appear very drunk, caused trouble and did a minor amount of damage in the reception area before being bounced out by the waiters.[10] When McCowan next saw the Krays it was pointed out that this sort of thing would not have happened had their men been there to prevent it. An agreement was reached that now 20 per cent would be payable. McCowan asked for and was told he would receive a written agreement. He telephoned the police.

The Krays were kept in custody until their trial at the Old Bailey the next year, despite a question in the House of Lords from their old friend Lord Boothby who wanted to know if it was the intention of the Government to imprison them without trial indefinitely. Meanwhile Read hoped that, with the Twins out of harm's way, people would come forward. He was wrong and now his case began to fall apart. Sydney Vaughan went to the Twins' home in Vallance Road to retract his statement before a local vicar. McCowan was offered money not to give evidence, but refused.

Vaughan maintained that the only reason he had made his original statement was because McCowan had threatened to withdraw his financial support. After three and a half hours, the jury announced it couldn't reach an agreement, and at the re-trial things went worse for the Crown. The defence had discovered that McCowan had spent some time in a psychiatric hospital. That information did not help the prosecution and this time the jury took less than ten minutes to acquit.

That same evening the Twins purchased the Hideaway Club from McCowan, renaming it the El Morocco. The police were badly wounded by the trial, and for the foreseeable future the Krays now had a licence to do what they wanted in both the East and West End. Further damage was caused to Read by an often repeated story that he had gone into the club and was photographed drinking champagne with the Twins. The photograph is in fact of the actor Edmond Purdom, but despite Read's denials it is a story that still circulates.

A month after the case, on 20 April 1965, Reggie married a young girl named Frances Shea. The ceremony was attended by *le tout* East End, with photographs by David Bailey and the *Sunday Times* in attendance to cover the proceedings. The writer Cal McCrystal, one of the journalists dispatched, remembers Ronnie stomping down the aisle trying to encourage congregational participation by calling, 'Sing, fuck you, sing.' The marriage was not a success and Frances committed suicide just over two years later on the night of 6 June 1967. At her funeral the Kray henchman,

Albert Donoghue, was ordered to make a list of those who had not sent flowers for future reference. The distraught Reggie now began to believe that Frances had been reincarnated as a robin which sang at her graveside. Ronnie was also beginning to show increasing signs of serious mental instability. Another list was compiled, this time of those by whom he felt threatened. All his energies were being channelled into revenge and retribution.

Much has been made of the rivalry between the Richardson brothers from South London and the Krays, something which some of the remaining participants are now anxious to play down. Indeed Frank Fraser, who had been courted by the Twins and who chose to throw in his lot with the Richardsons, perhaps ill-advisedly gave evidence at the Twins' trial. Nevertheless the memoirs of Twin defectors such as Albert Donoghue make it clear that the East Enders were on war alert.[11] Charlie Richardson was much more of a businessman than any of the Krays and was becoming extremely wealthy. His brother Eddie, along with Fraser, had a highly successful slot-machine business off the Tottenham Court Road. There were also definite signs that the Richardsons were operating in the East End. Their henchman, the giant Brian Mottram, ran a long firm in Hackney, Billy Stayton had another in Southend, and it was feared they might seek to extend their interests. A meeting was arranged between the Twins, the Nash brothers and Freddie Foreman – on whose support even as a South Londoner the Krays could count – on one side of the table, and the Richardsons on the other. The meeting, designed to forge agreement on who should operate where, was not a success.

The Twins now became convinced that Charlie and Eddie Richardson were about to try to take over their empire. They also believed they were on the edge of a big deal with the American Mafia with which the Richardsons could interfere. At one meeting with a *mafioso* chief visiting from New York, the Richardsons had been present and had apparently made sarcastic remarks. Ronnie also feared that the uneasy truce between themselves and the Richardsons would end.

Another meeting was called at the Friday-night gangland hangout, the Astor night-club off Berkeley Square, for a discussion between the Twins, Ian Barrie and Ron Hart, Charlie and Eddie Richardson, Frankie Fraser and George Cornell.[12] The meeting became heated because the Richardsons apparently wanted a substantial interest in the Kray–Mafia business arrangements. Some people say this was when George Cornell called Ronnie a big fat poof and told him to bugger off when he asked to be cut into the blue film racket. If so, it was not an insult that could be accepted lightly. Still the Krays did not believe they were strong enough without help. To counter the ferocity of Frankie Fraser, they wanted someone just as fearless on their side. The person they chose was Frank Mitchell. But there was only one problem – he was serving a sentence in Dartmoor prison.

However, they received an unexpected bonus. After a fight in Mr Smith's night-club in Catford on 7 March 1965, in which a Kray hanger-on Dickie Hart was shot and killed, Fraser and effectively all the Richardson team were arrested and held in custody on charges of murder, affray and later of grievous bodily harm in what became known as the Torture Trial. Two days later Ronnie Kray shot George Cornell in the Blind Beggar public house in the Mile End Road. Cornell had been visiting a Jimmy Andrews, in hospital with gunshot wounds, to inquire who had actually shot him. Ronnie had long carried a grudge against the former East Ender who had defected to the Richardsons. It was generally thought Ronnie had earlier shot Andrews.

It is not clear why in the autumn of 1965, with almost the entire Richardson organisation out of the way and no Frankie

Fraser to worry about, the Twins actually felt they had to obtain the release from Dartmoor of the 'Mad Axe-man', Frank Mitchell, a man with a record of appalling violence.

After the shooting of Cornell perhaps they were no longer as popular in the East End as they had once been. Some members of the Firm were now disrespectfully referring to them as Gert and Daisy, after Elsie and Doris Walters, the cockney music hall act. They had fallen out with Leslie Payne who had left them and whom they contracted Jack 'The Hat' McVitie to kill. The Mitchell release was really to be a show of strength.

On 12 December 1966 Mitchell went on a work party at Bagga Tor. The weather was too bad for work and so the party stayed in a hut playing cards. This was by no means uncommon. Some Dartmoor officers at the time took the view that a certain amount of licence and trust was the way to exercise control. Nor was Mitchell the only person given this freedom. At the time the model wife of Peter Scott the cat burglar was hoping to become pregnant and she would drive down to the Moor in a closed van with a mattress in the back. Scott would then temporarily absent himself to perform his marital duties before returning to the working party.

At 3.30 p.m. Mitchell asked if he could go and feed some ponies. At 4.20 p.m., when the prison officers took the remainder of the party to the bus pick-up point, there was no sign of him. Twenty minutes later the local police were notified, but by now Mitchell was on his way to London. By the time the hue and cry really went up he was safely in Whitechapel.

For a few days he lived in relative comfort. A night-club hostess and former girlfriend of Donoghue, Lisa from Winston's in the West End, was produced to provide him with sex and, rather sadly, he fell in love with her. What he had done, however, was to exchange one prison cell for another. Without his surrender he was never going to be given a release date; if he did give himself up, it would mean a loss of privileges, probably loss of remission and further time to be served. He began to say he would never be captured alive. Now he became more and more of a liability to his hosts. With Christmas approaching, he wanted to go and see his mother and sister at the family house in Bow. He was told that a meeting would be arranged but nothing came of it. He began to rave to his captors about going to look for the Twins, both at Vallance Road and 'all around the clubs'.

On Christmas Eve he was told by Albert Donoghue that he was being moved to a new address in Kent. He protested at being separated from Lisa, but was told she would be following on. That was the last time anyone can really say they saw him. At the trial of the Krays for the murder of Mitchell, Albert Donoghue gave evidence that the 'Axe-man' had been shot just as the van left the Barking Road by Freddie Foreman, the long-term friend of the Twins who was paid £1,000 for the killing, and the formidable Alf Gerard, who owned the Blue Plaice Restaurant and who died in 1981 in Brighton. Donoghue claimed that also in the van were Foreman's friends Ronnie Oliffe and Jerry Callaghan, of Pen Club fame. Foreman was acquitted after calling a substantial number of alibi witnesses, including the former champion boxer Terry Spinks. Alfie Gerard was on the run in Australia at the time and he and the others never stood trial. Later Foreman would write that he had indeed taken part in the murder. What he objected to was Donoghue saying he had been paid £1,000. He maintained that his participation had been wholly as a favour to the Twins.[13]

The third of the murders for which the Krays eventually stood trial was that of Jack 'The Hat' McVitie, another long-time friend of the Firm. At one time a highly respected thief, who along with Frank Fraser had been sentenced to be flogged for assaulting a prison officer in Exeter in 1949, he disappeared in the autumn of 1967. By now his wife had left him and he was existing on a diet of alcohol and pills.

He had fallen from favour for a number of reasons, principally that he swindled the Twins and then went about boasting that he had done so. He had been given money to kill the estranged financial adviser Leslie Payne and, half drunk, had gone to Payne's house with another member of the Firm, Billy Exley, who would also give evidence against his former friends and employers. They had arrived only to find the potential victim out. McVitie had simply turned away and had pocketed the advance fee.

Shortly before his death McVitie met George Dixon – one of the brothers who worked both for and independently of the Twins – who had tried, unsuccessfully, to persuade him to absent himself from the scene at least for a period.

Then, on 28 October 1967, McVitie was murdered at a party at a flat in Evering Road – the owner 'Blonde' Carole Skinner had been sent across the road to stay with friends that night. Reggie Kray put a gun to McVitie's head which failed to discharge. McVitie began to struggle and was hauled back whilst trying to escape through a window and told to behave like a man. Finally Reggie plunged a knife deep into his face and stomach. In a later remark which cannot have helped his case for parole, he commented:

I did not regret it at the time and I don't regret it now. I have never felt a moment's remorse.[14]

McVitie's body was placed in a candlewick bedspread and taken to South London by Charlie Kray for disposal – something the prosecution alleged had been arranged by Freddie Foreman.

There have been many accounts of the disposal of the body and theories as to its whereabouts. Nipper Read rather favoured the theory that it had been returned to East London and put in the furnaces of the local swimming baths. Another version is that McVitie was sent to a friendly undertaker and buried in a double coffin. He may have been buried somewhere in the country. Possibly the body was taken in a car to South London and ended as an Oxo cube in a scrap yard.

Freddie Foreman, who of all people should know, has been fairly reticent about the funeral arrangements. In his book *Respect* he says that he was rather aggrieved at being called out in the middle of the night to help clear up this difficult situation. The car which had contained McVitie's body was sent to a wrecker's yard and the body itself was tied up with chicken wire and buried at sea away from the fishing lanes. He also maintains that, at the outset, there had been no intention to kill McVitie but merely to scare him. Then things had got out of hand.

In the autumn of 1967 Nipper Read was appointed to the Murder Squad with the express task of forming a squad to bring down the Krays. He first went to see the estranged Leslie Payne, who was afraid that a rather more professional attempt than that by McVitie would be made to kill him. Read obtained an indemnity for him against all crimes except those of violence provided he admitted to them, and Payne made a long statement saying what he knew about the Firm. Now Read was able to obtain evidence from others on the fringes, promising that he would not use the statements unless and until arrests had been made. At this time he was looking at fraud, the Krays' involvements with long-firm frauds, some GBHs and their dealings in stolen bonds rather than murder.

Meanwhile, at the beginning of 1968, the Krays were moving once more into the international market. They had met Angelo

Bruno of the Philadelphia Family, who was looking at casinos in the West End. The Krays promised him a trouble-free life running those interests. They had successfully disposed of a batch of bonds, part of a number stolen in an armed raid on the Royal Bank of Canada in Montreal. Now their trade in stolen securities was expanding. They had also met an American, Alan Bruce Cooper, who took them into Europe and the stolen jewellery market in Belgium.

Nipper Read had had Cooper under surveillance for some time when he learned that a man named Paul Elvey was being sent to Glasgow to collect a briefcase. There had long been a two-way trade in villains passing between Glasgow and London and a similar trade of information and assistance between the respective police forces.[15] Now Elvey was arrested and the briefcase found to contain dynamite, something readily available from the mines around Glasgow. Interviewed by Read, he passed on a story of assassination attempts of Soho strip club-owner George Caruana and others, both in the street and incredibly in the foyer of the Old Bailey.

When Read arrested Cooper he knew that once he disappeared from the streets the Krays would suspect something was up. Apparently Cooper had a stomach ulcer and Read placed him in a Harley Street nursing home from where he telephoned the Twins. Read hoped the Twins would come and make damaging admissions. Instead they sent one of their henchmen along with Joey Kauffman, a Jewish-Sicilian small-time *mafioso*, who was dealing in the stolen bonds.

On 8 May, after an evening out at the Astor, the Krays went back to their flat and Kauffman to his suite in the Mayfair Hotel. The next day around 200 of Read's men swooped on more than twenty members of the Firm. The swoop included both their friend Freddie Foreman and their brother, Charles. Now, with the Twins and senior members of the Firm on remand in custody, Read was able to make further progress in obtaining statements from men such as Donoghue, who turned Queen's Evidence, and also other witnesses like Patricia Kelly, the barmaid in the Blind Beggar public house on the night Cornell was shot, and 'Blonde' Carole Skinner.

The Twins received life sentences for the murders of Cornell and McVitie. Charles Kray and Freddie Foreman received ten years for their part in cleaning up after McVitie's death.

Now began what amounted to a cottage industry with books being written by the Twins and their elder brother. There were videos made about them and their era and T-shirts and mugs sold bearing their names. Visits to meet them could be arranged for a fee, said to be in the region of £1,000. Ronald Kray married whilst in Broadmoor, the secure hospital to which he had been sent and where, apparently, he had enjoyed most of his creature comforts. He died suddenly of a heart attack on 17 March 1995. His funeral, in traditional East End style with six plumed black horses, was said to have cost £10,000. His pallbearers included his brother Charles, John Nash and the boxing promoter Alex Steene.

Shortly after Ronnie Kray's funeral, Charles was back in major trouble. He was by now sixty-nine and his son, Gary, who had serious educational problems throughout his life, had just died of cancer at the age of forty-four. Charles had been released in 1975 from his ten-year sentence for assisting in the disposal of the body of Jack McVitie and from then on had variously sold cutlery at the Ideal Home Exhibition and managed a pop group. He had also been the consultant on the film *The Krays*. Now he was charged with conspiracy to sell cocaine worth £39 million to undercover officers. It was a charge greeted with ridicule amongst the Underworld, who regarded Kray as a pathetic old man trading off the names of his younger brothers for handouts for old times' sake. He said he had been unable to pay for Gary's funeral, the money coming from Reggie.

The police version was that here was a man who was still deeply involved in the Underworld and one who had been investigated on at least three occasions. There were unproven allegations linking him to amphetamines, counterfeit videos and fake coins. He had neither a bank account nor a credit card; he never claimed benefit. This, said the police, showed that he was still an operator with whom to be reckoned.

He cannot have been totally broke because he had offices down the Commercial Road and, unless he was doing it as a favour, the porn merchant Ronnie O'Sullivan senior, father of the world-class snooker player, was said to have serviced Charlie Kray's car. O'Sullivan himself was jailed for life in September 1992 for the killing in October 1991 of Bruce Bryan in a night-club brawl in Stocks Night-club, Chelsea. Bryan had been with Angela Mills, the one-time girlfriend of Charlie Kray. According to the prosecution evidence, Edward O'Brien and O'Sullivan were making racist taunts and singing football songs. A fight broke out and O'Sullivan produced a hunting knife with which he stabbed Bryan who had hit him with a champagne bottle. O'Sullivan was then alleged to have kicked Bryan in the head as he was on the ground. Although O'Sullivan claimed mistaken identity he was convicted. He also received sixteen years for affray.

The police in the Kray drugs case were recruited from provincial forces and at Kray's seventieth birthday party he had been introduced to 'Jack', an undercover officer posing as a businessman dealing in drugs. This was, say his supporters, his first mistake. Frank Fraser, who gave evidence at the trial, points up what he sees as Kray's lack of touch with the real harsh world.

What I should have said at his trial was to prove what a fool Charlie was. Patsy Manning had unknowingly introduced him to undercover cops. There was no problem in saying, 'This is Tom, this is Dick and this is Harry' and having a chat, but once Charlie'd started talking serious what he should have said is, 'What's your surname?' 'Can't tell you.' 'Who do you know?' Any *bona fide* villain would ask. It shows you what an idiot Charlie was. And if you're dealing in anything serious like a robbery or anything then if the man can't put up names of people he's worked with or won't tell you his name you know the score and it's, 'On your bike, get back to your local police station.' You are brought up automatically to ask questions and protect yourself. It's instilled in you from the time you're ten years old. Charlie simply didn't have a clue about life.

That's how simple he was. I thought that was the most impor-tant bit of all.[16]

In subsequent taped conversations Kray offered to supply five kilos of 92 per cent pure cocaine every fortnight for up to two years. If the deal had gone ahead he and his associates would have grossed £8 million. His defence was that he was stringing the potential purchasers along in the hope of conning money from them. He told the court:

All my life I have advised people never to be involved in drugs. I swear on my son's grave I have never handled drugs in my life. Juries have got it wrong for me before and this jury has got it wrong.

Judge Carroll was not convinced. Sentencing him to twelve years' imprisonment on 23 June 1997, he said:

There was never a real question of entrapment by those officers but, when caught, you cried foul. I am pleased to say this jury saw through that hollow cry.

Robert Field received nine years and Robert Gould five for their respective parts in the affair. For a time it was thought that Charlie Kray might have his conviction quashed or at least have his sentence cut but, on 12 February 1999, his appeals against both conviction and sentence were rejected. He had been given leave to appeal the previous November. Now the court said that it was 'unpersuaded that the judge was wrong in attributing to Kray a central role in this affair'. He could seek his release on licence once he had served half his sentence, said Lord Justice Ian Kennedy. These apparently encouraging words did not assist Charlie Kray. During his time in prison he suffered from a heart condition and was eventually moved to a hospital on the Isle of Wight, where he died.

Efforts had been made to persuade Reggie Kray to give evidence on his brother's behalf, but he had declined. There was soon better news for the brothers, however. On 14 July 1997, a well-educated and successful businesswoman, thirty-seven-year-old Roberta Jones, joined the list of women who have married long-serving prisoners when she became Reggie Kray's second wife in a ceremony at Maidstone prison. It was celebrated by a laser-show on the prison walls. Two years on from the marriage the campaign to have Reggie Kray released had again gathered momentum, but it did not move the Home Secretary until Kray's terminal illness rather forced the issue in the autumn of 2000.

What was the Twins' lifestyle and wardrobe? According to Ronnie Hart, their cousin, it was very different from that of their spiritual father, Darby Sabini. Ronnie Kray was said to have had about thirty suits, some from Savile Row and the others rather more prosaically from the tailor Woods in the Kingsland Road. He never had fewer than fifty shirts at a time, seldom wearing one more than twice. Underneath he favoured Y-fronts and string vests. He would wear only black silk socks and had twenty-five pairs of shoes. Of his three overcoats one was a fawn camel hair, the second a single-breasted dark blue cashmere and the third a dark blue Al Capone coat which he acquired after seeing a gangster film. He wore an Albert watch and chain and, like many an Italian *mafioso*, had a penchant for opera and was partial to Gigli. According to Ronnie Hart, he believed himself to be a reincarnation of Capone – something which would be difficult, if not impossible, since Capone died when Ronnie Kray was thirteen. He liked gin and tonic and lager, but then moved to wine when he was told this was the thing to do. Both Twins drank tea throughout the day and when they ate with their parents their preferred dish was stew. Again according to Hart, Ronnie would wash his feet at night in rosewater and milk.

Reggie Kray kept his shirts on hangers and had a wardrobe of suits ranging from nearly all white to all black. According to Hart, he was a bad driver, once driving a Mercedes 220 into a hole in the road and abandoning it. His preferred music was Dean Martin and Timi Yuro. He was fond of children and horse riding. When on a Saturday he and others assembled at the Clock Tower Riding Stables, he was Billy the Kid to be chased by the other members of the Firm.

No doubt recalling the misadventures of many a gangster in a barber's chair, both had a barber, Maltese Chris, come to them to do the trimming and he massaged their hair with a mixture of olive oil and surgical spirits, a recipe apparently favoured by old-time boxers. Ronnie, in particular, feared becoming bald. Both were vain. Reggie had his teeth capped and Ronnie went to America to have four false front teeth inserted at a cost of £400.

They had a private masseuse and manicurist and for a time both used York Town toiletries until Reggie Kray changed to Brut.

Both collected weapons such as bayonets, swords and Gurkha knives and, extremely superstitious, both were visited regularly by Dorothy Brown, a gypsy, the wife of the enormous Tommy The Bear who was on the Firm, to tell their fortunes. Hart believes that they (in common with other twins) had the gift of knowing what the other was doing. He recalls that on one occasion Reggie told him he had a dreadful feeling that something was happening to his twin, who at that moment was temporarily getting the worst of it in a bad fight in the Regency Club. To some extent, Ronnie had political ambitions. A great admirer of Hitler, he spoke of founding the Kray youth movement.

When they were seen by Home Office psychiatrists at the time of their trial they presented themselves as being highbrow, cultured men. Reggie was described as being a 'rather nervous boy who was a bedwetter until he was 10 years old'. He was also recorded as admitting to being a heavy drinker – up to a bottle of gin a day, but 'Mentally he was alert, friendly, pleasant and indeed one might say charming,' wrote Dr Denis Leigh of the Royal Bethlem and Maudsley Hospitals after an interview in December 1968. Reggie told him that he liked reading, particularly books on sayings and proverbs. Ronnie had battled against schizophrenia for some sixteen years; it had been under control for the last ten years and he was taking 25 mgs of Stemetil three times daily. He had told the doctor he was fond of listening to the opera singers Maria Callas and Gigli and reading biographies including those of Gordon of Khartoum, Genghis Khan and Lawrence of Arabia. 'He says he is a friendly man, not bad-tempered normally, a believer in God but not a churchgoer.'[17]

Their elder brother Charles became something of their scapegoat, someone who from time to time they would torment in public. Married with a son, Gary, and a daughter, Nancy, whom he adored, he was well liked in the East End. Any cozying up by him to celebrities was only to obtain their autographs for the educationally challenged Gary, whom he protected throughout his life.

Charlie Kray had also survived another humiliation in his life. It came following one of the more celebrated East End trials when George Ince was charged with the murder of Muriel Patience in a robbery at the Barn Restaurant in Braintree, Essex, on 5 November 1972. In the first trial, despite the best efforts of Mr Justice Melford Stevenson to secure a conviction, the jury disagreed; at the second trial in the late spring of 1973, Ince called an alibi witness, a Dolly 'Gray', who was in fact Charlie Kray's wife with whom Ince had conducted a long-standing relationship. She had visited her husband in Maidstone prison and sought his permission to give evidence that at the time of the robbery she had been in bed with Ince.[18] Three weeks after Ince's acquittal a John Brook was found in possession of the murder weapon and was subsequently convicted of the murder. The case was one of a number at the time which led to the Court of Appeal (Criminal Division) setting new guidelines on what is acceptable identification evidence.

In September 1977 Dolly Kray married George Ince.

And what happened to the rest of the team? The Twins' cousin, Ronnie Hart, is said to have gone to Australia. Freddie Foreman, who received ten years for his part in the disposal of the body of Jack 'The Hat' McVitie, served nine years for receiving some of the money from the Security Express robbery and later published his memoirs, *Respect*. He admitted on television that the Twins had organised the Mitchell murder, something which brought their wrath on his head from afar. Connie Whitehead, convicted for his part in the McVitie murder and perhaps the best businessman amongst them, opened a club and then a wholesale liquor business. In one of the wheels which continue to operate in the East End he bought the Norseman Club in Canning Town, once owned by Alfie Gerard, which was where Nicky Gerard beat Mickey Gluckstead. Both the Lambrianou brothers, also convicted over cleaning up the McVitie murder, wrote books. Tony Lambrianou died in 2004. Another, Ronnie Bender, 'never put himself about', as one East End face described it. Bender had been a stevedore and 'although he mixed with heavies was really a straight man'. He also died in 2004.

Albert Donoghue, whose evidence failed to convict the Twins of the murder of Frank Mitchell, had a series of adventures – in one of which he was kidnapped by Billy Amies who would himself turn supergrass. He escaped and in turn wrote his memoirs, *The Krays' Lieutenant*, later appearing on television explaining his part in the killings. Convicted of housebreaking, he served another sentence of thirty months before, in 2004, he suffered a major stroke. He died aged eighty in April 2016.

Charlie Clarke, regarded as cantankerous and devious, who kept a room as a hideaway for Ronnie Kray in Walthamstow and who was a police informant, later became involved in setting up a relation of the fighter Lennie McLean to receive a beating. There was an attempt to strangle the unfortunate man with chicken wire but he escaped and, for his part in this misdemeanour, Clarke was obliged to pay substantial reparation. At the age of seventy-one, and after having had a leg amputated, he was eventually found murdered in his home in Dover on 10 March 1989. He had been stabbed by nineteen-year-old Shane Keeler when he was surprised in a burglary. Keeler pleaded guilty to manslaughter on the grounds of diminished responsibility and received life imprisonment.

Charlie and Reggie Kray died within a matter of months of

each other. Charlie died on 4 April 2000 in St Mary's hospital near Parkhurst prison aged seventy-three. He had been suffering from a heart condition and Reggie had been taken to see him in prison; the first meeting the brothers had had since Ronnie's funeral. Reggie was allowed out of prison for Charlie's funeral, which was said to have been the largest of the three. But by now, however, the surviving brother was a sick man suffering from prostate cancer. In August 2000 he was transferred from prison to hospital and then released on licence on 26 August. He hoped to be able to return one last time to the East End but, although he was visited by old friends such as Freddie Foreman, Johnny Nash, Joey Pyle and Frankie Fraser, he never left the Beefeater Town House Hotel in Thorpe St Andrews, near Norwich, where he was staying in a £37-a-night room. He died on 1 October. His funeral was the least spectacular of the three brothers and there were noticeable absentees amongst the faces at the graveside. The Evangelical minister, Dr Ken Stallard, praised Kray's 'generosity of spirit', saying, 'He was a man of great thought and great depth . . . so many people like to look at the bad instead of the good.'

Their nemesis Nipper Read died aged ninety-five in April 2020.

NOTES

1. D.M. Downes, *The Delinquent Solution*, p. 134.
2. Kenneth Leech, 'Human Casualties in a Crisis District' in *East London Papers*, Volume 11, No. 1, Summer 1968.
3. *Sunday Express*, 13 February 1994.
4. A pseudonym.
5. Stafford had a long criminal career, mainly as a long-firm fraudsman and later in the celebrated Stafford–Luvaglio case of January 1967 in

which Angus Sibbett, the manager of a gambling club in Newcastle, was killed. Both Stafford and Luvaglio were convicted and a long campaign began to clear their names. Eventually, after they were paroled Stafford told the *News of the World* that, in fact, he but not Luvaglio had killed Sibbett. He later retracted this, saying he had confessed only for the money. He resumed his life as a con-man. See James Morton, *Gangland II*.

6. In criminal slang, office creeping is burglary, and to fly a kite is to proffer a stolen or forged cheque.

7. Rachman, a friend and sometime protector of Christine Keeler, had an empire built from prostitution and high rents from slum properties, using a collection of wrestlers and strong-men as minders including the Berlin-born Norbert Rondel, who appeared as The Polish Eagle and whose claim to legal fame was bringing the case in which it was ruled that no person could sue their barrister for negligence. *Rondel v Worsley*.

8. Albert Donoghue quoted in James Morton, *Gangland*, p. 109.

9. For details of the 100-plus long firms thought by the police to be operating in England in the middle of the 1920s, see Nat. Arch. MEPO 2 2188.

10. Smith, who had written a play for radio and who was a part-time driver for the Twins, disappeared in the 1960s and was thought to have been killed in a quarrel over a boy in Steeple Bay, Kent. His body was never found and no charges were brought. It is now believed he went to Australia.

11. See for example Albert Donoghue, *The Krays' Lieutenant*, Chapter 7.

12. Other versions of the story say it was in Al Burnett's Stork Room club in Piccadilly. There is an account of the blue film racket and the quarrel in F. Fraser, *Mad Frank*.

13. See Leonard Read, *Nipper*; Albert Donoghue, *The Krays' Lieutenant;* Freddie Foreman, *Respect*, Chapter 13.

14. Albert Donoghue, *The Krays' Lieutenant;* Reggie and Ronnie Kray, *Our Story*, pp. 85–91; Freddie Foreman, *Respect*, Chapter 13.

15. When George Cornell had caused so much trouble to Ronnie Kray, a Glasgow hardman Frank 'Tarzan' Wilson was brought down to deal with him. All he was able to do was to cut him in the buttocks and return to Scotland before the shooting in the Blind Beggar. For some of the exploits of Wilson, see James Morton, *Gangland 2*.

16. F. Fraser, *Mad Frank and Friends*, p. 229.

17. The *Guardian*, 5 January 2000.

18. For a full account of the case see Peter Cole and Peter Pringle, *Can You Positively Identify This Man?*

14

THE DIXONS AND THE TIBBS

Just as the First World War was intended to ensure peace for all time, so the Kray trial was intended to stamp out major villainy in the East End. One proved as much a pious hope as the other, although in both cases there was calm for some time. Initially after the Kray trial there were press stories that there would be a take-over bid for the West End by other interests either from South London – which was unlikely since the Richardsons were well locked up and there were no other serious contenders – or from the East End which was more likely.

Certainly clubs were paying money to the remnants of the Nash enterprise but ...

It was being done in a very different way from the Kray's reign of terror. It was really rather a friendly business with this gang – almost a two-way operation with benefits to both sides. We thought they would jump and occupy the vacuum, but it never happened. I think they sensed that if they had done that they would have let themselves in for a major investigation and consequently all sorts of troubles. It was a good example of preventive policing.[1]

For a time Harry Mooney, who had been with Nipper Read's squad when it eliminated the Twins, kept watch over the West End, but when apparently no one had moved into the vacant seat the squad was allowed to run down. But suddenly the Scotland Yard regime changed when Commissioner Waldron died and Robert Mark took his place. Now, once again, there were feelings that certain elements in the East End, notably the Dixon brothers, George and Alan, and their friends were once more getting out of hand, and there was one Scotland Yard 'star' still left to be pulled out of the locker. His name was Bert Wickstead, variously referred to as the Gangbuster and the Grey Fox. As a young officer he had been involved in the Pen Club affair and had worked his way up with stints in the East End.

As Read had taken over the Kray inquiry with just a couple of officers and no office space, so Wickstead began with no squad and no telephone. It was then that a decision was made to target the Dixon family. But to the outside world, who were they?

They had grown up at the end of the War in Limehouse where, in time, they controlled the local public houses and clubs. At one time they had worked with the Krays in a semi-independent capacity and, until his marriage broke up and drink and drugs took hold of him, Jack 'The Hat' McVitie had been a close running mate of Alan Dixon. In fact Dixon had tried to persuade McVitie to absent himself from things when the failure of the attack on the Krays' financial adviser, Leslie Payne (for which McVitie had been paid in advance) became known.

They were also known as debt collectors in a world where borrowers sought to avoid and, if possible, escape payment altogether:

The Dixons were debt collectors. People would ask them to bring in money that was owed because that was their legitimate business. Remember, the people they had to go after were in the rumping game. That's why there was a problem – they were slags who borrowed money and never intended to pay it back. Being slags they go to the law and start squealing that the Dixons are leaning on them with menaces.[2]

Their mother, Rose Dixon, only had one leg and married 'three of the most handsomest men you could find'. The first was Jackie Fairbrass who had a paper stall outside the West India Dock gates; the next was George Dixon, a seaman, by whom she had George, Alan, Brian, Sandra and Gracie. Then she married a harbour master at the Royal Docks, Billy Knight; by him she had twins, Glyn and Lyn, and a younger son Billy. Says a friend:

George is a reasonably tough man, a family man, not a man I would call a gangster. He's got a couple of medals for bravery. A kid who'd broken out of the nuthouse and was shooting at everybody. George was driving past and saw what was happening and disarmed him. The second was when a geezer had a gun in the City Arms in Millwall. George knocked it up in the air.

The fact that the Dixons had been friends of, and worked with, the Twins did not stop Ronnie attempting to shoot him one night in a mock trial held at the Green Dragon club in Aldgate over some alleged misdemeanour. He pushed the gun in Dixon's mouth. It misfired and Kray gave him the cartridge, telling him to wear it as a souvenir on his watch-chain. He did.

'Alan Dixon is a big clown, always laughing, joking, extrovert, loves a sing-song and hasn't got an ounce of violence in him,' says the same friend.

Perhaps, but perhaps not always. One of the earlier skirmishes in which the Dixons found themselves was, as is so often the case in the East End, a quarrel over a girl. It concerned one of George Dixon's best friends who would eventually go on to give evidence against him.

> The fellow was going with a girl and so was young Paddy Harris who she preferred. The man went to the Queen's in York Square and sent Tinker Taylor in to tell Paddy to come outside. When he did he got cut in the cheek so bad it went through the other one. Whilst he was in hospital a number of his friends and a gang of dockers said they were going to spring the Dixons at the Prince of Wales, Duckett Street, Stepney. There was Ray Moore, Charlie Kray's brother-in-law and a number of others. When they got there George and Alan had locked the pub up.
>
> People were clamouring outside and they let them in one by one, did them and then threw them out another door. That same night Charlie Morris was going home to Dempsey Street and a man lay in wait for him. Charlie went up a 20 foot wall which had no grip on it and there was bullet marks all the way behind him.[3]

Several people including Ray Moore were arrested and charged, but the committal proceedings at Marylebone were a failure after faces in the East End intervened and persuaded some witnesses that there was little to be gained and a great deal to be lost in giving evidence. Moore was later shot dead in Greenwich in an unrelated incident.

The so-called leader of the Dixons was a publican, the 5' 2" Phil Jacobs, known locally as Little Caesar, whose houses were the Bridge House in Canning Town, the Royal Oak in Tooley Street, and the Plough and Harrow in Leytonstone which George Dixon minded. The Dixons had stood up for him when, shortly before their arrest, the Krays had tried to muscle in on his pubs and he put himself under their protection. Now Wickstead believed the Dixons were expanding their own empire under Jacobs' guidance, specialising in protection and long-firm fraud.

Jacobs had left school at the age of fourteen and had worked in various restaurants before he went away for his National Service. Unlike the Krays and the Richardsons he must have rather enjoyed it, becoming a Leading Aircraftsman. He married in November 1965 with only ten shillings to his name. His wife's parents bought them The Ship in Aylward Street and from then on, with hard work, he prospered. By the time of his arrest he had a Rolls-Royce with a personalised number plate.

> He was a vicious-tongued little bastard. The Twins gave him a slap one day and from then on he had the Dixons help him, minding his pubs. No disrespect by George but he didn't think very big. If he had £50, £45 would go straight into the bank. He didn't know where a bar was in a pub. If he knew someone was going to give him £5 he'd spend £8 in fares to get it. Alan was under George's thumb. Jacky Dixon was a very clever, deep man, mean with money. He worked on the docks all his life and for Philly on club doors.[4]

The Dixons seemed to get landed with much of Philly Jacobs' dirty work. When, much to the annoyance of her long-time lover Mickey Morris, later put away by Billy Amies, the former Bunny girl Patti Hardie became involved with Philly Jacobs it was they who were left to sort things out.

> Mickey Morris was madly in love with Patty from the time he was a kid and whilst he was doing six years Philly started fucking about with her. When Mickey came home he was not a man to be trifled with and he went to see Jacobs who promptly

hit Spain for safety reasons, leaving Patty behind and Lammy, his brother, to be looking after his businesses. The Dixons were left to sort things out. George contacted me and I contacted Mickey and there was to be a meeting at Mile End station at 6 a.m. Mickey hoped Philly would come along and then it would have been bye-bye Philly. George and the others thought it was just going to be a start off. I don't think they realised just how wild Mickey could be.

The meeting took place at 5 a.m. First thing Jackie Dixon walks up to Mick with a pair of scissors and cuts off his tie. It was very theatrical and really I wanted to laugh but I said, 'Jackie, we came here to have a talk or we're going. You came to me, I've gone to him and now you've cut off his tie which probably cost him fifteen–twenty quid.' George Dixon went to give him the money and Mick said, 'I don't want it. Buy me a replica.'[5]

George Dixon had already been acquitted at the Old Bailey along with Connie Whitehead, now serving a sentence with the Twins, of causing grievous bodily harm to a club-owner. The allegation had been that injuries were caused after he had refused the offer to have his club looked after. Wickstead's breakthrough in his inquiries came when a complaint was made to West Ham police station by one of the Dixons' brothers-in-law, Micky Flynn. He was immediately taken round to see Wickstead who wrote admiringly:

To say he was big was a little like saying that Rockefeller was rich or that Capone was bad. He was huge, one of the most formidable men I'd ever seen.

According to Flynn, he was one of the enforcers for the Dixons but now he had left his wife, Lynne, he had consequently fallen out with the brothers. They, he said, had retaliated with a bit of nastiness directed towards his (Flynn's) sisters; one had had her arm broken, another had been threatened.

A friend of the Dixons, and a participant observer in these matters, has it the other way around. 'He'd given his wife a beating and Brian Dixon went round to sort things out.' Translated this means 'sort *him* out'. Despite his size, Flynn, the Dixons maintain, ran for cover.

Wickstead sees him in a more heroic light, maintaining that he would have visited each Dixon brother in turn and dealt with him. 'But you see I didn't know how far I'd go,' the reformed character told the Commander. 'So I changed my mind. I wasn't going inside for the likes of them.' Since George and Alan Dixon were both built like tanks, it may well be that these were brave words spoken in the safety of the police station.

It would not have suited Wickstead to have the Dixons as victims:

> If the Dixons had then made a complaint, we would have had to charge him; and with his almost inhuman strength, it might not have stopped at grievous bodily harm. It could so easily have been manslaughter or even murder.[6]

When it came to it no charge was brought over the alleged breaking of Flynn's sister's arm.

It was the familiar pattern of an inquiry. Once one witness came forward it was easier for others and, following a raid on The Greyhound in Bethnal Green run by a man called Osborne in March 1971, when some fifty cases of gin were found, Wickstead had another witness. He was willing to give evidence about a fight between Michael Young and his cousin Mickey Bailey which he said had been the usual prelude to a demand for money for protection. The fight was witnessed by two off-duty police officers who were told not to interfere. Instead they withdrew and compiled notes of the incident.

The arrests came at 5.30 a.m. on 25 August 1971. Wickstead borrowed twenty-nine officers from the Flying Squad and, as a result, nearly came to disaster. His team was briefed at 4 p.m. and dispersed. Someone leaked the story to the *Evening Standard* which, by the time of the raid, had its early headline prepared: 'Yard Swoops on London Gangsters'.

Wickstead learned his lesson. In the future he used only his own squad and the special patrol group, locking them in a gymnasium from the time of the briefing until they left for the raid.

The Dixon trial began on 12 April 1972 and continued until 4 July. Much of the time had been spent challenging the evidence of the police. There had been no written statements of admission and much of the police evidence consisted of verbal admissions. There was also the now fashionable crossover from the dock to the witness-box as some defendants gave evidence against their former friends in return for no evidence being offered against them. Of the defendants who were left, Lambert Jacobs and Brian Dixon were acquitted; Phillip Jacobs, Leon Carleton and George Dixon received twelve years. Alan went down for nine and Michael Young and Michael Bailey, who had had the fight in The Greyhound, received five each.

Monty Sherbourne, defending in the case, had called it a 'storm in a teacup' but the judge, Mr Justice O'Connor, thought otherwise:

You have mounted a campaign of vilification during the trial against police officers in the hope of saving your skins. Such activity on your part cannot operate on my mind to increase the sentences I have to pass on you. On the other hand, it does show the nature of your guilt. And it removes entirely such compassion as I would have been willing to show.

O'Connor called Wickstead forward for a public commendation:

You and your men deserve the full commendation of the public for bringing this gang to justice. It was a difficult task, thoroughly, honestly, efficiently and fairly discharged.

The encomium did not appeal to the public gallery or the dock, from which someone shouted: 'The end of your reign in the East End is just beginning. We will get you, Wickstead. We will get you!'

But they did not. Instead Wickstead and his team remained a force to be reckoned with for some years, culminating in the inquiry into the murders of Billy Moseley and Mickey Cornwall. When George Dixon was released he took a pub in partnership with his father-in-law, then bought a run-down hotel in Hastings, did it up and sold it well. With the proceeds he purchased a caravan park at Frinton and then went into the motor trade. Later he moved to live in Spain.

On his release, Alan Dixon first had an eel stall outside The Swan public house run by Lenny McLean, who recalled helping him when some of the younger Watney Streeters attacked it late one night.[7] Ian Dixon later had a wine bar and then a public house, afterwards expanding into the entertainment business. Philly Jacobs was one of those who, never before having seen the inside of a prison, found doing time to be a demoralising experience. Whilst in Bristol prison, an article about Patty Hardie had appeared in *The People* saying she would wait for 'her Philly'. In an ensuing argument, boiling cocoa had been poured over Jacobs. On his release he faded from the East End scene.

Although the second of Wickstead's major inquiries produced the usual 'Gang War' headlines, it was a very different affair and, indeed, one which could have gone either way. This was the arrest of members of the Tibbs family which followed a long-standing feud with the Nicholls family from Stepney, described derisively amongst some East Enders as 'half gypsies' although that soubriquet could apply to many families. Other descriptions of them were 'not very nice', 'liberty takers' and the ultimate put-down 'not well liked'. The feud seems to have begun in 1968 when Georgie 'Bogie' Tibbs, then in his sixties and described by Tibbs supporters as 'a quiet man', was having a drink in The Steamship public house, managed by a friend of the Nicholls, Frederick Fawcett.[8] Bogie Tibbs was a drinking man and the story is told that when he awoke in hospital one day, on seeing a white-coated doctor he called out, 'Waiter, bring me a drink.'

Bogie Tibbs became involved in a row with Albert Nicholls, then in his twenties, who, legend has it, 'smashed into him'. Bogie's eyes were blacked and he lost two teeth. Reprisals were swift and suitable. Albert had a cab office in Poplar near the Blackwall Tunnel where he was visited by Jimmy Tibbs, his brother Johnny and Georgie's son, young George. Nicholls produced a shotgun. It was taken from him, he was knocked down and hit on the head with the stock.

What happened next is variously described. According to Wickstead:

A shotgun blast inflicted terrible injuries to his legs and to the lower part of his abdomen. There were three large lacerations in the scalp and cuts to the face. The tip of his nose was partially severed and he lost the tip of a finger.

And by an admittedly partisan East End historian as, 'Unfortunately the gun went off catching him in the leg.'

That seems to be just how the judge at the Old Bailey saw it because, on his direction, at the close of the prosecution case the Tibbs were acquitted of attempted murder and in a bargain pleaded guilty to minor charges:

> You have been guilty apart from anything else of the most appall-
> ing folly. I sympathise with your feelings but at the same time,
> living in the part of London where you live there is a great deal
> too much violence.

This was the comment of Mr Justice Lyell, to the fury of the Nicholls' supporters, when handing down suspended sentences of two years' imprisonment coupled with fines of £100 each.[9] Albert Nicholls was left with a limp. And he and other members of his family did not see this as justice being done.

This simmered for the next two years and then boiled over in November 1970 when Robert Tibbs had his throat cut outside The Rose of Denmark. Certainly Frederick Fawcett's brother, Micky, was there; but just who wielded the knife and who started what, Wickstead was never able to discover. Apparently the argument was over football.

Onlookers now say that the Tibbs 'went looking' and that anyone who was with Fawcett was their enemy. Efforts were made to quieten things down, but neither side was willing to stand back.

On Christmas Day, one of Fawcett's friends was attacked and severely beaten near his home. Later Michael Machin, brother of the later deceased Teddy, walked into the Steamship and shot up Freddie's ceiling. Teddy Machin himself was shot at whilst at home in bed. Two men crept up to his ground-floor-flat window and blasted him in the backside with a shotgun. Two weeks later, Michael was fired on by two men also armed with shotguns.

And so it went on. Ronnie Curtis, a friend of the Fawcetts, was badly beaten, as was Lennie Kersey who was said to have called the Tibbs pikeys.[10] He was attacked with knives and an axe as he left his flat in Mile End, receiving wounds which required 180 stitches. As his wife described the scene:

> I saw the men hacking at somebody on the ground and tried to stop the horrible thing. Then I saw it was my husband. His face was falling apart. I screamed the place down. My friend also screamed and dropped her baby.

Another to suffer was David Storey, who was said to look like Catweazle but who was described as 'having bottle'. He was attacked in the Upper Cut in Forest Gate, then owned by the former boxer Billy Walker.

Further attacks took place, both on the Nicholls and their friends and on the Tibbs family. Albert and Terence Nicholls were called out of The Rose of Denmark by Stanley Naylor and told to get into their car. As they did so, the windscreen was smashed and they were attacked. Albert was stabbed in the leg and a gun was produced. The police arrived and the attackers fled.

Terence was taken to hospital but while the police were questioning Albert, Jimmy Tibbs returned and drove his car at them. They all jumped for their lives. Albert then drove to the hospital to see his brother. On the way he was hijacked by Jimmy Tibbs and Naylor and hit with a golf club. He managed to push them out of the car as it approached the Blackwall Tunnel. For this attack Jimmy Tibbs was charged with attempted murder.

George Brett,[11] another friend of the Fawcetts and the Nicholls, was shot in the leg. He had tried to separate two men who were fighting in the Huntingdon Arms public house. Eight months later came what he said was the revenge. Finally came the incident which determined Wickstead that he must intervene. Until then, according to his memoirs, he seems to have been observing events with something approaching an Olympian detachment. Quite apart from which, he still had his hands full with the Dixon case.

On 22 April 1971, a bomb was placed under the engine of Jimmy Tibbs' car near the radiator and exploded outside a school when his four-year-old son was with him. They would both have been killed had the bomb been positioned properly. The attack came a week after his café, The Star in Star Road, had also exploded – although in this case possibly from a gas leak.

'Enough was enough,' wrote Wickstead.[12] Now he augmented his squad and started to liaise with Treasury Counsel, Michael Corkery, and the late Dai Tudor Price who himself became an Old Bailey judge. To the outsider it might seem that there was a problem as to which of the rival factions, if not both, should be prosecuted. Wickstead had no such doubts:

... which faction posed the greatest threat to law and order. The answer to that had to be the Tibbs. They were a highly organised gang. They were becoming steadily more powerful, more ruthless, more ambitious. They were also more wicked and crueller than their opponents. The Nicholls weren't a gang in the accepted sense of the word – more of a loose collection of criminal friends. The same thing could be said about Michael Fawcett and his associates. My decision, incidentally, was agreed and fully endorsed by the DPP.

It was not an opinion shared by the East End in general. Old man Jimmy Tibbs may have been doing well out of receiving the contents of stolen lorries, but there does not seem to be any suggestion that they were actively involved in protection.

Wickstead settled on Fawcett as the key figure for his prosecution and an arrangement was made with him outside Westminster tube station that he would give evidence. After the arrests, and whilst the Tibbs were in custody awaiting trial, a curious incident took place at Rook's Farm, Stocking Pelham, in Hertfordshire.[13]

After the Hosein case the farm had been bought for £17,500 by an East End publican Tony Wyatt, who also used the name Lewis. On 19 September 1972, at a reception at the farm following the wedding of his sister-in-law, Avril Hurst, Micky Fawcett, Lennie Kersey and Curtis, another prosecution witness, were guests. During the festivities a young man named John Scott was killed with a sickle. The holes in his body were plugged and he was dressed in fresh clothes; he was then placed in his van and driven to the East End where his body was found on the following Monday in Ranelagh Road, Leytonstone, by some school boys. A number of people including Terry Nicholls were arrested and taken to Leytonstone Police Station before being released.

Wyatt was charged with his murder. Scott, he said, had been an uninvited guest who had ridden one of the horses on the farm and had been a general nuisance:

> I asked Scott to leave [he told the police]. There was an argument. He pushed me and I fell on the hearth. I got up with something in my hand and I hit him twice with it and he fell down. I realised I had hit him with a sickle. The only reason that this happened was that Scott was making a nuisance of himself to the women of my family and he attacked me when I asked him to leave.

On 9 March 1973 he was convicted of manslaughter and sentenced to three years' imprisonment, most of which was served at Leyhill open prison. He was paroled after twelve months in jail. Although it is inconceivable that Wyatt managed everything in the way of re-dressing the body and transporting it to Leytonstone by himself, no charges seem to have been brought against any other people.

The Tibbs' trial, heard by Mr Justice Lawton who had disposed of the Richardsons, lasted forty-four days. In January 1973 seven members of the family and their friends were jailed. James Tibbs senior received fifteen years, Stanley Naylor twelve, Michael Machin – who was said to have 'egged others on to violence' – went down for eleven, and the boxer Jimmy Tibbs for ten. Immediately after the verdict Mrs Kate Tibbs, James Tibbs senior's wife, was found suffering from a drugs overdose and was taken to hospital for treatment. Later she defended her family, saying, 'They are not gangsters or Godfathers. They are good, honest workers. The Press and the court have crucified us.'[14]

Michael Machin died in prison in October 1973, having developed Bright's disease. His brother, Victor, provided a kidney transplant but it failed. It was thought that his disease had been brought on by the shock of being shot when a car pulled alongside him while he was out walking. Sadly, after his release young Robert Tibbs was one of many of that time who went into drug-dealing. In April 1993, now a company director, he received eight years for his involvement in a 1¼-ton cannabis shipment which had been moved from Morocco to Oban. He was also ordered to pay £200,000.

Overall this was not a terribly popular prosecution amongst the *cognoscenti*, and their sentences received less than universal approval in the East End where it was felt that the Nicholls were the villains.

'They stuck up for themselves, that's all,' was the general reaction Oliver Pritchett of the *Evening Standard* encountered when he canvassed the locals after the case. 'I bet you can go into any pub in Canning Town today and you won't hear a word against them,' said one. 'They've never been liberty takers and that's gospel,' said another.

The trial was not, however, quite the end of things. The dying Michael Machin named names in prison and Commander Reginald Davis was sent to investigate.

At the end of 1973, eight men including Albert Nicholls and Michael Fawcett were arrested and charged with crimes such as attempted murder and grievous bodily harm dating back twelve years and totally independent of the Tibbs trial. On 19 October the Director of Public Prosecutions decided not to proceed. Proposed witnesses had vanished and those who remained were said to be 'possibly reluctant to give evidence'. The *omerta* of the East End ruled once more. The eight defendants were released and were awarded £100 each for their costs.[15]

After his release from prison, Jimmy Tibbs worked with the boxing manager Terry Lawless and was eventually given a licence – first as a trainer-second and then as a manager – by the British Boxing Board of Control. In the late 1980s he became a born-again Christian. George Tibbs, who in a way had started it all, rather blotted his copybook with the family, tending to side with the Nicholls. While her husband, James senior, was in prison Kathy Tibbs would occasionally send her brother-in-law a bundle of grass at a weekend.

Amazingly the Tibbs' case was the last of the so-called protection racket cases for fifteen years. It was 1990 before Frank Salmon, a market trader from Dagenham, was jailed at the Old Bailey for seven and a half years. He had been convicted of blackmail, affray and an attack during which ammonia was squirted in a victim's face. Robert Mitchell, said to be Salmon's right-hand man, was sentenced to three years for blackmail, affray and possession of a firearm, whilst Gary Pollard received four and a half years and Donald Meason twenty-one months.

Salmon had reigned over a part of the East End and Essex for a little over a year, trying to obtain protection money from twenty-three wine bars, clubs and saunas. He had shot up one bar and pressed a gun under the nose of a barman. In 1989 disc jockey Russell Holt, who played the East End pubs, had forty-two stitches in his head and hand following an assault by four masked men. His ankle was broken by a pool cue and he too went to the police. He told detectives he had been asked to pay Salmon £1,500 as a share in his earnings.

The police used WPC Elaine Manson[16] as the person to trap Salmon. Acting as the friend and business associate of Holt's wife, Denise Seaga, who ran a dress shop, she met Salmon on five occasions paying out a total of £800. It was thought that Salmon, known as a womaniser, would be less suspicious than if a male officer had acted as a decoy. On one meeting she was patted down by him when he came to suspect she was a police officer. One time when she was with him he 'shook his arm and a knife slid down inside his left palm', she told the court.

When she asked if he had a knife, 'Brains of Britain ...' he replied. 'In this business you get wankers who don't play ball.' On 22 May 1989 she handed over money and asked Salmon why he referred to the cash as a present. 'I am not going to shout out it is protection money, am I?' he replied. Afterwards a detective commented:

He tried to model himself on people like the Krays, though he was never going to be as criminally successful as them. He was a plastic gangster, but he was also a dangerous and violent one.[17]

In the late 1990s Stanley Naylor's son Lennie was caught in a drug deal and served three and a half years. Within two years of his release Lennie was shot and killed in April 2001 in the driveway of his home near Gravesend by a man who escaped in a white Bedford Rascal van. One theory was that it was revenge for a machete attack in a Canning Town pub in 1996. Naylor had been arrested but no charges had been brought. In October 2017 Terence Barry, known at the time as Terence Richardson, who had fled to Spain, was jailed for eighteen years for conspiracy to murder. Two others were found not guilty. A fourth man had been acquitted on the direction of the judge.

NOTES

1. L. Read, *Nipper*, p. 266.
2. L. McLean, *The Guv'nor*, p. 111.
3. Conversation with author, August 1999.
4. ibid.
5. ibid.
6. The quotations come from Bert Wickstead, *Gangbuster*, Chapter 11.
7. ibid, p. 111.
8. ibid, p. 89.
9. Albert Nicholls seems to have been out of luck on another occasion. During one of the periods when the Kray Twins were seriously feuding with the Richardsons, he was knocked down on the pavement outside The Lion public house in Tapp Street and his leg was broken. He had been mistaken for Ronnie Kray.
10. A term of abuse meaning gypsies. The origin is harmless and comes from a user of turnpikes. Since the middle of the twentieth century, as *piker* it has, however, come to mean a thief or cheat.
11. For the end of George Brett, see Chapter 16.

12. Bert Wickstead, *Gangbuster*, p. 91

13. Mrs Muriel McKay, the wife of the chief executive of the *News of the World*, had been kidnapped and held captive there by the Hosein brothers, Arthur and Nizamodeen, in December 1969. They had demanded a ransom of £1m. She was almost certainly shot at the farm and her body fed to the pigs. The brothers were sentenced to life imprisonment at the Old Bailey in 1970.

14. *Daily Express*, 20 January 1973.

15. For an article sympathetic to the Tibbs, see Corinna Adam, 'War in the East End' in *New Statesman*, 7 December 1973.

16. A pseudonym.

17. James Morton, *Gangland*.

15

THE MALTESE GANGS

The Messina brothers – Carmelo, Alfredo, Salvatore, Attilio and Eugenio – began their career as *souteneurs* and pimps in the 1930s. Their father Giuseppe came from Linguaglossa in Sicily and in the late 1890s went to Malta where he became an assistant in a brothel in Valetta. There he married a Maltese girl, Virginia de Bono. His first two sons, Salvatore and Alfredo, were born there. The family then moved to Alexandria in 1905 where he built a chain of brothels in Suez, Cairo and Port Said. The remaining sons were all born in Alexandria, and their father ensured they were all well educated. In 1932 Giuseppe Messina was expelled from Egypt. Two years later Eugenio, the third son born in 1908, came to England. He was able to claim British nationality because his father had sensibly claimed Maltese citizenship. With Eugenio was his wife Colette, a French prostitute, and it was on her back that Messina founded his London empire.

More girls were recruited from the Continent and as the empire grew Eugenio was joined on the management side by his brothers. Property was bought throughout the West End and the brothers turned their attention to English girls. By 1946, with the family's weekly earnings at £1,000, the girls were earning

£100 a night and were being paid £50 a week. It was not until 1950 that the Messinas were exposed for what they were, and it was the work of Duncan Webb, a curious man who a little later caused so much trouble for Jack Spot. A devout Roman Catholic, Webb believed his mission was to clean the streets of London. After one triumph over the Messinas he put an advertisement in *The Times* offering thanks to St Jude. After the murderer Donald Hume, killer of Stanley Setty, had been convicted, Webb married Hume's wife Cynthia. On 3 September 1950 *The People* published the exposure, backing it with photographs of the Messina girls and the flats from where they operated. Eugenio and Carmelo fled, as did Salvatore. Attilio and Alfredo remained.

On 19 March 1951 Alfredo was arrested at his Wembley home charged with living off immoral earnings and trying to bribe a police officer. He had offered Superintendent Mahon, one of the arresting officers, £200. He received two years' imprisonment concurrent on each of the charges and a £500 fine. Attilio and Eugenio were eventually accepted by the Italian government. Salvatore lived in Switzerland whilst Alfredo, who could claim British citizenship, died in Brentford in 1963.[1]

Nevertheless in 1956, out of thirty-five convicted in local courts of living off immoral earnings twenty-seven were Maltese. It was not always a high-class operation, more one of subsistence. In May 1958 one Maltese received four months for living off the earnings of his wife. When the police raided the premises there was only 3/6d in the house and £30 was owed to a clothing club.[2]

A run through the local papers of the time indicates the problems. Four dirty rooms in Hessell Street were being let to prostitutes at £3,000 a year. Prostitutes paid £20 a week for an insanitary room: two Maltese, Joseph Xerni and Tony Cutajat, were jailed for two months; Spiro Camillieri (twenty-three), who received twenty-one months for living off immoral earnings, had three previous convictions; Carmel Falzon was also convicted.[3]

Mickey Bailey remembers:

Around Cannon Street Road in Aldgate there were drinkers all over the place. I could probably name a hundred but there were nearer two or even three hundred. There was whole streets of them. It was just like Soho except Aldgate was smaller and the brasses were a cheap touch. There were a few drinking clubs owned by white men but the brasses were under the control of Malts and blacks. When I had clubs we'd let some girls in but the Malts would have their clubs full – they were earning from them.

A Malt, Emmanuel Buttigieg was known as Farmer – he'd been a farmer in Malta and who kept rabbits and goats in his back garden, and the nickname stuck – owned Sanders Street. Down that street there were two up two downs with two girls and a maid working 24 hours a day. Then you had Swendenbourg Square – big Victorian houses turned into flats and furnished rooms where they were doing tricks. I should think there was more brasses there than in Soho. The big names were Joe Ferrugia, Big Frank Mifsud and George Caruana.

Then there was Henriques Street, named after Sir Basil, the magistrate, that was full of clubs. The Cockney Club was in the next street and there was Abdullah's, owned by Somalis but used by a lot of white people. That was very clean. There were others in Grace's Alley – they were all illegal drinkers. Brothels were run openly.

In one building there was the Sabre Club and another the Mark. There was the Lowndes Bar, Vincent's in Batty Street and Farmer's as well as Vincent's was owned by a one-armed Malt – he'd lost it in the war – but with that one arm he had the strength of three men. He had houses galore but he was very good to the people who worked for him. He'd always have front men for him.

A lot of money went through George Miesl, which meant it went to the Twins.[4]

On 29 February 1969 Buttigieg was shot dead outside his café by John Marie Borg, who was sentenced to ten years. It seems to have been a domestic dispute.

After his release, Borg was involved in West End properties with the powerful but shadowy Maltese-born John Gaul, who owned Sun Real Estates, a property company which had prestigious tenants including the Law Society, the National Coal Board and the Postmaster General. Unfortunately there were also prostitutes in properties the company owned in Wardour Mews and Gerrard, Wardour, Frith, Berwick and Old Compton Streets.[5]

Borg died in suspicious circumstances. His body was found on 3 May 1978 after a blast destroyed a mini-cab office and flats in Hackney Road belonging to Printing House Properties Ltd, a £100 company owned by John Gaul. Curiously no smoke was found to have been in Borg's lungs, a clear indication that he had died before the fire. Things were made more complicated when it became known that a Portuguese, Carlos Amazonas, had made a statement to the police that Borg had been approached to kill Gaul's wife, Barbara.

There is no doubt John Gaul, procurer to the rich and with a conviction for living off immoral earnings, set up the contract killing of his estranged wife, a former children's nanny, who died after being shot outside the Black Lion Hotel, Patcham, near Brighton, where she had been visiting her daughter Samantha on Monday 12 January 1976. She died eleven weeks later.

On the basis that when a wife is killed the first person to be questioned is the husband, John Gaul was taken into Cannon

Row police station but later released. Almost immediately he fled to Rio de Janeiro. Later that year he was found with a new nanny, Angela Pilch, in Switzerland before moving on to Malta.

It was not difficult for the police to trace the actual killers. On the way from the killing the shotgun used was dropped from a car window and recovered, and later the car was traced to a breaker's yard in East London. The contract had been arranged in Norfolk with two East End brothers, Roy and Keith Edgeler.

The brothers were jailed on 24 June 1976. In the witness-box Roy said that, from his limited knowledge, he did not believe it was John Gaul who had arranged the contract for which he was to have been paid £10,000. He was given a recommendation of a minimum of twenty years to serve.

On 3 April 1978, Gaul was arrested in Malta where he had high political connections and where he was living on a boat in the harbour, defying efforts to have him returned to the United Kingdom. Three years later the official explanation was that insufficient evidence had been supplied by the British police, but Gaul was now well established – he had built and leased out a 240-room hotel. In March that year he was reported to have had a serious heart attack. On 17 July a magistrate in Malta said the prosecution case was weak and refused to order extradition.

By April 1984 it was reported that the English police had given up. Even if he came back the passage of time had made witnesses' memories unreliable. Gaul was still said to be ill and medical certificates were sent to the Director of Public Prosecution, on whose orders the warrant was dropped. Gaul died in September 1989 in Italy. He had been reported missing, but it was three days before it was realised he had died in a Milan hospital.

According to the *Sun*[6] Keith Edgeler, then in Ford open prison, named Gaul as the man who had ordered the contract. It was, he said, because Gaul feared Barbara was about to expose shady property deals. He said he never received the payment for the murder. Despite offers by the police for a deal he had refused to talk on the basis that if a man could have his wife murdered, his own family was in danger. In the East End there were persistent stories that the shooting, which was explained as a bungled warning, had been brokered through Charlie Kray. 'I don't believe it. You'd never do business with him,' says one London figure. 'The only thing I do believe is that if this man had brokered it, it would have been botched.'

But back in the late 1950s there were troubles from the English who believed that some Maltese club-owners were actively recruiting East End girls for prostitution, and Vincent's was set on fire after a fight in January 1958.

They were getting girls whom we'd known as kids, giving them Preludin and putting them on the game. Funnily a lot of the girls came from Dagenham. A girl who'd lived in Billy Fisher's flat was with a Malt and Billy said he was taking her home to her parents, That's when the fight started. Six got arrested but there were probably about as many again and there were about thirty Malts. I had a cut head, a cut over the eye and bruising all over. About 11 that night I went to hospital and whilst I was there someone threw petrol down the stairs and a match after it. Shortly after that Jimmy Lawley, known as Jimmy the Pleaser or Jimmy Shovel Tongue, was cut in the Commercial Road in a fight with some Maltese. He believed that Johnny Gatt, known as American Johnny, was involved. In May that year they went searching for him.[7]

Jimmy was set on going back to see the Malt up the West End and his friend Derek said he'd come too. He always had a

gun – a big old piece – and they went into this restaurant in the
Edgware Road. American Johnny ran out the back and Derek
saw a shadow go past and fired. It was a bit of bad luck. It was
the cook. He got a ten and Jimmy a seven. He was away six to
nine months and he escaped from the Scrubs. He was out eight
or nine years and started a family. Then, as luck would have it,
his wife bought a crooked jumper from the woman below. Derek
took the blame, said it was his and told the cozzers who he was
before they even fingerprinted him. The judge didn't believe him
at the Sessions. He said he was sure he was covering and he said
he was recommending that he serve no longer than two years of
the original sentence. He came out, went straight and we never
heard any more of him.[8]

One of the reasons for the existence of the clubs and cafés
was the passing of the Street Offences Act 1957 which drove
prostitutes from the streets and indoors. It was to these cafés that
Lord Stoneham referred when he spoke in the House of Lords on
gangsterism in the East End. Up to 1954 there were only eighteen
registered clubs in Stepney; by 1960 there were ninety. Within
three minutes' walk of St Paul's Church, Dock Street, there were
thirty-two cafés and clubs, and in one spot within 25 yards there
were six cafés combined with clubs, four of them adjoining.

One problem was the linked café and club such as the
Cockney Café in Backchurch Lane, which only sold tea and soft
drinks. It had a capacity of twenty-eight people, but the owner
paid a weekly rent of £20. The reason he could afford this was
because of the number of girls who took men upstairs where it
transmogrified into the Britannia Club. All who mounted the
stairs and other things were members.

One of the worst problems was the frequency and speed
with which clubs reopened under other names after police raids

and prosecutions. The Play Box in Berner Street was regarded as just about the worst until, after serious effort in 1958, the police managed to bring a successful prosecution against the proprietor who was fined £140 on seven counts of allowing prostitutes to consort. He was also deprived of his licence to run a refreshment house. The same night the premises reopened as The Blue Heaven Club.[9]

The 9A Club became the Horseshoe Club and then the Corridor Club, but in all its guises it had one evening and two afternoon shows of teenage strippers with an audience of about fifty, mainly City workers. Membership was immediate and gained on the signing of a membership form. In this case its main purpose was to increase the sale of drink out of licensing hours rather than the sale of sex. After it closed as the Corridor, when it had the unhealthy total of 666 members, it reopened as The Ninepins.

However, some of the club-owners did display a limited concern, if perhaps mixed with self-interest, for the girls. With a view to obtaining a licence, one had the wit to set up a committee which never met and to which he appointed Edith Ramsay, the Head of LCC's Stepney Women's Evening Institute, a teacher and unofficial social worker whom Lord Stoneham described as 'the Florence Nightingale of the Brothels'. Over a period of time he brought some twenty of the girls to Edith Ramsay's institute in Myrdle Street, where she endeavoured to teach them dressmaking.[10]

The Cosmopolitan Club in the Commercial Road was run by a Ghanaian called Sherriff. It was populated by black men only and single white girls, and stayed open until 2 a.m. for the purposes of prostitution.

One long-running club was the St Louis which had opened at the end of the 1940s and in the twilight of its career was owned by Seriff Bambo Kaitay and used by servicemen from the US bases. Kaitay clearly did try to keep some sort of order and would not allow drugs to be sold on the premises. In April 1958 he handed over a dealer to the police, but despite his efforts eventually the Trustees of the United Jewish Friendly Society obtained a repossession order of the premises, for which the rent was £1,500 a year and which had a membership of 7,000, each paying six shillings a week, but not before Mr Justice Donovan had some remarks to make:

> I think the plaintiffs exhibited a high and suspicious degree of unworldliness if they thought for two years that this club, catering largely for coloured men and paying a very substantial rent, was serving only ginger beer or lemonade to its members.[11]

But sex was not simply an indoor recreation. Father Joseph Williamson, one of the clergy in the area who campaigned against vice, was also one of those prelates who had perhaps an unhealthily explicit attitude to sex. Somewhat unnecessarily and certainly graphically he told Edith Ramsay of four or five men on a street corner, two with their trousers down and the others 'driving up them like dogs'. He was not a Roman Catholic, but he would give a blessing if the girls wanted it and also would recite portions of Kipling's poem 'If ' to them, in this case unasked. Nevertheless, one Christmas he and his wife took a violently sick prostitute into their home; she was pregnant, mentally unbalanced and had broken wrists. He also set up Church House in Wellclose Square as a hostel for ex-prostitutes, managed by a Committee for Moral Improvement.

He was clearly a charismatic speaker, leading Edith Ramsay in a debate on housing and prostitution at the London Diocesan Conference, and recounting to the audience how coach loads of continental students pulled up in Ensign Square with the tour guide telling them, 'You'll find everything here.'

There are people in this hall who saw three men committing sodomy in the open in Wellclose Square.

Before the Sexual Offences Act 1957, at 7 p.m. one evening I found a group of my schoolchildren watching a coloured man and a white girl having sexual intercourse ...

... they know nothing of prostitution or the sordid and vicious level of slavery. Girls screaming and fighting for their money, girls taking man after man in the open street, girls being smashed to the ground, thrown down bodily and kicked ...[12]

In the summer of 1958 the residents took action, lobbying the council and politicians to do something positive about suppressing prostitution in the area. First another petition was presented to the town hall. At the end of June the police produced a record number of prostitutes before the Thames magistrate Cecil Campion. Instead of the usual three or four on a Saturday morning, twenty-four girls were on parade to be fined forty shillings. The observant magistrate pointed out that a number of these girls appeared to be Marlborough Street ones.[13] Not everyone accepted there was a problem and, to hectoring and calls of '—–fool', one of the younger Bethnal Green councillors C.F.F. Fleet argued, 'There are no prostitutes or pimps in the borough. What has been purported tonight is untrue. Ours is a good borough.'[14]

This was at a time when housing conditions were at their worst. In 1961 the Stepney Borough housing waiting list had 3,606 families and approximately 14,000 individuals; 326 families were on the LCC Borough clearance area lists and there was no prospect of rehousing the remaining 3,280 families and 13,000 people.

Independents rarely flourished for very long in the East End, or the West End for that matter. One who tried and died was

Tommy Smithson who, in his chequered and largely unsuccessful career, suffered at just about everyone's hands. Smithson, an ex-fairground fighter with a penchant for silk shirts and underwear, a man of immense courage and little stability or ability, was known as Mr Loser. Born in Liverpool in 1920 and brought to the East End two years later, he had served in the Merchant Navy until his discharge in the 1950s. Back in Shoreditch he found things to be different. The Maltese had now assumed control of clubs and cafés, and Smithson decided to set up his own protection racket devoted to these Maltese businessmen as well as working a spinner[15] with Tony Mella around the dog tracks.

Initially he protected George Caruana – said to resemble Tony Curtis, and whose gambling clubs included one in Batty Street, Stepney – acting as his minder and as a croupier. At the time Caruana and the other Maltese were keen to avoid trouble and Smithson soon extended his interest to a share of the takings in the clubs. A levy of one shilling in the pound from the dice games earned him up to £100 an evening. He also moved into a series of drinking clubs in the West End.

But now he had moved into competition with the Hill–Spot interests and he was involved in a fight with Frederick 'Slip' Sullivan, cutting him in the throat and arm while throwing him out of French Henry's. Unfortunately Sullivan, who was later murdered by his girlfriend, was the brother of Sonny, a member of the Hill–Spot firm, and reprisals were swift.

A week later Smithson was betrayed by the Maltese he had been protecting. Told there was a peace offer on the table, he was asked to attend a meeting at the Black Cat factory in Camden Town. On the dramatic signal of a cigar butt tossed onto the pavement, Smithson was dragged from the car and slashed over his face, arms, legs and chest. He was then thrown over a wall in Regent's Park and left to die. The slashes on his face were in the form of the letter V down each cheek, meeting at his chin. Smithson had not been wholly naive; two loaded revolvers had been taken from him before his slashing. Somehow he survived and forty-seven stitches were put in his face. Amongst those present were Hill, Spot, Moishe Blueball, Spot's aide-de-camp, and Sonny Sullivan. Smithson's reward for honouring the code of silence was a party, the soubriquet 'Scarface' and £500 with which he bought a share in a club in Old Compton Street, and then another for illegal gaming. This too was closed down by the police and Smithson took up fencing as an occupation. For a time he was successful, but then word began to spread that he was a police informer. This time he received a further twenty-seven stitches after another beating.[16]

He retreated back to the East End to provide protection for the Maltese, but yet again he miscalculated. Now a new wave of Maltese club-owners was becoming more powerful. They may not have wished to have trouble, but they were themselves preparing for a move into the recently vacated Messina territory and were not prepared to tolerate the likes of Smithson.

Smithson had also contracted an unfortunate alliance. He had fallen in love with Fay Richardson, one-time prostitute, then prostitute's maid and seemingly bad luck for most of the men with whom she took up. Three of her lovers were murdered and others suffered bad beatings. Now she was on remand in Holloway prison on forged cheque allegations. Originally from Stockport, where she had been a mill girl, she was what could be described both as a gangster's moll and a *femme fatale*. She said of the handsome Smithson:

[He was] a dapper dresser, very fussy about having a clean shirt every day. He was a big gambler. He could have £400 on the nose.

Money was needed for her defence and Smithson set about raising it with a will. On 13 June 1956 Smithson, together with Walter Downs and Christopher Thomas, went to a café in Berner Street, Stepney, and confronted his one-time employer Caruana and Philip Ellul, a Maltese who ran a second- or third-division string of prostitutes. Smithson said he wanted more than £50 from Caruana and in the ensuing fight Caruana's fingers were slashed as he protected his face from a flick-knife. Other Maltese in the café were held off at gunpoint by Thomas. A further £30 was produced. In accordance with standard gangland practice Ellul was told to start a collection for Fay and provided with a book to record the contributions.

On 25 June Smithson was found dying in the gutter outside George Caruana's house in Carlton Vale. He had been shot in the arm and neck. His last words were said to be, 'Good morning, I'm dying.'

Fay Richardson sent a wreath: 'Till we meet again.' Smithson's death worked well in her favour and she was placed on proba-tion with a condition she returned to Lancashire and did not visit London for three years. Although over the years there were reported sightings in the company of Australian shoplifters known as the Kangaroo Gang she faded into obscurity.

It was some years before the story behind Smithson's death was unravelled and the police, in the form of Bert Wickstead, believed that the pre-eminent mover was Bernie Silver whose operations can be traced back to the early 1950s when initially he ran clubs and brothels in Brick Lane. In 1956 he was arrested and charged with living off immoral earnings. Along with a man Cooper and acting as an estate agent, he had been carrying on an extension of the Messina trade by letting out rooms and flats to prostitutes at exorbitant rents. Silver appeared at the Old Bailey along with a prostitute, Albertine Falzon, and seven others in front of the eccentric Judge Maud who found there was no case for the defendants to answer. Albertine Falzon later married Silver. In the 1970s she committed suicide by leaping out of the flat in Peter Street, Soho, from which she worked.

Meanwhile Silver had been pursuing something of a parallel if more active course. So far as he and his partner Frank Mifsud were concerned, it blew apart again in 1973 when Silver was arrested for living off the immoral earnings of prostitutes and Mifsud went on the run. The girls, run by the Syndicate, as it was known, had been organised on a factory-line basis. One girl would run the flat from 1 until 7 p.m. when the next shift took over until the early hours of the morning.

Each girl would contribute £180 a week to the Syndicate. Silver had been responsible for the recruitment and placing of the girls and they clocked on and off their shifts on time. Strip clubs in Soho provided up to six shows daily, with the girls travelling from one to the next on a circuit and giving six performances a day. The flats above the strip clubs were owned by Silver, Mifsud and their nominees.

That scourge of East London, Bert Wickstead, had for the moment moved his operations from the East End and had been called in to investigate the Soho vice syndicates. His operation ran side by side with one against dirty bookshops and the investigation into the Porn Squad. One of the first men he wished to interview was George Caruana, who over the years had had three separate attempts made on his life, by any standards a risky one. In 1968 he had been the intended target of a Kray-led attack. Although they had interests in Soho this was to be done as a favour to Bernie Silver, with the possible fringe benefit that they would have a substantial hold over him. The plan to blow up his car was foiled when, as a result of a phone tap, the intended assassin, Paul Elvey, was arrested in Scotland with three dozen sticks of dynamite. There had been a considerable trade between the London gangs and Scottish mineworkers who supplemented their wages with the supply of explosives.

Perhaps sensibly, Caruana left the country to work a double act with his wife in a strip club in Hamburg. It was at his house that Smithson had been murdered in 1956. Now, in 1973, Caruana was located and made a statement – but then, when it came to it, he declined to give evidence. His retraction was to be only one of a series of early disappointments for Wickstead.

In fact Wickstead had considerable misfortune with his witnesses throughout the case. Apart from Caruana's defection another potential witness, Maltese Frank Dyer, was kidnapped in London and given a beating, with a gun held to his head, to try to make him disclose what he had told the police. In October 1973, the top men of the Syndicate took off on an extended holiday. An offer of £35,000 had been made for the Serious Crime Squad to drop the charge against Silver. It seemed as though Wickstead's work might have been wasted. One of the officers in his squad had been given the tip-off that raids were due. Wickstead went through the motions of having warrants he had obtained withdrawn, and then leaked a carefully prepared story that his work had been wasted and his investigation abandoned. For the moment he turned his attention to pornographic books.

Three months later the directors of the Syndicate started to filter back and on 30 December Bernie Silver was spotted at the Park Tower Hotel in London. He was arrested – along with his then girlfriend, Dominique Ferguson – as they finished dinner, and was taken to Limehouse police station where Wickstead felt more at home. He could not discount the fact that at West End Central he might run into corrupt officers who could impede his progress.

That morning a raid was organised on the Scheherazade Club

in Soho. Wickstead had stepped up on the stage to announce the wholesale arrest. 'What do you think of the cabaret?' called one reveller. 'Not much,' shouted another. The assembled company, including the band, was arrested and taken down to another East End police station which Wickstead considered was far from the eyes and ears of the police at West End Central.

But the sweep did not net Frank Mifsud. He had been living in Dublin but was tipped off with a phone call on the night of the Scheherazade raid. By the time the Garda went to arrest him he had gone.

One of the charges against Silver was conspiracy to murder Tommy Smithson. By now Wickstead had most of the story concerning the small-time hoodlum's death. His attempts to blackmail Silver to put up money for Fay Richardson's defence had come at a most unfortunate time. Silver was preparing his moves from Brick Lane into Soho and could not afford any hindrance. Nor could he allow himself to be seen as a weak man. Two contract killers, Philip Ellul and Victor Spampinato, were given the contract and executed their one-time friend Smithson, but they were never paid.

After the murder they had gone into hiding in Manchester where they received a message from the Syndicate telling them to give themselves up. A deal had been arranged that they would only be charged with manslaughter, and once their sentences had been served they need never work again. But they were betrayed, and both had been put on trial for murder at which Spampinato had been acquitted and Ellul sentenced to death before being reprieved on the eve of his execution. He served eleven years and on his release came to London to collect his money. Sixpence was thrown on the floor and he was told to pick it up. Later he was taken to obtain a passport and then to Heathrow.

Spampinato was found by Wickstead's officers working as a

wine-bar tout in Malta. Ellul was traced by the American police and telephoned Wickstead. Yes, he would come and give evidence. Spampinato gave evidence at the committal proceedings at Old Street Magistrates' Court but did not reappear at the trial. When next traced in Malta he owned a villa on the sea front at Sliema, a new car and was said to be in possession of £30,000. His contract had been honoured at last.

Ellul was given police protection in a flat in Limehouse. He was kept under close observation but complained, saying that his time in the death cell had left its mark on him and he did not like company. The watch was relaxed and later Ellul said he wanted to go back to the States, promising to return for the trial. There is no such thing as protective custody of witnesses in England and so no reason to detain him. He never returned. It is said he was paid £60,000, which would roughly equal the payment made to Spampinato.

Silver was found not guilty on the charge of conspiring to murder Tommy Smithson but guilty of living off immoral earnings. He received six years' imprisonment. Others in the case received up to five years. All that remained was the arrest of 'Big Frank' Mifsud.

He was found in Switzerland where he had been living in hiding in a small tent on the Austrian border and returned to London after fighting a losing extradition battle on the grounds of his ill-health. Mifsud was sentenced to five years' imprisonment, only for the Court of Appeal to quash the conviction. He did not remain in England long: he left and returned to Malta to live on the proceeds of his Swiss bank accounts along with the other members of the Syndicate before moving for a time to Dublin. He died in Malta in the autumn of 1999. Silver returned to the West End but, although now property-rich, he was never again quite a force with which to be reckoned.[17]

Gradually the slum clearances moved prostitution from the area and north towards Brick Lane. That does not mean to say there were not still some pockets left. However, the trade had changed.

In 1975 disued prefabs on Stoneyard Estate in Poplar were being used by under-age prostitutes[18] but a decade later saunas were keeping things more discreet and the prostitutes off the streets.[19]

Stepney was a £20–£25 beat, but by 1993 crackhead girls reduced it to £15–£20. Now in an effort to dissuade clients from approaching the girls the police were videoing punters, and it was estimated that fifty prostitutes worked the area. A Brick Lane resident recalls:

I have lived in the area since the early 1980s. When I first moved into the area the local prostitutes were a spillover from Spitalfields fruit and vegetable market on Commercial Street where most of the visible prostitution was centred. With the end of the market, Old Montague Street became a popular rat-run for kerb crawlers.

In the 1980s the local girls were mainly regulars, out on the streets with their own corner or stretch of the road; many either lived in the area or came from the neighbourhood. They were invariably white and their pimps were mainly white, though the punters were a mix of white and Asian men. Most of the girls and their pimps were on drugs – particularly heroin – or alcoholics but they were generally friendly to local people. They were tolerated by the likes of me and my neighbours. The police kept a low profile. The prostitutes I knew from that period are now either working from home or rented flats or dealing.

In the past few years the situation has changed. The girls and their pimps are a different, louder more hostile breed.

There is a lot more trouble with the mainly black pimps and much more violence on the streets late night. My neighbours' attitudes to the local prostitution have become much more hard-line as parked cars have been damaged, used condoms and syringes left in public hallways and residents threatened. My neighbours no longer regard the local streets as safe at night. People who complain in the early hours about the noise have been beaten up and verbally abused. One pimp urinating outside my front door even threatened me with a knife when I complained. There is a lot more visible drug dealing in the streets, day and night.[20]

Much of the prostitution in the area was of heroin-addicted white girls sent on the streets by Bangladeshis, but with some infiltration from outside.

There was still semi-organised prostitution in the Commercial Road. One enterprising doctor in need of money to pay her bills set up a brothel over a dry cleaning shop. The newly qualified thirty-one-year-old Ukrainian, Oksna Ryniekska, helped by her husband, imported nine young women from her homeland. Ryniekska told them she would get them visas so they could learn English. But the only English they learned was the sexual terminology required to service the clients. In just eight months in 1998 they had earned £130,000, half of which went to the girls and half to the good doctor.

She received a modest three months' imprisonment at Southwark Crown Court, had a confiscation order for £16,000 made against her and was recommended for deportation. Her husband, whose role had been to ferry the women to outcalls, received a suspended sentence. It is not recorded whether she had provided free medical treatment for the girls.[21]

Over the next ten years things changed again. In 2008 it was estimated that there were between 250 and 500 women working the streets in the East End on a regular basis in any one year.[22]

The year before, when Whitechapel sex worker Bonnie Barrett disappeared from her flat in Canning Town, what the newspapers lovingly called a copycat Jack the Ripper surfaced in the East End. This Jack was in fact Derek Brown, from Rotherhithe, a man who had previously served a six-year sentence for rape.

He was also convicted of the murder of twenty-nine-year-old Xiao Mei Guo, an illegal Chinese immigrant who sold pirate DVDs to pay off the money she owed to Snakeheads for smuggling her to Britain. The forensic evidence was against Brown. He was seen on CCTV speaking with Ms Guo on the morning of her disappearance on 29 August at Whitechapel Underground station, before both went into the tube. On 6 October he was arrested after he walked into a local Londis shop where officers were making routine inquiries and showing pictures of him. Brown was stopped immediately after he left the shop.

Two days later forensic teams found every room at his flat was spotted and smeared with the blood of both women. Bonnie Barrett's blood was found on the boiler cupboard, washing machine and fridge in the kitchen, and detectives believe she was attacked and murdered there. Xiao Mei Guo's blood was found near the front door, suggesting she may have tried to escape from the flat when Brown caught up with her. She may have agreed to go to Brown's flat to show him the DVDs because she was so desperate for money.

There had been attempts to clean up the flat. Police found three receipts from the local B&Q store where Brown had spent a total of £155 on materials to dispose of the bodies and clean the crime scene. Blood was found on a packet of scourers in a cupboard and a pair of industrial gloves and there were drip marks and spots on the hallway wall and carpet. Brown, who was completely redecorating his flat, had torn out bloodstained carpet and tried to give furniture away to neighbours.

At his trial Brown claimed that an Australian biker, who had spent the weekend with Bonnie Barrett, was responsible for her death and that Snakeheads were responsible for the death of Xiao Mei Guo. However, when after half an hour of cross-examination he refused to answer any more questions, his conviction was inevitable.

The bodies of the women have never been found and it is thought Brown may have either thrown them in the Thames or used an industrial compactor where he worked. The police also thought he might have killed up to another six women.

Based on anecdotal evidence from the Athens Olympics and events such as the Superbowl, it was thought there would be an influx of prostitutes trafficked or otherwise at the London Olympics in 2012. Dennis Hof, who owned the Moonlite Bunny Ranch, a large-scale brothel in Nevada, US, said that based on what he saw at the Winter Olympics in Vancouver he expected London to see '1,000 girls trafficked in by South East Asian, Albanian and African gangs, violent gangs involved in crime and drugs'. Brothels in the five East End boroughs were raided and closed but the feared influx does not appear to have materialised.[23]

The international nature of people-trafficking was, however, exposed fully in 2014 by the trial of a gang that imported more than 100 women into Britain. The trial ended with the gang leader, Vishal Chaudhary, being jailed for twelve years. Chaudhary, who lived in some style in Pan Peninsula Square, Canary Wharf, contacted young women through social networks in Hungary, the Czech Republic and Poland, offering work as receptionists, nannies or cleaners in England. However, when they arrived in the UK, the women were forced to work in brothels in Hackney and in other parts of London. Chaudhary's team, including his brother, Kunal, who worked as a manager for Deloitte in Manchester, were all jailed.

In 2018, Romanian women working as street prostitutes in Ilford were causing the same problems as those in Brick Lane twenty years earlier. But when they were cleared from the streets the result was that 'pop up' brothels – flats with security gates often rented by a couple of women through Airbnb for a weekend or a week – sprang up.

Just as Emma Smith had found out at the hands of the Green Gate Gang at the end of the nineteenth century, even with the security of CCTV and mobile telephones, prostitutes are still extremely vulnerable. In February 2020 a gang who preyed on working women in Tower Hamlets received long sentences. Over a seven-month operation working on the Isle of Dogs as well as in Hackney and Tower Hamlets, twenty-four-year-old Erlandos Vyte, twenty-one-year-old Joshua Coke Robertas Zilionas, and Jospin Blea, aged twenty-three, robbed a series of girls at knife-point. Vyte would usually telephone to make an appointment for an escort and when the girl opened the door one or more of the others would burst in. The women were tied up and their credit cards, money and mobile phones were stolen. Finally caught on CCTV the men received sentences of up to fourteen years.[24]

In June 2019 Edmilson Caimanque, David Fonseca and a third man broke into a brothel in Hackney brandishing knives and an axe before raping and robbing two sex workers who were sleeping there. It is a measure of the mistrust sex workers have in the police that they did not report the matter immediately. Instead one of the women went to a Sexual Health Clinic and told the staff she had been raped. She told the workers there was a second victim who had also been raped. The men were traced through DNA and CCTV; Caimanque received eighteen years and Fonseca fifteen. The third man, convicted of robbery, was sentenced to ten years.[25]

NOTES

1. For a fuller account of the operations of the brothers, see James Morton, *Gangland*, and for an in-house view Marthe Watts, *The Men in My Life*.
2. *ELA*, 16 May 1958.
3. *ELA*, July 1957, 6 September 1957, 9 July 1957; *East End News*, 9 August 1957.
4. Interview with author 27 May 1999. See *ELA*, 21 February and 20 June 1969. A white protection gang was said to be earning £350 a week from club protection. *News of the World*, 19 June 1960.
5. 'Put your houses in order, Mr Gaul' *Sunday People*, 25 March 1962.
6. *The Sun*, 31 October 1989.
7. Interview with author 25 August 1999.
8. For reports on the case, see *ELA*, 30 May and 11 July 1958.
9. 'The Shame of Vice in London' in *The Star*, 2 June 1960. It is the text of the speech by Lord Stoneham. See also letter to Edith Ramsay, 23 May 1957, quoted in B. Sokoloff, *Edith and Stepney*.
10. B. Sokoloff, *Edith and Stepney*, p. 138 *et seq.*
11. *ELA*, 27 June 1958.
12. Speech at Church House, Westminster, at the London Diocesan Conference on 13 February 1961.
13. *ELA*, 20 June and 1 July 1958.
14. *ELA*, 7 November 1958.
15. A crooked roulette wheel.
16. Slip Sullivan was stabbed to death in January 1955 during a quarrel with his Polish girlfriend. The coroner returned an open verdict. See James Morton and Gerry Parker, Gangland Bosses, pp. 166–7.

17. James Morton, *Gangland*; Bert Wickstead, *Gangbuster*.
18. *ELA*, 4 December 1975.
19. *ELA*, 1 August 1986.
20. Interview with author, 5 January 2000.
21. *The Herald*, 29 September 1999.
22. *Safe Exit*, Toynbee Hall, 2008.
23. Mario Cacciottolo, 'London 2012: Will the Olympics bring more prostitutes?' *BBC News*, 7 June 2012.
24. Elena Cruse, 'Gang who robbed sex workers at knifepoint in seven month spree jailed,' *Evening Standard*, 7 February 2020.
25. Neha Gohil and Lorraine King, 'Thugs smashed their way into brothel before two of them raped and robbed sex workers', *Daily Mirror* , 7 April 2021.

16

ROBBERS, ROBBERIES AND ESCAPEES

As the decades have passed the East End has been emptied of its white working-class old-style blue-collar criminals, and with it some of its larger characters. The former robber and now successful writer, John McVicar, was one who made the exodus.

He was by no means a successful career criminal but, like his contemporary Walter Probyn, he was a great escapee. He was not born into grinding poverty – his mother owned a shop in East Ham – but like many he trod the boards of the juvenile courts, remand homes and Borstal institutions from which he regularly escaped. One old East Ender remembers:

He was a bit of a hanger-on. Crombie overcoats was the thing in those days and he'd tell people he'd got his from thieving but in fact his parents had bought it for him. He worked with Georgie Nash on the thieving; nothing to do with the protection or other things. He was called Mad Mac in his early days. He'd do scatty things. He'd have money from a decent touch and then he'd go and nick a car wireless.[1]

In 1964 he was sentenced to eight years for armed robbery and, two years later, he was part of one of the most elaborate mass escape attempts in British prison history. A fight took place in Parkhurst prison on the Isle of Wight, with the result that one prisoner was charged with wounding another. Because of the supposedly poor facilities for trials on the island, the case was to be heard in Winchester and thirteen prisoners – nine of them known to be escape risks – were taken to give evidence. On the bus on the way back from court the prison officers were attacked. McVicar was one of the few successful escapees and remained at large throughout the summer. In fact the whole thing had been a sham to facilitate the escape attempt.

In 1967 he was sentenced to fifteen years after he was involved with Billy Gentry, who had survived an assassination plot by the Krays and who now received two more, in a failed South London armed robbery. Gentry, cornered in a yard, tried to shoot at a policeman at point-blank range but had run out of ammunition.

It was, however, McVicar's daring escape from Durham prison and his efforts, aided by his girlfriend Shirley, to remain out of the clutches of the police which brought him his reputation. Before he was sent to Durham maximum security prison in late 1967 he had nearly managed to escape from Chelmsford. On 28 October around 7 p.m. he escaped with Probyn and Joey Martin, convicted of murder during an armed robbery. Martin never managed to get far but Probyn and McVicar made it to the prison roof, and Probyn forced a trapdoor into the courthouse next door. He was trapped but McVicar stayed on the roof and eventually dropped into the garden of a terraced house, swam across the river Wear and, after sheltering in the backyard of a student house, again took to the river. He hid for three days until friends from London arrived to collect him.

He was out until 11 November 1970 when he was found in a

flat over a dress shop in Blackheath where a number of firearms were found. During his time on the run he had acted as a caretaker and armourer for various robbers. On one occasion the police announced, without any evidence to support the claim, that they thought he was one of three men who had killed a pawnbroker Frank Beiring in Marylebone on 20 February 1969. Two other men were later acquitted.

One old East End face thought:

> When McVicar was finally arrested he thought that he had been grassed by Johnnie D, but in fact he was grassed by Philly Herbert. It was his own fault. No one would listen to what was told them about Herbert. Their grubby fingers couldn't resist dealing with him and they had short memories and long hard lessons.[2]

He was sentenced to an additional three years, making a running total of twenty-six. He never again tried to escape and was released on parole in July 1978. He had read for a degree while in prison and became a well-known journalist and broadcaster. He later became a publisher.

Largely through jealousy McVicar has left behind some of his popularity. 'He's a preacher now, a reformed character and goes on the telly,' wrote Kray friend the dwarf wrestler Royston James Smith in his autobiography *Little Legs: Muscle Man of Soho*, and there is a feeling that he has crossed over to the other side. His loss of peer status may also be coupled with what many saw as his unfair comments about his wife and son Russell.

On 22 May 1998 Russell Grant-McVicar was sentenced to fifteen years' imprisonment at the Central Criminal Court after being found guilty of eight robberies and related offences. He told the judge they had been committed to make a 'spiritual

statement' on behalf of starving children. The former cat-burglar
Peter Scott received three and a half years for receiving Picasso's
Tête de Femme, stolen at gunpoint by Russell McVicar from a
London art gallery.[3]

One man whose career spanned forty years, for many of which
he was a hero to at least some, was Walter 'Angel Face' Probyn.
Then he too fell Lucifer-like from idolisation. Like John McVicar,
Probyn made his reputation in the East End as a great escapee
rather than as a robber of the calibre of, say, Charlie Knight. Born
in 1931 in a tenement in Shoreditch, he had been in trouble, as
the euphemism goes, from the age of ten when he broke a probation order after admitting he had stolen a tin of peas. From
then on he spent his time escaping from approved schools and
remand homes. He was yet another man who was impervious
to pain, and no amount of punishment or beatings would deter
him from his overriding concept of freedom. During his career
he escaped from the cells at Old Street police station no fewer
than five times. Because he was so small, weighing barely 8 stone
and 4' 10" tall, he was able to squeeze through the small hatches
in the cell doors. Now he was dubbed 'Angel Face' by the police
and press who wished to impress on the public that, whatever his
looks, Probyn was no angel.[4]

His career really took off when, at the age of fourteen, he hit a
policeman with the jagged edge of a sardine tin. He was fifteen
by the time he appeared at the Old Bailey where, because he was
too young for Borstal, he was ordered by Mr Justice Stable to be
detained for four years. In Wormwood Scrubs he began on yet
another escape by digging through the floor with a spoon. He was
making progress when he was suddenly transferred to Wakefield,
where he spent much of his sentence in the punishment block for
fighting and trying to escape. From there he was certified under
the Mental Defective Act and transferred to Rampton, outside

Nottingham, the Northern equivalent of Broadmoor. The regime in such institutions in the 1940s was much less socially orientated than it is today. Beatings, kickings and punishment by being choked with a wet towel were standard. In December 1949 he escaped while on exercise, hid out overnight in freezing conditions and made his way back to London where he was recaptured after five months. Pleas from the parents of a child he had saved from drowning in Victoria Park did nothing to prevent a return to Rampton. He tried another escape, but only succeeded in getting a few fields away before he was dragged back kicking and screaming. He was not released until May 1952 when his family threatened to bring *habeas corpus* proceedings. In all he had served six years because he had been too young for the two years of Borstal training.

Probyn lasted only six months on the outside before he received three months for stealing a car and a further three years for shop-breaking. This time he stayed inside, but on his next sentence – eighteen months for another office-breaking in October 1958 – he absconded from a Maidstone working party with less than a month of his sentence to serve. His then girlfriend Joan was in financial trouble and it was feared that her children might be taken into care. A 'This man is violent and dangerous' alert was issued.

He was found a month later looking at cars on a garage forecourt in Stamford Hill. Cornered, he pulled a gun and escaped over a low wall. The next day he was found in Shoreditch. He had arranged to meet a *Daily Mirror* reporter to give his version of the previous day's events, but had been betrayed. The result was both a picture of him in a police headlock on the front page and a further two and a half years' imprisonment for using an imitation firearm to resist arrest.

But he escaped again in September 1959 when he was

attending St James's Hospital, Balham, where he had been sent from Wandsworth for treatment for an apparent appendicitis brought on by a bar of carbolic soap. In his pyjamas he climbed off a trolley and barefoot dived through a window and into the street. It would defy common sense to think he did not have outside help. He lasted ten weeks before being recaptured shortly after Christmas, this time at a garage where he was getting a tyre repaired. Joan pleaded that if he was given a real chance he would go straight. Instead he received a further five years and was sent to Dartmoor from which escape attempts had not been noticeably successful or long-lived.

Until then those few who had escaped included Charles 'Ruby' Sparks in 1940, Stan Thurston, known as 'The Man No Prison Can Hold', and Roy 'Rubber Bones' Webb who lasted only a week on the outside. Cyril Mitchell Bond had inside help, but he was arrested within hours, as were the two warders who had helped him. The escape immediately prior to that of Probyn was Jimmy Jennings who, in June 1964, along with two others, hijacked an oil tanker which was delivering supplies to the prison. They also enjoyed only a few hours of freedom.[5]

Now there seems to have been some sort of conciliatory gesture by the prison authorities because, towards the end of his sentence, Probyn was given a week's home leave to get married. This was a success from few people's point of view. Certainly not from that of Joan, for she was not at the altar. Instead he married Beryl Smith from a seriously well-known Nile Street family. She was a very hard lady – 'I saw her put a milk bottle in Billy Rees' face' – known as the Jellied Eel Queen because she ran a stall in Hoxton Market. Unfortunately, whilst on their honeymoon in July 1963 they were arrested for shop-breaking and his five-year sentence was doubled. Now, back in prison, he learned that Beryl was having trouble with a former lover, Alfie 'Punchy' Hines.

She had lived with Hines for six months in about 1962. Now she maintained that he would not leave her alone and said that when the pubs closed he would come round to her flat to give her a beating.

In August 1964 Probyn escaped from Dartmoor in what was reckoned to be his nineteenth escape. It had long been the tradition that Dartmoor had relatively unstructured outside working parties for long-sentence prisoners. Transport in the 1960s was nowhere near as easy as it is today, and the prison authorities took the view that because of its isolation there really was nowhere for escapees to run. On a rainy 24 August, Probyn simply walked away wearing a white mackintosh and carrying a bag of plaster on his shoulder. He had also managed to hide a compass in one of the houses on which he was meant to be working. Within a day he had covered fifty miles, and five days later he arrived near Salisbury where he made a reverse charge call to London. Along with John McVicar's escape from Durham, it must rank as one of the great endurance escapes of the century.

As an East End villain says, to survive on the outside required not only help from friends and sympathisers:

When I first met him [Probyn] he was a little shabby man like Lonely in the Callan television series. He was on the run and I gave him a few quid. You did it for everybody.

But also by thieving:

Probyn and Beryl were just running around like Bonnie and Clyde. They went on a screwer with a man Jimmy M up in Stafford. He got spun and, rightly or wrongly I don't know, blamed Beryl. I had a flat off Hoxton Market at the time and he came round one day with a wooden mallet under his jumper.

Thirty minutes goes by and Beryl's brother Harry comes round with another brother, Charlie. He's pouring blood, asking me if he can wash and clean up. 'This bastard Jimmy M's done me in the caff.'

Harry then comes down after his wash and I asked Charlie what happened. He said Jimmy just come in and said, 'This is for your fucking sister.' I felt I was being put right in the middle both ways.[6]

Then came another small local problem. On 20 September 1964, a month after Probyn's escape, the ex-boxer Alfie 'Punchy' Hines was shot after drinking in the Royal Standard in Shoreditch, almost on the spot where Ted Berry had been shot the previous year. A dark-haired woman wearing sunglasses had beckoned to him and as he headed with her towards the White Horse public house, 50 yards down an alley, he was shot from behind.[7]

Although there is no proof whatsoever that Probyn was involved, his days of freedom were numbered. On 16 October, following a tip-off, the police were waiting when Probyn and his wife met by arrangement at a Post Office in Burdett Road, Stepney, only to find themselves in an ambush. Probyn grabbed his wife and ran into a fish and chip shop, climbed out from a back window and up onto the roof. With Probyn firing at the police, he and his wife made their way across the rooftops, through the window of a tobacconist's shop and down into the street. Probyn was rugby-tackled by a detective but wriggled away and Beryl was captured. He fired at the officer holding her and after fending off two more officers ran away once more. He was caught after leaping a fence. The police said he fired at them nine times. He said only two, and anyway he had thought they were friends of 'Punchy' Hines and not officers. When Beryl

Probyn's handbag was searched at the police station it contained 174 bullets.

By the time he reached Thames Magistrates' Court five days later Probyn was in a poor way. He had a broken arm, shoulder and ribs, and was missing two front teeth. Although he reserved the words for a later occasion, on 20 February 1965 at the Old Bailey Mr Justice Melford Stevenson thought society had earned a long rest from Probyn and he received twelve years for shooting with intent to commit grievous bodily harm. Beryl received five years and would later be one of a number of women to attack Myra Hindley in Holloway prison. She had been a wild girl in her youth, but after her sentence she faded from the scene; she never returned to Probyn.

Punchy Hines, denying he was the leader of a gang, told the newspapers that Beryl had married Probyn on the rebound. Probyn had broken out of jail for one reason only – to get the man he believed had stolen his wife:

> But I never took his wife away from him – he took the girl I had known since we were children together.[8]

Probyn's broken arm required a bone graft and whilst waiting in Wormwood Scrubs for the operation he tried once more to escape, but he and his partner were unable to throw a rope and tackle onto the wall.

He was sent to the new security block at Parkhurst to which he brought five hacksaw blades, but once he found they were useless against the manganese steel bars of this prison within a prison he bided his time before teaming up with the later police killer Harry Roberts.[9] Theirs was a highly elaborate plan which came to nothing when their replica Luger pistols, painstakingly made from cotton reels and wax, were found in a lavatory. In the leg of

Probyn's bed was an Ordnance Survey map of the Isle of Wight and a naval map of the Solent.

He was driven through the night to Durham, where he spent a good deal of his time in solitary confinement plotting his next escape through cell windows. Unfortunately the man with him could not cope with the physical aspects of the escape which, once they had gone through the cell window, involved descending the outside of the wall with a rope made from mailbags and climbing a drainpipe. Trying to help his companion, Probyn fell from three floors up. He went straight back into solitary confinement.

After his attempt to escape from Durham with McVicar and Joey Martin, Probyn never tried to escape again. While in prison he had been studying sociology. He was released in March 1974 on parole. Unfortunately his subsequent career was not as successful as that of McVicar.

Although now he was repaying his debt to society by helping battered mothers and their children in Hertfordshire, by March 1977 Probyn was once more back in jail serving eighteen months after being found guilty of breaking and entering an off-licence in St Osyth. He had already had another conviction, this time for the burglary of a vets' surgery in Hitchin, Hertfordshire; on that occasion it was said he was so depressed that he was trying to get drugs to kill himself. By the time of the court hearing, however, things were getting better. The band The Who were putting together a charity which he would run. It was sufficiently encouraging to get him a spell of probation.[10]

By the 1990s he was running a police monitoring unit from his flat in Shoreditch when he was arrested for indecent assault and possessing indecent photographs of children. On 25 May 1995 he was sentenced to three years' imprisonment.

More an absconder than an escapee, Malcolm 'Micky'

Gooch's career took off in the 1980s when he was in Brixton with the major drug-dealer Howard Marks who later supplied him with Thai grass. By the time of Gooch's arrest he was living in a substantial house in Essex owned by a Liechtenstein foundation. Convicted of one count of importing three tons of cannabis, he was jailed for eleven years.

Three years into his sentence Gooch left HMP Send on day release and was not seen again, at least by the authorities, until he surfaced at St Pancras station on a Eurostar train twenty-one years later in June 2016.

By this time the appeals of the Essex man, alleged to have run a £4.7 million cannabis ring, had long been heard and dismissed. He was returned to prison to complete his sentence.[11]

On 9 February 1970, the then-biggest daylight raid on a bank took place when a team of eight or nine men attacked a Security Express van while it made a stop at Barclays Bank, Ilford, and removed some £237,000. It was a case which had interesting repercussions both in England and in Canada. One of the men convicted was Arthur John Saunders, against whom the total evidence consisted of a series of verbal admissions made to Commander Bert Wickstead, who would go on to root out both the Dixons and the Tibbs.

Saunders was convicted but in December 1971 the first super-grass, Bertie Smalls, said in one of his statements that Saunders had not been on the raid. The Court of Appeal quashed the conviction, attaching no blame to the Commander and saying that Saunders had been drinking when he made the boastful wrongful admission. Saunders was released and awarded a substantial sum in compensation, but in 1985 he was found leading a gang of middle-aged men planning to rob a security van in Baker Street. This time he received fifteen years' imprisonment.

One problem for the prosecution was that John Short had

been named by Smalls as being on the robbery. If Smalls was to be believed about Saunders, what would happen if his evidence against Short proved to be wrong? Short solved the problem; when Smalls turned supergrass, he disappeared abroad, not returning until April 1978 when he pleaded guilty to other robbery charges and received twenty-one years. Released, he took up drug-smuggling, that new and healthier occupation of retired bank robbers, for which he would later receive nine and a half years for his part in the 'camper van' smuggling. While he was abroad he took up selling slow trotting horses with dubious pedigrees for racing in and around Montreal. When his partner was found dead in the St Lawrence River he returned to England to face the outstanding charges which, because of the difficulties caused by Bertie Smalls' exculpation of Saunders, in time were dropped.

Bigger by far, however, was the hijacking of a security van containing twenty tons of silver worth some £400,000 at the roundabout on the A12 near Mountnessing in Essex on 2 May 1972. It was a decent enough if straightforward job – the van was blocked and the security men kidnapped – but it was the fate of the participants and their relatives which provides the real interest. As for solving the robbery, the police had been targeting one of the participants, Golly Sillett, and when he was arrested he named names although he would not give evidence in court.

One of them was George Ince who was to be acquitted of the Barn Murder, and another was John Brett. Both received fifteen years. Brett's brother George and his ten-year-old nephew Terence were to disappear in early January 1975. At one point it was suggested that the reason behind the killing of Brett and his son, who had been given a teddy bear to hold whilst he was shot, was because he was investigating the whereabouts of the Mountnessing money too closely. But as is often the case, it was revenge for a simple quarrel. Brett had apparently beaten up a Leonard Thompson.

In November 1990 another of the Mountnessing team went down, but not in quite the same way. Frankie Simms from Stratford, who had also picked up fifteen years, now drew another thirteen for financing, along with his son Gary, what was said to be one of Britain's largest amphetamine factories run from a cottage in Ware. It was suggested that he had been supplying 40 per cent of the amphetamines in the country in an operation worth £200 million. This was a claim he denied. However, he lamented the change in attitude.

In *Respect*, Freddie Foreman tells the story of the 'Battle of Bow', on 14 December 1971, when a security van hired by Williams and Glyn Mills' Bank to deliver money in the East End was attacked at Bow Common Lane. A City of London policeman, PC Buckle, and his dog accompanied the run with two security guards, each of whom was armed. Buckle was badly beaten while his dog was kicked as it held onto another robber. When one of the robbers, Harry Wright, attempted to climb into the bank van he was shot. He was taken away by the robbers, who were obliged to leave the loot behind, and died. His family was told he had gone to Australia. In another version of the story, Wright was caught and made a statement before being released on bail and shot by friends of his former colleagues. A number of well-known players, mainly from South London and including Frank Fraser junior, Tony White and Alan Roberts, who later went down at the hands of John Hilton, were arrested over this and other robberies and later released without evidence being offered.[12]

Perhaps the greatest instance of the East End rallying to one of its own, but who was not, certainly at the time, a villain, came on the conviction – principally on identification evidence – of George Davis. A painter and decorator, he was convicted in March 1975 of a robbery at the London Electricity Board in Ilford for which he received twenty years. One of those acquitted was Mickey Ishmael, another whose story runs thread-like through the history of East End villainy, and who is regarded by some as perhaps the most talented of the players of his time. 'Trustworthy and one of two people – Harry Abrahams was the other – of whom the Krays were wary,' said an admirer.

Davis's loyal wife, Rose, and friends began a campaign to prove his innocence. Walls, bridges and the railway in the East End were covered with the slogan 'George Davis is Innocent O.K.' His campaigners, who genuinely believed in him, also engineered a series of publicity-catching stunts – digging up the wicket at the Headingley Test Match, driving through the gates of Buckingham Palace, streaking on an island in Victoria Park, Hackney, were just three – designed to secure his release. And although Peter Chappell, one of the heads of the campaign, was sent to prison himself, the campaign was successful. An officer from the Hertfordshire Constabulary was appointed to investigate the conviction and, in May 1976 whilst the inquiry was continuing, the Home Secretary ordered Davis's release. His supporters were overjoyed. Release was one thing, however, and the quashing of the conviction quite another. The campaign continued.

On 23 September 1977 the campaign came to a crashing halt when Davis, along with Mickey Ishmael, was arrested *in flagrante* whilst attempting to rob the Bank of Cyprus in the Seven Sisters Road. The story goes that Davis was sitting in a car when an officer approached him and asked him what he was doing. 'Shopping,' he replied. 'Well, take the balaclava off then,' said the officer. This time he received fifteen years, reduced to eleven on appeal.

Davis further blotted his copybook when, on 21 January 1987, he received eighteen months' imprisonment, with half suspended, for his part in a raid on the London-to-Brighton mail train in March 1986. His partner John Gravell received ten years. After that Davis dropped out of sight. Rose Davis died in 2009. She had been suffering from cancer.

It was not until May 2011 that Davis's conviction for the 1974 Ilford robbery was quashed by the Court of Appeal. It was something of a pyrrhic victory for Davis. One of the judges, Lord Justice Hughes, said that the conviction, based on dubious identification evidence, was unsafe but that the court was not able positively to exonerate Davis.[13]

Over the Easter Bank Holiday of 1983 a particularly unpleasant robbery took place, one which would effectively terminate the career of Ronnie Knight. A gang led by a 'toff' with a 'posh' accent, and a member wearing a monkey mask, carried out what came to be called the Great Bank Note Raid in Curtain Road, Shoreditch. £7 million was removed from the Security Express headquarters by six masked bandits who burst in at about 10.30 a.m. One guard had petrol poured over him and was threatened that if he did not hand over the combination for the safe he would become a human torch. The guards were then tied and blindfolded for the duration of the raid, which would last a further five hours.

As with the Great Train Robbery, it was a job which had been on offer for some years and one which had taken a considerable time in the planning. The Security Express building had been known as Fort Knox and was thought to be a virtually impregnable fortress. The underwriters put up the then staggering sum of £500,000 as a reward. But it was police work which paid off.

One of the men involved had been under observation for some time, and when he was being questioned about another major robbery he told the police he had stored Security Express money at his home. This led to the arrest of Allen Opiola who was later given three years and three months with a recommendation that he serve this in police custody. Opiola was to turn Queen's Evidence against the rest of the gang.

For a fee of £25,000 he had provided transport for 'a big one' and allowed his home – the money would fit into most people's living rooms – to be used for counting and laundering the proceeds. For this service, and for providing suitcases, making coffee, fetching a Chinese takeaway whilst the money was being counted and later doing a certain amount of laundering, he received in all £30,000.

On 10 June 1985 John Knight and Terry Perkins received twenty-two years; James Knight was given eight for handling stolen monies and Billy Hickson six years. John Horsley, who pleaded guilty at the outset, received eight. The police were convinced the gang had received inside help.

In November 1980 Ronnie Knight, John and James' brother, had been acquitted of the murder of 'Italian' Tony Zomparelli, shot while playing a pinball machine in the Golden Goose Arcade in Old Compton Street. The killing on 4 September 1974 by Georgie Piggott, a failed supergrass, and Nicky Gerard, son of the more famous and certainly more dangerous Alf, was said by Piggott to have been a contract by Knight at a price of £1,000. The reason for the killing was certainly the death of Knight's younger brother David who had been stabbed to death by Zomparelli in the Latin Quarter night-club in Soho on 7 May 1970. The reason behind it, said the prosecution, was that Zomparelli was acting on behalf of Albert Dimes in protecting the club from the likes of the Knights. No, said Ronnie Knight;

he, along with Billy Hickson and some others, had merely been in the club seeking the explanation for a bad beating David had received earlier in a club at the Angel, Islington. After David's death he, Hickson and the others had been acquitted of causing an affray.[14] Zomparelli received four years and on his release went for a time to Italy.

Now, Ronnie Knight went to Spain to remarry and become a club-owner and one of the so-called Famous Five London criminals on the Costa del Sol – reduced to four with the extradition and conviction of Freddie Foreman who in 1990, after having been found not guilty of taking part in the Security Express robbery, received a nine-year sentence for his part in the handling of the monies. The remaining three were Ronald Everett, himself once a close friend of the Twins, John James Mason, who was acquitted of conspiracy in the £8 million robbery of the Bank of America in 1976, and Clifford Saxe, one-time landlord of The Fox in Kingsland Road, Hackney, where the robbery is said to have been planned. Saxe was reputed to have bought two villas for just under £170,000 with part of his share. He died in 2002 awaiting extradition.

In 1990 Ronnie Knight published his memoirs. Blowing up safes, hurting innocent people and planning big robberies were way out of his league. He was quite prepared to return to England to clear his name of the Security Express robbery and also the Brinks-Mat robbery, which had followed and eclipsed it. All he wanted was the guarantee of a fair trial and bail pending it. These were clearly not forthcoming because he remained on the sands.

Then, amid a flurry of excitement and with the help of the *Sun* which financed the trip, on 2 May 1994 Ronnie Knight returned to England. It was said that up to £185,000 had been paid to his family for the story. All sorts of reasons were advanced for his decision to leave his home on the Costa del Sol. While one may have been that his money was running out, another may well have been that he was thought by the younger and more volatile newcomers to the area to be attracting adverse publicity, something they could well do without.

As might be expected, the *Sun* was triumphant and a number of faces began to wonder whether now was not the time for themselves to take a break in the sun. Again rumours abounded. Ronnie Knight was being kept under wraps and was about to tell all to the police; he was going to turn supergrass; he had been bailed to a secret address. If he had decided to peach on his old friends there was many an interesting story he could have told, but when it came to it he remained staunch and received five years for dishonestly handling some £300,000 of the Security Express proceeds. In the end there was no suggestion that he had been involved in the Brinks-Mat affair.

During Knight's time in prison the *Sun* reported on his progress. He went on work experience, he was allowed out at Christmas 1997 but did not drink because he knew he would be breath-tested on his return to prison. Sue, whom he had married in 1987 after his divorce from the actress Barbara Windsor, was waiting in Spain for him even though he might not get a passport until 2001. He was upset that the parole board did not recommend him for parole after a report had said he showed little remorse.[15] At the end of November 1998 he was released on parole.

What about poor Sue? She remained in Spain while Knight started a new life in Barnet with another girl and a replaced hip. He also republished his revised memoirs, in which he accepted that he had paid Nicky Gerard to kill Tony Zomparelli.[16]

One of the most ruthless of the robbery gangs was broken with the jailing for twenty-five years in November 1992 of John Calton, known as The German, and his henchmen Sean Wain and Robert Moore who received twenty years apiece. They had terrorised a series of bank and supermarket managers in Essex and Suffolk. In scenes reminiscent of the heyday of Billy Amies, the Tesco manager in Copdock in Suffolk had handed over £55,000 in 1991 after his sons had been threatened with castration, and two years earlier an assistant bank manager in Kelvedon was threatened with a stun gun to his testicles and his brother Philip was locked in a car boot. The gang was acquitted of two London robberies in which hostages were taken. The trio were caught after men involved in the planning told the police. Calton, a former paratrooper, who maintained throughout the proceedings that he was German, would take off his mask and then threaten the victims with death if they later described him.

Although women are not often active bank robbers there are of course exceptions; Monica Proietti led a gang in Montreal until she was gunned down on the traditional 'one last job'.

There have also been a number of female bandits. In October 1937 Elsie Florence Carey, who entered the dock dressed as a man, known as 'Lady Jack' or 'Queen Jack' and who was born in Canning Town, received four years' penal servitude after being convicted of breaking into a London store. She was described as hating men and ruling crooks and was the leader of a gang of breakers and enterers.[17]

One definite girl bandit was Lilian Goldstein, best known as the Bobbed-Haired Bandit.[18] It has been suggested that her real father was the old-timer Timmy Hayes, but the police records have her as being born Lilian Rose Kendall on 4 August 1902. Her brother was believed to be Victor Kendall, and for a time she was known as Ken. According to Scotland Yard, on 15 July 1920 when she was only sixteen years of age, Henry Goldstein, aka Harry Johnson, was sentenced to three months' hard labour at Old Street Police Court for living off her immoral earnings. On 9 October, after his release, she married him at a London register office and they lived together for four years. On 19 April 1928, under the name Hyman Johnson, he was sentenced at the Old Bailey to eighteen months' hard labour for having carnal knowledge of a girl under the age of sixteen.[19]

What is clear is that she was the driver and nurse for Charles 'Ruby' Sparks, the celebrated jewel thief who later became a smash-and-grab artist. By some accounts it was she who suggested that he turn from the country house burglaries, at which he had been a master, to the less skilled trade of throwing bricks through jewellers' windows. She was highly regarded, not only by Sparks and his friends but by the police. Detective Chief Inspector 'Nutty' Sharpe described her:

> She usually drove a big Mercedes car. Sitting at the wheel with a man's raincoat collar turned up around her close-fitting hat, there wasn't much to see of her.

When she was caught with him at Manchester in 1927, he pleaded guilty to protect her and received three years' penal servitude. In return she waited outside Strangeways when he escaped during the first few months of his sentence. Unfortunately he was hampered in climbing the wall and she was obliged to drive off without him. He had been lucky not to have faced a murder charge. On 20 November 1924 a woman was killed in Birmingham in an escape after a smash-and-grab. Sparks was not arrested until 27 May 1927 when it was decided that any identification would be wholly unreliable.

In 1930 Lilian Goldstein was arrested in Blackpool with Victor Kendall, John Wilson (Sparks) and Bernard Rayner and charged with receiving. Kendall was sentenced to eighteen months and Rayner and Wilson received three years apiece. The charge against Goldstein was withdrawn. Which was just as well if she was to be on hand on 30 June when Sparks made another escape attempt, this time from Wandsworth. The previous month at the Old Bailey he and a James Turner had been sentenced to five years for a series of motor-car robberies. On the same wing, they began to communicate with each other by putting cups to the walls of their cells. For security they put down saucers of water so that when the warders came down the corridor in heavy boots the water would ripple.

The escape took place early in the morning while they were on exercise, but Sparks failed to make the wall after a warder threw his truncheon, hitting him between the shoulders. Legend has it that he was badly beaten for his pains and was so covered in blood that when the Chief Officer asked his name he was able to say Turner, so giving his friend a little extra time. Lilian Goldstein had organised three cars – one waiting outside the prison, a second car which she had rented and duly returned and which she drove, and a third positioned just outside Barnet. Although the police were certain who was behind the escape they were never able to prove it.

Turner did not last long on the outside. The police lost the trail in Barnet and there were suggestions that he was on the Continent with a forged passport, but in fact he never left London. On 3 July he was found in a house in Rye Hill Park, Peckham, sitting in an upstairs room smoking a pipe and reading the evening paper. He leaped through the window and was injured in the 30-foot drop into the garden.

Sparks went on to serve a ten-year imprisonment and was involved in the Dartmoor Mutiny. He escaped from the Moor on 10 January 1940, together with Alec Marsh and Dick

Nolan, after serving two months of another five-year sentence.
Marsh was recaptured in six days and Nolan after four months.
Sparks – sheltered by Goldstein who led the police a merry
chase – survived for several years until both were arrested and
she was sentenced to six months' imprisonment for harbouring.
She served less than three weeks before the Recorder of London
substituted a probation order:

> I have decided to reduce the punishment, for I think I can under-
> stand the human element in this case. He was an escaped convict
> to the rest of the world, but that is not how you may have viewed
> him. In doing what you did, although it was breaking the law,
> you followed a natural womanly instinct in trying to succour
> and protect this man with whom you had intimate relations
> over the years.

She rather faded from the scene, although from time to time
she was noted as being in Soho when she could be called on by
the press for a comment on such things as the murders of Soho
prostitutes shortly after the war. Sparks married elsewhere, but
one ex-policeman recalls that by the end of his life he was back
with her.[20]

An East Ender who survived is Linda Calvey, who happily
assumed the soubriquet of the Black Widow and to whose house
a visit spelled considerable trouble on occasion. She came from a
family of blacksmiths and was one of eight children. The family
also built chalets on the Isle of Sheppey. After she left school she
worked as an optician's assistant, but she clearly had a wild streak.
A contemporary recalls her:

> What happened was when Mickey Calvey came out of doing
> an eight he was introduced to Linda as a sort of coming-home

present. Mick wasn't really a violent man. He was more genial but he could be difficult. Mick finished up marrying her. Sometime after, he got a four. He came home and they had another baby. She pulled herself together and then he got killed, and this time she went completely off her trolley. She went absolutely anti-police. Then she met Ronnie Cook. He was very good with her and when he got fourteen she ended up with Brian Thorogood.

A long-time friend of Mickey Ishmael, in 1953 Micky Calvey received eight years along with Ishmael for robbing Marks & Spencer. Linda had married Calvey in 1970, when he was taken from Wandsworth prison to a local register office. In 1977 he was acquitted of charges of burglary brought on the evidence of supergrass Charles Lowe.

Calvey died on Saturday 9 December 1978 in a shoot-out with the police, when he and three others tried to rob security guards at Caters supermarket in Eltham, South-East London. The other three men fled after discharging a shotgun over the heads of the crowd.

On hearing of his death Linda said, 'Mickey has been in trouble before, I know, but he's been trying hard since he came out of prison a year ago.' Some 200 people attended his funeral at the East London crematorium to which the currently imprisoned Mickey Ishmael sent a wreath in the form of the letters PAL.

Linda earned her nickname of the Black Widow by shouting 'murderer' at the police officer who stood trial for the shooting. There had been some evidence that Calvey was shot in the back, but the officer explained that this was the way he had been standing rather than that he had been shot while fleeing. He was acquitted and given a bravery award.

Shortly after that Linda became involved with robber Ronnie Cook, going with him on trips abroad including one to Las Vegas when it was said they spent £30,000 in just over a week. He lavished gifts on her – clothes from Harrods, jewellery, money, a car, even £4,000 for cosmetic surgery. Although other East Enders speak well of his treatment of her, there was apparently a downside. Cook was obsessively jealous, forbidding her to speak to other men, and apparently subjecting her to savage beatings and sadistic sexual practices.

Three years later in 1981, he was jailed for sixteen years for his part in Billy Tobin's Dulwich raid when a hijacked mobile crane was rammed into the back of a security vehicle containing almost £1 million.

Calvey promised to wait for him and as a mark of her fidelity had 'True Love Ron Cook' tattooed on her leg. Almost certainly Cook had had money salted away with her and now she began to spend it, taking up with one of his friends, Brian Thorogood, whom Cook had arranged to act as a 'minder' for him while he was inside. Thorogood left his wife, bought a house in Harold Wood, Essex, and moved in with her. Later he too was convicted, receiving eighteen years for a post office robbery. Linda, who seems to have supplemented her income by being the armourer for various robbery teams, served three of a five-year term for conspiracy to rob. That was the end of Thorogood, but now Cook was due for release.

Afraid that he would find out about both her infidelity and her dissipation of his money, she planned to kill him, offering a £10,000 contract. Finding no takers, she turned to Daniel Woods or Reece, a convicted rapist whose evidence had assisted the police to convict David Lashley, the killer of Australian heiress Janie Shepherd. Quite apart from the money, Reece too was enamoured with Calvey and agreed to do the job.

In theory Cook had a cleaning job outside the prison but, as with so many before him, he took to a more agreeable and less arduous way of passing his days out. On 19 January 1990 Linda Calvey collected him from Maidstone prison and drove him to London whilst Reece, whom she had already collected from another prison, waited outside her flat. Cook brought in the milk and as he stood holding it Reece followed him in and shot him in the elbow. He could not, he later told police, bring himself to kill the man.

Linda Calvey had no such qualms. She grabbed the gun from him, ordered Cook to kneel and then shot him in the head. Reece took a train back to the West Country to continue his thirteen-year sentence for rape, buggery and false imprisonment.

At first it seemed as though Calvey had been successful. The police appeared to accept her story that an unknown gunman had burst in and shot Cook while she cowered in a corner. Then it was discovered that Reece had been with her over the week-end and had been her lover. It was curious that he had not been mentioned in the statement.

Under questioning Reece cracked first, telling all. Later he withdrew his confession in court. Linda Calvey told the jury his confession was a fabrication. 'Ron meant everything to me,' she said. His gesture of solidarity did Reece no good; he too received a life sentence for murder.

Calvey does not seem to have held Reece's pusillanimity against him for long and the pair corresponded in prison. Reece was allowed to travel from Whitemoor to see her every three months until the point came when 'Ma', as she was known in Durham, decided to marry him. Arrangements were made for a prison wedding on St Valentine's Day 1994, but it was then announced that the wedding would be delayed until their release. However, given that this might be some years in the future, to the strains of 'Unchained Melody' they married in August 1996. The prison governor was the best man, a retired warder took the photographs and the bridesmaid, who wore black, was Bernadette McNeill, herself serving life imprisonment for her part in the torture and death of sixteen-year-old Suzanne Capper whose crime had been to lose a coat belonging to Ms McNeill.

Calvey's third marriage in April 2009 was after her release and this time was in Dymchurch to seventy-year-old businessman George Caesar. Both bride and groom wore white. In 2019 she published her life story, marked by a party at the Blind Beggar. Now she thought that it was indeed Reece who had fired the fatal shots which killed Cook.

The days of the Friday bank robbery or wages snatch began to die away in the 1970s. This was the result of the tightening of security, the coming of the supergrass, and the fact that drug- dealing was (a) becoming socially acceptable; (b) far more profitable; and (c) that if caught, sentences in those days were far less than for being caught on the pavement with a sawn-off shotgun.

Frankie Simms, robber turned dealer, thought, 'In the sixties if you were a drug taker, you could never be a proper thief. It wasn't accepted.'

Things had indeed changed. One of the Great Train Robbers, Tommy Wisbey, who had gone down for cocaine dealing in August 1989 along with his colleague, Jimmy Hussey, explained the change in attitudes:

We were all against drugs all our lives but as the years went on, towards the seventies, it became more and more the 'in' thing.[21]

But perhaps the main reason was that now the police were armed and prepared to open fire on robbers brandishing guns.

One of the first incidents when the police opened fire seems to have been on 27 December 1972, when Peter Slimon was going to work armed on Embassy guard duty. At the same time William Kellard, who was on the raid while on work release from prison, Robert Hart and others robbed the National Westminster Bank at 138 High Street, Kensington, during which Luka Prodanovic was shot in the leg.

Slimon went into the bank and when he called out that he was armed Robert Hart shot at him and in turn Slimon shot Hart. Slimon was knocked backwards out of the bank doors. He survived; Hart did not. Tony Baldassare, another robber who had worked with John McVicar, tried to help the injured Kellard who had also been shot. Another robber called out 'Leave him Tony, for Christ's sake leave him'. Hart was left in a beach buggy in the NCP in nearby Young Street, where he was found at 1.30 that afternoon.

At the end of January 1985 Baldassare killed himself in his attic after a two-day siege with the police who surrounded his Streatham home. He was wanted in connection with the death of police dog Yerba and a string of robberies. In March that year James Baigrie killed himself in a van in Earls Court during another siege. In October 1983 he had escaped from Edinburgh's high security prison during a life sentence for shooting a barman in the back. He had been on the run for sixteen months.

In 1987 Dennis Bergin went down as he tried to steal paintings at Sir John Soane's museum in Lincoln's Inn Fields. A bullet mark is still preserved in the wall. The same year Terry Ash was killed in a robbery set up by the police. In 1989 Terry Dewsnap and Jimmy Farrell were killed, shot by marksmen in a failed robbery at a Post Office in North Harrow.

It was always possible to be killed by your own men. When John Hilton robbed Leo Grunhut, a Hatton Garden jeweller, in Golders Green, he shot not only Grunhut but also his partner

Alan Roberts. Hilton managed to get Roberts into a car where he bled to death. He then buried him on a railway embankment. Later caught after a raid in Burlington Arcade, Hilton received a life without parole sentence.

Apart from the death of Harry Wright, these deaths may not have been in the East End but the word soon filtered through. Except for the very large organised robbery, investing in drugs was now a great deal safer. Robberies were often now only done to raise a stake to buy in.

Nevertheless there have still been some spectacularly successful and some spectacularly failed robberies. And some of both. One of these was the 1995 Snow Hill robbery, then the most lucrative robbery since the Great Train Robbery when Danny Woollard and Angelo 'Festus' Hayman held up a security van and stole £7 million in bearer bonds and £400,000 in diamonds. Both men were sentenced to lengthy terms of imprisonment. Acting as a minder Woollard, who owned dogs for illegal fighting, later became peripherally involved in the Hunt-Allen dispute over land near the Olympic Park. He died in November 2013.

In theory the profits can be just as good and in practice the penalties are much lower for staged robberies. At first blamed on East European criminals, a £1 million bullion robbery in Belgium was an all British, in fact more or less an all Essex affair. David Chatwood, the stepfather of the TOWIE girls Sam and Billie Faiers, was one of a gang of middle-aged men who staged a faked hold-up of Brian Mulcahay who, on 4 October 2011, rang his employers from his locked lorry to say he had been robbed. A week after the robbery most of the stolen bullion was found in a hotel room and flat in Antwerp. Despite the girls' evidence that Chatwood was invaluable help in their dress shop he was jailed for four years. He had already been returned to prison to complete a twelve-year firearms and drugs sentence imposed in 2001. Mulcahay was sentenced to three and a half years.[22]

NOTES

1. Conversation with author, August 1999.
2. ibid, August 1999.
3. For an account of John McVicar escapes, see J.P. Bean, *Over the Wall*.
4. Walter Probyn, *Angel Face: The Making of a Criminal*.
5. For these and other stories of prison escapes, see J.P. Bean, *Over the Wall*.
6. Conversation with author, August 1999.
7. *Daily Express*, 21 September 1964.
8. ibid, 16 February 1965.
9. The *Guardian*, 2 February 1993. See also Tom Tullett, *No Answer from Foxtrot Oscar*.
10. *Daily Telegraph*, 29 May 1976.
11. *R v Malcolm Gooch* [1998] EWCA 10626-2.
12. Freddie Foreman, *Respect*. For an account of the robbery and others together with allegations of corruption against, and the conviction of, Chief Inspector Phillip Cuthbert, see James Morton, *Bent Coppers*.
13. Rose Davis, *The Wars of Rosie*; Duncan Campbell, 'Rose Davis', *The Guardian*, 3 February 2009.
14. For a fuller version of the Knight–Zomparelli feud see Ronnie Knight, *Black Knight* (revised edition); and for a less partial account James Morton, *Gangland* and Duncan Campbell, *The Underworld*. For Freddie Foreman's account of his return to England and trial for the Battle of Bow robbery see *Respect*.
15. John Askill, 'Ronnie Knight fury at extra year in prison' in the *Sun*, 31 December 1997.

16. Ronnie Knight and others, *Gotcha!: The Untold Story of Britain's Biggest Cash Robbery*.

17. *Empire News*, 24 October 1937.

18. ibid, 24 October 1937.

19. Nat. Arch. MEPO 3 503.

20. For a full account of the chase she led the police after Sparks had escaped from Dartmoor, see J. P. Bean, *Over the Wall*; James Morton, *Gangland 2*.

21. Duncan Campbell, *The Underworld*.

22. Duncan Campbell *The Underworld;* Kate Kray, *Linda Calvey: The Black Widow*

17

DEATH IN THE EAST END

The first British murder case with a conviction based in part on palm prints was that of ex-Borstal inmates Samuel Dashwood and George Silverosa. In 1942 they were convicted of the murder of seventy-one-year-old pawnbroker Leonard Moules, found beaten to death in his shop in Bethnal Green on 30 April. No weapon was found but Silverosa's palm print was discovered on the shop safe. Although it provided conclusive evidence he had been in the shop, at first the print does not seem to have played that great a part in the investigation and it was the then unheard of offender profiling which led to the arrests. In this case Chief Inspector Ted Greeno was convinced the men must be local. Also, by chance, a soldier was heard to remark he had seen two men who called themselves Sam and George with a gun in a local café.

They were not helped by making statements in which each man blamed the other for striking the fatal blows. Awaiting execution in Pentonville prison, Silverosa asked for permission to burn his letters before he died. He was allowed to go to the prison bakery where there were ovens. He picked up an iron bar, bashed two officers and tried to escape but he was soon overpowered. He and Dashwood were hanged on 12 September 1942.[1]

George Cornell, who met his end at the hand of Ronnie Kray in the Blind Beggar pub in March 1966, came from a well-known East End family called Myers. Most of the brothers changed their name to Cornell but although George took the name he never did so officially.

In 1955 his forty-five-year-old brother Myer 'Johnnie' Myers was prosecuted for the murder of the prostitute Nancy Wojtasko, allegedly throwing her over the bannisters in a block of flats at Norfolk Buildings, Shoreditch. Certainly the few facts of the case which could be agreed were odd. The pair were found around 7 a.m. on the morning of 9 March at the bottom of the stairs in the block. She was wearing only stockings and a cardigan, and a coat and shirt had been thrown over her. She died in hospital that afternoon. She was suffering from syphilis and was partially paralysed following a cerebral haemorrhage a few months earlier. Myers made varying statements saying they had been out drinking and she had fallen down the stairs around 1.30 in the morning. He had not been able to lift her and had stayed with her until they were found.

Other tenants claimed they had heard her call out 'Don't hit me' around 3.30 a.m. and one woman had looked out and seen the pair before going back to bed. She had brought Nancy a cup of tea when she found she was still there in the morning. It was agreed the lighting was bad and the staircase with its narrow steps was dangerous. Two months later, after a three-hour retirement, the jury acquitted Myers of both murder and manslaughter.[2]

Jimmy Moody, who vanished after the 1965 Richardson gang shootout at Mr Smith's club in Catford, had been convicted of manslaughter in 1967 and then became part of the Chain Saw Gang which attacked security vehicles. He was arrested in 1979 on charges of robbery. While in Brixton he organised the escape of himself and his landing mate Stanley Thompson, and a Provisional IRA member Gerard Tuite for which he was said to have received £10,000. Tools were smuggled into the prison and were used to tunnel through the walls of their adjacent cells and then through the outside wall of Tuite's cell. The men then escaped across the roof.

Moody was shot dead on 1 June 1993 at the Royal Hotel Hackney by a man described as being in his forties with black hair going grey and a slight tan and wearing black clothes with a leather bomber jacket. His killer escaped in a white Ford Fiesta and was never arrested. After his death a number of contract killings were laid on Moody's shoulders. Some of them, including the killing of a couple, the Dixons, in Wales, were undoubtedly wrong. The Royal Hotel changed its name to the Royal Inn on the Park.[3]

One of the most notorious cases of East End violence, however, came not with a fight in a Maltese Club but in the Pen Club in Spitalfields, said to have been bought with the proceeds from a robbery at the Parker Pen Company and named as an Underworld joke.

At the time, however, the club was owned by former boxer Billy Ambrose – at one stage thought to be one of the most promising middleweights in the country – who was from a local family who, at the time of George Cornell's death, owned the Barley Mow public house around the corner from the Blind Beggar. His partner in the club was Jeremiah Callaghan, a member of another leading family from Walworth. Both were serving ten-year prison sentences but came home on parole at the weekends. The club was frequently raided by the police and at the time of the shooting it was being managed by none other than Tommy Smithson's girlfriend Fay Richardson, now renamed Fay Sadler after her marriage to Alec Sadler – an employee of David Barry, the West London club-owner.

Bert Wickstead, later a Commander of the Flying Squad but then a Detective Sergeant, believed that, no matter what was on the surface, the real reason behind the incident was that it was part of the West End power struggle as West End gangsters moved East in search of clubs and car sites to protect, with a chance accident providing an opportunity to establish a new pecking order.[4]

In any event Selwyn Keith Cooney, manager of the Billy Hill-owned New Cabinet Club in Gerrard Street, and no friend of the Nash family, was beaten and shot in the club. Jimmy Nash was charged with his murder and acquitted. He was later sentenced to five years' imprisonment for the beating Cooney received before he was shot.

Reports of the background to the incident on 7 February 1960 vary. One version is that Jimmy 'Trunky' Nash, who worked as a minder at the Astor Club in which the family had an interest, set out to avenge Cooney's beating of his brother, Ronnie, in a Notting Hill club. Jimmy Nash, together with his red-headed girlfriend, a hostess named Doreen Masters, and other former professional boxers Joey Pyle and John Read, arrived at the Pen Club a little while after Cooney. According to witnesses Cooney was pointed out to Nash by Doreen Masters and, together with Pyle and Read, he went straight over, broke Cooney's nose with one blow and proceeded to give him a severe beating. 'That will teach you to give little girls a spanking,' he said. Cooney, protesting he had done nothing of the kind, fought back and there was a cry, 'He's got a gun.' Two witnesses were adamant that Nash then shot Billy Ambrose in the stomach and Cooney in the head at point-blank range.

Others in the club attacked Nash and Read, who was hit over the head with a bottle. They ran out of the club and Nash was driven away by Pyle whilst Doreen Masters drove off with

Read. Billy Ambrose, although badly hurt, still managed with some help to carry Cooney's body from the club and put it on a pavement some distance away. He then drove himself to hospital, reporting that he had been shot outside a club in Paddington; he could not remember its name. With a death on the pavement and the wounds Billy Ambrose had suffered, it was clear the police would be notified by somebody sooner or later and they were – by the hospitals who received the body of Cooney and the injured Ambrose. Jeremiah Callaghan couldn't resist going back to the club to find out what was happening and was seen in Duval Street by the police. The bloodstains on his clothing came from a brawl outside a pub in Walworth, he said. Fay Sadler was seen leaving the London Hospital. Giving her name as Mrs Patrick Callaghan, she said she had simply called to see her friend Billy Ambrose. Then two others in the club were brought in for questioning. The first was Cooney's girlfriend, a nineteen-year-old barmaid from the New Cabinet called Joan Bending. The second was Johnny Simons, who had hit Read over the head with a bottle. Both were to point the finger at Jimmy Nash, Pyle and Read. When Fay Sadler was brought in for questioning, she too confirmed the picture and immediately disappeared, only resurfacing after the trial. Jimmy Nash's flat in the Charing Cross Road was searched and a mackintosh stained with blood of the same type as Cooney's was found. Of Nash himself there was no trace. Meanwhile Joan Bending had picked out both Pyle and Read at an identification parade. Two days later James Nash surrendered himself at City Road police station.

Nash, Pyle, Read and Doreen Masters were charged with the capital murder of Selwyn Cooney. The trial began on 21 April with the public gallery filled with 'faces' including members of the Billy Hill organisation, the Callaghan family, and the Kray Twins as well as the Nash family in force. Now only Nash, Pyle and Read stood trial. The charges against Doreen Masters had been dismissed.

The all-male jury took ninety-eight minutes to acquit Nash of Cooney's murder but, at a second trial which began an hour later, he was found guilty of causing grievous bodily harm and was sentenced to five years' imprisonment. Mr Justice Diplock, imposing sentence, said:

> You have been found guilty on abundant evidence of a brutal assault upon a man who is now dead, in a drinking club frequented by crooks. An example must be made of you and people like you . . .[5]

Within days of the incident the Shamrock, which backed onto the Pen Club, opened in its place. That was then raided and closed and was reborn as Ricardo's.

Over the years Billy Ambrose's name cropped up including an unlikely suggestion that he had been one of the six men said to have been on the Great Train Robbery who were never caught. More recently, although he was never prosecuted, it was suggested that he was either part of or involved in what was called the Hungarian Circle run by the con-man Henry Oberlander which tried to defraud banks of millions. Sentenced at the Old Bailey to fourteen years, Oberlander was another who was released after only a few years on the grounds of serious ill health from which he immediately recovered. Ambrose died in 2009.

One of the great East End mysteries – at least to outsiders – was the apparent disappearance of the well-known figure Tommy 'Ginger' Marks on 3 January 1965 in Cheshire Street outside the Repton Boxing Club and near the Carpenters Arms. All sorts of rumours circulated about his whereabouts, which soon turned into rumours about his death.

Of course the Krays' name was once more in the frame but this time any part they may have played was peripheral. However, after Marks disappeared Ronnie, showing his kindly side, had Firm member Pat Connelly buy a puppy in Brick Lane and take it round to Anne Marks to cheer up the children.

From a bullet chip in a wall in the street, the police believed Marks had been shot in the stomach. A dig in a local bomb site turned up nothing. *The Sketch* now thought his body had been thrown in the Thames in concrete and the *News of the World* put up a £5,000 reward. Next, the police thought it might have something to do with the Great Train Robbery – one story is that Marks had been the man paid to burn down the robbers' hide-out at Leatherslade Farm and had failed to do so. The *News of the World* had the better intelligence, however. 'It is accepted that he was the unintended victim of a "crime of passion" feud between two South London gangs,' wrote Peter Earle, their major crime reporter.

It was ten years before anybody appeared in court and the man who did so was George 'Jimmy' Evans, accused of the attempted murder of Freddie Foreman's brother George. The prosecution's case was that on 17 December 1964 Evans had shot George Foreman because he suspected he had been carrying on with his wife. Foreman, maintaining the best traditions of the Underworld, refused to identify Evans and he was acquitted both of the attempted murder and of possessing a sawn-off shotgun. He gave a triumphant interview to the *News of the World* denying he and Marks had been up to no good the night of Ginger's disappearance. Indeed he was fed up with the police leaning on him over the whole thing.

In January the next year, with Evans now serving a seven-year sentence for manslaughter, he was able to tell a different tale. Yes, he accepted he had tried to shoot George Foreman, and yes, he, Ginger and two others had been out to do a raid on a jewellers. They had failed to notice a red car was following them. When it drew up beside them a voice called out, 'Jimmy, come here'. A shot rang out and Marks fell. He had thought the call was 'Ginge' and for him. Evans ran round the corner and climbed under a lorry. Marks' body was bundled into a car and driven off. He named a not unfamiliar quartet – Freddie Foreman, Alf Gerard, Jerry Callaghan and Ronnie Everett – as the men involved. They were all charged with Marks' murder.

Evans made a poor showing in the witness-box and early in the trial Mr Justice Donaldson discharged Everett. At the end of the prosecution case the judge told the jury, 'The problems with identification are very real. This crime is ten years old. The first time Mr Evans condescended to say it was these three men who were in the car was last year'. Found not guilty, it was off to Micky Regan's A & R club in the Charing Cross Road to celebrate. Alf Gerard commented, 'This is the end of a nightmare for us. Justice has been done at last.'

Well, perhaps rough justice because in his autobiography *Respect* Freddie Foreman admitted he had shot Marks with Alf as the driver. Asked if he had any regrets, he said, 'Yes, I regret I did not shoot the two of them that night.'

Anne Marks remarried and never told her son Phillip of his father's career. He obtained seven 'O' levels and was given a medal for encouraging children to help the police. On 10 February 1997 he was sentenced to twelve years for his involvement in a raid on a security van in Limehouse. His step-brother received ten years for the same offence.

A criminal and a customs officer died when a drugs run went wrong. George Francis – not the popular boxing trainer – had led a colourful life. Long suspected in the Underworld of being a grass, he had been a relatively small-time thief and enforcer until in late 1979 he took up with a number of armed robbers who were moving into the very much more lucrative and very much less dangerous drug-trafficking. 'Silly' Lennie Watkins, also known as Teddy Bear, proprietor of Edward Bear Motors, Fareham, hatched the plot when he was serving a sentence in Maidstone for a supermarket snatch. Blocks of high grade cannabis embossed with the Rolls Royce symbol were smuggled in with shoe containers from Pakistan, which produced millions for the gang. Four runs produced a street value of £10 million but, unfortunately, the team did not conceal their new-found wealth. In particular Watkins took to lighting cigars with £20 notes.

A joint police and customs operation was mounted and on the fifth run officers watched as a container was fitted with a false bottom and loaded with sanitary ware for a trip to Karachi. On its return, driven by Watkins, it was filled with shoes and £2.5 million of cannabis in the false bottom of the container. It arrived at Harwich and for some days meandered around the Suffolk countryside before the shoes were dropped off in Saffron Walden. The officers also saw a bag of guns being handed to Watkins.

The lorry was then driven to the Commercial Road on the borders of the East End and the City where the officers realised there had been a 'show out' and their cover had been blown. Watkins also knew he had been watched and parked his lorry, leaving two sawn-off shotguns inside to use a telephone box to ask for further instructions from his team. He was told to stay near the box until an orange van arrived which would guide him to a 'slaughter' or safe house.

As he waited by a bus stop he was approached by customs officer Peter Bennett and a detective sergeant John Harvey.

Watkins, who had a Lady Beretta in his parka jacket, fired at both men, hitting Bennett in the stomach. A seventy-six-year-old pensioner came to the men's aid and began beating Watkins with his walking stick as other officers arrived.

At his trial for the murder of Bennett at Winchester Crown Court, Watkins' story was that he thought a rival gang was trying to hijack his lorry and he had fired in self-defence. He did not do well in the witness-box, telling prosecuting counsel, 'I am not going to answer any more questions from made up note-books and rubbish from your firm, from the trickery department who pull more strokes than an Oxford blue'. He received life with a minimum of twenty-five years and told the judge he hoped he would die of cancer. A number of other luminaries, who included Freddie Foreman, were also on trial over the drugs. Foreman received two years after pleading guilty. George Francis was acquitted after a retrial amid suggestions that witnesses had been got at. The Kray Twins' friend and armourer Duke Osbourne died before he was arrested. His body was found on a playing field on Hackney Marshes. It was said he died of natural causes but another view is that it was from a drug overdose and that his body had been kept in a deep freeze before being deposited on the football pitch.

An East Ender recalls:

Ronnie Cook put him up for a bit after Lennie Watkins killed the customs officer. By now Dukey was depressed. He reckoned it was only a matter of time before he was picked up and there was going to be a lot of bird handed out. He'd already done a lot and he couldn't face any more was the general opinion. They put his body on Hackney Marshes and that's where the police found it.[6]

Within a month an effort to free Watkins failed when a ladder was found propped against the Winchester prison wall and a lorry parked nearby. Watkins later committed suicide in prison. As for Francis, in 1975 he was shot at point-blank range in the shoulder in the Henry VIII pub he owned near Hever Castle in Kent, in what was said to be a reprisal for his failure to pay for the nobbling of the jury. His survival came because he turned his head at the last moment.

There may no longer have been the seriously active old-fashioned East End gangs and families of the 1960s and 1970s, but as the fifty-seven-year-old Tommy Hole, a top-class villain and senior figure in the East End, found to his cost it can still be a dangerous place. On 5 December 1999 he and Joey 'The Crow' Evans, two years younger, were shot dead at the Beckton Arms, Beckton, while they were watching Italian football on the pub's giant screen. The balaclava-wearing killers waited until 3.20 p.m. when the pub was emptying and six shots were fired at point-blank range, killing 'The Crow' first and then Hole as he tried to flee. A third man survived the shooting and made himself scarce.

Hole's is a complicated story interwoven with gangland figures in East London and Soho and laced with double dealing and betrayal. He was born in Poplar, the son of a boiler-maker, and at the age of twenty-three had his feet firmly on the criminal career ladder when he received three months for possessing forged banknotes. He escaped while attending Hammersmith Hospital. The next year he received five years for an attempted payroll snatch. Progressing up the ladder, at one time he owned a hotel in Benidorm.

In 1976 Hole was convicted of attempted murder when he repeatedly drove a car across a man who had fallen foul of him, and that year was acquitted, along with George Davis, of the whisky robbery in which Charlie Lowe gave evidence. For the attempted murder he received seven years.

On his release he was charged with the murder of Nicky Gerard who, like his father, was a feared enforcer. Gerard is unofficially credited with the death of the royal hairdresser André Mizelas on 9 November 1970. Mizelas, a partner in the André Bernard chain of hairdressers, was killed as he drove in Mayfair traffic. A number of suggestions were made as to the motive including thwarted lovers, but no one was charged. It is now believed that Mizelas owed £100,000 to a South London money lender who put out the contract to Gerard for £5,000.

Gerard was not popular. Whilst he was serving a seven-year sentence for causing grievous bodily harm to an ex-boxer Micky Gluckstead in the Norseman club in Canning Town, a gangland kangaroo court sentenced him to death in his absence. His wife, Linda, was sent a wreath with the message, 'Nicky Gerard, rest in peace.'

In the days before his death, Gerard made the fatal mistake of thinking that the men he knew were following him were undercover police officers rather than Underworld members. On Sunday, 27 June 1982, only a few months after his release, Gerard went to his eleven-year-old daughter's birthday party in Peckham, South-East London. As he got into his Oldsmobile, gunmen wearing boiler suits and balaclava helmets ambushed the vehicle. Gerard was hit in the stomach but he managed to get out of the car and staggered 100 yards, chased by the men. He was then hit so hard on the head with a gun that the stock of the gun broke. He was beaten unconscious before the gunmen shot him to death. Tommy Hole and his son Kevin were charged. One possible reason for Gerard's death was that he was said to have been paying too close attention to Kevin's wife while Tommy Hole was seeing Gerard's estranged wife.

They were acquitted at the Old Bailey when a witness failed to follow through with his identification evidence. Hole then went into drugs and received a sentence of thirteen years to run alongside eighteen years he was now serving for armed robbery.

It was while he was in Whiteside prison that he found his son, Kevin, hanging in his cell. Shortly after that he spent some time in Rampton Mental Hospital where in March 1995 he married. On his release his temper became more changeable and shortly before his death he is said to have threatened neighbours with a gun. His wife said that he had settled down and his criminal career was over.

As for 'The Crow', Joey Evans, he was generally regarded as a nobody enforcer but he was the man shot first. Hole was killed as he tried to escape the gunmen. He and Evans had been lifelong friends from the time when they attended the same school in Canning Town.[7]

Again all sorts of explanations for the killings have been offered, including a drug deal in which Hole and Evans ripped off their partners for £80,000 and insults allegedly offered by Hole at the funeral of James Gerard, Nicky's uncle, in the previous November. Hole's wife Christine denied her husband had even been at the funeral.[8]

In 2010 Hackney had the dubious distinction of hosting what was then the youngest convicted contract killer in England. Fifteen-year-old Santre Sanchez Gayle had killed Gulistan Subasi, mother of a nine-year-old boy, in what was thought to be a domestic dispute. CCTV footage showed Gayle ringing the doorbell and waiting for Ms Subasi to open the door before shooting her at point-blank range. He was caught only because he boasted of the killing.

A member of the Kensal Green Boys (KGB), Gayle, known as Riot, had taken the contract to boost his gang status. He was sentenced to life with a minimum of twenty years.[9]

Murder ran in the Gayle family. In December 2006 his half-brother, Lloywen Carty, was jailed for a minimum of thirty years for the murder of twenty-seven-year-old Lee Subaran at the Notting Hill Carnival. A month earlier Carty's half-brother, Donnel Carty, another KGB member, was given a life sentence for murdering City lawyer Tom ap Rhys Pryce, stabbed to death for his mobile during a botched mugging in Kensal Green.

Contract fees can range from £200 to £100,000, said to have been paid for the murder of Robert McGuill in 2015, with an average price of just over £15,000. Gayle was the one who received the £200. The money was spent buying a Dolce and Gabbana beanie.[10]

And still the street killings go on. Gang status can be raised immeasurably by carrying out a broad daylight stabbing in front of witnesses. In late April 2021 a string of killings took place in Canning Town. The brother of one youth who died had been killed two years earlier.[11]

NOTES

1. Nat. Arch. DPP 2 985 and 2 1019; Frank Fraser, *Mad Frank and Friends*.
2. Nat. Arch. Crim 1 2589; *The Times*, 26 May 1955; 'A sordid story of the slums', *East End Advertiser*, 27 May 1955.
3. Wensley Clarkson, *Moody: The Life and Crimes of Britain's Most Notorious Hitman*; Frank Fraser, *Mad Frank's London*; Terry Kirby, 'Gangland war linked to murder of fugitive', The *Independent*, 23 October 2011.
4. It was suggested the going rate was £5 or £10 for cafés, clubs and second-hand car dealers. He thought that the West End gangsters sent down girls to flirt with the dockers in the daytime and 'the attentions of these women appeal to the ego of the men in working clothes and they soon pass over information about lorry movements without

realising what they are saying'. Harold Mitchell, 'The vice boys move into the East End' in *Evening News*, 8 February 1960.

5. For a full account of the fight and the incidents leading up to the trial see James Morton, *Gangland*.

6. Conversation with author August 1999.

7. There were thought to be up to twenty hitmen operating in the South East, with the price of a simple contract around £1,000 going up to £10,000. As was predicted, the ban on firearms has had no effect on the professional criminals. Automatic weapons are smuggled in from Eastern Europe, with a semi-automatic priced between £300 and £800. See *The Times*, 7 December 1999.

8. Nick Paton 'Once upon a time in the East End, *The Guardian*, 19 March 2000.

9. Jacob Dirnhuber, 'Running Riot' in *The Sun*, 12 November 2018.

10. *Daily Mail Online,* 24 May 2011.

11. Matt Townsend, 'London Killings. It's like a war zone. How did it come to this?', *The Guardian*, 1 May 2021.

18

VICE

Serious vice problems began again in the East End at the end of the Second World War, and in 1944 local churchmen produced a report into conditions amongst black and Asian people. Naturally, sex featured prominently.

It was thought that in the Stepney area there were a minimum of 400 resident people described as coloured, of whom 136 were children and twelve were women. All except twenty of the children had white mothers; seventy-eight of them were under five years old and fifty-eight were between the ages of five and sixteen.[1] The floating population rather appropriately depended on the number of ships in the docks at any one time. The section on the health of the men found that a high number signing off from the Merchant Navy pool had both venereal disease and a general distrust of hospitals and treatment clinics. The report continued:

ATTITUDE TO WHITE WOMEN

When the coloured man first arrives in Stepney he is attracted by the white woman who wishes to trade on him; only after he has lived with her for a short period does he realise this. Thus, in the vast majority of cases, he very soon begins to adopt this attitude towards the white woman who associates with him.

When he has money he is generous and as long as the woman pleases him, affectionate: but this does not prevent him from beating her if she displeases him or even turning her away and taking another woman if he feels so inclined. Even superstition may influence him towards her: a Negro in a café one day explained that he had lived with three different women and although a dark woman had been the most beautiful, he had had to beat her and throw her out because her black hair had brought him bad luck in betting: he had been luckier when living with fair women.

. . . In most instances the coloured man has taken the woman to administer to his physical needs only, for either a short or a long period.[2]

The next section was devoted to the white woman:

Among the women married to coloured men in the area there can be found a few of the nicer type who have been genuinely attracted to the man and have married him for affection, but the vast majority have come into the district with the deliberate intention of trading on the coloured men.

The report found that some of the women were themselves daughters of prostitutes who, having had an illegitimate child, had lost their self-respect:

Almost all of these women are below normal intelligence and, according to officials who have dealt with them, over-sexed.

With the exception of those few who have married, these women have very little moral sense. They will leave one man to

go to another if the second will give them more. While accepting
a monthly allowance from one man while he is at sea, they will
live with others until he returns, and will encourage men in any
activity, such as black-marketing, that will help to provide more
clothes or food.[3]

This section of the report concluded that a large number of
the women also suffered from venereal disease and that syphilis
was on the increase.

The report then turned its attention to café society, something which would trouble the clergy and authority for the
next thirty years. There were thirty-four cafés, thirty-two of
which were within the area, used by black men and white
women. They were often run by 'men from Malta' who usually
provided a wireless set. Although the cafés operated as local
clubs, their main function was as a rendezvous between black
men and white women. There were often rooms over the cafés
which were let at five shillings a week – and more if a woman
was brought to stay. If there were no rooms, then the man
would be directed to a nearby house. If a woman joined him,
part of the additional rent would be paid to the café proprietor. The cafés catered separately for Muslims or for 'Negroes',
but all were frequented by white women. In 1943 there had
been twelve prosecutions for brothel keeping; in nine cases
women were the keepers. There was also some evidence of trade
between similar cafés in the Tottenham Court Road area and
as far afield as Coventry.[4]

Although the figures seem ludicrous by today's standards, the
cafés were highly profitable and when they were sold the goodwill
could reach as much as £1,000. A manager might receive £9 a
week and a share of the profits. Street soliciting, however, did not
become a serious problem until the 1950s. There were two cases

in the Stepney area in 1946; nine in 1949; but by 1965 the figure had grown to 500.[5]

It had been a growing problem for some time. In October 1947 a 3,000-strong petition was presented out of the blue to Stepney Borough Council, protesting about the conditions in Cable Street between Christian Street and Leman Street:

> ... Grave moral and physical danger exists for both young and old people in this area, and we demand that the Borough Council take active steps in consultation with the Home Office and the Food Ministry to rid us of this pestilence. We express the opinion that the contributory causes are the excessive number of cafés in the street open at a late hour and the disgusting conditions in some public houses.[6]

This brought protests and counter-protests in the council chamber. The police representative said that there was no evidence to support the contentions raised and as for suggestions that women were afraid to – and perhaps more importantly their husbands were afraid to let them – walk in Cable Street, not a single complaint of molestation or assault had been lodged.

The reply to this was an invitation for councillors to take off their rose-tinted glasses and to go to Cable Street or the top of Pell Street to see for themselves. The demarcation line between 'good' and 'bad' Cable Street was the traffic lights at, appropriately enough, Christian Street.

Taking up the scent of a good story, Harry Procter in the *Daily Mail* wrote:

> The girls who haunt the cafés and pubs are not London girls, they come from South Shields, Newcastle, Cardiff, Liverpool: many of them are on the run and some have escaped from

remand homes. They are safe in Cable Street. Most of them are teenagers, they get drunk, and the coloured seamen they are with get jealous.[7]

He went on to say that the cost of living in Cable Street for a week at that time was between £100 and £150, the sum the seamen had when they came off the boats. In the flats around Cable Street he estimated there was a gang of about 150 men and some 200 women who preyed on the seamen, saying that sometimes the gangs would arrange fights during which the unfortunate sailors would be robbed.

The ever crusading *John Bull* weighed in that December with some comments which fifty years later might cause problems with the Commission for Race Relations:

Seamen from all over the world know of Cable Street, and if their tastes lie that way, make for it as soon as their ships dock. Some of them are coloured boys just off their first ship. A few months ago they were still half naked in the bush. You can pick them by their speech and the awkwardness with which they wear their unfamiliar clothes.[8]

It took the local clergy a little while to muster a reply, but when they did it was to emphasise that the difficulties were not of a wholly racial nature. They suggested that the problems had been grossly exaggerated and:

... first, and most important, to make known, with the widest possible publicity the fact that the blame for the immorality and the undesirable conditions in the Cable Street area should not, in the first place, be laid upon the coloured population of the district.[9]

They went on to say that black people had not been asked to sign the petition. Not so, said one of the organisers. Many had been asked. Some had signed, some had declined.

The black journalist Roi Otley, writing in 1952, was appalled by what he saw in Cable Street:

> Today, down by London dock in about a square mile of back streets there exists a dismal Negro slum. The neighbourhood, situated in the borough of Stepney, abounds with brothels and dope pads in tumbledown old buildings. Few slums in the U.S. compare with this area's desperate character, unique racial composition, and atmosphere of crime, filth and decay.[10]

Three years later, M.P. Banton was similarly perturbed if less hostile:

> To the passer-by the area is a strange and definitely a frightening one; if he enters a café or a public house the other customers will scrutinise him thoroughly and there is an atmosphere so hostile that anyone but a coloured man, a seaman, or one of the poorest of the local population will come to feel that he does not 'belong' there and that he is not wanted.[11]

However, by 1957, in another church publication, the clergy was displaying its fears over the moral welfare of men from overseas:

> The advent of many coloured men is not responsible for the situation to be described later in this report but it does aggravate the gravity of that situation. It will certainly colour the picture of Christian England that they will send home to their countries.[12]

It is clear that by 1957 the fears of the *Daily Mail* ten years earlier had been realised and that the Commercial Road prostitutes who operated over a long stretch of the street came from all parts of England, although there were disturbing signs that local girls were taking up the game. That year there were 795 convictions for prostitution at Thames Magistrates' Court. Many were younger and less stable than prostitutes in other parts of London and, in a survey of girls in a reception area, over 50 per cent were mentally unstable *per se* or drink made them so.[13]

However, there was evidence that prostitution in Stepney was more organised than simply pathetic and feeble-minded amateurs. In his study of East End crime D. M. Downes suggested that: 'since the early and mid-1950s, the girls have been more organised and a pattern established.'[14]

It was now the Maltese who were the suggested organisers. There was a grain of truth to lend a little substance to the stereotype of the Maltese as profiteer, exploiter and pimp, but not everyone condemned them. The East End priest Father Fitzgerald asked, 'Who taught them to sell their sisters and other girls, but the visiting Imperial British?'

The problem of the Maltese in the East End was that over the years the community had been tarnished severely by the activities of the Messina brothers who had run organised prostitution in London overall from the 1930s until final deportations in the 1960s.

NOTES

1. Phyllis Young, *Report on Investigation into Conditions of the Coloured Population in a Stepney area*. The report gives a breakdown of the nationalities in the area. Of the group described as colonials which

comprised just under half the survey, 69.4 per cent were West Indians, with the British West Indians providing another 17 per cent.

2. ibid, p. 21.

3. ibid, p. 22.

4. It should be remembered that two women working from the same premises constituted a brothel.

5. See Gilbert Kelland, *Crime in London*; James Morton, *Bent Coppers*.

6. *ELA*, 31 October 1947.

7. Harry Procter, 'Street Scene' in *Daily Mail*, 31 October 1947.

8. Vivien Batchelor, 'The Citizen versus Vice' in *John Bull*, 6 December 1947.

9. *ELA*, 12 December 1947; 26 December 1947.

10. Roi Otley, *No Green Pastures*, p. 29.

11. M.P. Banton, *The Coloured Quarter*, p. 92.

12. 'Vice in Stepney,' 1957. Pamphlet in the local history section of Tower Hamlets Library.

13. Wellclose Square Fund, Progress Report 1962.

14. D.M. Downes, *The Delinquent Solution*, p. 161.

19

DEATH IN ESSEX

In the 1960s, with slum rebuilding and improved transport both contributing, East Enders – criminals and general public alike – moved more regularly out to Essex for work, play and living purposes. The trend was nothing new; rather it was the pace that had changed. Few lived in the East End by choice. In the nineteenth century when 'Baron' Nicholson, the confidence trickster who would go on to be the proprietor of the Judge and Jury shows, was apprenticed in Hackney, he would be behind to mind the premises whilst his master went to his cottage in the far more salubrious area of Shadwell for the night. Now Romford's Emerson Park would in time become a place where 'only the very rich and villains can afford to live'.

'We had a beautiful life, with cows, a big garden, a swimming pool. Dad used to say you don't get the lifestyle in the East End that you can have here. But obviously his motive for moving us was it was less dangerous,' said Nicola Collins, film producer daughter of East Ender Len Falco.

Not always.

The murder trial of Frederick Guy Browne and William Kennedy for the shooting of PC George Gutteridge in Essex is now regarded as yet another where a miscarriage of justice may have taken place.

Around dawn on 27 September 1927, thirty-six-year-old PC Gutteridge was found dead at Howe Green on the road between Romford and Ongar some 20 miles from central London. The officer had been shot in the head but a particular feature was that he had also been shot in both eyes; the belief in some circles is that a person's pupils reflect the last thing a dying person sees and, in Gutteridge's case, the imprint would have been that of his murderer. Shortly after a Dr Edward Lovell reported that his car in which he had left his medical bag had been stolen in nearby Billericay. The car was later found abandoned and in it was an empty cartridge.

The bullets with which Gutteridge's eyes had been shot out were obsolete ones which had not been used for several decades but all the experts at the Royal Arsenal could say was that the shots to his head had come from a .455 Colt, Webley or Smith & Wesson. The fashionable ballistic expert Robert Churchill, using his comparison microscope, was convinced they had come from a Webley. Four months later Frederick Guy Browne was arrested at a garage in South London after he had sold a stolen car. In another car in the garage was Dr Lovell's medical bag along with a Webley and ammunition of the type which had killed Gutteridge.

Churchill compared the Webley and the cartridge case found in Lovell's car and found the patterns on the breechblock of the Webley and the base of the cartridge case matched, marking for marking. William Fox, an arms inspector from the Royal Arsenal, examined over 1,300 small arms which were at the Royal Arsenal for repairs and it was only after he had failed to find a single breechblock whose markings corresponded with those on the cartridge case that he agreed with Churchill. It was the first time in a British court that modern forensic ballistics had played a prominent part. Browne and his employee William Kennedy were both convicted and hanged. Browne maintained his innocence to the end and re-examination of the case suggests that, while the forensic evidence may have been impeccable, Kennedy may have acted alone.

Four decades later the small but flamboyant villain, Tony Maffia, disappeared on 27 May 1968 soon after he returned from Belgium, where he had shown an interest in forged notes. Together with his long-time friend, prison escapee Alfie Hinds, Maffia had acquired a copper mine in Portugal and they worked together in various enterprises. They also both knew Manchester coal merchant Stephen Jewell.

For outside purposes Maffia was a car trader with a small firm, Justice Motors, who couldn't keep his hands off a quick deal. He was also one of the largest receivers of stolen goods to be found in England at the time. A man of some personality, he had the nerve to stand up to the Krays when they wished him to contribute to a whip for the repatriation of brother Charlie (then in a spot of bother in Africa), telling them to get it the way he did by grafting. It was over this that the old-time villain Buller Ward was cut. He warned Maffia in the Regency Club that the Krays were about to do him over. Maffia escaped through a back door but, for his treachery, Ward received 110 stitches in his face.

On the day Maffia disappeared he met with Jewell, who hoped to sell him forged £10 notes and on whom Maffia hoped to unload his cruiser, the *Calamara*, then in a marina at Wallasey Island. The price for the notes was £8,000 in real money as against £32,000 paper value.

According to Jewell, when he saw Maffia's house in Buckhurst Hill he liked it so much he suggested buying it. The price of £12,000 was even then a bargain. Maffia was separated from his wife and a sale was needed. The pair then drove in Maffia's green Jaguar MCC 932 to the marina to see the boat. Jewell carried a gun which, he said, Maffia had instructed him to bring. The gun, with its magazine housing bullets with a hole in each nose, was put on the front seat covered with a cloth. Jewell's car was then left in a pub car park. They certainly went to the marina, where Maffia reversed a call to London to say he would be back in about an hour, but after they left there he was never seen alive again. Maffia had been planning to fly to Jersey, where apparently he had important papers to sign, later that day.

Tony's older brother, the much shyer Arthur, who at the time was wanted over a long-firm fraud, was missing as well. Negotiations were opened with the police by the long-time bedridden wrestler, Alf 'Man Mountain' Dean, who arranged the surrender of Arthur Maffia. The long-firm inquiries came to nothing but Arthur could not explain where his brother might be.

Four days later on 1 June it became quite apparent where he was. On the Whit Saturday one of the staff at the Midway Restaurant – so-called because it was midway between Southend and London – saw a dog sniffing at a green Jaguar which had been in the car park for the last few days. In the front passenger seat, covered by a tarpaulin, was Maffia. It had been a hot few days and his body was so bloated it was recognisable only from fingerprints and a gold ring he wore. He had been shot twice, by the right eye and behind the right ear.

Two days later Jewell, of his own volition, arranged to see Detective Chief Inspector Kenneth Drury.[1] His story was that, shortly after he and Maffia left the marina, they were stopped by three men in a Ford Zodiac who told Jewell to go away while they talked to Maffia about a deal. When he returned both Maffia and the Zodiac were gone, as was the pistol and ammunition from the Jaguar. The car itself was still there. Jewell's overcoat, which he had left in the car, was bloodstained. He described the men, saying that one had a scar on his cheek.

Jewell said he drove off in the Jaguar for London and after a time stopped to throw the overcoat into a field. It was just as well he admitted that, for the coat was found containing a live bullet and sale particulars of Maffia's house. A witness would later say he saw Jewell wipe the passenger door with the coat before it was thrown away. Jewell agreed he had left the Jaguar in the car park of the Midway Restaurant.

Jewell was convicted by a 10–2 majority. Throughout the trial he had repeatedly tried to implicate Alfie Hinds, answering questions by saying that Hinds should be asked about the subject. After the trial Hinds was allowed to have counsel, Roger Frisby, make a statement in court denying any knowledge of the murder.

While he was in Wandsworth Jewell continually wrote to Arthur Maffia denying, yet again, that he had been his brother's killer and giving descriptions of the men whom he said had stopped the car. He maintained the old East End hardman Mickey Bailey had been one of them, and indeed before Jewell's arrest Bailey had been placed on an identification parade but not picked out. Buller Ward had also been on another parade and he too had been eliminated from the inquiries.

Arthur Maffia and other friends made what are quaintly described as 'their own investigations' and were satisfied the killer was Jewell. But Jewell still could find supporters for his story and in 1991 a television programme was made advancing his version of events.

Once the police began their investigations into Maffia's background, they unearthed a series of safe boxes containing the proceeds from a string of robberies in the Home Counties including a gold bar from the £750,000 gold bullion robbery in Bowling Green Lane, East London, a year earlier. There were also coins, diamonds, Dresden porcelain and jewellery. His nickname 'The Magpie' had been completely justified.

Many reasons were advanced for the killing – a contract hit; because Maffia would not join a forgery racket; a reprisal for being swindled by Maffia and Hinds. But perhaps the best theory is that on the way back to London Maffia, said to have had a spiteful tongue, simply taunted Jewell over a simple trick he had played and Jewell shot him in temper.

An old Spot man, George Wood, was charged along with Donald Alexander Mooney, Edward Henry Robins and James Tibbs senior with the so-called Ranch House murder of Ronald Thomas Coomber on 23 December 1960. Coomber and five other men had been drinking and had gone into the Ranch House in Ilford, caused trouble, insulted a woman and, when the owner Bob Patience had intervened, bashed him. Wood and the others threw them out and the prosecution alleged they then beat Coomber to death outside the club, one of them stamping on his throat. When the trial was heard at the Old Bailey there were no witnesses who could identify the men as being involved and Mr Justice was highly critical of the police investigation. On 8 March 1961 the case was stopped and all were awarded their costs. Later Patience said he had been picked up by gunmen who said the witnesses should not be able to make any identification.[2]

By a long series of coincidences thirteen years later Patience became involved with Charlie Kray. It came after the Barn restaurant in Braintree, of which he was the licensee, was robbed and his wife was killed.

In 1973, this time through little fault of his own, Charlie Kray became involved in one of the more sensational murder trials of the decade when George Ince, later convicted of a major bullion robbery, was accused of the murder of Muriel

Patience in what was known as the Barn Murder. Again the judge was Melford Stevenson whose acidity had not sweetened over the years.

Ince had first met Charlie's wife Dolly towards the end of the 1950s either in the Double R or at one of the many parties thrown by the Kray Twins. By the mid-1960s Ince had fallen in love with Dolly and once the three Kray brothers were in custody from the summer of 1968 he was a regular visitor to her flat in Poplar. In arguments with Charlie, Dolly would tell him that Nancy, their daughter, was in fact Ince's and although she later denied it, it was something that Charlie appears to have accepted as true. Charlie Kray in his book says, 'Deep down I knew Nancy was not my child.' 'Even though I knew Nancy was not my child I still wanted to see her' and '...I'd thought the world of her. Even though she was another man's child.' Charlie was indeed enormously proud of her, producing photographs of her at every possible opportunity.[3]

It was in November 1972 that Muriel Patience was shot and killed in a bungled robbery at the Barn restaurant. A description of the robbers was compiled from descriptions given by her husband Bob and their daughter Beverley. Ince had been in hiding since earlier in the year when he was suspected of being part of the Mountnessing bullion robbery team, but when an informer put his name up for the Barn Murder he believed he could prove his innocence and went to see the now qualified Ralph Haeems whose clerk George Stanley took him to the police. Dolly Kray gave Haeems a statement providing an alibi for the night of the murder but Ince never expected that it would be required to be produced.

Later that November, after the police had shown Ince's photograph to Beverley, she picked him out at an identification parade whilst Bob Patience identified another man. The trial opened at

Chelmsford Crown Court on 2 May 1973 and it did not go well for Ince. From the start there was trouble with Melford Stevenson whom Ince considered, probably correctly, to be biased. He was defended by Victor Durand QC, then regarded as one of the top five criminal silks in the country, and his junior was the vastly experienced Robert Flach. Beverley Patience was unshakeable in her identification of Ince. At one point Ince called out, 'Why don't you tell the truth?' Beverley Patience began to cry. A furious Stevenson commented, 'I have been making notes on that outburst' and adjourned the court for twenty minutes. On his return Ince said he apologised but added, 'I am not the man who did it'. Stevenson then sent him to the cells for the rest of Beverley Patience's evidence. On the fifth day, with Ince convinced he was going to be convicted by Stevenson let alone the jury, he said he wanted a different judge. Stevenson told him he was not going to get one and Ince said he wanted to go down to the cells. Stevenson refused him permission and Ince yelled that he was 'biased, rude, everything'. Stevenson told the warders to 'keep him there' and now Durand told the judge that his client had decided to sack him and Flach.

Over the weekend Ince's family sent a telegram to the Lord Chancellor asking for Stevenson to be replaced. Of course he was not. As a result Ince sacked Durand and Flach who sat in court taking no part and Ince elected not to cross-examine further witnesses. He turned his back on the judge for the remainder of the trial and called no witnesses, instead asking to be given a truth drug. That was also refused and Ince angrily interrupted the judge sixteen times during the summing up.

After they had retired for three and a half hours the jury returned to say they were worried that they had heard no evidence for the defence and Stevenson told them it was Ince's choice. Now, he said, he would accept a majority verdict of ten votes to two, but by 9.30 that evening they were unable to reach any verdict and they were discharged.

Ince's second trial began four days later with a reinstated Durand and Flach and this time the judge was the far more approachable Mr Justice Eveleigh, the antithesis of Stevenson – the pair were known by members of the Bar as the Rough and the Smooth. It was conducted in a very different atmosphere and when Ince complained he was being prejudiced because everyone else had been given glasses of water while, as a supposed security risk, he had to have a plastic beaker, Eveleigh, who actually believed Ince was not guilty, then arranged that everyone should drink out of plastic. During the second trial the question of the killer's accent, described as a Yorkshire one by both the Patiences, was brought up but Beverley Patience remained certain that she had correctly identified Ince.

On 18 May, the fifth day of the second trial, George Ince's defence began. On the evening of the murder he had been with a Mrs Grey at an address which he was allowed to write down. If correct, this put Ince more than sixty miles from the Barn ninety minutes before the murder.

Mrs Grey was in fact still Charlie Kray's wife, and it was to protect her from her husband and his family that Ince had not called her during the first trial – he himself had already had a number of beatings from Kray friends over his relationship. When Charlie was told she was coming on a visit, extra security was arranged. She had come to tell him she was going to give evidence. Kray wanted to know if Ince had some sort of hold over her but she told him it was true and he had been with her the night of the murder.

The prosecution wanted Mrs Grey's true identity known to the court but it was ruled that the jury should be told that she had changed her name but were not to be given her real name.

During his questioning prosecuting counsel, John Leonard QC, did in fact refer to her as Mrs Kray, something which Eveleigh considered to be 'most unfortunate'.

When Eveleigh summed-up on the eighth day, he told the jury that, 'if Mrs Grey had had any bad character this would have been disclosed to the court because she was a vital alibi witness' and contrasted Ince's alibi of having been with his mistress with the certainty of Beverley Patience's identification.

The jury returned after three hours and to uproar in the public gallery found Ince 'Not Guilty'. He left the court shouting abuse at the detectives in the case. In August 1973 the northerner John Brook and Nicholas Johnson were charged with the murder after Brook had confessed to a petty crook he had been working with. In February 1974 Brook was convicted of the murder and sentenced to life imprisonment and Johnson was convicted of manslaughter and sentenced to ten years. Ince's case was one of a number at the time which led to the Court of Appeal (Criminal Division) setting new guidelines on what is acceptable identification evidence.

Poor Dolly. After the hearing Violet Kray told reporters, 'I never liked Charlie's wife but now I hate her. The family has cut her off completely.' Ince later received fifteen years for his part in the Mountnessing bullion robbery, something he again denied. Dolly Kray received £20,000 from a newspaper for the story of her involvement with Ince. Now she said that the relationship was over but Kray told her that their marriage was at an end. Even before the Barn case Ince had paid heavily for his devotion. He was beaten up and shot on two occasions, the first in 1969 in the leg and a second time two years later when, in an attempt to emasculate him, a shotgun was pushed down his trousers. This time he received ninety-three pellets in his left calf.

Ince had a hard time in prison. While watching a football

game at Long Lartin he was cut by Harry Johnson, known as 'Hate 'Em All', who was serving eighteen years. Ince refused to identify him at Evesham Magistrates' Court, telling the justices 'I wouldn't like to take a chance on identifying anyone. You know what I think of identification parades'. Johnson still received five years. He was said to have been given a Rolex gold watch by the Twins as a reward for the cutting.[4]

Dolly may no longer have been in love with her husband but she was still supportive, lobbying for more visits and for him to be moved from the Special Security wing in Chelmsford to the general prison population. In its turn the Home Office told her he was getting more privileges than most.

In September 1977 Ince was allowed out of prison to marry the now divorced Dolly. After his release Ince returned to live with her in the East End with her daughter Nancy. Gary went to live with Charlie's family.

A man who seems to have been in the wrong place at the wrong time was Jimmy 'The Wad' Waddington, so-called not because of his surname but because he was said to have always carried a wad of notes. He had the misfortune, so the prosecution alleged, to have been in the Kaleli restaurant on Station Parade, Barking, in the late evening on Valentine's Day 1984 with the hardman and bouncer David Elmore. Neither man was seen again. The search for them did not begin for a week, by which time the Kaleli had undergone a spring clean.

According to the prosecution there had been a long-standing feud between Elmore and the Maxwells, another East End family, which had included an axe attack on Mickey, brother of David Maxwell who eventually stood trial for the Elmore and Waddington murders. One witness told the jury that they had been bound hand and foot and then decapitated with a samurai sword stolen from a local sports club and strangled with a table-cloth. Brian Wilson told the jury that Elmore had been reciting the Lord's Prayer during the attack and when he reached 'Thy will be done', one of his tormentors interrupted saying, 'You're dead right, son'. David Maxwell and Ronnie Reader were acquitted after a retirement of less than an hour, as was Reader's brother David who had been accused of helping dispose of the bodies. David Maxwell told reporters he had had nothing to do with any killings, adding 'We only got the word of the police that these two men were murdered in the first place'. A senior detective said the police were 'not looking for anyone else'. In November the next year two heads were thrown at the door of Harold Hill police station. After that incident Waddington's mother told the *Daily Express* sadly, 'I felt desolation not knowing where his last resting place might be or what exactly happened to him. I wanted to have him found in one piece but it looks like it could be him.'[5]

On 16 July 1991 publican Alan Brooks, also the landlord of the Gunmakers Arms pub in Chester Road, Loughton, was killed at his new pub, the Clydesdale in Loughton, Essex. He had only been the landlord of the Clydesdale pub for a fortnight when he was dragged from behind the bar and frog-marched into the car park where he was attacked by an armed gang with machetes.

Many suggestions have been put forward for the reason behind his death but perhaps the most likely is that the murder had been in relation to an incident a week earlier when Alan Brooks had barred third-generation members of a London family from entering the Gunmakers Arms pub. A man was arrested for his murder in June 1994, but no charges were brought.

With international travel the Costa del Sol opened itself to British villains. East Enders who pitched up there included Freddie Foreman who arrived there with Ronnie Knight, Clifford

Saxe and John Mason after the £6 million Easter Monday 1982 Shoreditch security van robbery, then the largest cash robbery in the United Kingdom.

At first it was sun and sangria and living off the proceeds of earlier villainy but as the years went by the old men left Puerto Banus and Marbella and a new breed of drug-dealers and international criminals moved in.[6]

On 6 December 1995 came the more celebrated murder of three Essex drug-dealers. Anthony Tucker, Patrick Tate and Craig Rolfe were found shot at point-blank range in a Range Rover in a field just outside Rettendon.

None of them were wholly admirable characters. They had all been members of the Inner City Firm, the West Ham football hooligan gang, before moving to Essex where they were part of a loose syndicate who controlled the doors of night-clubs and also dealt in drugs. Known as 'The Enforcer', Patrick Tate was a cocaine-addicted bodybuilder who, the night before his death, had badly beaten the manager of a local pizzeria when he failed to put adequate toppings on the food. Prior to that he had served a six-year sentence, and in December 1988 gained heroic status when he escaped from Billericay Magistrates' Court. He had jumped over the dock and disappeared on a conveniently parked motorcycle. He was in Spain within a few days, where he remained until he foolishly went to Gibraltar for the day and was arrested. He controlled a club in Southend and at one time had been physical trainer to Kenneth Noye, acquitted of the murder of a police officer, jailed for fourteen years for receiving part of the proceeds of the Brinks-Mat robbery and convicted in March 2000 of the murder of Stephen Cameron, stabbed in an apparent road-rage incident on the M25.

Craig Rolfe was simply the driver and gofer. He had an unfortunate start in life. He was born in Holloway prison where his mother, Lorraine Rolfe, was serving an eighteen-month sentence for impeding the arrest of nineteen-year-old John Kennedy, who received life for murdering Lorraine's husband, Brian, on Christmas Eve 1968. The prosecution's case had been that Rolfe and Kennedy were having an affair and that Kennedy had murdered Brian Rolfe with a tenpin-bowling skittle in the bedroom of his home in Linford Drive and then dumped the body on the A13 near Vange in an effort to make the death look like a botched robbery. By the time of Craig Rolfe's death, he too had a serious cocaine habit.[7]

It was, however, the third of the bodies which attracted the most attention – that of Anthony Tucker of Fobbing, who acted as minder for the boxer Nigel Benn, leading him into the ring before his contests. More seriously, he controlled the doors of sixteen night-clubs from Southend to East London. Control of night-club doors is essential in the drug-dealing world. Only those favoured by the management or the bouncers are let in, and rival organisations have their salesmen excluded. If a door can be properly policed, a fortune is there for the taking. Tucker certainly had links with South London criminals and probably with the Triads and Yardies.

There had been a good deal of activity in the area in the previous weeks. In August, Darren Kerr, a friend of Tucker, had been abducted and then had acid thrown in his face, blinding him in one eye and completely disfiguring him to the extent that he had to wear a plastic mask as favoured by ice-hockey goalkeepers. Whilst he was in Billericay Hospital he was shot in the chest by a man disguised as a clown with a clown's wig, red nose, Dracula teeth, and carrying a bunch of flowers. The man had asked the staff where Kerr was and, on being told, fired at him with a shotgun, hitting him in the shoulder. Kerr survived. Leah Betts, daughter of a police officer, did not. On 16 November she died after taking an Ecstasy tablet bought in Raquels night-club in Basildon.[8] It was said that a North London gangland leader offered to put a contract on the man who had given it to her. Later, after two retrials, a man was acquitted of supplying her with the drug.

The men's funerals were in the best gangland tradition, with twenty cars following a horse-drawn carriage for Craig Rolfe on 21 December. The next day there was another horse-drawn carriage for Pat Tate, and the same afternoon Tony Tucker was buried. Within weeks Raquels was closed down.

It was some time before the whole convoluted story, or at least one version of it, behind the three deaths emerged and, as is often the case, it did so through the good offices of one of those involved but who wished to preserve his relative freedom. Before that it was suggested that their deaths had been a reprisal for that of Leah Betts, or for that of Keith Whittaker who had died following an overdose when a £60,000 drug deal had gone wrong.

In many ways a drugs hierarchy works on exactly the some principles as an ordinary business. If you are a junior executive on a drugs gang then you must be careful not to upset senior management. If you do, life as a drug courier can be very nasty and even fatal. So if you are used as a courier and are somehow ripped off by the supplier or indeed the purchaser then the loss could be said to be down to you. You are expected to pay for the lost drugs or cash deficit. This was a trap into which Keith Whittaker fell in his dealings with Tate, Tucker and Rolfe. In April 1994 he was sent to collect cannabis from a team in Manchester but when he returned a kilo was found to be missing. Management takes a serious view of what it sees as defaulting. From experience they know when they are being ripped off. Sacking is not an option. At the least a bad beating is. Rolfe refused to accept Whittaker's story that he was innocent and demanded he pay over £2,500. Whittaker borrowed the money from his parents and paid up. From that time Whittaker deteriorated, smoking more cannabis, not bathing or washing and sofa-surfing. Finally in the November came an opportunity to make £5,000 out of a deal with Rolfe. However, when it came to it he was told he would get £2,000 maximum which would show him nothing after he had purchased the drugs. Now he made a serious error of judgement and complained.[9]

First he was injected with ketamine, which is usually used on horses and known as Special K. This had the effect of paralysing him but not knocking him unconscious. Pleading for his life he was then injected with a dose of lignocaine which killed him. His body was left by the roadside in a ditch in Dunton Road, Laindon.

In fact the murders related to yet another drugs rip-off worked by Tucker.

The supergrass was Darren Nicholls, who went on to claim that there was a price of £500,000 on his head. Nicholls was, he said, the driver of the getaway car after Michael Steele and Jack Whomes lured the three men to the field. He maintained that he thought he was only driving the men to a drug deal, not to a killing. At the trial the prosecution's version of events was that a consignment of bad cannabis had been supplied to Tate by Steele who, along with Whomes and a Peter Corry, rather daringly smuggled drugs from Holland using fast open boats to bring the cargo to the East coast. One of the cargoes in November 1995 had been of such poor quality that refunds were demanded and paid, but Steele had further rows with the increasingly unstable Tate and had decided that he and his colleagues had to be killed before Steele and Whomes became the victims.

Now Steele claimed he was bringing in a consignment of cocaine and that he would ensure that Tate, Tucker and Rolfe had a chance to hijack that consignment. Arrangements were

made to meet in the lane at Rettendon, where Whomes and
Steele opened fire at point-blank range. In improved versions of
the stories the men were offered the chance of immediate death
or having their fingers cut off first. In May 1996 the pair, along
with Corry and Nicholls, were arrested with 10 kilos of cannabis.
Faced with a long sentence, Nicholls, who had been in a corrupt
relationship with an Essex detective, decided that co-operation
was the better part of valour. The trial, which began at the Old
Bailey on 1 September 1997, was estimated to have cost £1.5
million – of which protection for Nicholls was £300,000. In his
cell, he had a multi-gym as well as a colour television. He also
had a take-away meal service provided.

The Crown case depended wholly on Nicholls. As far as he
was concerned he was merely driving Whomes and Steele to a
drug deal, and had driven in convoy to the Halfway House near
Rettendon where Steele joined Tucker, Tate and Rolfe in the
back of their Range Rover. Whomes had put on a boiler-suit
and told Nicholls to drop him off at the bottom of Workhouse
Lane, saying he would ring to let him know when he wanted to
be collected. At 7 p.m. Nicholls received the call and noticed
the two men had blood-covered surgical gloves. He had been so
alarmed, he told the jury, he had nearly crashed his car.

When it came to it Steele did not exactly help himself in the
witness-box. Against the advice of his lawyers he regaled them
with his previous convictions, mostly for drug offences.

Was Nicholls to be believed? Certainly his evidence was
riddled with inconsistencies and the defence had an alternative
scenario for the murders. This was that the men had been killed
by members of the Canning Town Cartel. The source of this
information was Billy Jasper, an East End hardman who had
himself been arrested in January 1996 and had given the police
his version already. It seems he had met Jesse Gale, another East

End heavy, at Moreton's Bar in Canning Town together with a third man. They had then gone to a local Mexican restaurant where they had discussed the future prospects of Tate, Tucker and Rolfe. Apparently the Cartel had negotiated a sale of drugs to the trio, who planned to roll the Cartel and not pay for the drugs. This was, according to Jasper, standard practice and with this in mind the trio had purchased a submachine-gun. Tate and Tucker had also taken Gale and the third man for some £200,000. Now Jasper was to be the driver for a fee of £500. He had driven a grey Fiat Uno from outside the Peacock Gym in Canning Town to Hornchurch, where he had collected the third man from Moreton's Bar. Gale had been left behind and Jasper had been told to drop the third man off near Rettendon and to wait while he went to collect 4 kilos of cocaine. Forty minutes later he reappeared and then telephoned Gale to say that everything was sorted.

Rather bravely, Jasper had later confronted this third man in Moreton's Bar when he went to collect his £500 and had said, 'You took them out.' The third man had merely smiled and told him not to be inquisitive.

Although Jasper appeared for the defence, much of his evidence was ruled inadmissible by the trial judge. Investigative reporter Jo-Ann Goodwin from the *Daily Mail* made inquiries around Canning Town and found that in general the locals accepted Jasper's version of events.

Sadly Gale cannot now be asked to give his version of events. He was killed in a five-person crash when he lost control of his Range Rover in October 1997 crossing the central reservation near Swanley in Kent and smashing into a Vauxhall Carlton. The driver and his passengers who all died had been returning from a day trip to France. The Coroner's Court heard Gale had been over the drink-driving limit and was speeding.

On 20 January 1998 Whomes and Steele were jailed for life with a recommendation that they serve at least twenty-five years. The jury had been out for some four and a half days and although the verdict was unanimous it had clearly been a long struggle in the jury room. Three women jurors wept as the foreman announced the verdict. Nicholls, who had received fifteen months which he served in police custody, wrote a book about the affair.[10] Whomes and Steele have continued to protest their innocence. Their appeals were rejected by the Court of Appeal and in 2006 the Court of Appeal upheld the convictions. They had then heard that before the trial Nicholls had negotiated a book deal said to be worth up to £15,000 with a publisher. This had not been disclosed to the defence but the court held it would not have affected the jury even if they had been told about it. Whomes, who behaved in an exemplary fashion, had his sentence cut by two years and was eventually released in March 2021.[11]

In January 2021 Steve 'Nipper' Ellis told the *Essex County Standard* that his father Sid had killed Tucker and the others. He said that Tate had threatened to cut off Ellis' daughter's fingers in retaliation for remarks made by Nipper Ellis about Tucker's girlfriend Donna Garwood. Tucker and Rolfe had been at Nipper Ellis's house where they had threatened him with a machete and smeared excrement on the walls so in a way it was a form of pre-emptive self-defence even if the courts might not have seen it in that way. Sid Ellis had told his son about the killings before he had died four years earlier.[12]

Another version of the reason for their executions was that money had gone missing from the Brinks-Mat robbery which one of them had been looking after. Certainly Pat Tate had been the minder for one of the robbers.

A matter of days after Linda Millard, living in Portsea, contacted the police to say she had overheard a telephone conversation which might assist them regarding the murders, she disappeared. Since then there has been no hint that she might still be alive nor has her body been found. A man's house was searched but no arrests were made.

Another murder of an Essex man said to have been carried out by the Canning Town Cartel may have been linked to Tate and co., say locals. Not so, say the police. It was that of Tate's friend John Marshall who, according to Jo-Ann Goodwin, had been given £120,000 drug money to mind by Tate and who was found shot in his car in May 1996. He had been missing for a week after leaving his home in Billericay with some £5,000 in cash, telling his wife he was going to buy a car. His Range Rover was found parked on a yellow line in Round Hill, a residential part of Sydenham. It had a parking ticket attached to the windscreen. Marshall's body was under a dog blanket in the boot; he had been shot in the head. The £5,000 had been left in the car.

The police issued a statement that there was no suggestion that Marshall had been a drug-dealer.[13]

Following the March 2000 conviction of Kenneth Noye for the killing of Stephen Cameron in an apparent road-rage incident on the M25, it was suggested that Marshall's death was linked to the fact that he had disposed of Noye's car after the stabbing incident.

At the end of the 1990s one of the more dangerous spots in Essex was the Epping Forest Country Club in Chigwell, earlier owned by Bobby Moore and Sean Connery. It was in fact a collection of three night-clubs, Atlantis, Casino and Woolston Hall, known as The Night-club and meant to be for over twenty-fives. Behind

Casino was a complex where over 5,000 clubbers could attend 'Splash' events.

After a fatal stabbing of Darren Pearman, whose father Christopher was alleged to be a member of a Canning Town firm, at the club on 3 October 1999, Pearman was put in a taxi and taken to nearby Whipps Cross hospital but he was found to be dead on arrival. Pearman's brother was also stabbed but he survived.

Bouncer Ron Fuller was arrested and charged with violent disorder. He and another bouncer at the club were kept in custody for their own safety but, when the charge was dropped because witnesses could not be found, they were released on 25 November.

One version of the story is that the brawl in which Pearman was killed was the result of earlier differences that started when Dave 'Rolex Dave' King, a man described as a well-known Underworld figure, had Fuller eject Pearman from a pub in North London. Then, sometime later when Pearman saw Fuller in the club, there was a fight that developed into a mass brawl during which Pearman and his brother were stabbed.

Reprisals – if indeed they were reprisals – came within the year. On 27 August 2000 after a fight in Atlantis had spilled outside – there were said to be 7,000 people in the club at the time – two bouncers were shot, one in the stomach and one in the back. The next day at about 7. 45 a.m. Fuller, who knew there was a contract on him, was shot and killed outside his home in Grays as he left for his daytime job as a builder. His killer, who shot him twice in the head and twice in the body, escaped on a motorcycle with L plates. No one has ever been charged with the murder.

The surviving bouncers could not help the police with the identity of their attackers but not long after, Christopher Pearman, Darren's father, survived an attempt on his life. His car tyres had been let down and when he went to the car, shots were fired at him.

'Rolex Dave' King, described by his parents as 'a devout Muslim' and by an associate as 'a violent bully' and the man said to have started it all, survived until October 2003. After an early morning workout he was shot in a drive-by contract killing by three men armed with a Kalashnikov AK47 as he left the Physical Limit gym in Hoddesdon. Twenty-six bullets were fired, five of which hit King. It was the first time the gun had been used in a British killing.

Earlier King had been charged, but later released, when a 14 kilogram (30 pound) shipment of heroin was intercepted by customs officers. As a result the word in the East End was that he had become a police informer. Even before this he had not been a popular man. He had served a prison sentence and on his release had begun to bully his way into taking control of the doors of night-clubs in Essex before opening his own, the Renaissance in Stevenage, said to be a home from home for drug-dealing.

It was the second contract on King. The first failed when Dean Spencer lost his nerve after seeing King's sheer size. The second was carried out by Roger Vincent, from Penn in Buckinghamshire. After he was unanimously convicted of murder at Luton Crown Court he was told he would serve a life sentence of at least thirty years. The driver, David Smith, was sentenced to a minimum of twenty-five years. A third man was acquitted.[14]

Immediately after the death of Fuller, Peter Pomfret, owner of the Country Club, said that while there had been problems in the past, now the club was 'rocking'. In 2002 the club was closed after allegations of stabbings, fights and drug-dealing as well as complaints from neighbours. In May 2010 Pomfret was sentenced to ten years – reduced to eight on appeal – for his part in a £37 million VAT fraud.

The curse of the club lingered on.

In similar circumstances to the Fuller murder, in May 2006 Christopher Pearman shot and killed Rocky Dawson as he was putting his young daughter in the back of a Fiat Punto. He received life imprisonment. Another man, James Tomkins, fled to the Costa del Crime where he lived for four years. He was returned and in April 2011 he also received life imprisonment with a minimum of thirty-three years. The killing was thought by the police to be one of mistaken identity and in 2012 Pearman told Dawson's mother that he and Tomkins had been paid £5,000 each to kill Rocky's brother Ross. Apparently a businessman suspected Ross of burgling his home. There were allegations that corrupt police had interfered with the initial investigation but these were never proven.[15]

In July 2007 Daniel Smith fled to Spain after he shot Douglas Turner by mistake at his home near Chelmsford. He had intended to shoot Turner's son. Smith lasted three years on the run before he went down, shot outside a bar in Mijas. Eric Wilson received twenty-three years for the shooting, said to be over a quarrel in the bar, but there was more to Wilson than just bad temper. When Wilson's home in Coin was searched a quantity of weapons and explosives was found.

A month after Turner was shot, fifty-two-year-old Keith Cowell, his seventeen-year-old son Matthew, and thirty-three-year-old Tony Dulieu were shot at a house in Bishop's Stortford with a sub-machine gun. Ian Jennings survived after hiding in the garden. Cowell's wife had just left for work at Stansted. Matthew's girlfriend Claire Evans was repeatedly stabbed as she tried to protect her daughter Courtney, who was unharmed.

In June 2008 twenty-three-year-old Miran Thakrar, who had

also shot the family dog and fled to North Cyprus, was jailed for life with a forty-two-year minimum. He had claimed two other men had burst in and shot Dulieu and the Cowells before he had been forced to go upstairs to stab Claire. Earlier his brother Kevan Thakrar, aged twenty, received a thirty-five years minimum sentence. Their father Atul Thakrar, forty-six, Yilay Tufensoy, twenty, from Enfield, and his girlfriend Amanda Dansie, twenty, were jailed for four years each for assisting an offender. The killings were apparently linked to the quality of cocaine supplied in a £30,000 deal. Thakrar had been sold an inferior cocaine known as Repress instead of the better-quality Shine he had hoped for.[16]

In November 2011 Kevan Thakrar was acquitted of two counts of attempted murder and three counts of wounding with intent after an incident at Frankland Prison in County Durham. He admitted he had lashed out with a broken bottle and injured three prison guards but claimed he'd acted in self-defence in a pre-emptive strike after suffering years of alleged racist bullying. The next year he lost an action claiming his human rights had been breached over the use of telephones in prison. In March 2020 a demonstration was held by the Industrial Workers of the World (the Wobblies) to mark ten years of his being held in a Close Supervision Centre.

In 2011 self-confessed serial criminal Billy Martindale, son of unlicensed boxer and doorman Lew 'Wildman' Yates, published his memoirs, *Wanted: My Life on the Run as Billy Boy Yates*. In it he maintained that he had begun to 'tax' drug-dealers after the death of a boyhood friend Tommy Shepherd, a twenty-four-year-old agricultural worker, whose naked body was found wrapped in a carpet in Chatteris. This was in April 1997, a few years after Martindale left Cambridgeshire.

'He was killed by drug dealers, and that sort of kicked me off the direction I went,' Mr Martindale recalled.

I got involved in 'taxing' drug dealers in London - relieving them of their ill-gotten gains.

I never took a penny off a working man. I'm not a scumbag.

He went on to write he was completely reformed and that the book had been a cathartic experience for him.

The book has been a bit like a counselling session for me. I'm completely legit now and both spiritually and mentally, I'm a completely different person. Being legit is the best feeling in the world.'[17]

In October the next year Martindale was killed at his farm in Ongar in an argument over growing cannabis; he was clubbed to death with a pickaxe handle. In May 2013 Paul Groves was given life imprisonment. He claimed that the fight had been over his right to grow cannabis on the farm for himself and he had merely been defending himself.

One of Reggie Kray's prison sons and lovers Bradley Allardyce demonstrated that those who believe prison will cure criminality are likely to be sadly disabused. After Reggie's death, from which Allardyce was to inherit a substantial part of the estate, he went to Spain where he opened a gay bar in Altea, but in 2002, a few days after house hunters Anthony and Linda O'Malley were kidnapped and murdered, he closed everything and returned to England.

The O'Malleys had been lured to a villa by Venezuelan brothers-in-law Jorge Real Sierra and Jose Velazquez Gonzales, and while Mrs O'Malley was bound and held hostage in the cellar, her husband was forced at gunpoint to empty their bank account with a series of card transactions for cash and goods. They were then killed. Sierra and Gonzales were sentenced to an aggregate of 116 years in prison. In 2006 Sierra wrote to a civil rights lawyer protesting his innocence and trying to lay the blame on Allardyce.[18]

By then Allardyce, then aged thirty-six, was back in serious trouble. The money left him by Reggie brought no happiness. His wife Donna had gone and now a David Fairburn became involved with Amy, sister of Allardyce's girlfriend Tracey Cooper. The relationship turned sour and Allardyce, along with Shane Porter and Wayne Turner, attacked Fairburn on a Barking street, stabbing him in the heart. In 2005 they were all jailed for life with a recommendation they serve a minimum of eighteen years.[19]

NOTES

1. Drury was later implicated in the great Porn Squad inquiry, convicted and sentenced to eight years' imprisonment reduced to five on appeal.

2. *The Times*, 14 January, 9 March 1961.

3. In June 2004 Nancy was reported in *The People* newspaper to have wanted Charlie Kray's body exhumed so that DNA tests could prove if he really was her father. Charlie Kray, *My Brothers and Me*. For an account of the Ince trial and its repercussions, see Peter Cole and Peter Pringle, *Can You Positively Identify this Man?*

4. Charles Bronson, *The Krays and Me*, p. 120.

5. *Today*, 21 March 1985; *Daily Express*, 6 November 1985.

6. Freddie Foreman, *Respect*; Dan Bilefsky, 'Once He Was the "Godfather of British Crime". Now He's Just a Grandfather', *The New York Times*, 19 April 2019.

7. Bernard O'Mahoney, *So This Is Ecstasy?*

8. The club itself had serious problems with violence and discontented customers. On one occasion, after a youth had been refused admission he returned and petrol-bombed the doors. For an account of

club minding and drug-dealing in Essex during the period and an account of the violent Jason Draper and the Bullseyes from Basildon, see Bernard O'Mahoney, *So This Is Ecstasy?*

9. Tony Thompson, *Bloggs 19.*

10. Ibid.

11. *R v Steele and ors* [2006] EWCA Crim 195. Nicholls' account of the killings has been subsequently challenged by Bernard O'Mahoney in his updated version of *So This Is Ecstasy?*

12. Steve Ellis with Bernard O'Mahoney, *Essex Boy: Last Man Standing*; *Essex County Standard*, 10 January 2021.

13. See Jo-Ann Goodwin, 'Bloody Revenge and a Cosseted Supergrass' in *Daily Mail*, 2 August 1999.

14. Nigel Rosser, 'Hoddesdon gym victim's past revealed', *Evening Standard*, 9 October 2003.

15. Tom Pettifor, 'Eight murders that have been covered up according to ex-Met Police detective', *Daily Mirror*, 9 November 2015.

16. *The Queen v Thakrar and anr* 2010 EWCA Crim 1505, http://news.bbc.co.uk/2/hi/uk_news/7503118.stm.

17. BBC Cambridgeshire, 18 January 2011.

18. Danny Collins, *Nightmare in the Sun.*

19. *The Times*, 27 January 2005.

20

FOREST MURMURS – THE DISPOSALISTS

'He was good as a killer but not as a disposalist,' said Jason Ryan of his uncle Dennis Allen, the Australian crime lord, so adding a new word to the English language.

Over the years many people have used Essex and in particular the 5,900-acre Epping Forest – 19 km long but a bare 4 km wide – as a disposal ground; an easy way of getting rid of a body and without much thought that it will more or less inevitably be found. Some just leave the body or its parts in the open air.

The Krays were said to have disposed of a rent boy killed during sex at Steeple Bay, as well as their friend Mad Teddy Smith when they thought he was turning against them. The latter was certainly wrong. Smith lived to go to Australia before returning to Wales to die many years after the Twins.

One of the earlier examples of Essex as a repository for the unwanted bodies of victims killed elsewhere was in October 1949. After the Second World War one of the bigger car dealers in Warren Street off the Tottenham Court Road was the Iraqi-born Stanley Setty. His brother Max, with whom he had quarrelled, owned the very fashionable night-clubs, the Orchid Room in Brook Street and then the Blue Angel in Berkeley Street. Stanley Setty, whose real name was Sulman Seti, would, however, turn his hand to anything which might produce a profit for him. He had a conviction in Manchester in 1928 for obtaining credit by fraud and associated bankruptcy offences. Apart from dealing in cars he was regarded as a black market banker, putting up money for jobs and then taking a cut but not handling the merchandise himself. According to the police, as a sideline he was a small-time pimp. He disappeared on 4 October 1949 and his sister-in-law reported him missing the next day.

On 22 October parts of Setty's body were found wrapped in parcels near Tillingham on the Essex marshes where they had been dropped from a light aircraft. It was not difficult to trace the pilot Donald Hume who had hired an Auster from a flying club at Elstree and then left the plane at Southend airport. Hume, married with a three-and-a-half-month-old daughter – a typical wide boy of the time, involved in smuggling and indeed anything else which might turn a profit – was known to be short of money. Four days later when interviewed he said, 'I'm some kind of bastard, aren't I?' He claimed that two men, 'Mac' and Green, came to him to pilot a plane to drop out at sea hot plates used for forging clothing coupons. For a fee of £50 he had dropped the plates and when he returned to his Golders Green flat he found them and a third man, 'Boy', offering him £100 to drop a third package. He cannot have really thought they were plates because he had heard a gurgling noise from this third parcel and indeed he had thought it might even be Setty, of whose disappearance he had heard.

The prosecution's case was that Setty had been killed – stabbed in the chest – at Hume's flat at 623 Finchley Road and on the face of it the evidence against him was strong. There was a good deal of blood in the flat and Hume had taken a carpet to be cleaned on the morning of 5 October. He had also taken a knife to be sharpened locally just before the killing. On the other hand there were no fingerprints of Setty, nor had neighbours heard anything sounding like a quarrel or fight, certainly not the noise of someone dismembering a body. In the days when a jury's verdict had to be unanimous it was sufficient for Hume to get a disagreement. Hume was re-tried and this time pleaded guilty to being an accessory after the fact. He expected to receive a shortish sentence and was not at all pleased with his twelve years.

While he was away his now divorced wife, a former night-club hostess Cynthia, married the crime reporter Duncan Webb. As Hume was nearing his release Mad Frank Fraser and others used to tease the journalist that Hume would be coming after him. He did not. Instead on his release in 1958 he sold his story 'I killed Setty' to the *Sunday People* for £2,000, saying he had, in fact, killed him in a quarrel over Setty kicking Hume's dog.

That year Hume went to Switzerland where in August he shot a bank cashier and another in November. Both survived but Arthur Maag, a taxi driver who tried to prevent him escaping from a bank robbery in Zurich in January 1959, was not so fortunate. Hume was sentenced to life imprisonment and the President of the Court announced, 'Life imprisonment for this kind of man means life.' It did not. He was returned to England in 1976 and sent to Broadmoor from where he was later released. Shortly afterwards Hume died in a wood in Gloucestershire. His badly decomposed body had to be identified through dental work. Setty is buried in the Jewish cemetery at Golders Green in Row 57 Plot 11.

Forty years later, on 2 July 1990, another body was found on Rainham Marshes, about four miles from where parts of Setty had been dropped. It was that of millionaire garage owner and one-time saloon car racing champion Nick Whiting. He had run All Car Equipe in Wrotham Heath, Kent, almost at the gates of Brands Hatch. He and five high-performance cars from his garage went missing on 7 June, although the cars were all recovered within a few days. Following a tip-off the police found Whiting's body in a shallow grave on the marshes.

He had been stabbed nine times and shot twice and the police thought that he had been beaten, bound and gagged and then put into the boot of a car. He was taken to the marshes and then frog-marched for two miles before being shot in the head and buried. That month a man was charged with his murder but the charge was later dropped.

Whiting was said to have been involved in the Brinks-Mat robbery and it was thought he had been shot because he was an informant. He was said to have been a close friend with another high-profile person who was also associated with the robbery and who had later been found with some of the gold.

Whether it was murder or merely a kidnapping that went wrong, the death of the one-time Mayor of Stepney, Solomon Lever, remains unsolved. Lever was the secretary of the Workers' Circle Friendly Society to which members could pay in money and borrow against their capital. Shortly after 1 a.m. on the night of 19 July 1959 Lever was with his wife when he received a telephone call at his home in Victoria Park, Hackney, to say there was a fire in the timber yard next to the Society's offices just behind the Hackney Empire. The police would come and collect him and take him there. Lever fell for the bait. A bogus police-man turned up at the Lever door – tall and dark, said Lever's wife. Neither of them asked the man for identification. Lever was taken to the offices where there was no fire; he was made to open the safe and £7,000 was taken. A couple of hours later his body was found 100 yards from Rangers Road in Epping Forest. A passer-by thought he had been the victim of a hit and run but he had been gagged and his wrists tied. Lever had had a bad heart and probably the strain had been too much. The coroner returned a verdict of manslaughter by persons unknown. All the usual suspects were rounded up, including the old Clerkenwell expert safe-breaker Bert Rossi, but no charges were ever brought.[1]

As the blue film industry developed there was a demand for stronger and stronger material. No longer would punters pay to see large Scandinavian women playing volleyball in long shot. More was needed. And a film maker and distributor who upped the story lines was Michael Muldoon. One of his bodyguards and actors was Gerry Hawley, known as the tattooed man. In the summer of 1989 Hawley's body was found in a grave in the Forest. He had been stabbed more than eighty-nine times.

At his trial Muldoon admitted that he had stabbed Hawley but it was in self-defence, saying that Hawley had burst into Muldoon's Balham flat and was standing over him and attacking him, but the pathologist maintained that the stab wounds were all in a downward direction, indicating that the attacker was standing over the victim, not below him. Muldoon was convicted and sentenced to life imprisonment. Two others were convicted of assisting him.

The prosecution's case had been that the extremely violent Hawley, who had once slit a woman from her groin to her breasts, had been muscling in on Muldoon's extremely lucrative porn film industry and Muldoon's had been a pre-emptive strike. Another theory was that Hawley had been recruited by the Krays, acting on behalf of the Obscene Publications Squad (OPS), to kill Muldoon who had overstepped the boundaries of their contract with him. Muldoon had turned the tables. This is difficult to accept because at the time of the killing the Krays had been in custody for the better part of a year.

Muldoon maintained that the investigating officer, Bert

Wickstead, wanted him to inform on corrupt OPS officers whom he was tracking down at the time but Muldoon turned him down. After his release Muldoon changed his name, continued in the porn business and served another sentence before moving his operations to Holland. From the time of his murder conviction Muldoon has maintained his innocence and has written his memoirs.[2]

Another poor disposalist was police officer Peter Swindell who had once stood guard outside No 10 Downing Street. In March 1981 he received five years for preventing the burial of 18 stone lesbian prostitute Pat Berkeley, who had choked to death wearing a mask at Swindell's Walthamstow home. He had kept the body in the bath but, when neighbours complained about the smell, had cut it up with a hacksaw and left the parts in the Forest where a boy found them after shooting at them with his air rifle. Swindell was found not guilty of manslaughter. The Director of Public Prosecutions had decided there was not sufficient evidence to proceed with a charge of murder.

Eight years later in 1989 Terence Gooderham, an accountant, and his girlfriend, Maxine Arnold, were both killed with a double-barrelled shotgun in a hit-man-style slaying. Although unsolved, one suggestion is that James Moody, described as 'Britain's most notorious hitman', may have been responsible for the killings. Another theory in the press is that Gooderham was targeted because he had creamed off £250,000 in drugs money that he was involved in laundering and that the hit was ordered by the Adams family criminal organisation, lovingly dubbed by the press as the Clerkenwell Crime Syndicate.

In July the following year forty-three-year-old Debbie Lee Parsons, who ran a massage parlour, disappeared. She had left her home in Muswell Hill, North London, to help out at her boyfriend's restaurant but never reached it. Her body was found in her open VW in Upshire. She had been shot in the head with a cross-bow. Again it was never established quite why she was killed or by whom, but the officer in charge of her case described it as an execution by any other name. One suggestion was that she had a 'black book' of clients and was subject to a contract killing following the possibility that she was going to sell details to a newspaper. The murder remains unsolved.

There is a tendency when a noted hardman disappears, or is killed, to put the blame of any unsolved contract killing within a fifty mile or more radius on his shoulders. Teddy Machin was one example, and this time again in the blame frame for being the actual hitman was Richardson member Jimmy Moody.

But there again it might just as easily have been undertaken by an Adams family associate, Gilbert Wynter, who himself disappeared on 9 March 1998. Wynter left the house he shared with his girlfriend in her Nissan Micra. Later that day, he spoke to her by phone but after that Wynter was neither seen nor ever heard from again. The car was found abandoned in June. His bank account, credit card and mobile phone remained untouched. The main suggestion advanced over his death is that he stole a shipment of cannabis worth £800,000 which went missing. The prosaic version is that Wynter double-crossed the Adams family, stole the drugs and was killed, with his body being buried in the foundations of the Millennium Dome. In this version the killer is said to be a Bristol-based drug-dealer. The more romantic, but probably less likely, version is that he fled to the Caribbean with the drugs and has successfully remained in hiding. If so he would now be in his early sixties.[3]

Another naked body, this time that of thirty-one-year-old Wendy Woodhouse from Rugby, was found on 18 April 2001 near the back of Snaresbrook Crown Court. She had been singularly unlucky. Courtney Peters, an illegal immigrant from Jamaica, now living in the Midlands, had given her £1,300 to buy crack cocaine but she mistook the man from whom she was to buy the drugs and bought parsley wrapped in foil from a small-time crook instead. Peters wanted to know where his money had gone and his girlfriend, Fiona Jamison, lured Woodhouse to Epping Forest. Jamison remained in the car while Peters and his cousin Ewing Thomas stripped Woodhouse and beat her to death with a snooker cue and pistol butt. 'It was brutal, it was violent, and it was final,' said Victor Temple QC prosecuting. The trio received life imprisonment.

In 2005, after passers-by heard gunshots, Rafal Czapczyk was found at Wake Arms, Loughton, with wounds to his head. He died later in hospital. The body remained unidentified for several months until his family in Poland recognised mortuary pictures that had been released by police. Four men were later arrested but not charged.

Another poor-quality disposal was unearthed when the partially buried body of Hidir Aksakal, known as Boxer Cetin, was found wrapped in blue plastic Ikea bags close to Hollow Ponds, near Epping Forest, on 9 September 2015. A passer-by had noticed a number of rats scurrying about near the bags and had called the police. He had last been seen a month earlier in Green Lanes, Haringey, then the home of the Bombaciar gang which at one time was responsible for the import of much of the heroin coming into the United Kingdom.

Cetin had had something of a chequered past. Although he was living in Margate at the time of his death, back in 1998 and then known as Musa Yaut, he had been acquitted of killing a Glasgow drug-dealer Bulent Giritli, shot in the head in a Turkish café in Lordship Lane, Tottenham. His co-defendant, Mustafa Sungur, was found guilty. Giritli had failed to pay for £40,000 worth of drugs.

This time, however, the argument had not been about drugs

but over a woman. Cetin was killed in the living room in an execution killing. The last bullet of four had been fired with the gun in Cetin's mouth. His killers were Remzi Akguc and Yilmaz Coskun. After the shooting, Akguc then went shopping for equipment to clear up the evidence, spending over £260 on a shovel, tarpaulin, rope, trolley and gloves. The gun, stained with the victim's blood, was found stashed in a sock in the garden of Coskun's home. In August 2016 the men received life imprisonment with a minimum of thirty-two years to be served.[4]

One man whom East Enders believed had ended up in Epping Forest was the supergrass Billy Amies. Given the soubriquet 'The Snake' and described by a lawyer as 'one of the worst', although he named fifty-eight criminals, it seems Amies was responsible for the conviction of only five.

An only child, Amies came from Carr Street, Stepney. He grew up a thief and graduated into robbery. In 1964 he was arrested with two others for tying up a woman in a robbery. Amies was convicted and received four years' imprisonment. The others were acquitted. Whilst in Maidstone prison Amies developed a relationship with another prisoner and when that man was upset by another inmate Amies attacked the third person, for which he received a further eighteen months. On his release he resumed his occupation. In 1970 he was arrested and sentenced to seven years for a robbery in Portsmouth.

Detective Inspector Martin Lundy, who turned Amies into a supergrass and who seems rather to have admired him, described him a trifle politically incorrectly in today's terms:

In some ways Billy was a nutter. He was also known as Billy the Queer because he's a raving homosexual. A big hard man, over six foot, a real animal, a compulsive armed robber who was really feared, but clever too.

Amies was one of the more unpleasant of armed robbers. Amongst his other roles, dressed as a policeman he had threatened his victim in a robbery with castration and had the man's daughter stripped to her underwear, asking, 'How would you like to see your daughter raped?' He had also been at work on Merseyside. In the first of his three cases there a middle-aged woman had been repeatedly punched in the face; in the second another middle-aged woman, her Down's syndrome daughter and her son had all been tied up; the latter had also been threatened with castration. In the third incident a garage owner and his family had been tied up and the owner had had his testicles bitten to persuade him to open his safe.

But, so far as the police were concerned, the most serious incident had involved the Flying Squad's Detective Sergeant Bernard Craven who suffered brain damage while guarding Amies in Liverpool. Versions of exactly what happened and how vary.

Amies was in serious difficulties. He was caught out of his territory and had been arrested with one of Liverpool's real hardmen, John Tremarco, on robbery charges. Lundy was told by another supergrass, David Smith, that Amies wanted help because he feared a corrupt Liverpool police officer, John Keating, was trying to lighten Tremarco's load by placing it on Amies' shoulders. It appears Amies was being pressured into pleading guilty. Lundy went incognito to Walton jail and saw Amies who, once he had read Smith's statements involving him, decided that the path to safety was for him to turn supergrass. Much to the fury of the Merseyside police, Amies was transferred to Brixton on Rule 43 and then to Acton police station. There he told his version of his life of crime, implicating Tremarco and also Keating.

In October 1977, he went back to Liverpool to plead guilty. His statement was then shown to the solicitors for the other defendants who, as soon as Amies walked into the witness-box, in turn were forced to put their hands up. The public gallery howled revenge and the case was adjourned until the Monday for the sentencing of everyone including Amies.

The new and reformed supergrass was, unsurprisingly, unhappy about staying in the North West for the weekend and wanted to do the round trip to the safety of London. It was agreed that he should be returned on the Sunday evening to be lodged overnight in a Liverpool police station. So far so good, except that on the Sunday night the London sergeants who had custody of Amies could not find him a home; nor could they manage to contact the local Serious Crimes Officers. They turned up with Amies in tow at the hotel in Liverpool where Lundy was staying. Further efforts to find Amies a bed in a cell failed, and so he was booked into the hotel along with his guarding officers Craven and O'Rourke. On a toss of the coin it was decided that Craven should sleep in the room with Amies, with O'Rourke outside.

Unfortunately Amies thought it would be a good idea to go out for a last drink. This was by no means an uncommon situation with supergrasses and the officer agreed. Off he and Craven went to The Crow's Nest, a pub in the docks. Even more unfortunately, it was the haunt of Tremarco's friends. Lundy seems to have been full of admiration for his protégé:

> Typical of the fearless animal he is, off goes Amies with Craven into the lions' den. But as soon as they walk in, they're set upon! Amies, big strong beast, fights his way out and escapes, but Bernie Craven gets an almighty kicking. He's almost kicked to death but he manages to stagger out of the pub, he's found in the front garden of a nearby house and he's rushed to hospital.[5]

Amies was badly cut and had a broken arm by the time he returned to the safety of the hotel. Craven was not so fortunate; he had severe concussion, a broken nose and a fractured cheekbone. He never really recovered and retired from the force on health grounds. The next morning Lundy managed to have Amies' case remitted to London where he could be sentenced for all his offences. Tremarco received fifteen years; back in London Amies served only two years. Two years later Keating was convicted of attempting to extort half the money an insurance company had paid to a police informer; he received two and a half years.

The story in the Underworld was that Amies had been punished in the pub by a Liverpool hardman Billy Grimwood, assisted by two London brothers from a well-known and influential family. The mystery remains as to why Amies chose The Crow's Nest, of all Liverpool pubs, in which to drink.

Amies served his sentence and, according to an East Ender, died outside London at the beginning of the 1990s 'of natural causes', whatever that may mean. In fact, other sources suggest that Amies' nemesis may have been a much more popular and respected London figure, the small and deceptively harmless Mickey Morris. It was Amies' evidence which had convicted him when, on 27 July 1979, he was found guilty along with the Twins' cousin, Richard Smith, of robbing a scrap-metal dealer in Hampshire.

Morris, who was in Spain at the time when Amies told more or less all to the police, was lured back to Heathrow and in July 1979 received fourteen years; Smith got a year longer.[6]

Mickey Morris was wild, remembers an East End face:

We'd all grown up together and he could be devious. He might say, 'Come and have a meal' and you'd go with him to this restaurant and he'd have a hidden agenda. The moment he walked in the door he might shoot someone. Because he was little and blond and very baby-faced you didn't believe the damage there was in that man.

Once in 1971 he shot the doorman [the wrestler Bully Boy Muir] in the Candy Box off Regent Street because he wouldn't let him in the previous night. He took his wife along with him. Put four shots in him, but when it came to it the doorman couldn't recognise him.

Amies disappeared after his release and there have been numerous suggestions as to his ending. One is that Mickey Morris caught up with him and that Amies is one of many who lie in unmarked graves in Epping Forest. If the story is correct it was one of the better bits of disposal. Morris himself later took to drugs and died of a heart attack.

However, not everyone who was taken to Epping Forest has been left there. In 2002 Shpetim Lisha was jailed for thirteen years at the Old Bailey for kidnapping Albanian businessman Arap Mytaj as he walked home from his car-wash business in Romford. Lisha was demanding a £50,000 ransom. Mytaj had been tied to a tree and told that if he informed the police he would be beheaded. Lisha and his younger helpmate also made him telephone his relatives who had to listen to Mytaj's cries for help. During one attempt to escape he managed to snatch a screwdriver and stabbed one of them in the hand, only to be quickly overpowered and given a 'good beating'. The family eventually did contact the police. Lisha left Mytaj tied up in the boot of a car outside Harlow railway station while they collected the money. This was when the police swooped, discharging distraction grenades as they did so. The incident was over a finance deal which had soured. The slightly younger boy received ten years.

One man who left Epping Forest alive when, had he been found there, might not have expected to do so, was Harry Roberts. On 12 July 1966 Roberts, John Duddy and John

Witney were stopped by police officers in West London when they were on their way to rob a rent collector. Roberts shot the three officers before an informant tipped off the police. The car number was traced and Witney and Duddy were arrested in short order. Roberts, a survivalist who had served in Malaya, hid out in the Forest for three months before the police were tipped off that he was at a farm near Bishops Stortford and arrested him. They were all given life sentences with a minimum recommendation of thirty years. Duddy died in prison. Witney was released in 1992 and was killed in Bristol in 1996 in an incident unrelated to the shooting. In an interview from prison, Roberts commented:

> The police aren't like real people to us. They're strangers. They're the enemy. And you don't feel remorse for killing a stranger. I do feel sorry for what we did to their families. I do. But it's like the people I killed in Malaya when I was in the army. You don't feel remorse.

Over the years he made over twenty escape attempts before he was finally released on 11 November 2014 after serving forty-six years in prison.[7]

One East End hardman recalled another who survived a visit to the Forest:

> Around 1968–69 we kidnapped a man who was a detective at an East End station who was making a nuisance of himself. He was taking money from all the little firms at the jump-up with anything crooked but he made sure he kept to a certain level and didn't overstep.
>
> Then his shoes started to get too big for him and he made himself busy over a sum of money which had been taken from some Greeks in north London. This involved certain people I

knew. We thought this is the time the silly bastard is going to start making a pest of himself.

And it was only a matter of time before he was going to start on us. So we decided to make some enquiries about him. He was a Scotsman. Married to a very nice Scots lady, a wife beater and not a very good father – all the traits of a coward; and a drunkard.

We acquired his address. Where he lived he had to go down the back of some shops to get to the entrance of his flat. We waited three nights and then the fourth he showed up at 3 a.m. completely out of his crust.

Two of us got out of the van – we was wearing boiler suits and balaclavas. I had a gun; the other guy had a sawn off shotgun. We slung him in the back of the van, taped his hands and our driver took us to Epping Forest. On the way over I took the clip out and kept clicking the gun and there was a nasty smell of shit and piss. Once we was there we uncovered his head, took the tape off, give him a spade and told him to start digging a grave. There he was on his knees weeping and pleading for his life. Of course we didn't have any intention of killing him, just frightening him. At the end our plan was for the driver to take over as boss. 'He's got three kids,' he said, 'I think we should reprieve him but if he ever goes out of line again he knows we know where to pick him up'. We argued a bit to make it look good and then drove the man back to his flat.

I've no doubt this man knew we were responsible as he tried his hardest to make friends. We started getting him to do small favours which grew into larger ones and there was always a £1 note for him.

We kept on using him of course. He may have been above the law but he wasn't above ours.[8]

NOTES

1. See, *inter alia, Daily Mirror*, 20 July 1959; *News of the World*, 26 June, 3 July, 10 July, 17 July 1960.

2. Michael J. Freeman, *I Pornographer*; Bert Wickstead, *Gangbuster*.

3. Duncan Campbell, 'Vanity "cost gangland enforcer his life"', *The Guardian*, 19 April 1999.

4. BBC News, 'Epping Forest body: Two jailed over "execution" style murder', 3 August 2016.

5. M. Short, *Lundy*; A. Jennings and others, *Scotland Yard's Cocaine Connection*.

6. There is an account of the trap set for Morris in Martin Short, *Lundy*.

7. *The Guardian*, 2 February 1993. See also Tom Tullett, *No Answer from Foxtrot Oscar*.

8. Conversation with JM August 1999.

21

THE FALL OF THE GANGBUSTER

The case which brought the posthumous downfall of Scotland Yard's soi-disant Gangbuster Commander Bert Wickstead began when parts of a body were found, not in Epping Forest, but in the Thames in Rainham on 26 September 1974.

In his lifetime the gaunt and gangling North Londoner Billy Moseley was a relatively successful bank robber. Standing well over 6 feet, when he and his equally tall half-brother George Arnold were arrested for a raid, soldiers from the nearest Guards' barracks had to be sent as foils so that a realistic identification parade could be held.

Moseley was probably not quite top class and he went to prison in the early 1970s following a failed armed robbery. Before then he had been having an affair with Frankie, the wife of robber Ronnie Fright, who was himself serving a seven-year sentence at the time. This at the very least was regarded as bad form and certainly worth a bad beating, even a non-fatal shooting. On his release Moseley took up once more with Frankie. He also discovered that his close friend Bobby Maynard had begun to associate with Reggie Dudley, a man he certainly disliked, and although he had badly beaten him in a fight some time earlier he now probably feared him.

The lean and saturnine Reginald Dudley was a thoroughly undesirable character. He was a receiver and police informer, jobs which often go together. Despite rumours of his being a grass he was well respected in the criminal fraternity. One police officer recalled:

> I always thought he could go as far as the Krays and the Richardsons. He had a team and he had ability and the sense of purpose to do to North London what the Krays did to East London.
>
> Another story about him was that after his wife had in some way offended him he had chained her to the pilings on Brighton Pier and left her there for the tide to come in. True or not, he had certainly served a six year sentence for slashing her face.

By the middle of the 1970s he would only deal with high-quality stolen goods and it was suggested that he was also working with the corrupt police officer Alec Eist, shaking down robbers and relieving them of their proceeds.

Robert 'Fat Bob' Maynard was much more rotund and far jollier. He had been hit over the head with a plank in a fight in a club in London's Tottenham Court Road, resulting in brain damage which affected his speech. He would stammer over the telephone, 'He-llo it's Bob-by May-....' and when interrupted would ask, 'How – do - you – know - it's - me?'

Together Dudley and Maynard were known as the Legal and General Firm after an advertisement of the time for the insurance company that showed two men in overcoats, something they both habitually wore. The name was said to have been coined by Dudley's friend Eist.

On 26 September 1974 Moseley set off for a meeting at 6.30 p.m. with Ronnie Fright 'to clear the air' at the Victoria Sporting Club in Stoke Newington, a rather less grand venue than its name suggested. He was never seen alive again. A week later parts of a body began to surface in the Thames near Rainham in Essex. The head and hands were missing which, in the pre-DNA days, made identification extremely difficult and for a time it was thought to be that of the IRA robber Kenneth Littlejohn who had escaped from Mountjoy prison in March. However, Moseley had suffered from a rare skin disease as well as from gallstones. An X-ray taken while he was in Bedford prison showed the gallstones, and blood samples from the body matched those of his children. As a result the not always reliable pathologist Professor James 'Taffy' Cameron identified the body as that of Moseley.

Another friend of Moseley was Micky Cornwall, an armed robber known as 'The Laughing Bank Robber' who was released from his eight-year sentence for robbery on 18 October that year. Back in 1962 another robber, Ray Barron, had been convicted with Colin Saggs and Cornwall of a bank robbery in Barnet. He had met Reggie Dudley in prison and had taken up with Dudley's daughter, Kathy.

Cornwall was also involved with Kathy Dudley, once married to a John Dann, known as 'Doughnuts' possibly because he was once a baker and possibly because he cut holes in people who offended him. Her marriage to him had broken down and it was then she had taken up with Barron. It was when he went back to prison she began an association with Cornwall. Neither her father nor Ray Barron seem to have taken umbrage.

As so many criminals do, in the short time he was in circulation Cornwall was looking for 'one last big one'. He also had a new girlfriend, Gloria Hogg, with whom he wanted to buy a home in the country. Meanwhile he contented himself with a string of hotel robberies and rented a room from Colin Saggs, now a police informer. Cornwall confided his plans for a 'final job' to another North London criminal John Moriarty, who also turned supergrass after he had been shot in the leg for a second time. It seems Cornwall left his digs for 'the big one' on 3 August 1975 in a mustard-coloured Range Rover. Some days later two men, identified by Saggs' fourteen-year-old daughter Sharon as Dudley and Maynard, came asking for him. Moriarty claimed to have seen Cornwall at a bus stop in Highgate, North London, on 23 August and that seems to have been the last sighting of him before his body was discovered by picnickers in a newly dug grave in Hatfield, Hertfordshire. He had been shot in the head.

During the next year the *Islington Gazette* published an ambiguous letter signed 'Fat Bob'. 'It's been said that Mick was asking too much about Bill's death. The police seem to have forgotten Billy. They may forget about Mick.' Maynard went to their offices to complain, saying he had never been interviewed by the police about the death or the letter. He certainly had not written it. The paper published an apology but said they had been told by the police it was genuine. Maynard also received a .22 bullet wrapped in cotton wool. So had an acquaintance, car dealer Phil Luxford.

Meanwhile an inquest into Moseley's death was held and Professor Cameron told the coroner that he had been tortured before his death. He had been burned with a naked flame and his toenails had been pulled out. He also told the coroner that he thought Moseley had been killed with a gunshot to the still missing head.

Initially the Hertfordshire police had absolute control of the inquiry into Cornwall's death but when no progress was made, and such leads as there were led straight back to London and the name Moseley, a joint Hertfordshire and London squad was assembled. Now the officer in charge of the inquiry was Scotland

Yard's Commander Albert Wickstead, known as Bert and a man who, as with many other policemen around the world, liked to be called The Grey or Silver Fox. He was known for his success rate in clearing up cases but was not regarded as being over fussy about the quality of the evidence, provided it stood up in court. 'A horrible man,' recalls one detective sergeant who worked with him. 'He hated everyone and everyone loathed him. You look at all his cases and it's the same the whole way through. Everything was verbals and he blew cases up for more than they deserved.'

It was not until nearly eighteen months later that on 22 January 1976 Wickstead swooped. Eighteen people were taken to Loughton police station and seven were finally charged. Dudley and Maynard were charged with the two murders, as were Ronnie Fright, Ernie Maynard (Robert's brother) and George Spencer. Charlie Clarke, a market stall-holder, and Kathy Dudley were charged with conspiracy to murder. Others who were rounded up but not charged included Ernie Maynard's wife Sylvia and the grass John Moriarty.

The trial opened in November 1976. 'The story I have to tell is a terrible one. The evidence will disclose no shortage of cruelty and no shortage of sheer evil,' Michael Corkery dramatically told Mr Justice Swanwick and the jury in his opening speech for the prosecution. He was keen to point out that he was not obliged to provide a motive and this indeed was a problem for the prosecution. Eventually a selection of motives to suit all tastes was offered: (1) Moseley had had an affair with Frankie Fright and had to be punished. (2) He had fallen out with Dudley ten years earlier. (3) He had been suggesting Dudley was a grass. (4) He, Moseley, was sitting on the proceeds of a large jewel robbery. (5) Sheer sadism. (6) Cornwall had set out to avenge Moseley's death. (7) Cornwall had discovered Maynard and Dudley were the killers and so had to be silenced. (8) Cornwall had had more than a brief liaison with Kathy Dudley and had to be punished as well. Corkery was 98 per cent sure that Moseley had been killed with a single shot to the head, which was still missing.

The case against Ronnie Fright was that he was deliberately late for his meeting with Moseley outside the Victoria Sporting Club and so had lured him to his death.

Much of the evidence against the defendants was delivered by a ragbag of serving prisoners who, having seen 'The Light' (and the prospects of an early release), were able to give evidence against their former cellmates. Principal amongst them was thirty-year-old Tony Wild who asked the judge if he could sit down to give his evidence because he had an anal fissure. He had, he said, been raped as a young man and apart from contracting syphilis, he had this permanent reminder of the experience. His criminal career had begun as a shoplifter, car thief and office-breaker before he graduated to armed robbery and a series of attacks on Securicor vehicles. The proceeds had disappeared into the Golden Nugget casino in Piccadilly, major London hotels and on a fur coat which cost him £1,200.

Bertie Smalls had paved the way for supergrasses to obtain a semi-official five years for their crimes instead of up to twenty and Wild took advantage of this when he was caught on another Securicor vehicle raid which stood to net him over £7,000. He shot at the guards and escaped, crashed his Volvo and was arrested hiding in a field. His co-accused picked up eighteen years. As thanks for his evidence in the case Wild, who was fortunate not to have been charged with attempted murder, received a mere five. In his cell he kept a record of alleged conversations with other inmates including the Brighton publican Oliver Kenny, then landlord of the Horse and Groom in the Hanover area of the town and an old friend of Dudley. When he offered these to the police there was initially no reaction and he wrote:

Although I have passed on information that I believe would be useful to your inquiries, I have received from your office not even an acknowledgement of the receipt of my letters let alone a routine questioning as to the validity of their content. Perhaps you feel that I am trying to work a ticket or something.

Next he offered them Reggie Dudley, writing to Wickstead:

I hope you will appreciate that I have been very forthright in this letter and that, in itself, will indicate to you that I have other more serious matters to impart to you.

And when he did make a statement:

It's almost a relief to be in the police cell and get it off my plate. I am caught and am going to spend a long time in prison. When I come out I only want to spend the rest of my life quietly with those I love.

Now where have we heard that before?

Wild told the police that Dudley had boasted about killing Cornwall, saying, 'He went up in the fucking air, didn't he boys?' And as for Maynard, he had apparently said, 'I didn't know guys would squeal like a pig.' But most damaging came from his conversation with Oliver Kenny who, Wild said, had told him he nearly died of fright when Dudley brought Moseley's head into the pub one night.

Wild held his own in cross-examination. Attitudes in the 1970s were different and Michael West, for Dudley, suggested that real men such as Dudley would have had nothing to do with a disgusting pervert such as Wild. Dudley would not have given him the time of day, let alone a confession.

Wild, who had a good line in psychological gibberish, would have none of it:

> I have been to bed with literally hundreds of women and I could call five hundred into this court to testify to that fact. My crimes, I know, have got progressively more serious, ending up with armed robbery. I would interpret that as an attempt – or at least a subconscious attempt – to regain my manhood.

As for Fright, Frank Read, a fellow prisoner in Pentonville, said he had confessed saying, 'We done one, we sawed one up.' This evidence was effectively destroyed when two other prisoners said that they were sure Read was perjuring himself. An assistant governor at the prison told the jury that the police had tried to trap Fright by putting him in a cell with a known grass. Yet another prisoner said the police had tried to recruit him to get a confession out of the defendant George Spencer.

Wild apart, the only evidence against the defendants was a certain amount of circumstance and their apparent and hotly disputed half admissions to Wickstead. They had been kept in custody and interviewed over a period of four days. According to the police, Dudley had, during a journey in a police car, said, 'The cunt [Moseley] had it coming. He tried to fuck me so I fucked him good and proper.' Later Dudley was said to have told the police questioning him about Cornwall, 'You can take it from me it is not on my conscience...He deserved what he got and that's it.' Maynard had supposedly told the police after his arrest, 'It's about time you came for me.' He was also alleged to have said of Cornwall, 'I told him if he had sex with her [Kathy] I would kill him.' Maynard, asked why he had gone to Saggs' house looking for Cornwall, had replied, 'It was business'. Had he told Fright to be late for the meeting at the Victoria Club? 'I'm not answering that, otherwise I'm finished.' Kathy Dudley was alleged to have said of her father, 'Now he's got us into murder.' Charlie Clarke had admitted his involvement but said he had thought the pair were only going to be beaten up.

What was so surprising was that there had been the opportunity to tape record most of these interviews, so eliminating any doubt. There had been a recorder fitted into Wickstead's desk at the police station but it had never been switched on. Why not?

I am a police officer who believes in police methods and tape recorders are not used in police interviews.

Another officer went on to explain that tape recording was not an option because it would not have been admissible. In which case why have one? And that the street noise would have made the answers inaudible, as would the noise of officers scraping their chairs and coughing. The room was, in fact, carpeted.

The case, initially estimated for eight weeks, had dragged on until on 17 June 1977 when summing up, Swanwick told the jury:

In no case here, none of the cases against any of the accused, is there any physical evidence directly connecting any of them with any of the crimes charged. There is no evidence of where or exactly when either Moseley or Cornwall died. There are no eyewitness of any crime; there was no forensic evidence, no finger prints, no blood stained clothing, no murder weapon to connect any of the accused with either killing, and no written and signed confessions. The evidence against the accused consists largely, and in some cases almost wholly, of alleged oral confessions to police and others. So you must consider – such questions by themselves would not be sufficient – motive and opportunity, relationships, previous and subsequent conduct and see whether in each case they support and confirm the alleged confession or make it less likely to have been made or to have been intended as a confession.

The judge directed the jury to find Ernie Maynard not guilty. Dudley was found guilty with a unanimous verdict. Bobby Maynard was found guilty by an 11-1 majority of killing Moseley and by a 10-2 majority of the murder of Cornwall. Ronnie Fright had already been acquitted, as had George Spencer. Dudley and Maynard each received life with a minimum of fifteen years; Kathy Dudley, convicted of conspiracy, received two years suspended. Charlie Clarke also received two years but not suspended.

On 28 July, six weeks after the trial ended, Moseley's head was found in a public lavatory in Islington, thawing in a plastic bag along with a copy of the London *Evening News* dated 16 June 1977, the day the jury began to reach their verdicts. On 18 October that year Professor Cameron told an inquest that Moseley's head had been kept in a deep freezer possibly for up to three years. It had also previously been buried and, because of paint traces, had possibly been kept in a garage. There was no evidence it had ever been in the sea. He now thought Moseley had not been shot in the head but had choked on his own blood.

It seems the police were not interested in who had been keeping the head over the years because when the investigative journalist, Duncan Campbell, asked Scotland Yard what inquiries were being made, he was told there were none in progress.

Immediately after the appeals were dismissed in April 1979, Moseley's widow, Ann, and his eldest son became keen members of the campaign led by Maynard's wife Tina to have the guilty verdicts reversed. Leaflets and badges MDC – NOT GUILTY, RIGHT √ were distributed and in September that year a march took place from Camden Town to Hyde Park Corner.

In 1980 Wild was released from prison and told Duncan Campbell that he had made up his evidence about the head in the pub following a scenario police officers had outlined for him. On 23 April 1982 he received a further ten years for another five armed robberies. His luck was still in. Although he had fired shots in the raid the trial judge accepted he had done so only to frighten. He was paroled in a little over three years.

The years went by and Maynard, Dudley and Clarke took truth drug tests and Kathy Dudley a lie-detector test. All passed but the results were not admissible in court. Wild was released again and in 1995 made further statements. Initially he would not go to court but, offered an indemnity against prosecution for perjury, he said:

> I would like to make it clear that the whole of my evidence against Reg Dudley, Bob Maynard and other co-defendants was entirely false in so far as it relates to comments made by them that were incriminatory.

In 1991 Liberty, formerly the National Council for Civil Liberties, adopted the Maynard–Dudley case as one for special consideration in a campaign against wrongful convictions. It took another eleven years before the case finally came to court. Scientific techniques including the technique of ESDA (electrostatic document analysis) had been developed and it was now possible there was a chance to prove that the compromising remarks to police were never made. If writing is fashioned on a sheet of paper resting upon other pages, the indentations or impressions produced are transferred to those below. These transferred impressions, although often invisible to the human eye, can be detected using an electrostatic detection device. Dudley and Maynard applied for access to the interview notes but the

Metropolitan Police replied that the papers had unfortunately been destroyed by a sergeant who had been told to make space.

After his retirement from the bench, Swanwick generously gave his time to listen to and discuss the case with some of the campaigners and in later years was certainly not convinced of the rectitude of the convictions. He died in June 2003.

In the appeal in 2002 there was new evidence to the effect that a statement said to have been taken by the police could not have been written within the times stated. Although it was timed as from 4.05 p.m. it was said to have commenced at 4.28 p.m. and concluded at 5.18 p.m. The statement was handwritten. However, an independent document examiner stated that studies had shown that the number of characters written in the statement could not have all been handwritten in 50 minutes. The average person can write 140 to 150 characters a minute. One or two people can do 180, but 250 is impossible. By this time Wickstead and the note-taker Trevor Lloyd Hughes were both dead.

Victor Temple QC for the Crown submitted that it was obvious that either the commencement time of the interview or the finishing time must have been noted down incorrectly and that the jury would have appreciated that point. The court said that whilst it accepted that such an explanation could well have been a possibility, it also appreciated that there could have been other, less innocent, explanations.

Temple argued that Dudley had come across as 'prone to angry outbursts, challenging and arrogant' at the trial, and these same traits could be found in his answers to questions put in the interviews. But Lord Justice Mantell replied, 'Just because the person in the dock is a known villain and thoroughly unpleasant, it does not mean his convictions are therefore safe.'

The court said that it was not for it to determine which scenario was correct. Once it had determined that there had been a defect in the evidence not disclosed at trial, and that defect might have affected the decision of the jury, then the court was obliged to overturn the verdict. Indeed, the court ruled that the defect in one statement could have led the jury to look differently at other pieces of evidence against the other co-accused. As a result, they overturned all four convictions, even though the statements which the others had given appeared to be without such defects. The court said the suggestion that the jury concluded that the police made a mistake would require the Appeal Court to look into the minds of the jury and to speculate as to their reasoning in a way that is clearly forbidden.

Dudley and Maynard had not been thought suitable for early release because they had refused to accept their guilt. Dudley, who had been finally paroled in 1997, served twenty-one years and Maynard, who had been given bail in November 2000, twenty-five.

'If you look at Wickstead's cases, they're all the same. They're these verbal half confessions, never signed,' says one detective who knew him.

Certainly there was one embarrassing case in his career when Arthur John Saunders was jailed for fifteen years for his part in a raid on Barclay's Bank in Ilford. His conviction was based on partial admissions in questions put to him by Wickstead. Two years later bank robber and supergrass Bertie Smalls turned Queen's Evidence and provided details of the many robberies in which he had been involved, including the Ilford one. He was adamant that Saunders had not been on it. If this was not accepted, the whole house of cards built around Smalls' evidence must tumble.

In an appeal heard in October 1973 Lord Widgery commented:

In the course of this interview as recounted by Police Superintendent Wickstead, one does not find Saunders positively admitting that he had anything to do with the llford Bank robbery; on the other hand there is a noticeable absence of any positive denial of such association and indeed many of the answers which I have read, equivocal in themselves were certainly, one would have thought, answers which did not lie readily in the mouth of an innocent man, who would have asserted his innocence in a positive way.

Rather than find Wickstead had fabricated the confession, His Lordship decided Saunders had been drinking before the interview and was boasting. His conviction was quashed and he was awarded compensation. He later led what was called 'the Grandfather Gang' of bank robbers and received fifteen years.

Dudley and Maynard were finally awarded six-figure sums in compensation and Dudley died in 2008. Neither were ever reconvicted. For some years Billy Moseley's ashes remained on the mantelpiece in Tina Maynard's house in Camden. Ronnie and Frankie Fright were reconciled. Wickstead had died in 2001 aged seventy-seven.[1]

NOTES

1. R v Robert Maynard, Reginald Dudley, Kathleen Bailey and Charles Clarke [2002] EWCA Crim 1942; James Morton, *Justice Denied*.

22

OPERATION TIBERIUS

By the beginning of the twenty-first century the problem with professional crime in the East End was that it had been infiltrated by the gangs and there was no great enthusiasm amongst some officers to eradicate it. One gang was uncovered by the crime squad in Newham in 2006 when a scrap yard in the Docklands was searched for stolen metal. When another nearby property was raided, forty-two containers were unexpectedly discovered to contain the contents of eighteen lorry thefts and a commercial burglary. Counterfeit goods were also seized. Dave McKelvey, head of the crime squad, discovered that the gang had been corrupting police officers for over a decade and that, despite a gang insider leaking information to the police, the information was never acted upon. In spite of overwhelming evidence, the case collapsed after a corrupt anti-corruption detective sent a dossier to the Director of Public Prosecutions suggesting the senior investigating officer was dishonest. McKelvey was then investigated for two years before he was exonerated. As a result of the raids, the officer was told that a known contract killer, linked to the street gang Tottenham Man Dem, had been contracted for £1 million to kill three police officers including him.

Throughout the 1990s the Metropolitan Police ran a series of anti-corruption investigations of retired and serving officers suspected of involvement with major criminal gangs in North and East London. The operations included *Operation Othona* set up in 1994 and *Operation Zloty* but they came to little, possibly because they had been infiltrated and possibly because what was described as a lorry load of documents from *Operation Othona* was mysteriously shredded in 2001.

Now, on 15 October 2001, *Operation Tiberius* began investigating more or less the same allegations that officers were active players in eight named gangs or syndicates and that three murder investigations had been interfered with. The alleged gang involved was the Adams family from North London but with links throughout the East End, the rest of Britain and abroad. Then came the Bowers Syndicate, members of which were later convicted of an attempted theft at Gatwick airport. They had, they said, been trying to finance their gymnasium after their landlords had upped the rent. Whatever the police may have thought of them, they were thought of highly in the community and there were plenty of locals who were prepared to give evidence in mitigation on their behalf.[1]

There were the Hunt Syndicate from Canning Town; the Palmer Syndicate led by timeshare fraudster John 'Goldfinger' Palmer, late of Brinks-Mat and said to be experienced drug importers and money launderers; the Kean Syndicate; the Camp Syndicate operating out of Loughton and allegedly involved with drug importation; the Chrysostoinou/Panayiotou Syndicate based in the Green Lanes area of North London and said have operated unchecked since the 1970s. This syndicate was thought to be responsible for the large-scale importation and distribution of heroin. The Kaan Syndicate, a North East London group, was also said to be involved in large-scale heroin importation.

These syndicates were said to include thirty career criminals amongst their members and to have criminal connections with thirty-four serving and twenty-two former Met Police officers. The syndicates would have an association with a former officer who would liaise with serving officers to provide information about any inquiries which might be ongoing and sometimes bring them into the operations.[2]

It was possible for one officer to be involved with more than one syndicate. For example, DC Martin Morgan, who was allegedly involved with both the Kean and Chrysostoinou Syndicates, had a share in two racehorses with a member of the latter. At the time of *Tiberius* he was awaiting trial on a charge of attempted kidnapping of an alleged drug-dealer Alan Smith (a pseudonym) who was said to owe property developer Robert Kean £600,000 over a drug deal. If Morgan was successful in luring Smith to a meeting at the Post House Hotel, Guildford, where the unfortunate man would be tortured, he was to be paid £50,000. In fact the police took Smith and his family into protective custody first and set up a sting operation at the hotel. Kean and both Morgan and another officer Declan Costello pleaded guilty to conspiring to unlawfully and injuriously imprison a man and to detain him against his will. Costello pleaded guilty to conspiracy to assault, causing actual bodily harm. Morgan and Costello were sentenced to seven years' imprisonment. Back in 1997 Morgan had previously been investigated but not disciplined over disappearing evidence.[3]

The murders in which corrupt officers were said to be involved were those of Kenneth Beagle, shot in November 2000, plumber Richard Rayner in May 2001, and Patrick Pasipandoya in August that year.

Beagle, a man with convictions for kidnapping and drug-dealing, was shot as he went to pay a parking ticket at Oakchurch Hospital, Romford. The police said they could find no motive but the word on the street was that it was over a failed drug importation. A serving detective sergeant was believed to have made inappropriate approaches to the team investigating the murder and also to have facilitated checks on behalf of a suspect in the Ricky Rayner murder.

Forty-five-year-old plumber Richard Rayner, who was working for his brother, was shot dead as he waited for his breakfast in the River Bank café in Bow. A man wearing dark clothes and with a black motorcycle helmet was seen to come up to him, shoot him and then walk away in the direction of the A12 before possibly climbing onto a motorbike. It was thought his case was one of mistaken identity and the intended victim was an Essex businessman who had once served a seven-year sentence for robbery. A £10,000 reward was never claimed. It is thought that after checks had been made on him on the UK police computer, the principal suspect was tipped off and fled to Spain.

Television actor from *The Bill* and *Minder* and doorman Patrick Pasipandoya, who had a female friend with him, was shot around 9 p.m. on 22 August 2001 whilst driving his VW Golf at Pickett's Lock, Enfield. Earlier he had been seen talking to two men on motor scooters in Edmonton. As a part-time occupation he had been thought to work as an enforcer for the Kaan Syndicate and had been using garden shears to finger snip those who had offended his employers. The son of a former detective sergeant was thought to have been involved and his father had intervened to scupper the inquiry. In June 2002 Soner Kaan, the head of the Syndicate, was jailed at Woolwich Crown Court for eighteen years over a drug importation.

A fourth case which ended nowhere was the 1995 murder of

Michael Olymbious. He was shot on 3 April as he was getting into his car on the Brandon Estate, Walworth.

A large consignment of Ecstasy tablets with a street value of £1.5 million had been found by a cleaner at a flat in Chelsea Cloisters in February 1993. The cleaner then informed the police. Olymbious had allegedly been minding the drugs for the Adams family. On 5 April and 15 May 1995 his minder Ron Johnson made statements to officers from *Operation Heaton*. In the second eight-page-long statement, he also spoke of Olymbious' illegal cigarette/drugs trade, his financial situation including the debts of £600,000 to the family and various criminal activities. Crucially there had been a meeting in March 1995 when a man connected with the family reminded him of the debt to the family and the necessity to pay it, £40,000 of which had to be paid by 15 March 1995, otherwise there would be 'no debt'. The 'no debt' was taken by Olymbious as a death threat.

On Wednesday 11 October 1995 at 6.30 a.m. raids were carried out by officers from *Operation Heaton* including on the Belugas Club, Finchley Road. Terry Adams was not at home. He had suddenly left at 10 p.m. the night before with his wife and child. In a flat above Belugas officers found a running shoe and in it a photostat copy of Johnson's hand-written original statement. A report made it clear it was 'obvious' the probe had been 'effectively infiltrated and corrupted'.

These were not the only murders which are thought to have been covered up over the years by the police on behalf of criminal families. The others included those of Lennie Naylor in Kent and Del Croxson, who in 1994 apparently overdosed himself in Belmarsh prison. Croxson was himself suspected of the murder of ex-bare knuckle fighter, bouncer, and minicab-owner Barry Dalton who had been interfering in East End business. In 1992 Dalton had been shot in the back of the head in his car in the grounds of Alexandra Palace. There was also the Gooderham and Arnold double murder in Epping Forest, that of Nicky Gerard and the killing of Bruno Hrela, found shot twice in the head by the side of his silver Mercedes in Enfield. One theory was that he was minding gems stolen in a raid on a Hatton Garden jewellers.[4]

In the mid-1980s, David Hunt, known as 'The Long Fella', one of eleven brothers, joined The Snipers street gang from Canning Town who were involved in lorry hijackings in Essex and East London. According to police intelligence six members of his family were already members, with reports identifying David and his brother Stephen as two of the six main leaders. He was arrested on seven occasions during his time with the gang, but witnesses would drop their allegations. In 1986, he was given a nine-month suspended jail sentence for handling stolen goods and possession of a sawn-off shotgun. He then was alleged to have moved into the Soho sex trade, purchasing a property at 2 Green's Court off Berwick Street that operated as an adult bookshop and brothel with a partner Jimmy Holmes. Hunt denied he knew the premises were used in this way, saying it had merely been a property investment. The club was firebombed in April 1996. Police intelligence also put him at the centre of a criminal network involved in protection rackets of night-clubs and pubs in the East End. After he fell out with Hunt, Holmes, writing as Horace Silver, published *Judas Pig*, a factional account of their time together.

Hunt had also sided with another old-time villain turned businessman Chic Matthews in his dispute with Billy Allen over the ownership of a strip of land in Silvertown which had increased enormously in value when London was awarded the Olympic Games of 2012. The dispute went to court where a mass brawl broke out between minders for Matthews and Allen. Later Hunt told a court that he had been present but had not seen what was happening because he was on the telephone.

Generally it is not a good idea for alleged criminals to sue the newspapers. Darby Sabini went bankrupt as a result of his action; Frank Fraser failed in an action against a newspaper which said he had been a 'grass'. How could an allegation he had helped the police injure his reputation in the minds of right-thinking people? Gordon Goody, the Great Train Robber, did little better in his action against Odham's Press. David Hunt went the same way in an action against the *Sunday Times* and journalist Michael Gillard who had been investigating him and his role in the East End for some eleven years. Boiled down, the allegation against him in an article in May 2010 was that he was a violent 'underworld king'.

The judge ruled that had Hunt won he would have awarded him something in the region of £250,000 but he found Gillard's allegation to be substantially proven.

Martin Ivens, acting editor of the *Sunday Times*, said:

This expensive and risky libel battle against a notorious crime figure in East London was made possible by the courage of investigative journalist Michael Gillard and several witnesses.

Hunt has been brought to justice by a libel action where the authorities have failed for more than two decades. The judgment highlights the role of journalism for the public good. The *Sunday Times* welcomes the judgment of Mr Justice Simon.[5]

Those who know him say that since the action Hunt has become a changed man, something of a recluse . 'A good man to have as a friend but a hard man if you cross him.'

The end for sixty-four-year-old John 'Goldfinger' Palmer came in what was certainly a contract killing on 24 June 2015. He was in the back garden of his home at South Weald near Brentwood when he was shot three times at point-black range and a further three times whilst he was lying on the ground. He had been due to stand trial for money laundering and firearms offences in Spain. Earlier he had undergone keyhole surgery and almost inexplicably for several days it was thought he had died from a heart condition rather than being shot. As a result considerable time was wasted before a start was made looking for his killers, said to be Spanish and who, if they were, presumably were long gone. This was all the more surprising because Palmer had been under electronic surveillance at the time of his death and had been so for the previous sixteen years.[6]

Palmer had had a star-studded and very successful career as a criminal. He owned Scadlyn, jewellery and gold dealers, which as part of its business also melted gold. In 1985 the company plant was raided after the Brinks-Mat gold robbery two years earlier. One director received ten years but days before the raid Palmer had moved his family to the Playa de las Americas in Tenerife from which, at the time, there was no extradition treaty. Whilst there he set up a timeshare business. When the extradition treaty was signed Palmer tried to move to Brazil, travelling on an expired passport, but he was deported.

In his 1987 trial the jury accepted Palmer's explanation that while gold had indeed been melted in his back garden he had no idea that the metal came from the robbery. Six years later, still denying any involvement in the smelting of stolen gold, he settled a civil action with Brinks-Mat's insurers, paying a reported £360,000.

In 2001 Palmer was jailed in the UK for eight years after defending himself for a £20 million Spanish timeshare fraud involving 16,000 victims. He served half his sentence and in May 2003 a confiscation order for £33 million was overturned at the Court of Appeal. In 2005 he was declared bankrupt with debts of £3.9 million, despite a reputed wealth of £300 million. In 2007 he was charged by the Spanish police with fraud, firearm possession and money laundering. He was released on bail two years later.

At the time of his death he was said to have a mansion in Bath, a castle in France and numerous planes and helicopters. At one time he was considered to be one of the largest landowners in the Canaries.[7]

Three months before Palmer's murder, fifty-eight-year-old Dennis New, who was said to have run the Spanish timeshare industry with a rod of iron for twenty-five years, was found dead in his bungalow near Phuket, Thailand. His death was thought to have been from a heart condition but those of Billy and Flo Robinson certainly were not. In 2006 they had been ambushed on their way home from a restaurant in Tenerife. She had been bludgeoned to death and he had had his throat cut. Robbery was not a motive. A £100,000 watch worn by Robinson was left on his wrist, and Flo Robinson's diamond earrings weren't taken either.

In 2010 Garry Leigh, who ran holiday clubs in Spain, was knocked down and killed while cycling near Marbella. During his career there he had made enemies. Eight years earlier his office had been stormed by masked gunmen. In 2005 another Palmer associate, former guardsman Dale Moore, now in the security business, had been found dead in a container in Tanzania. He was said to have had a heart attack.[8]

NOTES

1. *Bowers & Ors v Regina* [2006] EWCA Crim 1433.
2. *Operation Tiberius Strategic Intelligence Report Main Report*, March 2002; Mike Sullivan, 'Bent coppers nobble four murder probes', *The Sun*, 11 January 2014.

3. Paul Cheston, 'Seven years for Criminal Cop', *Evening Standard*, 6 June 2002.
4. Tom Pettifor, 'Eight Murders that have been covered up according to ex-Met Police detective', *Daily Mirror*, 9 November 2015.
5. David Hunt v Times Newspapers Ltd [2013] EWHC 1868 (QB).
6. *London Evening Standard*, 26 September 2015.
7. Marnie Palmer with Tom Morgan, *Goldfinger And Me: Bullets, Bullion And Betrayal*.
8. Mike Lockley, 'Solihull Gangster John Palmer's murder linked to five other hits', *Birmingham Live*, 23 August 2020.

23

FROM POSTCODES TO COUNTY LINES

By 2000, overall the mood amongst the former East End players was elegiac. One resident thought:

> You aren't going to get people like Spotty and Georgie Wood any more. All you get now is drug dealers. People like Alfie [Gerard] wouldn't stand for what goes on today.

While there were still pockets of Jewish crime in the East End involving the protection of amusement arcades, clubs and discos, what had now arrived was a new breed of ethnic criminal to replace the generations of Irish, gypsy, Jewish and Maltese criminals of the past century. Prominent amongst the new kids on the block were the Bengalis, whose parents in the 1960s and 1970s came to Brick Lane where Arthur Harding had plied his trade a hundred years earlier. The pattern is an ever-repeating one.

Just as the Irish, the Jews and the Maltese had banded together, so did the Bengali youth who came from a clannish community with very strong family ties and family culture. 'They feel they should be in gangs,' said award-winning journalist Hilary Clarke of the *Independent*. Again street behaviour has echoed the pattern of earlier communities. 'There is horrendous violence among the Bengali street gangs. It is, "You looked at my girl", "You trod on my shoes"', she says. Instead of taking and driving away sports cars as did their predecessors, now these were hired with stolen credit cards and licences.

The origins of the Bengali gangs may well have stemmed from the series of racist attacks on the community in the late 1970s. The most serious of these was when, in the summer of 1979, a gang of National Front supporters chased Altab Ali down Brick Lane and eventually kicked him to death in the nearby St Mary's Churchyard. In a chapter on Asian gangs in his book *Gangland Britain*, Tony Thompson points out that this incident substantially reduced support for the National Front which had been steadily making a comeback in Bethnal Green and, coupled with the strict immigration control policies of the Thatcher government, racist incidents were at least on hold.

In fact from the demise of the National Front, whose headquarters in the area were forced to close, arose the Anti-Nazi League. Unfortunately in recent years Combat 18, an extreme right-wing organisation, has flourished amongst disaffected Essex white youth and associated itself with the football gangs including the ICF. Combat's name derived from the position of Adolf Hitler's initials in the alphabet. Apart from its self-proclaimed anti-Government stance – it suggested that it would mount an international terrorist campaign regarding the Government as ZOG (Zionist occupation government) – it is heavily involved in drug-dealing and a lucrative neo-Nazi music business.

Then, with Asian communities making their mark in various cities throughout Britain in the 1980s, came another right-wing backlash. Now Bengali youth was not willing to rely on the often tardy police protection. They were prepared to band together to deal with their attackers. And so the youth gangs were born, doing exactly what the Odessians had done eighty years earlier and Jack Spot had done in the Mosley days. For a fee they provided protection for shopkeepers and ensured that in the demonstrations and counter-demonstrations their windows were not smashed. The difficulty was that, just as with Jack Spot and his forebears, out of community protection were born gangs just as unpleasant and dangerous as those they originally sought to fight.

But, as is often the case, from wholly understandable beginnings groups splintered and became rival factions until in early 1998 fifteen members of the Cannon Street Gang were attacked in the East End by an alliance of fifty youths from smaller groups. Then later that year the largest gangs – BLM (Brick Lane Massif), the Stepney Posse, the East Boys and the Cannon Street Gang – joined together to broker a peace amongst the ethnic minority gangs. Probably about 2,500 youths were affiliated to one of the local gangs.

Award-winning journalist Hilary Clarke believed, quite correctly, that the East End was awash with drugs, a problem exacerbated by the fact that very few local police officers could speak Bengali. In a 1999 survey published by the community drugs team, one of six drugs clinics in Tower Hamlets, 57 per cent of its under-twenty-five-year-old clients were Bangladeshi, and of those under eighteen the figure was 64 per cent.[1]

Clarke also believed, however, that much of it was not organised crime in the strict sense but, 'It is taking a risk. One bottom of a bag filled with heroin and you can buy a restaurant. It comes from Burma and is better quality and purity.' In return, new restaurant owners could expect a welcoming firebomb, not in the sense of protection but as a gesture from existing competing owners.

Just as generations ago the Sabinis and later the Nash family had an impact on the East End, so now did much heavier black gangs from Stoke Newington lean on the less organised Bengali youth gangs. It is also something about which the local fundamentalists were organising protests. A public house reputed to be the centre of drug-dealing and which featured lap-dancing was closed 'for refurbishment', and members of the local mosque ran a vigilante campaign against prostitution in Spitalfields. Now the prostitutes who once frequented Brick Lane were moved on, albeit only a few streets away, but there was still semi-organised prostitution in the Commercial Road.

Another of the problems the police faced in dealing with the Indian/Pakistani groups in the East End was that, like the old-fashioned white working-class gangs, they were family-based. Blood is thicker than water and so they were difficult to infiltrate. One thing denied to the old-fashioned white gang was that the families had links abroad and as such were able to deal in illegal immigration as well as heroin smuggling.

In April 2000 the London Transport Police claimed that a gang of six men were operating a massive child pickpocketing ring from an East London council estate. As many as forty children, mostly aged ten and under and mostly girls, would be taken on the Underground to central London. On the way they would change into flowing ethnic costume then, splitting into groups of six or seven and minded by one of the men, they would commence work. In one week-long operation against the gangs forty-six children were arrested. It was not made clear from where the children originated; possibly from Kosovo, Romania or Bosnia.

Just as the early East End and New York street gangs were at first territorially inclined and at first the Vietnamese youth gangs in Australia had self-protection rather than profit in mind, so were the twenty-first-century youth gangs. In time, as with motorcycle gangs, the smaller ones were subsumed into the larger; some splintered off and some just faded away. New gangs emerged, many of which have transformed into what have come to be known as postcode gangs. By 2018 it was estimated there were around 250 such gangs in London with around 4,500 people in twelve active gangs in Waltham Forest alone. Of the original gangs, surveyed ten years earlier, only the Beaumont Crew, Priory Court, Drive and Boundary were still active. In October 2017 the Mali Boys were said to be in alliance with the Boundary Boys, the Drive/DM Crew, Stoneydown and Coppermill.[2]

The London Fields Boys, one of around two dozen gangs still operating in the Hackney area, seem to have begun life around the beginning of the twenty-first century. On 31 August 2008, fourteen-year-old Shaquille Smith was stabbed to death while sitting on a park bench with his dog in Hackney. His sister, sixteen-year-old Tahira who was with him, was also slashed but survived. Six members of the London Fields Boys were jailed for life, with a minimum of fifteen years to be served before parole could be considered. It seems they had killed him for no real reason except to show their control of the area.

Two years later, by which time the London Fields Boys had been running the area for a decade, sixteen-year-old Agnes Sina-Inakoju was caught in the cross fire of a feud between LFB and the Hackney Boys. She was simply in the wrong place at the wrong time, queuing in a takeaway when LFB member Leon Dunkley opened fire with an Agram 2000 machine gun said to be capable of firing 1,100 rounds a minute. He and a lookout were both jailed for life, with a minimum of thirty-two years to be served.

The gun, which had been used in at least six separate shootings in the previous three years, was found under the bed of a gang wannabee who had been seen by a police officer to throw a bag into a garden. When his room was searched an arsenal of weapons was found.[3]

In the five-year period from 2006 the local gangs expanded their activities into more profitable operations. Around 700 children aged between ten and twelve were arrested after being recruited by gangs and drug runners and used to take part in muggings and burglaries.

By 2018 LFB, Stratford Mandem, Tottenham Mandem (strictly speaking meaning men over there) who emerged after the 1985 Broadwater Farm riots, and Northumberland Park Krew (NPK), a split-off from Tottenham Mandem, were thought to be amongst the top gangs in the North and East London areas.[4]

In the decades when white blue-collar gangs ruled the East End, relatively few innocent by-standers were caught up in their internecine feuds. However, at about 9.35 p.m. on Easter Monday 2018, seventeen-year-old Tanesha Melbourne was shot dead from a passing silver-coloured Vauxhall Meriva outside her home in Tottenham while she was talking with friends. She was the forty-eighth murder victim in London that year. A forty-ninth victim followed in a matter of hours in an unrelated incident in Walthamstow. Later NPK claimed responsibility on social media. Although a number of arrests were made no one has been charged with her murder.

The Browning gun used to kill Tanesha, which was eventually found in Highgate, had earlier been used when Joseph Williams-Torres was shot dead on 14 March in Walthamstow in an unrelated incident. It was thought the handgun was one which was hired out between gangs.

Within days Tanesha's father, Conrad Kingdom, was charged with conspiracy to deal in heroin said to be worth £1 million, some of which was found in his house. He was refused bail so that he could attend her funeral. In 2019 he pleaded guilty and received a seven-year sentence.[5]

In 2017 the highly sophisticated Mali Boys, named because so many of the founder members came from Somalia, had around fifty members. It has been in existence for only five or so years and came from a splinter of the older gang the Beaumont Boys or Crew, also known as Let's Get Rich. The Mali Boys, who try to avoid publicity, are known to control drug-dealing in the Walthamstow area backed up by a justified reputation for violence and intimidation.

In complete contrast a group with little interest in anonymity are the Hellbanianz (motto 'We are God of the Streets'), a gang of young Albanians based in Barking who have not heard of, or at least not learned from, the maxim that the best criminal is the invisible one. In 2017 they went online via Instagram and YouTube rap videos to demonstrate both their ill-gotten wealth and their firepower.[6]

Albanian criminals masquerading as Kosovan refugees began arriving in Britain in the 1990s. Along with Turkish gangs they quickly took over control of London's sex industry from the Maltese. They have a reputation for violence far and above the usual 'pimp beat' to control the women. By 2003 the Albanians were already well established in people smuggling. That year twenty-six-year-old Luan Plackici was jailed for twenty-three years. He was said to have made more than £1 million from trafficking between fifty and sixty 'poor, naive and gullible' young women who thought they were on their way to jobs as waitresses or barmaids. Some had to service up to twenty men a day to pay for their £8,000 'travel bill' from Romania and Moldova. After Plackici had married one teenager he told her she would spend her wedding night working as a prostitute. The girl later had two abortions and Plackici forced her to work within hours of each.[7]

From prostitution the Albanians moved into cocaine smuggling and dealing. In 2016 one of Hellbanianz' most prominent members, Tristen Aslanni, was sentenced to twenty-five years for drug-dealing and firearms offences which included possessing a Škorpion sub-machine gun. He had been caught with a suitcase containing 21 kilograms of cocaine after a police chase in North London which ended when he crashed his car into a computer repair shop in Crouch End. A photo of Aslanni, showing him stripped to the waist after he had apparently spent long hours in the prison gym, appeared on a social media page called 'My Albanian in Jail', with a caption reading 'Even inside the prison we have all conditions, what's missing are only whores'.

The flashy cars – one man Azen Dajci drove a gold-coloured Mercedes with the number plate HE11BOZ – and bundles of banknotes shown in the Hellbanianz videos mainly come from the importation of cocaine and cannabis, but the gang has also been involved in the weapons trade. The pictures showed £50 notes wrapped around a cake and their HB logo written in cannabis.

In 2019 Dajci and two other Hellbanianz members were caught when they raided a cannabis factory in Mill Hill. They had been seen by an off-duty special constable. They received sentences of six years plus. After being jailed, gang members have posted pictures of themselves, taken with smuggled mobile phones, from inside prison. Dajci had a picture of himself doing press-ups. There were then around 700 Albanians in British jails.[8]

Unlike other gangs who flaunt their status on social media, the reclusive Mali Boys are the most business-driven, violent and ruthless of the gangs, shunning social media in favour of keeping their activities a secret. For example, they have used old-fashioned Nokia phones because they are less easy to track.

On 14 March 2018 Joseph Williams-Torres was shot and killed in Walthamstow by members of the Mali Boys. He had been mistakenly identified as a gang member and was not the intended target. Prosecuting, Allison Hunter QC said the killing was part of a set of related and retaliatory acts of violence rooted in a dispute between rival groups. In particular, violence had begun to escalate after Mali Boys member Elijah Dornelly was murdered in May 2017. The Mali Boys were reported to be then in a 'turf war' with a group known as Priory Court or Higham Hill. One of the defendants accused of murder, Hamza Ul Haq, had previously been squirted with acid in November 2017, whilst another member of the Mali Boys had been stabbed in Walthamstow.

The Mali Boys did not always have things their own way. In December 2018, nineteen-year-old Daniel Fakoya, a member of rival gang Priory Court, and two other men armed with a loaded gun, a knife and ammonia, drove a stolen car into Leyton High Road, territory of the Mali Boys. They met and chased four members of the Mali Boys until they ran into an off-licence, locking themselves into a back room, eluding Fakoya who gave up his chase. In an attempt to escape the police, Fakoya then returned to his car but took a corner too quickly and crashed into a shop, narrowly missing pedestrians. He ran from the scene, leaving blood on the car's airbag identifying him as the uninsured driver of the stolen vehicle. A loaded handgun was found in the footwell of the driver's seat.

Undaunted, while in prison awaiting trial, he ran a drugs line from inside. A search of his cell turned up over sixty dealer wraps containing cocaine and other drug paraphernalia.

Finally, Fakoya pleaded guilty to aggravated vehicle taking and the jury found him guilty of eight other counts, including conspiracy to possess a firearm, conspiracy to cause grievous bodily harm and conspiracy to supply controlled drugs. He was sentenced to fifteen years in prison.[9]

On 8 January 2019 fourteen-year-old Jaden Moodie was stabbed to death by a group of Mali Boys in Leyton. Moodie, who was associated with rival gang Beaumont Crew, had allegedly been out drug-dealing. Mali Boys members drove into his scooter and stabbed him as he lay on the ground. Ayoub Majdouline was sentenced to life in prison with a minimum term of twenty-one years for the murder.

Earlier Majdouline had himself been identified by the National Crime Agency as a victim of modern slavery used for drug-dealing. His life had gone downhill after his father was murdered when he was fourteen. In January 2015, his father Othamane Majdouline and his Portuguese friend Leandro Da Silva were beaten with a hammer and stabbed at his flat in King's Cross. Their killer, thirty-seven-year-old Paul O'Shea, originally from Portlaoise, Ireland, had argued with them after visiting Majdouline to buy Class A drugs but it seems he had had no money. He returned later in the day with a computer monitor which he tried to exchange for drugs and a dispute broke out. After killing the men O'Shea set fire to the property in an attempt to destroy any evidence. In 2015 he was jailed for life with a minimum term of thirty-two years for the murders.

For a time in the early 1990s, Jason Lee Vella reigned unchallenged as a dealer in South East Essex. Of Maltese extraction, he was educated at a Catholic school in South Ockenden. When he left school, he began helping his father on market stalls. By the time he was twenty-two he was running a drug empire based on Ecstasy from Dutch dealers and then wholesaled to the street with outlets throughout England and Scotland. Steeped in Mafia and Kray lore, Vella had two piglets named Ronnie and Reggie. More or less immune to pain, he was happy to inflict it on those who upset or betrayed him. One member of his outfit who had the temerity to send a Christmas card to Vella's girlfriend was, in true *mafioso* tradition, invited round for dinner after which, however, things started to go wrong for him. He was stripped, his head and eyebrows shaved, cigarettes were stubbed out on him, knives were stuck into him and he was forced to snort cocaine and take LSD tablets. Finally he was left shoeless in the local park.

Another of Vella's victims was Reggie Nunn, who had been found guilty by Vella's court, held at 65 Hollands Walk in Vange, of selling 1,000 tabs of Ecstasy bound for Scotland on his own behalf and then spending the £8,000 profit. His face was sliced with an épée and to escape he leaped from a first-floor window. By chance this flight was recorded on CCTV and the police began an investigation which would lead to the break-up of the Vella enterprise.

In all it was estimated there were no fewer than twenty-six victims of Vella's controlled violence. Of that number, only four would give evidence and two sent solicitors' letters to the police indicating that they did not wish to co-operate. In July 1995 Vella was sentenced to a total of seventeen years for a wide variety of offences, including conspiracy to supply drugs and false imprisonment. Judge Alan Simpson, using the traditional judicial sentencing language, said:

> You set yourself up as a criminal tsar of south east Essex. You imposed your will on those who argued with you with a regime of torture and terror. There is no doubt in my mind that many people have breathed more easily since your arrest.

He added that had he been older Vella would have received thirty years. Not that Vella had not been good to his cohorts when they pleased him. Some were taken to Las Vegas to see Lennox Lewis fight, and as a bonus he had paid cash at the airport to upgrade to Club Class. One man, ten years older than Vella, had named his son Bobby Jason Lee Vella Barker in homage. In a year, Vella's operation had turned over in excess of £1.2 million.

In recent years the so-called County Lines have developed and expanded to operate in every area. In 2012 only a handful of police forces recognised their existence. Today County Lines, through which illegal drugs are transported from one area to another, often across police and local authority boundaries, are acknowledged by all forces. The drugs are collected from a city dealer and then sold over a mobile telephone – the County Line. They are then distributed to the customers, often by children and vulnerable people groomed by the gangs. Temptations such as a takeaway chicken and chips are sometimes enough to lure them.

Importing areas (areas to which the drugs are taken) are reporting increased levels of violence and weapon-related crimes as a result of this trend. With County Lines has come the unattractive practice of cuckooing – the flats or rooms, again of lonely, elderly or vulnerable people, are taken over on a temporary basis for storage and distribution purposes. The vulnerable householder will often be prevented from leaving or will actually leave and make themselves homeless to avoid the gangs.

Once in, getting out is extremely difficult. It is the distributors who are responsible for any shortfall in money or goods. The vulnerable and young are effectively trapped and can be subjected to threats and what is known as 'taxing' or debt bondage when a member of the gang has done wrong in the eyes of his superiors. This can be a failure to account properly or from a fake robbery set up by the leaders. For every bag of drugs found by the police some young person is going to be held accountable, threatened and beaten, if not worse.

Another feature is that County gangs are using consenting females to a far greater extent than the traditional gangs. They can be used to book hotels, hire cars, pay into bank accounts and look out places for cuckooing. There are reports they are occasionally used as enforcers.[10]

The criminal who operates on his own is usually the safest, but not always. West Ham based Armand Mpita operated his own one-man County Line, collecting heroin and crack cocaine and then telephoning around before delivering the orders personally. Unfortunately he was trapped when he came into sight while the police were investigating another County Line in Chelmsford. In May 2021 he was sentenced to three years and seven months. He was also made the subject of a serious crime order preventing him for five years after his release from using more than one mobile telephone and SIM card.

In 2020 Lee Chapman, a Southend courier for a County Line known as Max, fell foul of the second-in-command Tyrell Thompson. Like Keith Whittaker and the Essex Boys twenty-five years earlier, he had lost the gang's money. His crime had been to be robbed of £3,000 worth of drugs he was delivering for the Line. His punishment was to be held by two teenagers while Thompson stabbed him to death. Thompson received a minimum sentence of twenty-six years and the teenagers fourteen and twelve respectively.[11]

Cannabis-growing in Essex can itself be dangerous, as Asqeri Spaho found to his cost in December 2019 when he was working on a cannabis farm in a flat in Westcliff. An early morning attack on the flat by six men led by Wesley Henderson and Leon Wright with the aim of stealing £50,000 worth of plants ended with Asqeri being stabbed to death. Another man, who was stabbed in the stomach and jumped through an upstairs window to escape, survived. They were being paid £5,000 to look after the plants, which were due to be harvested the next day. The gang, which had driven down from London, fled but dumped swords, knives and gloves which the police later retrieved. They were also caught on CCTV. In April 2021 Henderson stormed out of court when one of the others was found not guilty of murder. He and Wright received life sentences with a minimum of thirty-two years to be served. The other men were convicted of aggravated burglary and received thirteen years.

In the first three months of 2021, Essex police arrested 178 people in sixty-eight raids breaking up nineteen County Line gangs.[12] In May a nationwide crackdown on County Lines ended with 1,100 arrests and 300 firearms and knives seized. Eighty County Lines were broken.

For all their efforts the police usually only manage to pick off the low- and medium-level hanging fruit. And if they actually reached higher would things be any better? History has repeatedly shown that where one gang leader is picked off, another replaces him almost immediately. Former undercover officer turned author Neil Woods believes that every time officers bring down organised criminals, they open up opportunities for more efficient gangsters to move in. He points out that what police do is get rid of the competition for them.

> It's like any marketplace – the more efficient ones grow and become bigger monopolies. The people in control of drug supplies now are in charge of big international businesses. [13]

And so we beat on, boats against the current. The times and mores of Albert Dimes are long gone. 'Dimes would seem more like an Ealing comedy gangster to the Albanians and Kurds,' says Professor Mark Roodhouse of the University of York. But there are new, more modern, more dangerous Dimes by the basketful. The more things change, the more they remain the same.

NOTES

1. Sanjiv Bhattacharya, 'Streets of Shame' in *Evening Standard*, 24 September 1999.
2. Andrew Whitaker *et al*, *From Postcodes to Profit*.
3. Rebecca Evans and Colin Fernandez, 'Found under a nine-year-old's bed: The weapons arsenal of gang who killed schoolgirl, 16', *Daily Mail*, 12 April 2011.
4. Paul Harper, 'MAPPED: The London Gangs running the Capital's streets as violence escalates', *Daily Star*, 14 April 2018.
5. Sam Truelove, 'London's most fearsome gangs, their nicknames and how they became notorious on the streets', *MyLondon*, 13 November 2020.
6. Jacob Dirnhuber, 'Running Riot', *The Sun*, 12 November 2018.
7. 'Prison for sex slave gang leader', *BBC News*, 22 December 2003.
8. Richard Wheatstone and Jake Ryan, 'Dealing in Death', *The Sun*, 8 July 2019.
9. Ben McVay, 'Violent Waltham Forest gang member who ran prison drugs line jailed for 15 years', *MyLondon*, 11 October 2019.
10. NCA County Lines Violence, Exploitation & Drug Supply, 2017.
11. *echo-news*, 15, 17 December 2020, 26 April 2021.
12. Lewis Berrill, 'Essex Police targeting county lines', *Epping Forest Guardian*, 27 April 2021.
13. Neil Woods, *Good Cop, Bad War*.

SELECTED BIBLIOGRAPHY

Allen, T., *Underworld: The Biography of Charles Brooks, Criminal* (1931) London, Newnes.

Aronson, T., *Prince Eddy and the Homosexual Underworld* (1994) London, John Murray.

Aykroyd, P., *The Dark Side of London* (1973) London, Wolfe.

Banton, M., *The Coloured Quarter* (1955) London, Cape.

Bean, J.P., *Crime in Sheffield* (1967) Sheffield, Sheffield City Libraries.

Bean, J.P., *Over the Wall* (1994) London, Headline.

Bell, L., *Bella of Blackfriars* (1961) London, Odhams Press.

Benney, M., *Low Company* (1936) London, Peter Davies.

Benney, M., *Almost a Gentleman* (1966) London, Peter Davies.

Bermant, C., *Point of Arrival* (1975) London, Eyre & Methuen.

Berrett, J., *When I Was at Scotland Yard* (1932) London, Sampson Low & Co.

Besant, W., *The East End and Its People* (1901) London, Chatto & Windus.

Biron, C., *Without Prejudice* (1936) London, Faber & Faber.

Bishop, C., *Women and Crime* (1931) London, Chatto & Windus.

Booth, C., *Life and Labour of the People in London* (1902) (reprinted 1969) New York, Augustus M. Kelly.

Brimson, D. and E., *Everywhere We Go* (1996) London, Headline.

Brimson, D. and E., *Capital Punishment* (1997) London, Headline.

Bristow, E.J., *Prostitution and Prejudice: The Jewish Fight Against White Slavery 1870–1939* (1982) Oxford, Oxford University Press.

Bronson, C., *The Krays and Me* (2004) London, John Blake.

Browne, D.G., *The Rise of Scotland Yard* (1956) London, George G. Harrap & Co.

Burke, S., *Peterman* (1965) London, Arthur Barker.

Burke, T., *Limehouse Nights* (1961) London, Brown Watson.

Campbell, D., *The Underworld* (1994) London, BBC Books.

Campbell, D., *Underworld* (2019) London, Ebury Press.

Cancellor, H.L., *The Life of a London Beak* (1930) London, Hurst & Blackett.

Cannon, J., *Tough Guys Don't Cry* (1983) London, Magnus Books.

Cartwright, F., *G-Men of the G.P.O.* (1937) London, Sampson Low.

Champly, H., *The Road to Shanghai* (1934) London, John Long.

Champly, H., *White Women, Coloured Men* (1936) London, John Long.

Chesney, K., *The Victorian Underworld* (1972) Harmondsworth, Penguin Books.

Cheyney, P., *Making Crime Pay* (1944) London, Faber & Faber.

Chinn, C., *The Real Peaky Blinders, Billy Kimber, the Birmingham Gang and the Racecourse Wars of the 1920s* (2014) Studley, Brewin Books.

Chinn, C., *Peaky Blinders, The Real Story* (2019) London, John Blake.

Clarke, F.G., *Will-o'-the-Wisp* (1983) Oxford, Oxford University Press.

Clarkson, W., *Moody: The Life and Crimes of Britain's Most Notorious Hitman* (2004) Mainstream Publishing Company, Edinburgh.

Cole, P., and Pringle, P., *Can You Positively Identify This Man?* (1974) London, André Deutsch.

Collins, D., *Nightmare in the Sun* (2007) London, John Blake.

Cornish, G. W., *Cornish of the Yard* (1935) London, John Lane, The Bodley Head.

Critchley, T.A., and James, P.D., *The Maul and the Pear Tree* (1977) London, Constable.

Crocker, W.C., *Far From Humdrum* (1967) London, Hutchinson & Co.

Davis, V., *Phenomena in Crime* (n.d.) London, John Long.

Deakin, N., *Colour, Citizenship and British Society* (1969) London, Panther Modern History.

Deakin, N., 'Immigrants and Minorities' – Essay in *Colour, Citizenship and British Society* (1970) London, Panther.

Dean-Davis, R., *The Wars of Rosie* (2009) London, Pennant.

Dench, G., *The Maltese in London* (1975) London, Routledge.

Dew, W., *I Caught Crippen* (1938) Glasgow, Blackie & Son.

Dey, T.H., *Leaves from a Bookmaker's Book* (1931) London, Hutchinson & Co.

Divall, T., *Scoundrels and Scallywags* (1929) London, Ernest Benn.

Donoghue, A., *The Krays' Lieutenant* (1995) London, Smith, Gryphon.

Downes, D.M., *The Delinquent Solution* (1966) London, Routledge & Kegan Paul.

Fallon, T., *The River Police* (1956) London, Muller.

Farson, D., *Limehouse Days* (1991) London, Michael Joseph.

Fawcett M., *Krazy Days* (2013) Brighton, Pen Press.

Felstead, S.T., *The Underworld of London* (1923) London, John Murray.

Felstead, S.T., *Sir Richard Muir* (1927) London, John Lane.

Fido, M., *The Krays, Unfinished Business* (2000) London, Carlton Books.

Fishman, W.J., *East End Jewish Radicals 1875–1914* (1975) London, Gerald Duckworth.

Fishman, W.J., *The Streets of East London* (1980) London, Gerald Duckworth.

Foreman, F., *Respect* (1996) London, Century.

Fraser, F. and Morton J., *Mad Frank* (1994) London, Little, Brown.

Fraser, F. and Morton J., *Mad Frank and Friends* (1998) London, Little, Brown.

Fraser F., and Morton J., *Mad Frank's London* (2002) London, Virgin.

Freeman, M.J., *I Pornographer*, Book 1 (2013), London, kindleunlimited.

Friedland, M., *The Trials of Israel Lipski* (1984) London, Macmillan.

Gainer, B., *The Alien Invasion: The Origins of the Aliens Act 1905* (1972) London, Heinemann Educational.

Goldman, W., *East End My Cradle* (1940) London, Faber & Faber.

Gordon, C.G., *Crooks of the Underworld* (1920) London, Geoffrey Bles.

Green, J., *A Social History of the Jewish East End of London* (1991) Lampeter, Edward Mellen Press.

Greeno, E., *War on the Underworld* (1960) London, John Long.

Greenwood, J., *The Wilds of London* (1874) London, Chatto & Windus.

Guerin, E., *Autobiography of a Crook* (1948) London, John Murray.

Hanshaw, P., *Nothing is Forever* (1992) London, Wapping Neighbourhood.

Harding, J. with Berg, J., *Jack 'Kid' Berg* (1987) London, Robson Books.

Harrison, M., *Peter Cheyney: Prince of Hokum* (1954) London, Neville Spearman.

Hart, E.T., *Britain's Godfather* (1991) London, True Crime Library.

Hicks, S., *Sparring for Luck* (1982) London, Thap Publishing.

Hill, B., *Boss of Britain's Underworld* (1955) London, Naldrett Press.

Hobbs, D., *Doing the Business* (1988) Oxford, Oxford University Press.

Hobbs, D., *Bad Business* (1995) Oxford, Oxford University Press.

Huish, R., *The Life of James Greenacre* (1837) London, William Wright.

Humphreys, C., *The Great Pearl Robbery of 1913* (1929) London, Heinemann.

Humphreys, T., *A Book of Trials* (1955) London, Pan.

Ingram, G., *Cockney Cavalcade* (n.d.) London, Dennis Archer.

Jackson, R., *Coroner* (1963) London, Harrap.

Jansen, H., *Jack Spot: Man of a Thousand Cuts* (1959) London, Alexander Moring.

Jarvis, S.M., *The Essex Murder Casebook* (1994) Newbury, Countryside.

Jennings, A., Lashmar, P. and Simpson, V., *Scotland Yard's Cocaine Connection* (1990) London, Jonathan Cape.

Jones, J.P., *Gambling Yesterday and Today* (1973) Newton Abbot, David & Charles.

Jones, S., *London The Sinister Side* (1986) London, Tragical Tours Publications.

Jones, S., *When the Lights Went Down* (1995) London, Wicked Publications.

Kelland, G., *Crime in London* (1986) London, The Bodley Head.

Kerner, A., *Further Adventures of a Woman Detective* (1955) London, Werner Laurie.

Knight, R., *Black Knight* (1990) London, Century.

Knight, R., and ors, *Gotcha!, The Untold Story of Britain's Biggest Cash Robbery,* (2003), London, Pan.

Kohn, M., *Dope Girls* (1992) London, Lawrence & Wishart.

Kray, C. with Robin McGibbon, *My Brothers and Me* (1997) London, HarperCollins

Kray, K., *The Black Widow, The Life and Crimes of Linda Calvey* (2019) London, Mirror Books.

Kray, R., *Villains We Have Known* (1993) Leeds, N.K. Publications.

Kray, R. and R., *Our Story* (1988) London, Pan.

Leeson, B., *Lost London* (1934) London, Stanley Paul.

Lewis, D. and Hughman, P., *Most Unnatural* (1971) London, Penguin.

Linehan, T., *East London for Mosley* (1996) London, Frank Cass.

Linklater, E., *The Corpse on Clapham Common* (1971) London, Macmillan.

Lock, J., *Dreadful Deeds and Awful Murders* (1990) Taunton, Barn Owl Books.

Lucas, N., *Crooks: Confessions* (n.d.) London, Hurst & Blackett.

Macdonald, J.C.R., *Crime is a Business* (1939) Stanford, N.Y., Stanford University Press.

McDonald, B., *Gangs of London* (2010) Wrea Green, Milo Books.

McLean, L., *The Guv'nor* (1998) London, Blake.

Mills, L., *Crimewatch* (1994) London, Penguin.

Morton, J., *Gangland* (1992) London, Little, Brown.

Morton, J., *Bent Coppers* (1993) London, Little, Brown.

Morton, J., *Gangland 2* (1994) London, Little, Brown.

Morton, J., *Supergrasses and Informers* (1995) London, Little, Brown.

Morton, J., *Gangland International* (1998) London, Little, Brown.

Morton, J., *Justice Denied* (2015) London, Robinson.

Morton, J., *Bert Rossi, Britain's Oldest Gangland Boss* (2017) California, National Crime Syndicate.

Morton, J., *Krays: The Final Word*, (2019) London, Mirror Books.

— and Parker, G., *Gangland Bosses*, (2004) London, Time Warner.

Moulton, H. Fletcher, *The Trial of Steinie Morrison* (1922) London, William Hodge.

Newman, A. (ed), *The Jewish East End 1840–1939* (1981) London, The Jewish Historical Society of England.

Ny, K.C., *The Chinese in London* (1968) Oxford, Oxford University Press.

O'Donnell, E., *Great Thames Mysteries* (1929) London, Selwyn & Blount.

O'Mahoney, B., *So This Is Ecstasy?* (1997) Edinburgh, Mainstream.

O'Mahoney, B., *Essex Boys* (2000) Edinburgh, Mainstream.

O'Mahoney, B., *Wanna Be in My Gang?* (2004) Edinburgh, Mainstream.

Odell, R., *Jack the Ripper in Fact and Fiction* (1965) London, George G. Harrap.

Otley, R., *No Green Pastures* (1952) London, John Murray.

Palmer, A., *The East End* (2000) London, John Murray.

Palmer, M. with Morgan, T., *Goldfinger And Me: Bullets, Bullion And Betrayal* (2018) London, History Press.

Parker, R., *Rough Justice* (1981) London, Fontana.

Parr, E., *Grafters All* (1964) London, Max Reinhardt.

Pearson, J., *The Profession of Violence* (1977) London, Granada.

Probyn, W., *Angel Face* (1977) London, George Allen & Unwin.

Ramsey, W.G., *The East End: Then and Now* (n.d.) London, After the Battle.

Read, L. and Morton, J., *Nipper* (1993) London, Warner Books.

Richardson, C., *My Manor* (1991) London, Sidgwick & Jackson.

Rocker, R., *The London Years* (1936) London, Robert Anscombe & Co.

Rogers, C., *The Battle of Stepney* (1981) London, Hale.

Rose, A., *Steinie* (1985) London, The Bodley Head.

Rose, L., *Rogues & Vagabonds: The Vagrant Underworld in Britain 1815–1985* (1988) London, Routledge.

Rose, M., *The East End of London* (1951) London, Cresset Press.

Roston, W.W., *British Economy of the Nineteenth Century* (1948) Oxford, Clarendon Press.

Rubenhold, H., *The Five, The Untold Lives of the Women Killed by Jack the Ripper* (2020) London, Black Swan.

Rudé, G.F., *Hanoverian London* (1971) London, Secker & Warburg.

Rumbelow, D., *I Spy Blue* (1975) Bath, Chivers.

Rumbelow, D., *The Complete Jack the Ripper* (1987) London, W.H. Allen.

Rumbelow, D., *The Houndsditch Murders and The Siege of Sidney Street* (1988) London, W.H. Allen.

Russell, C. and Lewis, H.S., *The Jew in London* (1900) London, T. Fisher Unwin.

Russell, J.F.S., *My Life and Adventures* (1923) London, Cassell & Co.

Samuel, R., *East End Underworld: Chapters in the Life of Arthur Harding* (1981) London, Routledge & Kegan Paul.

Savage, P., *Savage of Scotland Yard* (n.d.) London, Hutchinson & Co.

Sellwood, A. and M., *The Victorian Railway Murders* (1979) Newton Abbot, David & Charles.

Sharpe, M.C., *Chicago May – Her Story* (1928) New York, Macaulay.

Shaw, R., *Prettyboy* (1999) London, Blake.

Shore, H., *London's Criminal Underworlds c.1720–c.1930 A Social and Cultural History* (2015) Basingstoke, Palgrave Macmillan.

Short, M., *Lundy* (1991) London, Grafton.

Sidelsky, R., *Oswald Mosley* (1975) London, Macmillan.

Simpson, A.W., *In the Highest Degree Odious* (1992) Oxford, Clarendon Press.

Smith, A., *The East Enders* (1961) London, Secker & Warburg.

Smithies, E., *Crime in War Time: The Black Economy in England Since 1914* (1982) London, George Allen & Unwin.

Smithson, G., *Raffles in Real Life* (1927) London, Hutchinson & Co.

Sokoloff, B., *Edith and Stepney* (1987) London, Stepney Books.

Sparkes, H., *Iron Man* (1964) London, John Long.

Spencer, J.C., *Crime and the Services* (1954) London, Routledge & Kegan Paul.

Sturley, L., *The Secret Train Robber* (2015) London, Ebury Press.

Sutton, C., *The New York Tombs* (1847) San Francisco, A. Roman and Co.

Symons, J., *A Reasonable Doubt* (1960) London, The Cresset Press.

Thompson, T., *Bloggs 19* (2000) London, Warner Books.

Thompson, W., *Time Off My Life* (1956) London, Rich & Cowan.

Thorogood, H., *East of Aldgate* (1935) London, Allen & Unwin.

Tietjen, A., *Soho* (1956) London, Allan Wingate.

Totterdell, G.H., *Country Copper* (1956) London, George G. Harrap.

Tremlett, G., *Little Legs: Muscleman of Soho* (1989) London, Unwin, Hyman.

Tullett, T., *No Answer From Foxtrot Eleven* (1967) London, Michael Joseph.

Walpole, K., *Dockers and Detectives* (1983) London, Verso.

Watts, M., *The Men In My Life*, (1960) London, Christopher Johnson.

Wensley, F., *Detective Days* (1931) London, Cassell & Co.

White, J., *Rothschild Buildings, Life in an East End Tenement Block 1887–1920* (1990) London, Routledge.

Whitehouse, J.M. (ed.), *Problems of Boy Life* (1912) London, P.S. King.

Whittington-Egan, M., *Scottish Murder Stories* (1998) Glasgow, Neil Wilson.

Whittington-Egan, R., *The Quest for Jack the Ripper* (2000) New Jersey, Patterson Smith.

Whittington-Egan, R. and M., *Mr George Edjali* (1985) London, Greyhouse Books.

Wickstead, A., *Gangbuster* (1985) London, Futura.

Wilkinson, J., *Father Joe* (1963) London, Hodder & Stoughton.

Wilkinson, L., *Behind the Face of Crime* (1967) London, Muller.

Woods, N., with Rafaeli, J.S., *Good Cop, Bad War*, (2016), Ebury Digital.

Woolton, Lord, *Memoirs* (1959) London, Cassell.

Worby, J., *The Other Half* (1937) London, J.M. Dent & Sons.

Worry, J., *Spiv's Progress* (1939) London, J.M. Dent & Sons.

Wray, V., *Pay Up and Play the Game: Professional Sport in Britain 1875–1914* (1998) Cambridge, Cambridge University Press.

Wray, V., *The Turf, a Social and Economic History of Horseracing* (1976) London, Allen Lane.

ARTICLES ETC.

Baxter, L., 'Behind the Suffolk Sting', *Ipswich Star,* 28 February 2002.

Berridge, V., 'East End Opium Dens and Narcotic Use in Britain' *The London Journal*, Vol. 14 (1978) pp. 3–18.

'Opium and Oral History' in the *Oral History Journal*, Vol. 7, No.2.

Berrill, L., 'Essex Police targeting county lines', *Epping Forest Guardian*, 27 April 2021.

Bilefsky, D., 'Once He Was the "Godfather of British Crime". Now He's Just a Grandfather', *The New York Times*, 19 April 2019.

Cacciottolo, M., 'London 2012: Will the Olympics bring more prostitutes?' *BBC News*, 7 June 2012.

Cheston, P.C., 'Seven years for Criminal Cop', *Evening Standard*, 6 June 2002.

Daly, P., *Heavyweight Champion of England* c. 1927. Unpublished manuscript deposited in Islington Library, London.

Dickinson, L., 'Gangland General from Hornchurch sent down', *Romford Recorder*, 12 November 2010.

Dirnhuber, J., 'Running Riot', The *Sun*, 12 November 2018.

Evans R. and Fernandez, C., 'Found under a nine-year-old's bed: The weapons arsenal of gang who killed schoolgirl, 16', *Daily Mail,* 12 April 2011.

Hill, A., 'Girl Gang's Grip on London Underworld Revealed', The *Guardian*, 27 December 2010.

Harper, P, 'MAPPED: The London Gang's Running the Capital's Streets', *Daily Star*, 14 April 2016.

Kirby T., 'Gangland War linked to murder of fugitive', *The Independent*, 23 October 2011.

Leech, K., 'Human Casualties in a Crisis District' *East London Papers*, Vol. 11, No. 1, Summer 1968.

London Diocesan CETS and Churches, *Commission on Gambling Funfairs and Delinquency: A Survey in London 1941–42*.

McVay, B., 'Violent Waltham Forest gang member who ran prison drugs line jailed for 15 years', *MyLondon*, 11 October 2019.

Marks, L., 'Jewish Women and Jewish Prostitution in the East End of London', *Jewish Quarterly*, February 1987.

NCA, 'County Lines Violence, exploitation and drug supply', 2017.

Operation Tiberius Strategic Intelligence Report Main Report, March 2002.

Paton, N, 'Once upon a time in the East End', *The Guardian*, 19 March 2000.

Pettifor, T., 'Eight murders that have been covered up,' *Daily Mirror*, 9 November 2015.

Pocock, T., 'Odd but the "red light area" will be pulled down at last' *Evening Standard*, 17 November 1960.

Richardson, F.E., 'Social Conditions in Ports and Dockland Areas', Joint Committee of the British Social Hygiene Council and the British Council for the Welfare of the Mercantile Marine, 1935.

Rownsend, M.M., 'London Killings. It's Like a War Zone', *The Guardian*, 1 May 2021.

Rosser, N., 'Hoddesdon gym victim's past revealed', *Evening Standard*. 9 October 2003.

Rupp, J.C., 'Was Francis Thompson Jack the Ripper?' *The Criminologist*, Winter 1988.

Sullivan, M., 'Bent coppers nobble four murder probes', The *Sun*, 11 January 2014.

Swarc, D., 'Background and conditions contributing to Jewish prostitution in the East End of London 1890–1914' (1987). Unpublished manuscript deposited in the Jewish Museum at the Sternberg Centre, Finchley.

Sweeney, J., 'Jason Lee Vella' *Observer Life,* 19 May 1996.

Temple, R., 'The Metropolitan Police and the British Union of Fascists 1934–1940'. Unpublished manuscript deposited in Bancroft Road Library, Tower Hamlets.

Thompson, T., 'Crime bosses run empires from jail' *The Observer*, 8 August 1998.

Truelove, S., 'London's Most Fearsome Gangs,' MyLondon, 13 November 2020.

Warren, N.P., 'Dr Merchant was not Jack the Ripper' *The Criminologist*, Spring 1992.

Wheatstone, R., and Ryan J., 'Dealing in Death', *The Sun*, 8 July 2019.

White, K., 'Downfall of the drug barons' *The Law*, February 1996.

Whittacker A., and ors., 'Post Codes to Profit', South Bank University, 2018.

Whittington-Egan, R., 'Miss Nina and the Anarchists' *New Law Journal*, 11 January 2000.

Williams, S., 'Brick Lane and Beyond', Commission for Racial Equality, 1979.

Young, Rev. E., 'Vice Increase in Stepney', 1957. [A copy may be found in the local history section of Tower Hamlets Library in Bancroft Road.]